# DEFINING
# THE MANAGER'S JOB

# DEFINING THE MANAGER'S JOB

## Second Edition

Max S. Wortman, Jr.
JoAnn Sperling

## *A Manual of Position Descriptions*

amacom

A DIVISION OF AMERICAN MANAGEMENT ASSOCIATIONS

**Library of Congress Cataloging in Publication Data**
Wortman, Max Sidones, 1932–
  Defining the manager's job.

  Bibliography: p.
  Includes index.
  1. Executives—United States—Job descriptions.
I. Sperling, Jo Ann, joint author.  II. Title.
HD38.W63   1975    658.4'0023    75-19253
ISBN 0-8144-5377-5

Second Printing

# PREFACE

When the first edition of this book was published, few unified managerial position description programs existed. Today many excellent programs have been developed. Programs that existed fifteen years ago have shown an amazing ability to change in coverage, usage, format, and style. Companies have built new programs on the experiences of other companies, public agencies, and nonprofit corporations, and have developed unique, innovative characteristics of their own.

The purposes and uses of managerial description programs have broadened extensively since the first edition. Today they are used in the design of organizations; manpower planning; individual career planning; results-oriented appraisal programs; recruitment, selection, and placement of executives; executive orientation; compensation administration; management development; and task forces, project teams, and matrix teams. These uses are a far cry from the uses described in the original study. Such programs no longer are the exclusive instrument of manufacturers; they are used widely in financial institutions, utilities, transportation corporations, hospitals, educational institutions, and governmental agencies.

The analysis of current practices in several types of organization makes it clear that there is no one best way of preparing or using managerial position descriptions. However, by describing current practices of 136 organizations we have identified some of the factors used in determining the proper program to be instituted or changed in a given situation.

In organizations that have description programs, this book can be used to compare their present programs with those of other similar organizations. After making such a comparison, the organization may wish to use some of the suggestions in the book to make alterations in its questionnaires and guides, organization manuals, position description manuals, and in its managerial position descriptions themselves—in format, content, length, and language. In organizations that do not have description programs, this book can be used as a major source of information on organizing and designing a program, obtaining executive approval for the program, preparing descriptions, and implementing the program.

In the future, managerial position descriptions probably will change even more dramatically than in the past two decades. This book attempts to point the directions in which those changes will occur. For example, with the present shifts in management styles, organization structures, and environmental operating conditions, managerial descriptions are apparently moving toward a much stronger results orientation with more individual career planning for each manager.

Thanks to the generosity of many organizations, the book provides useful data and specimens on current practice as well as current and future problems in such programs. Some of the most important and newest managerial positions in the country are described.

MAX S. WORTMAN, JR.
JOANN SPERLING

# CONTENTS

# PART ONE

---

## *A Survey of Organization Practices*

# 1

## An Introduction to
## Managerial Position Descriptions

Managerial position descriptions have achieved a significant role in every type of organization, business and nonbusiness. They are one of the major ways of obtaining, maintaining, and retaining an outstanding corps of executives in our rapidly changing technological society. As they have evolved during the past fifteen years, these descriptions have shown an amazing ability to change in coverage, usage, format, and style to meet the increasing demands of organizations for additional, current information on executive jobs. Many of the programs have shifted their descriptions from a historical data-base approach to an almost current approach, from a strictly compensation-administration-oriented approach to a performance-oriented approach, and from a single-purpose approach to a multipurpose approach.

At the present time, position descriptions are widely used in the design of organizations, in manpower planning, individual career planning, results-oriented appraisal programs, the recruitment, selection, and placement of executives, the orientation of executives, compensation administration, management development, and task forces, project teams, and matrix teams. Since the first AMA study on managerial position descriptions fifteen years ago, their uses have been broadened extensively and they now serve many purposes not even considered when they were established. Furthermore, the coverage of these programs has expanded into many different types of organizations, including manufacturers, financial institutions, utilities companies, transportation firms, entertainment and travel corporations, hospitals, universities, professional sports, and government agencies of many types.

In the future, position descriptions probably will change even more dramatically. In response to anticipated shifts in management styles and in organization structures and environments, position descriptions appear to be moving toward even stronger results orientation and greater individual career planning. As more valid descriptions are formulated and applied to meet the requirements of affirmative action programs, more minority group and female employees will have a better chance at managerial positions. In the very near future, computerization of modular, standardized descriptions may be instituted. Furthermore, shorter, more current (almost on-line) position descriptions may become available because of their interrelationships with results-oriented performance appraisal systems.

During the past fifteen years there has been some standardization of the procedures to develop managerial position descriptions. However, even today, form, content, coverage, usage, and program procedures vary considerably according to the basic purpose behind the description program. Similar jobs in different organizations are often described in significantly different terms.

This book analyzes current practices in managerial position description programs in several different types of organizations. It does not attempt to tell the reader a *one best way* to prepare or use these programs. Instead it describes the current practices of 136 organizations that have had considerable experience with position descriptions on managerial levels, and it attempts to identify some of the factors that encourage particular approaches in particular situations. It does this in three ways: The first part of the report presents information gathered in a mail survey; the second presents brief examples of managerial position description questionnaires and guides, organization manual materials, and position description manuals; and the third presents an ordered set of sample managerial position descriptions.

The survey presented in Part One was conducted among organizations that have already used—in some cases, for many years—managerial position descriptions. Their methods differ primarily according to the basic purpose or purposes behind the programs. The different procedures in the 136 programs are described. Part Two, "A Handbook of Methods for Preparing Position Descriptions," provides information on techniques, methods, and procedures used in the programs. They can serve as a source for new programs and revisions of older ones.

The specimens in Part Three, "A Handbook of Position Descriptions," are almost self-explanatory. They can be employed as a source of ideas on content, style, and format. Much can be learned from a detailed examination of these descriptions, which are the final products of well-developed programs, but they cannot be used as a source of standardized descriptions. As the report itself demonstrates, managerial position descriptions (even more than rank-and-file descriptions) must be exactly tailored to the needs and structure of each individual organization.

Not all descriptions in Part Three can be classified as "top management" or "executive management." Also included are middle management positions such as operations manager, manager of corporate accounting, director of marketing, and manager, environmental production, along with professional positions such as senior manufacturing engineer, corporate patent attorney, and management development administrator. These were included because there is a great demand on the part of top managers for descriptions of positions held by their immediate subordinates. In addition, many of these specialized positions in larger organizations involve the supervision of sizable groups of personnel and make substantial contributions to organizational success.

## DEFINITIONS AND TERMINOLOGY

Although many managerial position descriptions have by now been written and rewritten several times, terminology is still far from standardized. The reason for this is probably that each writer or user tends to adopt his or her own terms, with little regard for ordinary dictionary meanings. In writing these descriptions, both executives and compensation specialists have been constantly obliged to use such words as "function," "responsibility," "relationship," "accountability," "objective," and "duty" in special senses. For example, what one organization calls "duties and responsibilities" may be another's "scope and specific accountabilities." One organization's "purpose" may be another's "accountability objective." Hopefully, a little language clarification at this point may assist executives and analysts to move toward some standard terms.

One of the most quoted definitions of a managerial position description appeared in a "Management Guide" published by Standard Oil of California. This shortened version of an organization manual for top management contains much information on how to prepare descriptions. The manual uses the term "management guide" in two senses: (1) as an individual description of an executive's position, and (2) to denote the entire manual in which the descriptions of all managers are gathered together with an organization chart of the business. The company's definition reads: "The Management Guide is a delineation of the functions, responsibilities, authorities, and principal relationships of a particular position in a business enterprise, or a series of such delineations of positions." The series referred to would be a full-fledged organization manual if appropriate organization charts were added.

This company assigns particular meanings to the words "function," "responsibility," "authority," and "relationship." These definitions are specific to this organization. "Function" implies a brief statement of the whole job, whereas the phrase "responsibilities and authority" implies a much more detailed statement. With just as much logic, the terms probably could be reversed so that "function" would be used to define the detailed duties of the manager. Yet this individualistic use of words is still quite common, and just what a given organization means by such terms can usually be determined only by reading a number of its position descriptions or by reference to definitions that appear in its manuals.

### Job Descriptions versus Management Guides

In the first edition of this book, job descriptions and management guides had essentially different uses and were therefore clearly definable. Job descriptions were terse, factual, and designed primarily for compensation administration, whereas management guides provided the intangible aspects of positions and their interrelationships and served to inspire the job incumbent to fulfill the pattern of the job as outlined in the guide. At that time the distinction between the two types turned out to be theoretical rather than practical.

Today position descriptions and management guides are quite similar. Furthermore, descriptions that originally served a single purpose (such as compensation administration or management development) have evolved to the point where they serve many different functions of management and personnel operations within an organization. Position (or job) descriptions, position guides, and management guides are sufficiently similar in nature that they can be termed "managerial position descriptions."

This report primarily covers managerial positions and will refer to its subject matter as "managerial position descriptions," which will be defined rather simply as *a brief, clearly written statement of a manager's job in terms of job objectives and the scope and level of job responsibilities, accountabilities, and authority.* This definition is based on the hundreds of position descriptions obtained in this study. Depending on the use of the descriptions, they may be written as the job exists presently or as the job should exist in the future. As the descriptions are oriented more toward performance, the definitions will have to be rewritten and clarified. (For additional information on what constitutes a good description, see Chapter 6.)

### Specifications versus Descriptions

In recording information about jobs a distinction is frequently made between a "specification" and a "description." Managerial position descriptions are written statements outlining the work and responsibilities of managers, whereas managerial position specifications are written statements outlining the qualifications required of persons seeking to hold those positions.

Thus a position description might state that the chief industrial engineer is to "direct and coordinate all industrial engineering operations within the firm." It would also describe some of the more exact ways in which this broad assignment is to be carried out and what specific accountabilities would be entailed. On the other hand, position specifications might state that anyone to be employed as chief industrial engineer must have "at least ten years of experience as a top executive of a manufacturing firm's industrial engineering department" and must also have "a graduate degree in industrial engineering from an accredited university with a regularly established graduate program in this subject area." The individual who fails to meet these specifications cannot, at least theoretically, satisfactorily perform the activities outlined in the description. With the advent of affirmative action programs, these specifications must be bona fide occupational qualifications and there must be a demonstrated relationship between the qualifications and the job.

Job specifications are often prepared for recruitment, hiring, and promotion. Such specifications are also referred to as "job qualifications," "position qualifications," or "minimum hiring requirements." In many cases specifications or qualifications are kept apart from job descriptions. Typically, specifications for each position are kept on file by the personnel department or other departments or by executives directly involved in the recruitment process. On the other hand, position descriptions may be distributed much more widely throughout the organization simply because they have so many useful applications.

A few organizations do include the qualifications in the individual executive's description. This practice is particularly common among organizations that prepare the descriptions with recruitment and selection as primary objectives. In such cases the qualifications form one more section *within* the position description. In the future more position descriptions may include such sections because of the impact of affirmative action programs on the entire personnel process.

**Position Specifications and Organization Charts**
The AMA has defined another concept in description programs as follows: "A position specification consists of three parts: a position description; an organization chart; and position qualifications." The word "specification" is used as the broadest term, with "position description," "organization chart," and "qualifications" (elsewhere commonly referred to as "specifica-

tions") denoting parts of the whole. This approach is probably just as logical as any other, but again it shows that terminology varies from authority to authority.

Perhaps the most interesting thing about this definition is that it points out a relationship between organization charts and position descriptions. A person new to a managerial post would find it quite difficult to understand his or her place in the organization without a careful study of an organization chart. From a glance at the chart, it is usually quite easy to see the position's relation to other managerial positions throughout the organization. If well drawn, the organization chart makes it possible to omit much detail in the written description. Analysts who attempt to translate all possible relationships traceable in an organization chart into words in the description are probably wasting valuable time and space.

Normally, most of the discussion of relationships in a written position description is meant to supplement the facts readily discernible from the organization chart. The written description can be particularly helpful in clarifying vertical relationships that may not be clearly defined by the chart. For example, consider the factory manager who reports to a vice president in charge of manufacturing. The chart indicates that the vice president is responsible for the acts of the factory manager. But to what extent has authority been delegated? With which person should a question on purchases of capital equipment commonly be discussed? Would one of the positions require extensive and detailed knowledge of production-control systems, while the other involves only general direction of such an activity?

## PROBLEMS IN INITIATING
## NEW POSITION DESCRIPTION PROGRAMS

Before an organization decides to institute managerial position descriptions, serious consideration should be given to the very basic question of whether such a program is worthwhile. Managerial descriptions require the expenditure of time on the part of participating executives, and the money outlay may be considerable, especially if outside consultants are called in to help the program along.

More than 95 percent of the respondents in this study have managerial position description programs. Their problems in developing and continuing their programs can serve as guides for an organization that is seriously considering whether or not to install such a program. (For additional information on these problems, see Chapter 4.) Most of the considerations outlined below were mentioned by respondents in both this and the earlier AMA surveys.

1. Many organizations do not consider managerial position descriptions worthwhile when an organization is small (under 200 employees), has a closely knit, highly personal top management group, and has little prospect for expansion. In such a situation, duties, responsibilities, and accountabilities are fairly well understood, and carefully written delineations of them may be superfluous. Of course, small organizations may wish to *change* managerial relationships and job content; a position description program can then be a useful tool.

2. Descriptions written during a period of spasmodic and unplanned expansion are mostly wasted (which is often the case in large public agencies and nonprofit corporations), since they are soon outmoded and bear no visible relation to the actual work being done by executives. However, an organization that wishes to undertake an expansion program of an organized, *planned* nature can use descriptions advantageously for organization design. For example, a complete set of descriptions can be written before a new department or division is set up and, if well conceived, can form a fairly satisfactory outline of the new unit when combined with a well-drawn organization chart. Needless to say, descriptions written in this circumstance are invaluable as induction and training aids.

3. Descriptions are a means whereby an organization may take a candid look at itself. When the first set of position descriptions for managers is written, anyone studying them will find considerable overlaps in authority and responsibility, ambiguities in the chain of command, and even duplication of work by whole departments. Well-formulated descriptions bring this out clearly, provided someone in authority takes the time and effort needed to study them. If immovable unwillingness to make any changes in basic organization structure is encountered at this point, the descriptions lose much of their value.

4. Position descriptions are not likely to pay off if they are hurriedly written to conform to a sort of "management fashion." Inherently useful tools of management (such as managerial development, performance appraisal, organization charts, and operations research) at times go through a period in which they are somewhat in vogue, and an organization may decide that it will seem behind the times if it does not jump on the bandwagon. So the word goes out: "Put it in operation—starting yesterday, if possible." If purpose or sincerity is lost in the rush, most of the potential value will probably be lost too. Many organizations have certainly found real use for descriptions of managerial and top executive positions, but it seems unwise to go through the lengthy, demanding process of formulating them just because "it's the thing to do."

5. Managerial position descriptions are probably not worthwhile if they are to be used only on a single occasion. The effort that goes into prepar-

ing them is too time-consuming and expensive. For instance, if an entire set of descriptions is prepared merely to give a new president an overall look at the organization, it may be somewhat out of date by the time it is presented. Furthermore, the executive may have gained the requisite information through personal observation before the descriptions are ready. This single-occasion situation is unlikely because most descriptions are soon used for multiple purposes, even when just one purpose was considered at the outset.

6. A well-considered description project is time-consuming. It is likely to take a minimum of three months to organize and initiate. Several more months may pass before any sizable number of descriptions are complete (written, compared, adjusted, approved, and distributed). Three more months may elapse before all the bugs are eliminated and the program is really part of routine operations (with descriptions being revised regularly). It takes approximately a year from the starting point to establish a program that operates routinely. This is understandable if it is remembered that a top management description sometimes determines the nature of an entire department or division employing thousands of persons. Actually, a well-formulated description at the executive level is very important, and considerable judgment must be used, especially because the description constitutes a type of "charter of authority" to an individual manager. It is wise to go slowly; the damage resulting from poor descriptions can be enormous.

7. Position descriptions should be formulated to serve many purposes, ranging from compensation administration to individual career planning to designing the organization to performance appraisal. Although many organizations begin programs with a single purpose in mind, almost all of them expand their use after they discover their value to management and to the personnel function. Perhaps it would be better to formulate the descriptions from the beginning with the understanding that they will be used in many different areas. This affects the content of the descriptions in a very marked way.

8. Managerial position descriptions are not a panacea. Many of the respondents stated that the process of formulating the descriptions is beneficial to both the incumbent executive and the organization. Relationships, overlaps, and sensitive areas are openly discussed with a resulting stimulus toward better performance. This is the developmental aspect of position descriptions. Descriptions are worth more if they are kept current and are used regularly after they have been formulated. Accurate revisions must be made whenever job content changes significantly. Descriptions placed in a confidential file because the work involved in keeping them current seems onerous are not serving the organization.

9. Can your organization afford them? A good program needs the full-time (or nearly full-time) effort of at least one person. It also absorbs a great deal of the time of the executives whose positions are being described. The expense increases if an outside consultant is called in. It often takes considerable time to convince the individual manager of the immediate value and continuing usefulness of the descriptions.

## THE OPERATING DECISIONS INVOLVED IN PROGRAMS

After the basic decision to describe managerial positions has been reached, a series of operating decisions must be made and continually expanded during the life of the program. Each decision will influence others, and the sum of the decisions may determine the success and perhaps even continuance of the program. The following summary attempts to provide a rough, overall guide to most of these major matters. Factual information on these items is given in greater detail in succeeding chapters of this report. Naturally, the same problems do not occur in the same order and at the same level of complexity in all programs. Yet this summary can be useful, even if it suggests only a few of the major items.

### Coverage of Description Programs

More and more organizations are covering larger numbers of their employees with position descriptions. Indeed, more and more managerial positions are being covered by position descriptions. Regardless of the type of organization (private, public, nonprofit), almost all of them cover approximately the same types and numbers of positions with descriptions. Of course, some organizations still do not have position descriptions, for reasons ranging from types of jobs to size of operations to costs of the program. In many of these cases the reasons appear to be legitimate. In others there seems to be a distinct lack of understanding by top management as to the nature and uses of managerial position descriptions and how these can strengthen management. Statistics on the use of programs in organizations, the overall coverage of such programs, and the noncoverage in a few organizations are provided in Chapter 2.

In deciding which positions to describe, the purpose and uses of the descriptions must be borne clearly in mind. For example, one can plan a drastic reorganization on the basis of as few as ten carefully written, top-level descriptions. Each description in such a program represents a major part of the organization. For instance, by rewriting the description of the vice president of marketing, one can radically change the entire character of the marketing department. If it is done for every top manager, the entire nature of the organization may be changed. This use of descriptions constitutes the very essence of a description program designed for organization planning.

On the other hand, if an organization plans primarily to establish a just basis for the entire organization's managerial salary structure, a far greater number of positions must be covered. Having decided on the total number and the kinds of positions that will be covered, the organization has a better idea of the basic nature and magnitude of the task. If the organization plans to use the finished descriptions for a wide variety of purposes, the number of positions to be described will be affected by each separate proposed use.

At this stage some thought should be given to the basis for deciding which jobs are to be described. This is in part a matter of prestige. If it is announced that a managerial position description program is to be carried out and several positions are not included, it is tantamount to a statement that one or two individuals are not in management. This can cause considerable dismay and irritation. Some organizations set definite criteria for deciding which jobs are to be covered. For instance, the question can be decided by salary level. All those receiving a certain amount or more will be included in the program; all those below it will be excluded. At least this has the advantage of establishing a firm criterion that everyone can understand. Other organizations decide on looser criteria such as the nature of the job titles, degrees of responsibility, specific accountabilities, and even "the degree of interest" shown by incumbent executives.

**Objectives for Description Programs**

When the initial objectives for a managerial position description program are formulated, they are usually oriented toward (1) compensation administration only, (2) a combination of compensation administration and other managerial purposes, or (3) managerial purposes excluding compensation administration. After a period of time managers invariably begin to use these descriptions for other purposes. Organizations that formulated descriptions primarily for compensation administration often use them in manpower planning and organization planning; other organizations, intending to use the descriptions only for executive development, have found they can serve in performance evaluation and personnel budgeting. Seldom are the descriptions used exclusively for their originally intended purpose. Specific information on the original stated objectives is found in Chapter 2.

**Uses of Managerial Position Descriptions**

Over the past fifteen years, many new ways to use managerial position descriptions have been discovered. Among the purposes they now serve are *organization design,* including long-range planning, organization planning, organization clarification, job design and redesign, and work-flow review and improvement; *manpower planning; individual career planning; management by objectives; recruitment, selection, and placement; orientation of new executives; compensation administration,* including both internal and external salary comparisons; *management development; performance appraisal,* including the establishment of standards of performance; and *task forces, project teams, and matrix teams.* Apparently, new uses of position descriptions will continue to be formulated by organizations. Chapter 3 provides an extensive discussion of the uses of the descriptions.

Our survey discovered that most organizations with managerial position description programs find additional uses for their descriptions after they are formulated. The possibility of multiple uses should be considered at the outset of the program so that further developments will permit the same descriptions to continue to be used. In this research, a few programs had a stylized format appropriate for only one use. For instance, they may have emphasized such sections as accountability, ultimate financial responsibility if errors are made, and number of persons supervised for compensation-administration purposes. Later on, other uses for the descriptions were found—recruitment, selection, and placement; organization design; and individual career planning. Descriptions formulated later in the program were changed significantly to permit their use in other areas. They were very different from those written at the outset of the program.

The ideal is to write the first description so well that a format for the entire program can evolve from it—one that can be used for a considerable period of time. However, this concept is changing because of the increasing demand for performance-oriented descriptions requiring greater applicability and flexibility in job descriptions. With the initiation of these new results-oriented programs, there is also substantially more interaction between the descriptions and the annual worksheets prepared for these programs.

After all the descriptions are written, they are compared. If all the descriptions do not contain comparable information (or do not cover the same subjects for each job), no valid comparisons can be made, thus obviating their usefulness for any purpose at all. Before embarking on the program it is perhaps best to formulate a written outline of what each description should contain. If additions or omissions are later decided on, *all* previously written descriptions should be adjusted to fit the new format. This provides for both consistency and some flexibility. Chapter 6 covers this subject in detail; there are also materials in Part Two of this book that pertain to the organization's efforts to achieve consistency in writing descriptions.

## Creating New Managerial Positions

In the past five years many new managerial and professional jobs have been established. Most of them reflect the changing concerns of organizations today. For example, many of them are related to consumer affairs, environmental protection, occupational health and safety, and equal employment opportunity. These types of new positions are sprinkled throughout top, executive, and middle management ranks.

In addition to these new concerns, corporations are apparently becoming sufficiently anxious about the increasing acceleration of change and the unforeseen fresh challenges and problems of the future to begin to establish long-range planning positions at both top and middle management levels. These planners hopefully will provide information and plans far enough in advance to allow managers to optimize opportunities and act on them rather than react to them under extremely unfavorable circumstances for their organizations.

In terms of traditional functions, new positions have appeared primarily in marketing at top management levels and uniformly among all functions at middle management levels. In addition, new positions seem to be appearing in computer technology, management information systems, and administrative services. The study indicates a substantial proliferation of jobs throughout both public and private sectors. Apparently there is an attempt to actually define some jobs for given individuals in some organizations. New management positions and related problems are discussed in Chapter 3.

## Establishing New Programs

In launching a managerial position description program successfully, top management support is one of the vital requirements. High-level authorization of the program emphasizes its importance to executives whose positions are being described. Furthermore, top-level support is important when these descriptions may be used in major projects such as reorganization programs, management-by-objectives programs, and organizational attempts to adjust compensation rates. Chapter 4 emphasizes the necessity of strong top-level support for the program.

In general, a personnel executive is placed in charge of the program at the outset. Personnel men and women are chosen because they already have had experience in handling similar programs for nonexempt salaried and hourly employees and are dealing with similar functions in their daily personnel operations. Furthermore, they are familiar with the operations related to the potential uses of the descriptions. Occasionally, other managers are placed in charge of the program initially. Such executives may have proposed the idea, may have an intimate knowledge of the jobs to be described, or may have a reputation for impartiality and fairness. In these cases the responsibility usually shifts toward the personnel function after the programs have been initiated and are successfully accomplishing their missions.

Although top and executive managers are preferred for the initial stages of the program, frequently lower-level managers are placed in charge of it. In some cases it may be better to choose a lower-level executive who has more time to devote to the project than an overloaded superior. In others it is better to avoid putting a junior manager in charge, since it is inevitable that the positions of his or her superiors must be described and it may not be possible to obtain their cooperation.

It is almost unnecessary to remark that the person guiding or coordinating such a program should have great understanding and appreciation of its purpose and a detailed knowledge of position descriptions. It is not enough to have participated in the description of office and shop jobs, since *managerial* position descriptions are usually more complex and involve such things as status and prestige. The assignment requires a diplomat. Sometimes individuals were chosen to head programs simply because they had the requisite personalities to handle prestige conflicts and the ability to brush over technical details of position descriptions rapidly. Lack of specific experience was far outweighed by demonstrated ability.

In instituting a new program, consultants are occasionally used. In these cases the management consulting services available range all the way from installing an entire program—writing the descriptions and training an organization's employees to continue and maintain a project—to offering a few days of consultation and advice. Outside assistance in initiating programs is often obtained from some other source, such as by attendance at seminars or training courses on the subject. Some organizations indicate that an outsider has the benefit of "neutrality" in organizational politics and can therefore do a more objective job. Others note that consultants are not used because they do not have enough intimate acquaintance with the organization's problems and structure. Although it is a difficult question to decide, the major consideration is probably whether or not persons within the organization have the abilities and talents to carry out the program without external assistance. Outside assistance is described in Chapter 4.

Up to this point in the planning, it is possible that incumbent executives have no knowledge of the impending description program. Sometimes this is where a program ends, simply because it encounters icy rejection by the management group. It is easy to see that if the program is introduced carelessly, at least a few executives may believe that an effort is being made to prune dead wood, to adjust compensation (perhaps downward), to cut some jobs down to a smaller size, or to inflate other jobs. Prestige and status are definitely involved.

What should be done about this problem? The program will be initiated best if it has the full force of the organization's top management behind it. The introductory announcement outlining the program to managers is frequently sponsored or actually conducted by the chief executive. The favored method appears to be a group meeting of top organization executives at which the need for descriptions is outlined and the method to be used in describing their positions is explained. Each executive then may hold a meeting of the department's managers and explain the program to them as fully and frankly as possible. Other organizations prefer to announce the project by means of a letter signed by the president, and some feel that the matter is vital enough to require both a meeting and a letter. If a consultant is employed, it is generally felt that he or she should be introduced at the meeting. It is also advisable to state what each executive may expect in the way of results and what he or she must do to prepare for job analysis.

The basic purpose of the program should be explained at this meeting or in the introductory memo. Reassurances are often given that compensation will not be reduced as a result of the description program and that no one will lose his or her job. Sometimes it is carefully explained that the study is being conducted for equality in compensation only and that job content will not be altered as a result—or, on the contrary, that the balance of duties is being reviewed and compensation will not be affected. In this connection, consideration should be given to the statistics in this report that tend to demonstrate that the eventual uses of descriptions in actual practice frequently go far beyond the purposes planned and expressed at the outset of the program (see Chapter 3). Whatever the intent, descriptions *are* used for many different purposes once they are formulated. They are too valuable to neglect. A statement at an introductory meeting that descriptions will be used for a single purpose is almost certain to prove confining or embarrassing later. Further information on how programs are introduced is given in Chapter 5.

### Continuation of Existing Programs

Once a program has been instituted, an organization tends to shift the responsibility for its administration downward. After the program has been routinized, a lower-level manager is placed in charge. Theoretically, at least, most of the major problems have now been resolved. In almost all these cases the new manager in charge is from either personnel or compensation administration. Shifts in responsibility for the program frequently occur after the first full set of managerial position descriptions has been finalized. Furthermore, after the program has been in existence for some time, the responsibility is shifted even lower in the organization, usually to someone in compensation administration. Hierarchically, the programs continue to move downward through management levels as the programs become more and more regularized. For a discussion of responsibility for these programs, see Chapter 4.

Continuing programs usually develop a fairly consistent set of problems. Most of these fall into the following classes: (1) the maintenance of managerial involvement in managerial position description programs as time passes; (2) the relative inflexibility of managerial position description programs, particularly in organizations that are rapidly growing or have high technological bases; and (3) the continually changing job content of position descriptions. An analysis of these problems and some suggested solutions are noted in Chapter 4.

**Top Management Control of Programs**
Although the direct supervision of managerial description programs usually rests in the personnel function, top management usually continues to maintain control. It is critical that such control continue. In describing their positions, executives may attempt to assume additional authority (which the organization does not want them to have), or understate the requirements, or gloss over the weaknesses in the position. Thus there must be some control over the process of writing position descriptions. Top management control of the program may be instituted at any step in the writing of the descriptions, or the organization may throw primary responsibility for the development of descriptions entirely on the shoulders of those managing the program. However, flexible controls are usually instituted by top management so that it can step in at any point if the program begins to develop problems. (See Chapter 6 for a discussion of some of these controls.)

**Preparing Position Descriptions**
After an organization has decided on a managerial position description program, determined the coverage of the program, clarified the program's objectives and uses, appointed an executive to guide the project, hired (or refrained from hiring) outside assistance, and communicated the existence of the pending program to incumbent executives, the next step is to consider the most practical means of formulating the descriptions themselves (unless, of course, the entire project has been turned over to a consultant).

In nearly every organization participating in this survey, the process falls into four stages: (1) gathering the job content information; (2) writing a first draft of the description; (3) reviewing, revising, and approving this preliminary version, usually after comparison with other position descriptions throughout the organization; and (4) writing and approving the final authorized version. For the details of the steps used, see Chapter 6.

The executive in charge of the project must decide how each of these stages is going to be accomplished and who should participate at each stage. In general, the three persons who are most active in all stages are the organization's description specialist (not necessarily the head of the program), the executive whose position is being described, and the executive's superior. In rare instances the incumbent executive has little or no part in preparing the description of his or her position. Even more unusual, the incumbent executives in a few organizations are not even informed that their positions are being described. This has the disadvantage of cutting out all the beneficial thought and training that occurs in the formulation of a description. Discussions with the incumbent executive are often quite valuable to the superior as well as the incumbent.

Interviews, observations, questionnaires, and previous position descriptions are the major sources of data for position descriptions. Other sources include personal knowledge of the job, personal knowledge of the organization, information from professional associations like the AMA, and personnel directors in other parts of an organization. In each of these methods, the specialist, incumbent executive, and immediate superior are all deeply involved (see Chapter 6).

In writing first drafts of descriptions, the immediate supervisor, incumbent executive, and specialist are all writing about the same number of first drafts. Significantly, the incumbent executive is now less involved— and his or her superior is much more involved in more of these efforts— than was indicated in the 1958 AMA study. For discussion of these changes in writing first drafts, see Chapter 6.

When first drafts of positions have been written, at least two executives are usually involved in their review—one line executive and a personnel specialist. Among the many different combinations used are (1) incumbent executive and specialist; (2) incumbent executive, immediate supervisor, and specialist; and (3) immediate supervisor, supervisor's supervisor, and specialist. Inevitably some conflicts occur between position descriptions because of dual responsibilities, joint accountabilities, and even overlapping reporting relationships. These conflicts are normally resolved by the lowest-level executive with direct authority over *both* positions.

In general, most organizations have only one person writing the final version of the descriptions. In two-thirds of the programs this person is a personnel or compensation specialist of some type. Hopefully, this step is a relatively simple one because the first draft should have been fairly good or should have been written and rewritten until it was at least adequate. Review of the first draft is a critical step in lowering the work level at the authorized final-draft stage. Final approval of these drafts still rests with the line managers. In only a few cases does an incumbent executive approve the final draft of his or her job. Statistics on these steps in formulating descriptions are found in Chapter 6.

### Maintaining Current Position Descriptions

Shortly after an organization has completed its first series of descriptions, the question of maintaining them on a current basis inevitably arises. This is no easy task. To be of real value, the descriptions must be kept up to date on as current a basis as possible. Almost all the organizations with description programs understand the necessity for reviewing them. Indeed, many of them regularly review programs at intervals ranging from one to five years. Almost all of them review and revise their descriptions at irregular intervals whenever (1) the job content changes, (2) the organization structure changes, (3) the incumbent executive changes jobs, and (4) a review is requested by the executive and his or her supervisor. In almost all cases these organizations have standardized procedures for review and revision.

Many of the organizations have different methods and procedures for reviewing and revising managerial descriptions after they have been established. Most programs apparently evolve through a series of steps: (1) The first authorized descriptions have a short outline form with some variation in the sequence and presentation of materials; (2) the first set of major revisions has improved formats and is more uniform, but tends to be too long, too detailed, and too wordy; and (3) the second set of major revisions shows uniform organization of materials and format with shorter, more concise, and better-worded sections. For information on maintaining descriptions up to date, on timing for revisions, on differences in procedures between initial operation of the program and revisions in the program, and on recent new methods of describing jobs, see Chapter 6.

### Content of Position Descriptions

Another important consideration in developing or maintaining a description program is the content desired for the position descriptions. Earlier we stressed the importance of multipurpose descriptions. Yet it is conceivable that at least a few programs have been designed to meet a *primary* need. Although the survey results indicate that this is not the wisest procedure, it may be necessary if a program is being conducted on a "rush" basis. For instance, an organization that definitely plans to use its descriptions (at least in part) as recruitment, selection, and placement guides should plan to include job qualifications or specifications. In other words, it should state the qualities and previous training and experience necessary for the position. As another example, an organization may be using descriptions to clarify promotional lines within the organization. Therefore, an effort should be made to make the section on reporting relationships longer and more detailed than usual.

Another matter affecting the content of descriptions and requiring careful consideration at the program's inception is whether the descriptions are intended to describe the job as it is *currently being done* or as it *should be done* (see Chapter 6). In general, organizations writing descriptions for purposes of salary administration and organization design tend to describe the jobs as they exist. Organizations writing their descriptions for multiple uses tend to describe the positions as they should be. In other words, the latter organizations are providing a target for the incumbent to shoot at—at least in many cases.

Today the content of position descriptions is changing significantly. With the advent of performance-oriented management (management by results and management by objectives), more and more organizations are using job descriptions that provide some means of measuring a manager's performance. Position descriptions include such terms as "accountability objectives," "end results," "specific objectives," and "specific accountabilities." By using these expressions, management is clearly attempting to establish measurable indicators of managerial performance in position descriptions.

Although many different satisfactory arrangements and styles are used in preparing managerial descriptions, the typical description is divided into three or four major sections. Depending on the specific managerial orientation, these sections may be divided in one or the other of these arrangements: (1) Function, Duties and/or Responsibilities, Authority, and Relationships; or (2) Accountability Objectives, Dimensions, Nature and Scope, and Specific Accountabilities. The first tends to be more widely used; however, the second is rapidly gaining popularity as more managements move toward results-oriented performance. Other sections of job descriptions include organizational relationships involving the status of the person to whom the incumbent reports, titles of jobholders reporting to the incumbent, and internal and external relationships with others and with other organizations; qualifications or specifications; position dynamics; and challenge. Thorough descriptions of these many different sections of position descriptions are provided in Chapter 7 and actual illustrations are shown in Part Three of the book.

**Accessibility of Descriptions and Description Manuals**

This study also analyzed the openness of the managerial position program. Apparently, organizations that do not use these descriptions for compensation administration are more likely to allow all employees free access to them than are organizations in which the descriptions are an integral part of compensation administration. Organizations using descriptions for salary purposes are much more cautious in the distribution of their manuals and their position descriptions. In almost all organizations, nonexempt salaried and hourly employees are not allowed to examine manuals or position descriptions except when an organization's basic structure must be explained. With the drive toward participative management by many organizations, these closed attitudes toward the use of descriptions appear to be heading in the opposite direction. In light of the many positive uses of position descriptions in the development of managers, a relatively open system seems far more in order. Statistics on accessibility of descriptions and description manuals and suggestions on accessibility are given in Chapters 4 and 7.

## THE FUTURE OF POSITION DESCRIPTION PROGRAMS

Many of the organizations surveyed anticipate significant shifts in managerial description programs in the future. These organizations believe that management description programs will have to relate to the decline in population growth, the effect of continuing automation, the consequences of the information explosion, and the effects of changing methods of management.

Coverage of these programs will continue to expand upward in the managerial hierarchy. Because their uses probably will change dramatically with the increasing orientation toward results-oriented performance by managers, position descriptions will have to become more current and more flexible. In response to affirmative action programs, position descriptions will add new sections emphasizing career ladders (including the many different promotional opportunities) and qualifications. Modules of positions perhaps will be instituted to standardize descriptions and eliminate overlapping responsibilities and accountabilities. Parts or modules of jobs will be computerized so that jobs can be better designed with less overlap. Such uses of modular components would be quite compatible with newer management concepts of job enrichment, job enlargement, and job redesign. In preparing position descriptions, validity (relation of description to actual job) will be emphasized to meet the requirements of equal employment opportunity programs. The format and contents of position descriptions will become shorter, less detailed, more current, and more flexible. For an additional overview of the future of new methods in position descriptions, see Chapter 8.

## THE SURVEY RESEARCH

This study represents the collective experience of the 142 organizations that returned a six-page questionnaire on managerial position description programs. Of these respondents, 136 had successful programs (see Chapter 2). The organizations in this study represented: *manufacturing; non-manufacturing,* including banks, insurance companies, transportation firms, utilities companies, hotels, and restaurants; *nonprofit organizations,* including hospitals and a museum; *educational institutions,* primarily public and private universities; and *government agencies* at municipal and county levels. These organizations ranged in size from corporations with less than 250 employees to those with over 400,000 employees. Furthermore, the study covered organizations with widely varying types of managements and description programs.

The respondents to AMA's questionnaire were asked to outline the purposes behind their managerial position description programs, the coverage of their programs, the uses to which the descriptions are actually put, the creation of new managerial positions during the past five years, the basic organization of the original and subsequent programs, the use of consultants in establishing and maintaining such programs (if any), the problems encountered in developing and using position descriptions, the introduction of the description program to executives whose positions are being described, the exact methods of gathering the information, the preparation of the first draft and the approval of the final version, the description of the major sections of position descriptions, the maintenance of programs once they are in existence, and significant changes foreseen in managerial description programs in the next five years. The answers to questions concerning these and related issues are summarized in Part One of this book.

This survey part of the book may prompt the reader to assume that the authors consider the majority practice to be the *best* practice. For example, the data may tend to indicate that a majority of the respondents believe a job should be described as it is presently being done rather than as it should be done. However, to conclude that a job should always be described as it is presently being done would not be correct. It is simply common practice as reported by the organizations in this study.

In any one of the areas covered by this survey, the majority—or most popular—practice may be exactly the wrong thing for the individual organization. The statistics in this report are intended to give the reader an idea of the range of possibilities, as seen in the variety of arrangements in current use among the respondents. Selecting the right arrangement or practice, or creating a still better one, is quite another thing.

Sample position descriptions and related exhibit materials reproduced in this report were obtained from two sources: (1) survey respondents, and (2) *AMA Research Study No. 33*. Brief examples of organization terminology, position description manuals, managerial position description questionnaires, and managerial guides appear in Part Two of the book. The descriptions in Part Three attempt to show the full range of management positions from Chairman of the Board of Directors to lower-level professionals in specialized staff positions.

In preparing this report, an effort was made to eliminate descriptions that could not be readily understood by a reader having little knowledge of the program under which they were developed. However, no description should be regarded as "standard" or "ideal." The very essence of managerial position description programs is that the descriptions be tailored to the needs of an individual organization. For instance, the description of a top marketing executive in one company may be entirely different from the description of the same position in another company.

Position descriptions given in this report can be used as sources for ideas on style, content, language, and structural organization, but in no sense should they be regarded as ready-made models of finished descriptions for any organization. An effort has been made to present an ordered series of descriptions whenever possible, as well as a fairly wide sample of job descriptions at every managerial level. Some specialized positions and less well-defined staff activities have been omitted from the collection, primarily because of lack of space.

# 2

# The Extent of
# Coverage and Distribution

When top executives are examining the possibility of establishing a position description program for managers or the potential for revising their present programs, they frequently are faced with questions related to the extent of the coverage of such programs. For example, are there really any differences in how such programs are used by private, nonprofit, and public organizations? Are they used differently by manufacturing and nonmanufacturing organizations (including financial institutions, utilities companies, transportation companies, and hotels and restaurants)? Do such plans vary by size of organization? Do they vary in different types of formal organization structures? What distinguishing characteristics, if any, exist in such programs between different types of organizations?

Executives might wish to analyze their position description programs internally in terms of whether or not every job in the organization is included, which positions or groups of positions, if any, should be omitted, and what objectives should be established for such programs.

This chapter attempts to analyze the use of managerial description programs, the overall internal coverage of such programs, and the original objectives of the programs.

## USE OF PROGRAMS IN ORGANIZATIONS

Of the organizations responding to the questionnaire, almost all had some type of job description program (see Table 1). For purposes of analysis, these organizations were initially broken down into five categories: manufacturing, nonmanufacturing (including banks, insurance companies, railroad companies, airlines, utilities companies, hotels, and restaurants), non-

*Table 1. Organizations that use job descriptions, by type of organization and number of employees.**

| NUMBER OF EMPLOYEES | Type of Organization † | | | | | |
|---|---|---|---|---|---|---|
| | MFG. | NON-MFG. | NON-PROFIT | EDUCATION | GOVERNMENT | TOTAL |
| 0–4,999 | 32 | 16 | 6 | 2 | 2 | 58 |
| 5,000–9,999 | 19 | 4 | — | 2 | — | 25 |
| 10,000–49,999 | 23 | 13 | — | 2 | 2 | 40 |
| 50,000 and over | 7 | 3 | — | — | — | 10 |
| Total | 81 | 36 | 6 | 6 | 4 | 133 |

* 136 organizations had job descriptions; 3 did not answer the question.
† Nonmanufacturing includes banks, insurance companies, transportation companies, utilities companies, hotels, and restaurants. Nonprofit includes museums and hospitals.

profit (including museums and hospitals), education (both private and public institutions), and government.

A close examination of the questionnaires seemed to show that the position description programs were used for the same purposes regardless of the size or type of organization. Analysis of the formal organization structures of the various corporations and agencies revealed little or no difference in how the programs were used by the different levels of organization (such as total structure, subsidiary or affiliate, and division). Because of this uniformity of use throughout industry, nonprofit corporations, and government agencies, it was assumed throughout the study that these could be treated in the same manner.

## OVERALL COVERAGE OF THE PROGRAMS

Approximately 48 percent of the organizations participating in the study have descriptions of one type or another for all jobs—from corporate president or agency head down through production workers and clerical employees. This is a significant shift from the AMA study fifteen years ago which indicated that 30 percent had coverage for all jobs. More and more organizations are adopting total description programs—and spending a great deal of money on them. Some planned to include all jobs from the beginning; others started with small pilot groups either at the top or at the bottom of the organization and gradually expanded the program to fill in the gaps.

Apart from those organizations with complete position description programs covering all employees, the coverage is quite spotty. However, it appears that programs tend to cover middle management and below much more thoroughly than top and executive management (see Table 2). Apparently there has been a significant shift since the last study when most of the job descriptions extended upward only through first-line supervision. Obviously more and more organizations have felt the need to optimize their coverage and have quite thorough coverage up through middle management. Some organizations still feel that top management positions should not be described. For example, one respondent commented: "Managerial jobs are difficult to describe in a brief manner. Also the positions tend to change with the incumbent." Another stated: "Our administration does not believe that a manager's job should be detailed through a description. His or her job consists of everything . . . to make the area or department run effectively and efficiently."

Fewer than 10 percent of the organizations stated that salary level was used as a factor in determining which jobs were to be included in the description program. In such organizations the annual minimum salary level of the lowest-paying job described ranged from $3,500 to $9,152, while the range for the highest-paying job described was from $6,720 to $100,000. However, the annual minimum salary level of the highest-paying job described usually was over $25,000.

Some organizations are still in the experimental stage and have pilot projects in which position descriptions cover only a few managers. Other organizations are experimenting with various forms of management by results and management by objectives. In describing the work of an executive it should be remembered that the interrelationships and complexities of their many responsibilities make their jobs more difficult to reduce to writing than the work of lathe operators, stenographers, assemblers, and shop foremen. Descriptions of lower-level jobs are usually written for wage and salary comparison and for recruitment and selection. Managerial position descriptions are often written for organization clarification and planning and for developmental purposes. It would be foolish to ask a person to describe managerial positions solely on the basis of earlier experiences with shop service or with clerical jobs. Describing managerial positions and lower-level jobs in the same manner could be almost worthless, particularly if the descriptions are to be used for organizational or developmental purposes.

**Who Is Covered?**
Some of the responses to a question on who is covered indicate that some organizations have not rationally thought out their programs in any planned way, but are trying to describe all positions and are getting the work done whenever and wherever it is possible. For instance, a large di-

Table 2. Percent coverage of position description programs, by type of organization and by type of employee.

| PERCENT COVERED | TOP MANAGEMENT | EXECUTIVE MANAGEMENT | MIDDLE MANAGEMENT | FIRST-LINE SUPERVISORS | SALARIED PROFESSIONALS | SALARIED NONEXEMPT | HOURLY |
|---|---|---|---|---|---|---|---|
| Manufacturing | | | | | | | |
| None | 30 | 19 | 3 | 4 | 5 | 5 | 12 |
| 0–25 | 5 | 1 | 5 | 3 | 5 | 4 | 6 |
| 26–50 | 4 | 5 | 8 | 6 | 3 | 4 | 8 |
| 51–75 | 2 | 5 | 4 | 6 | 7 | 4 | 5 |
| 76–100 | 3 | 5 | 12 | 13 | 11 | 15 | 11 |
| All | 35 | 45 | 47 | 46 | 46 | 43 | 31 |
| Nonmanufacturing | | | | | | | |
| None | 11 | 5 | 1 | 1 | 2 | 4 | 7 |
| 0–25 | 1 | 3 | — | — | — | 3 | 5 |
| 26–50 | — | 1 | 1 | 1 | — | 2 | — |
| 51–75 | — | 2 | — | — | — | — | — |
| 76–100 | 2 | 2 | 10 | 9 | 11 | 7 | — |
| All | 19 | 20 | 22 | 23 | 20 | 19 | 17 |
| Other | | | | | | | |
| None | 8 | 7 | 4 | 2 | 1 | 1 | 2 |
| 0–25 | 3 | 1 | 2 | 3 | 3 | — | 2 |
| 26–50 | — | 1 | 1 | — | 1 | 1 | — |
| 51–75 | — | 1 | — | — | — | 2 | 1 |
| 76–100 | — | — | 2 | 3 | 3 | 4 | 4 |
| All | 7 | 8 | 9 | 9 | 10 | 10 | 9 |
| Total* | 130 | 131 | 131 | 129 | 128 | 128 | 120 |

* 136 organizations were covered by programs. If a column does not total 136, the organization had no employees in that category, no answer was given, or the information was not available.

versified conglomerate reported: "Twenty percent of top management are covered; executive management, 50 percent; middle management, 80 percent; first-line supervisors, 80 percent; salaried exempt professionals, 80 percent; salaried nonexempt employees, 15 percent; and hourly workers, 25 percent." In a large entertainment conglomerate, a very different pattern appeared: "Top management, 100 percent; executive management, 100 percent; middle management, 80 percent; first-line supervisors, 40 percent; salaried exempt professionals, 80 percent; salaried nonexempt employees, 10 percent; and hourly workers, none."

Table 2 provides some information on the coverage of description programs in manufacturing, nonmanufacturing, and "other" organizations. In their responses to a checklist question about the coverage of their programs for all employees,* all the different types of organizations represented in the table indicated that employees are covered by programs fairly consistently up through middle management. However, large numbers of top and executive managers are not covered by job descriptions. Approximately one-half of these positions are covered (top management, 47 percent; executive management, 56 percent).

**The Top Executive**

Top executives were classified in Table 2 under two categories: top management (including chairman of the board, president, director, and the president's office) and executive management (including group vice president, executive vice president, senior vice president, general manager, deputy director, corporate and division vice president, including both line and staff officers). Middle management included all managers below the officer and above the supervisory levels. The latter classification is admittedly loose and includes a great variety of positions. Job descriptions covered approximately the same percentages of middle managers as of all levels of employees below them.

Position descriptions for middle managers are significantly more common than for top executives (approximately 60 percent of all middle managers are covered). It appears that descriptions for top officials are the most difficult to formulate. In addition, many of the responding organizations seem to believe the duties of the highest officials are perfectly under-

---

* The seven categories of employees were (1) *top management* (chairman, president, director, president's office); (2) *executive management* (group vice president, senior vice president, general manager, deputy director, corporate and division vice president, including both line and staff officers); (3) *middle management* (all managers below officer and above supervisory levels); (4) *first-line supervisors* (first supervisory level exempt from FICA with responsibility for operating employees); (5) *salaried exempt professional employees* (engineers, chemists, technical workers, etc.); (6) *salaried exempt employees;* and (7) *hourly workers.*

stood and require no formal description. Probably both factors cause the lower coverage of top officials.

During the past fifteen years there has been no significant change in the percentage of organizations using position descriptions for top executives. The significant shift seems to be from partial position description programs to programs covering all positions in the organization. Organizations apparently have discovered the importance of such programs for all their employees, not just their lower-level ones.

In organizations using position descriptions primarily for salary administration, top executives appear to be particularly reluctant to have their positions described in writing. They become much less resistant when the descriptions are formulated and used "to help executives acquire greater understanding of their present jobs by analyzing their duties"—that is, the descriptions are used as a developmental tool to assist managers in their work.

It is probably less necessary to write careful descriptions of top executive work if the program is primarily for salary administration. After all, the salaries of presidents and other top persons are often subjects of business gossip and are used by leading firms in their competition for executives. If one is to be president of a 2,000-employee manufacturing corporation, the salary or total compensation should roughly approximate the salary or total compensation received by other presidents in similar corporations in the same industry. Often, confidential salary comparison surveys are used for this purpose.

Type of company, type of industry, and geographical location are far more important in determining a top executive's salary than a detailed statement of his or her exact duties. This is further brought out by the fact that quite a number of top executive position descriptions are quite simple. One large corporation describes the duties of its president as follows: "The president is the chief executive officer of the company and is responsible for the accomplishment of the company's objectives." Whoever formulated this description evidently believed the duties of a president are so well understood that it was not necessary to go into detail. This same firm has formulated quite detailed descriptions for middle management positions. When it comes to setting the compensation of a middle manager—for example, a product division head or the manager of a branch—a well-written position description is invaluable precisely because, without it, one cannot make logical comparisons with other jobs within the company and with similar positions in other organizations.

Some organizations started their description programs by formulating the very top executive jobs in some detail. Often this has been done when a fairly drastic reorganization was contemplated and top posts had to be interrelated properly before organizational changes at lower levels were attempted. How the descriptions are used seems to be the determining factor in deciding the coverage of the description program.

**Who Is Not Covered?**
In this study the organizations that do not use managerial job descriptions are divided into two groups: those that have never used them for any positions and those with only partial coverage (excluding managerial positions) in an existing position description program. Only six organizations have never used job descriptions (three manufacturing, two nonmanufacturing, and one nonprofit). These organizations gave the following reasons for their policy: (1) Management had decided beforehand against job descriptions; (2) the entire staff consisted of the executive officers and the secretary; and (3) the company did not feel they were needed. However, in four cases, the organizations have plans to establish position description programs in the future on either an all-level organizationwide basis or with just partial coverage at lower levels of the organization.

Some organizations with partial position description programs have formal units operating without managerial job descriptions by actual design. Twenty-one percent of the organizations in this study do have some such units. Reasons for not having job descriptions are usually grouped into the following categories:

1. *Types of jobs.* This usually includes professionals of all types including attorneys and research and development personnel. For example, one corporation stated: "A major research and development engineering unit operates without descriptions in the belief that a description would be restrictive and that maturity curves are a more appropriate means of gauging salary levels."

2. *Scope of jobs.* The positions themselves are too broad, too complex, and too changeable to be clearly delineated. One utilities company stated: "Top management positions are too broad and such positions are not included in the job evaluation program." Another company thought they should not be described because of the "tremendous fluctuations in these jobs."

3. *Circumstances of jobs.* In certain instances the jobs are either temporary or special assignments and no definitive position descriptions are necessary.

4. *Size of operations.* In some cases the operations may be extremely small and/or require much flexibility.

5. *Costs of the programs.* One organization noted: "We do not regard the benefits as commensurate with the costs of developing and maintaining the descriptions."

6. *Insufficient support from top management.* "No useful purpose is served by having descriptions." There is "no motivation to extend those presently described."

7. *Types of management style.* "The descriptions themselves are inconsistent with the management style and interrelationships we endeavor to promote among our people."

8. *New concepts of management.* Some of the newer concepts of management encourage either defining jobs broadly in terms of job enlargement or job enrichment or defining jobs continuously through the establishment of goals, results, and so on. For example, one company stated: "All jobs follow the concept of 'job-enlargement–job enrichment.' The man makes the job. Descriptions may be too limiting." A large manufacturer commented: "MBO descriptions of responsibilities are more up to date and tend to boil out the super verbiage. Focus is on 'key' measurable responsibilities, not on prestige building or compensation-evaluation factors."

9. *Insufficient staff.* Some organizations do not have sufficient staff to extend the description program to all or to other managerial positions. In some instances the staff is too poorly or too inadequately trained to establish any program at all.

Some of these reasons are obviously legitimate. Others, however, show a distinct lack of understanding by top management as to the nature and uses of a position description program and how it can strengthen the management of the organization.

## ORIGINAL OBJECTIVES OF THE PROGRAMS

In the past fifteen years at least one-half (68) of the respondents had established managerial position description programs. Indeed, of the 104 respondents who were able to report when their programs had been established, all but two stated that they were established after 1945. It appears that in the decades of the sixties and seventies there has been an increasing interest in position description programs for managerial personnel.

The original objectives of a position description program are usually oriented toward (1) salary administration only, (2) a combination of salary administration and other managerial purposes, and (3) managerial purposes excluding salary administration. This study indicates that 50 percent of the organizations established their programs originally for salary administration, which includes such functions as job analysis, job evaluation, job grading, job classification, salary evaluation, and salary structures. Two statements of original objectives primarily stressing salary administration are given:

(1) to describe and evaluate all exempt positions; (2) assign salary grades and develop a salary structure for these grades; and (3) establish policies and procedures for administering salaries. (A manufacturing company in 1957.)

The purpose is (1) to analyze the duties, responsibilities, and authorities of the positions and to prepare complete and objective descriptions of them; (2) to arrive at an objective evaluation of the positions through the application of a uniform rating scale applicable to the position evaluations; (3) to develop a sound and competitive salary structure which will incorporate the results of the analysis and evaluation of the positions and meet competitive conditions of the industry and with other employers having similar professional positions. (A utilities company in 1972.)

Seventeen percent of the organizations founded their programs for a combination of salary administration and other managerial purposes, including manpower planning, organization planning, recruitment, selection, orientation, budgeting, organization design, organization development, performance evaluation, management development, and career planning. In addition, such programs in recent years have been used to provide opportunities for disadvantaged minority groups and women and to fulfill the requirements of federal, state, and local laws requiring that position descriptions be related to the work actually being performed. The original objectives statements of two organizations that use their programs for salary administration and other purposes follow:

The description could be adapted to salary evaluation, job training, selection and placement of personnel, appraisal of personnel performance, organization and methods improvement, integration of the efforts of personnel, and development of promotional sequences. (A manufacturing firm in 1948.)

The program serves the purposes of organization planning, compensation, evaluation, aid in placement and orientation, definition of position roles, and definition of company expectations. (An airline in the 1960s.)

Some of the organizations in the study (33 percent) initially did not use their programs for salary administration. As noted above, many personnel and managerial uses can be made of position descriptions. Two examples of original objectives statements for programs that exclude salary administration are given:

(1) define responsibilities clearly; (2) eliminate duplication of effort; (3) position evaluation; (4) organization planning; and (5) management development. (An airline in 1967.)

To delineate new and revised managerial duties in connection with a major reorganization. (A bank in 1965.)

Naturally, all the uses an organization makes of the job descriptions are not of equal importance. Though it is enough to say the descriptions are used primarily for salary administration and/or for "other purposes," "and" appears more frequently than "or" in the answers of participants in this and the prior AMA study.

Current uses of managerial position descriptions often bear little relationship to those originally envisioned. Almost all organizations find additional uses for the descriptions as their programs evolve. These subsidiary uses are often quite important. In fact, "by-product" uses sometimes overshadow the planned uses in value to the organization. The many initial and subsequent uses for position descriptions will be examined in the next chapter.

The philosophy seems to be: The descriptions are there—let's use them. Of course, this might lead to the use of salary-administration descriptions in organization planning. Whether or not this is a wise practice is quite another point. If descriptions are to be used for both purposes, one might conclude that they should contain the two types of descriptive material— that is, "specifics" and broad management blueprints. Part Three of this book shows that at least a few companies do attempt precisely this.

# 3

# *The Uses of*
# *Position Descriptions*

There have been frequent discussions in articles and books about the uses of managerial position descriptions, but most of these are entirely theoretical or based on the experience of one organization or one practitioner. This study reports on the experience of 142 organizations. Participants were asked to outline the uses to which managerial position descriptions are put in their organizations. Many differences were found between the original uses (described in the previous chapter) and their present uses. Most organizations found additional uses for the descriptions after starting their programs.

In principle, a description appropriate to compensation administration is terse and inclined to be specific—how many people are supervised, the ultimate financial liability incurred if the incumbent makes a mistake, and so on. But a description designed for use in a management guide or position guide is inclined to be broad, to stress relationships, and to provide a blueprint for management. The statistics developed in this report tend to indicate that this sharp theoretical difference between one type of description and another is really quite academic, simply because most organizations develop descriptions for one or two basic purposes and then, in reality, appropriate them for use in other areas.

This chapter discusses typical uses of position descriptions, enumerates how such descriptions are presently used in organizations, analyzes shifts that have occurred from original uses to present uses, and describes new types of managerial positions that have come into existence during the past five years.

34

## TYPICAL USES OF
## POSITION DESCRIPTIONS IN ORGANIZATIONS

To give the reader a clearer idea of how managerial descriptions have proved useful, the authors have taken the responses of several participants in the study and have put them together to make a complete statement of one idea. The composite quotations represent only the more common statements of the respondents. Such a procedure, perhaps, is even more illuminating than exact quotations, since each composite statement represents a group opinion. Numerical analysis of the comparative use of position descriptions is presented in the next section.

The following brief paragraphs have been systematically laid out to show how organizations use managerial position descriptions in management and personnel administration. The discussion begins with information and quotations on organization design, progresses through manpower planning and individual career planning, and continues through various aspects of personnel operations in management.

*Organization Design.* Many organizations have used position descriptions in the structuring and restructuring of their operations. They have used them in long-range planning, organization planning, organization clarification, job design and redesign, and work-flow review and improvement. Approximately 10 percent of the respondents (14) stated that they used position descriptions for long-range planning. However, none of their actual descriptions indicated this use. Apparently they are used informally in such planning efforts.

In the areas of organization planning and organization clarification, position descriptions serve to clarify managerial relationships and responsibilities. By providing descriptions for all managerial jobs and permitting every manager to see them, management is able to delimit these jobs and eliminate duplicate efforts in several closely related activities. Organizations are thus able to use job descriptions to discover faults in organization, reporting relationships, and work flow, and then to correct these deficiencies.

In recent years managers have been exposed to the terms "job enlargement," "job enrichment," and "job redesign." They have found that the restructuring and the redesign of both managerial positions and positions lower in the job hierarchy are much easier if the organization already has a position description program. In similar fashion, position descriptions have been useful in reviewing and improving work flow—in checking lines of authority from the point at which a decision is made, to the manager whose approval is needed, and back to the point of origin where the decision is put into effect. Through such analysis, authority chains are discovered that may be so long and complex that they are inhibiting the organization from achieving its basic purposes. Position descriptions in the authority area can be redrawn so that the organization is thereby made more efficient and effective. Similarly, other parts of job descriptions can be traced and work flow improved.

The following composite statement indicates the use of position descriptions in organization design:

> Managerial descriptions are used to analyze and improve the organization structure. Descriptions of executive and key managerial positions determine whether all corporate responsibilities are fully covered and show when a reallocation of responsibilities leading to a better balance of assignments is necessary. Job descriptions frequently uncover duplications of effort and activities that are no longer required. Later, as responsibilities are added, descriptions determine to whom the new tasks should be assigned. As jobs are changed or duties reassigned, position descriptions to fit the new situation are circulated to notify company personnel of the changes.

A second composite statement continues the argument:

> They clarify who is responsible for what within the organizations and they record the relationships that exist within and between various organizational departments. Where line and functional authorities cross, or where there are scrambled facilities within one location, clearly written job descriptions tend to maintain balance and harmony and reduce conflict, since they leave no doubt as to the several executives' responsibilities and authority. Where widely separated facilities must work together, job descriptions establish their most practical lines of contact and result in improved communications and better coordination of effort between them.

*Manpower Planning.* In recent years manpower planning has achieved a prominence it has not had since our nation used compulsory manpower planning for all organizations in World War II. Today, manpower planning in many organizations covers all types of personnel from managerial to blue collar. In managerial manpower planning, position descriptions are used to determine if there is a natural evolution from one managerial position to the next so that dead-end jobs can be eliminated. Planners are using such analysis to determine if there are sufficient promotable managerial personnel within the organization or whether additional personnel must be brought in from the outside to staff the organization. They are also discovering whether women and minority group employees have been shifted into dead-end or token positions within the organization. Manpower planning can establish a real relationship between position descriptions and the actual criteria for recruitment, selection, appraisal, and promotion. In this way, affirmative action programs can provide maximum opportunities for all persons both inside and outside the organization. Through the use of position description programs, manpower planners are able to establish career ladders.

The following composite statement describes promotional aspects of manpower planning:

> Descriptions are used to establish the organization's promotional sequences more clearly. They define career ladders and opportunities for all employees. Women and minority groups can clearly see these promotional ladders. In addition, job descriptions are useful when considering an executive for promotion, since they facilitate comparison of present and prospective responsibilities. The two position descriptions, when placed side by side and measured against the incumbent's latest performance appraisal, provide an accurate yardstick with which to measure his or her potential for moving up into the new post.

*Individual Career Planning.* More and more executives are beginning to come from the younger generation that insists on fuller utilization of its talents and abilities. Furthermore, these same young people expect to be given a better understanding of their opportunities and challenges within a given organization. Thus, clearly defined, readily available position descriptions provide additional inputs into an executive's decision on whether to stay in or leave the organization. A composite statement on career choice and self-understanding summarizes this view:

> Position descriptions help the executive to arrive at a clear understanding of the ramifications of his or her position and to analyze and assess the relative importance of his or her responsibilities and duties. For this purpose, the process of preparing descriptions (and the critical thought, discussion, and self-examination that this step entails) often has as great a value as the finished description.

*Management by Objectives.* As a new method of management, management by objectives (MBO) has gained great popularity during the past decade. By establishing routine, problem-solving, and innovative objectives for a stated period of time, executives have gained a clearer understanding of what is expected of them. In some organizations, managerial position description programs exist side by side with MBO programs. The formal position description provides the executive with a clearly defined statement of duties and responsibilities; the MBO program sets clearly defined actionable duties and responsibilities (hopefully with measurable standards) for a stated period of time. Under management by objectives, formal position descriptions are usually changed after one to three years of operation. Position description programs benefit from MBO programs by being fed additional information on what should be added to or deleted from the position description as the MBO program progresses. Through the interaction of these two programs, the executive gains a much better understanding of his or her job.

The use of position descriptions in superior-subordinate relations is clarified in this composite statement:

> They provide the means by which an executive and his or her superior may reach common understanding on the meaning and scope of a position. Spelling out aspects of the job—such as its degree of delegated authority, its indirect relationships, its freedom of action, and even the position's actual duties and responsibilities—often brings to light long-standing (and perhaps unconscious) differences between the incumbent's interpretation of the job and that of the boss. Once brought out, these varying interpretations may be reconciled in the final job description.

*Recruitment, Selection, and Placement.* Attacks on many personnel procedures by minority groups and women during the past two decades have intensified the need for position descriptions that accurately reflect the actual content of the jobs themselves. For example, the whole field of testing has come under broad attack because the tests lack validity—that is, they failed to reflect the actual job content. For the same reason, position descriptions may be attacked under affirmative action procedures. More than ever, these descriptions are critical to the recruitment, selection, and placement processes. A composite statement reads: "Managerial descriptions are a recruiting, hiring, and placement aid—since they form the basis for written position specifications which list the requirements that are necessary for satisfactorily filling a position."

*Orientation of New Executives.* In orienting new executives to a position within the organization, the best possible aid seems to be a clear and definitive statement of job duties and responsibilities. To maintain the value of position descriptions for this function, however, continual updating appears to be crucial. Strangely enough, many organizations do not use these descriptions for orientation purposes.

A composite statement on the use of position descriptions for orientation reads:

> They quickly and efficiently orient new incumbents to their positions and the requirements of those positions. Written managerial job descriptions are particularly helpful and comforting to two groups of newly promoted executives: those who are placed in freshly created positions with a job description as their blueprint of responsibility and authority, and those who have been promoted out of the straight line of progression into new posts embodying duties with which they are unfamiliar.

*Compensation Administration.* Many organizations use position descriptions for evaluating managerial jobs and placing them in equitable salary grades. Position descriptions are also used to determine equitable salaries for all managers doing the same type of work. In this way, illegal inequities in pay are more likely to be eliminated. Without position descriptions severe inequities may creep into compensation—for example, it is frequently impossible to determine whether or not managers are doing the same or similar kinds of work. Managerial position descriptions are also used as a basis for external salary comparisons. By describing the work of an organization's managers accurately, fair comparisons with organizations of a similar nature are possible. Thus compensation rates within the organization can be maintained at comparable rates with other, similar organizations.

A composite statement on external compensation reads:

Managerial position descriptions provide a foundation on which to compare positions inside the organization with others outside it in order to take full advantage of industry, community, interorganization, interdivision, and other managerial compensation surveys so as to pay salaries in line with the current market.

Similarly, a composite statement on internal compensation reads:

Managerial position descriptions provide a basis for executive position evaluation and represent an integral part of a soundly aligned managerial salary administration program, since they crystallize the meaning of the job in the minds of the evaluators. Later, revisions of the original descriptions are used to detect changes in job content sufficient to justify reevaluating and repricing the position. Written descriptions also assure the incumbents and their department heads that the persons evaluating their work have a proper understanding of the position's duties and responsibilities.

*Management Development.* Although position descriptions are frequently cited as being used to determine the need to develop managers, few organizations are able to specify exactly how they are used. Position descriptions, of course, are easily translated into job specifications. If the record of an incumbent is measured against such a job specification and several critical skills are found to be lacking, the need for management development is clear. By entering developmental programs for areas of weakness and by strengthening presently existing skills, a manager can better fulfill the requirements of his or her current position and be better prepared for any potential promotion. In some cases, individual plans of development may have to be established.

The composite statement on management development reads:

Position descriptions are a necessary part of a management development program in that they permit more accurate analysis of the requirements necessary for satisfactorily filling an executive position. These "target" requirements then serve as a guide for selecting, training, and developing the men and women who may later fill these positions.

*Performance Appraisal.* In some organizations, position descriptions are used as "standards of performance." For example, during the regular performance appraisal of a manager, the position description may be used as a standard of performance to determine if all the duties delineated in the description are being performed effectively. However, some organizations use position descriptions and standards of performance separately. As noted above, an MBO program is frequently used side by side with a position description program.

Standards of performance cannot be developed unless an accurate statement of job content exists. Normally the job content is spelled out in a managerial position description. In that description, the authority and responsibilities of a job are clearly spelled out in the general part that precedes a detailed listing of duties and the specific ways in which those duties are to be implemented. Standards of performance usually concentrate on a few key criteria that can be used as a check on performance. However, the practice of including standards of performance in job descriptions is still relatively uncommon. With the evolution of MBO and similar types of objectives-appraisal systems, the interrelationship between position descriptions and appraisal systems probably will continue to grow.

The composite statement on performance appraisal reads:

> Managerial position descriptions form the foundation for a periodic appraisal of the executive's performance of his or her job. By measuring how completely and how well the executive is carrying out the responsibilities of the position, areas of strength and weakness can be located, and the executive can be counseled accordingly.

*Task Forces, Project Teams, and Matrix Teams.* Approximately 60 percent of the respondents in the study used task forces, project teams, or matrix teams. Of these, only six respondents used special descriptions for these specialized types of management operations. One organization indicated that specific responsibilities were spelled out for task forces if the work of the task force was to last 90 days or longer. Another organization stated that "a concise document of guidelines and objectives is prepared to guide the task force."

## PRESENT USES OF POSITION DESCRIPTIONS

By means of a checklist, respondents indicated the specific uses to which they put managerial position descriptions and the three most important uses. At the end of the checklist, space was provided for additional uses not considered when the checklist was drawn up. Table 3 provides a good comparative picture of the present uses of managerial position descriptions. As seen in the table, 107 of the 121 organizations answering the question indicated that position descriptions provide a basis for setting salary ranges for jobs. Clearly, the next two items—defining areas of accountability and describing all functions, duties, responsibilities, and relationships needed to accomplish basic organizational objectives—are closely related to salary administration and the overall performance of managers. Similarly, the three most important uses are also the same: they are clearly

Table 3. Present and most important uses of managerial position descriptions.*

| USES OF MANAGERIAL POSITION DESCRIPTIONS | PRESENT MAJOR USES | MOST IMPORTANT USES † |
|---|---|---|
| Provide a basis for setting salary ranges for jobs. | 107 | 73 |
| Define areas of accountability. | 96 | 39 |
| Describe all functions, duties, responsibilities, and relationships needed to accomplish basic organizational objectives. | 93 | 52 |
| Provide a basis for developing position specifications for recruitment. | 74 | 14 |
| Provide a basis for performance appraisal. | 70 | 28 |
| Define limits of authority. | 63 | 5 |
| Orient new executives to their jobs. | 61 | 5 |
| Provide a basis for preparing or revising organization structure (and charts). | 59 | 14 |
| Provide a basis for developing performance standards. | 52 | 10 |
| Provide a basis for identifying reasonable promotional ladders for managers, including members of minority groups, women, and older employees. | 43 | 5 |
| Provide a basis for designing and redesigning managerial jobs (including job enrichment and job enlargement). | 41 | 3 |
| Insure that all work necessary to accomplish organization objectives is brought together in jobs that use present personnel effectively. | 39 | 10 |
| Provide a basis for assigning job objectives for a management-by-objectives program. | 35 | 8 |
| Aid in structuring management development programs by providing a basis for determining knowledge and skill required to do job. | 35 | 2 |
| Forecast the number of managers that will be needed in the future and their knowledge and skills. | 11 | 1 |
| Other uses.‡ | 5 | 1 |

* 136 organizations had job descriptions; 15 did not answer the question.

† Each organization was asked to rate the three most important uses.

‡ This classification includes budget, position evaluation ranking, determining title of position, basis for compensation surveys.

related to salary administration and the overall objectives of the organization.

Three items have achieved significance since the previous AMA study on managerial position descriptions. First, position descriptions are being used as a basis for identifying reasonable promotional ladders for managers, including members of minority groups, women, and older employees. Certainly this use is related to pressures from federal, state, and local governments for affirmative action programs for these groups. Such programs attempt to improve and clarify the process of upward mobility in the organization and to eliminate dead-end jobs. Second, there seems to be a significant use of position descriptions for designing and redesigning managerial jobs. This may be related to the demands of managers for more meaningful and more satisfying work—the need for self-fulfillment on the job. The same objective may be sought through job enrichment and job enlargement programs. Third, position descriptions are significantly related to MBO programs. Fifteen years ago there were few programs of this type. Today position description programs are beginning to provide a basis for assigning job objectives for an MBO program.

Many of the other uses of position descriptions have not changed significantly since the first AMA study in 1958. Today position descriptions are used for many different purposes. Certainly they are used for many purposes other than compensation administration.

## ORIGINAL PURPOSES VERSUS ACTUAL USAGE

As noted in the previous chapter, organizations shift significantly from the original purposes of their position description programs as time passes. Generally more and more uses are made of the descriptions. If the original intent was compensation administration, the uses will shift toward many of the functions listed in Table 3. If the original intent was some area other than compensation administration, certainly compensation administration will be picked up as one of the many uses of the program.

Almost all the description programs (93 percent) cover more job titles than they did five years ago. The trend is expected to continue. Also, more specific and more distinct titles of new positions are continually being added. Approximately one-half of the organizations (56 percent) now have more detail in their position descriptions than initially. As time passes, there is apparently a need for additional information and different coverages in the position descriptions because of the many new uses to which these descriptions are put.

In some organizations (only seven in this study), job descriptions have been discontinued in one area or another. These discontinued descriptions covered mostly nonexempt jobs, both blue collar (production and maintenance) and white collar (primarily secretarial). For example, one organization stated: "When a description exists for a nonexempt job and must be changed, there is pressure from the union always to upgrade the salary." Another said: "An elaborate program was implemented for the hourly production group some years ago and the present labor relations section prefers to work without the position descriptions."

Two organizations have moved toward generic rather than specific descriptions of professional and technical positions for certain types of employees. An air transportation company reported: "We no longer require job descriptions for each analyst position. We have combined 60 positions into three generic descriptions—analyst, senior analyst, and staff analyst." And similarly in a manufacturing company specific descriptions for individual positions have been replaced by more general descriptions covering groups of jobs (for example, foremen, engineers, and engineering group leaders).

Two organizations have discontinued top and middle management job descriptions because these positions change too rapidly. One organization noted: "We are a changing, evolving organization. Therefore descriptions for top management and corporate staff positions tended to become obsolete."

Even these organizations that have discontinued or significantly modified certain types of position descriptions have retained the major portions of their programs. The remaining 95 percent of organizations with programs have continued or expanded them as more and more uses have been found for the information provided by the descriptions.

## NEW MANAGERIAL JOBS CREATED

During the past five years, 116 respondents in this study have created 262 new positions. Although some of the positions have duplicate titles in other organizations, there has obviously been a tremendous expansion of new positions. (See the accompanying list.) Of the 262 newly created positions, only 10 were in top management, with 117 in executive management and 135 in middle management. In this study, no new first-line supervisory positions were reported. This finding is consistent with the earlier data indicating that many companies do not have job descriptions for their top executives. Obviously, organizations are not establishing new positions in the top management category.

Analysis of the data at the executive management level shows that new positions have been established mainly in marketing (20), finance (13), operations (11), planning (10), and research and development and engineering (10). At the middle management level the growth appears to be fairly uniform. It has been led by new positions in finance (23), operations (21), personnel (20), and marketing (18). Outside these areas new positions seem to be appearing in computers and management information systems and administrative services.

## NEW MANAGERIAL POSITIONS CREATED DURING PAST FIVE YEARS *

### Top Management

Chairman, Board of Directors
Vice Chairman, Board of Directors
President and Chief Executive Officer
President
Division President
Chancellor

### Executive Management

Senior Executive Vice President
Executive Vice President, Banking
Executive Vice President, Trusts and Investments
Executive Vice President, International Operations
Executive Vice President, Marketing
Executive Vice President

Senior Vice President
Senior Vice President, Financial Administration
Senior Vice President, Law and Corporate Development
Senior Vice President, Energy Supply and Utilization
Senior Vice President and Economist
Senior Vice President, Research and Development

| Vice Presidents—Planning | Vice Presidents—Operations |
|---|---|
| Corporate Planning and Research | Group |
| Corporate Planning | General Manager |
| Planning, Expansion, and Diversification | Operations |
| Planning and Economics | Operational Coordinator |
| Corporate Development | Long Haul |
| Strategic Planning | Inflight Services |
| Long-Range Planning | Material Services |
| | Material |
| | Manufacturing |
| | Traffic |

* Although titles of positions are listed, the number of citations of each title is not noted. Seldom was any title listed more than five times.

**Vice Presidents—Administrative Services and Legal**
Administrative
Administrative Services
Special Administration
Staff Services
Corporate Staff Services
Management Services
Legal
General Counsel

**Vice Presidents—Finance**
Finance
Financial
Finance and Administration
Financial Administration
Finance and Planning
Financial Planning
Investments
Controller
Revenue Requirements

**Vice Presidents—Marketing**
Marketing
Passenger Marketing
Communications Projects
Advertising and Public Relations
Product Group
Product and Services
Consumer Products
Ordnance Marketing
Consumer Affairs
Customer Relations
General Sales Manager
Sales and Services

**Vice Presidents—Personnel**
Employee Relations
Manpower
Human Resources
Personnel and Planning
Labor Relations

**Vice Presidents—R&D and Engineering**
Research and Development
Research and Technology
Venture Technology
Technical
Corporate Engineering
Environmental and Safety Engineering
Business Research

**Vice Presidents—Computers and Information Systems**
Electronic Data Processing
Management Information Systems
Business Information Systems

**Vice Presidents—Other**
International
Public Relations
Public Information
Medical Research and Medical
    Education
Purchases
Regional
Organization Development

**Middle Management**

**Managers—Planning**
Corporate Planning
Planning and Development

**Managers—Operations**
Group
General
General Division
Assistant City
Corporate Distribution
Facilities Services
Plant Materials
Material
Real Estate
Waste-Handling Systems
Inventory Control

**Managers—Administrative Services and Legal**
General Services
Administrative Services

**Managers—Finance**
Corporate Credit
Corporate Accounting
Financial Planning
Financial Analysis and Taxes
Investments

**Managers—Marketing**
General Sales
Division Sales
National Sales
Industrial Specialty Products
Product
Product Development
Aftermarket Products
Marketing Services
Advertising

**Managers—Personnel**
Personnel
Personnel Administration
Salaried Personnel
Safety
Compensation and Benefits
Compensation

**Managers—Research and Development and Engineering**
Mine Development
Pollution Control
Value Control
Technical Services
Engineering Staff Operations
Engineering

**Managers—Computers and Information Systems**
Administrative Systems
Management Information Systems
Programs and Systems
Software Systems

**Managers—Other**
International

**Directors—Planning**
Planning
Corporate Planning
Long-Range Planning
Operations Planning
Business Planning and Analysis

**Directors—Operations**
Production
Distribution

**Directors—Administrative Services and Legal**
Administration
Service
General and Supportive Services
Management Services
Environmental Management

**Directors—Finance**
Financial Planning and Analysis
Fiscal Affairs
Taxation

**Directors—Marketing**
Product Planning
New Product Development
Diversified Products
Marketing Management Controls
Market Research

**Directors—Personnel**
Personnel
Assistant Personnel
Industrial Relations
Labor Relations
Professional Services
Corporate Safety
Security

**Directors—R & D and Engineering**
Technological Administration
Facilities Engineering
Product Reliability and Quality
    Assurance

**Directors—Computers and Information Systems**
Computer Services
Office Management Systems
Management Information Systems
Systems and Data Processing

**Directors—Other**
International
Public Relations
Purchasing and Transportation

**Other—Operations**
Model Cities Director
Operations Controller
Relay Coordinator

**Other—Administrative Services and Legal**
Program Coordinator
Purchasing Agent
General Counsel
Commerce Attorney

**Other—Finance**
Controller
Group Controller
Assistant Controller
Assistant Controller for Auditing
Internal Auditor
Actuary
Financial Analyst
Consolidation Accountant

**Other—Marketing**
Chief Product Stylist

**Other—Personnel**
Executive Officer, Human Resources
Work Measurement Analyst
Salary Administrator

**Other—R & D and Engineering**
Management Engineer

**Other—Computers and Information Systems**
Management Information Systems Administrator

New titles reflecting new concerns of organizations in environmental and consumer affairs have appeared; among these titles are senior vice president, energy supply and utilization; vice president, consumer affairs; vice president, environmental and safety engineering; manager, waste-handling systems; manager, pollution control; and director, environmental managements. In response to the continuing and ever increasingly critical shortages in human and material resources, shortages in energy, and environmental problems, organizations have begun to initiate many new positions related to planning at both executive and middle management levels. For example, they have established such positions as vice president, long-range planning; vice president, corporate planning and research; vice president, financial planning; manager, planning and development; manager, financial planning; director, operations planning; director, business planning and analysis; and director, financial planning and analysis. Organizations are beginning to clearly understand the necessity for planning operations in the future and for continually establishing new positions in this area.

In the personnel area, intensified concern for safety, in response to the Occupational Safety and Health Act, and for security, in response to increasing amounts of theft and industrial espionage, are evident in newly created managerial positions. Among the new safety positions are vice president, environmental and safety engineering; safety manager; and corporate safety director. The title of security director certainly manifests top management's interest in security.

Many new positions are appearing in the field of computer technology and management information systems, including vice presidents, managers, and directors of computer services, management services, and management information systems. Another new title that may reflect a new trend is that of vice president for organization development. As they become increasingly concerned about achieving greater efficiency, effectiveness, and productivity from the workforce, organizations are looking harder at their structures and their ways of managing. Organization development is one method of analyzing such problems and attempting to resolve them.

This study seems to show a significant proliferation of jobs throughout both public and private sectors. Apparently some organizations are attempting to be specific in defining individual positions. Some, too, have begun to believe this is a significant problem and have started to move toward generic position descriptions and away from specific descriptions. Hopefully, that movement will lead to empirically derived equitable salary structures.

# 4

# *The Organization and Design*
# *of a Program*

Top management support appears to be vital to launching a managerial position description program successfully. High-level authorization of the program serves to emphasize its importance to executives whose positions are being described. This is particularly true when executive positions are to be described by staff specialists who do not have great authority in the organization. For instance, it would be difficult to ask a personnel manager to conduct a searching interview with a vice president about his or her work unless the personnel manager had the support of top management.

This chapter discusses the establishment of a new position description program, the responsibility for existing programs, the accessibility of position description information, problems in the development of position descriptions, and problems in the use of position descriptions.

## ESTABLISHING A NEW PROGRAM

In most organizations, managerial position description programs are authorized by the organization's top executives. This is quite natural, since these descriptions are often essential to such important projects as reorganization programs, management-by-objectives programs, and organizationwide attempts to adjust compensation. In most instances, any large-scale project of this type can be instituted only with approval from the highest authority in the organization.

Generally, new programs are instituted by either a single top executive or a group of two or more top executives. Approximately one-third of all new programs are authorized by a single executive who usually comes from top or executive management. Such an executive might be the chairman of the board, the president, the executive vice president, or the vice president of operations. The other two-thirds are approved by two or more executives or by a committee of some type. In most cases the committee consists either of the board of directors or of top executive managers. Usually these committees comprise the chairman of the board of directors, representatives from the board, presidents, senior and executive vice presidents, controllers, secretaries, and treasurers.

Once the program has been authorized, the next step is to place an individual in direct charge of implementing it.

### Original Supervisors of the Program

Generally, a personnel manager is directly in charge of the program at its inception. At least one-half of those originally in charge are classified as personnel vice presidents, personnel directors, personnel managers, industrial relations directors, compensation administration directors, compensation administrators, and other personnel officers (sometimes on a fairly junior level). Most of those placed in charge are either top, executive, or middle managers. Personnel officials are chosen frequently because they already have had experience in handling similar programs for lower-level employees and are already dealing with similar functions in their daily personnel operations.

Occasionally, managerial description programs are headed by top or executive line managers at the beginning. In some instances the president or other top-ranking officer may have personally instituted the program and remains in charge of its operation. In other instances major reorganizations or mergers may have caused the programs to be headed by a top official of the organization. In these latter cases the president or chief executive officer may be using the program to assist in the reorganization.

Other groups of nonpersonnel managers may head the program. Although these managers may come from practically every part and function of the organization, the majority come from organization and administrative work and from finance. Those in the first group usually have such titles as vice president, organization planning; vice president, organization development; vice president, administrative research; manager, organization planning; director of organization; and general administration planning superior. The titles of those in the second group—financial executives— range from financial vice president to controller to assistant to the treasurer.

When nonpersonnel officials are placed in charge of a program at its inception, it is usually for one of the following reasons:

1. The executive and the executive's superior first proposed the idea to the organization. The program's author is usually given control because of his or her interest in the program.
2. The executive has an intimate knowledge of the jobs to be covered, the managers in these jobs and their actual interrelationships, and the overall workings of the organization. This information is usually gained by close personal association with these managers over a period of years and by broad experience within the organization.
3. The executive is a person with a reputation for impartiality and is therefore considered well suited to take an unbiased look at the various positions and their interrelationships.

In almost all programs initially oriented toward compensation administration, the primary executive in charge is from the personnel function. In programs with additional uses, approximately two-thirds of the executives originally in charge are not from the personnel function. In time, almost all the programs are headed by executives from the personnel function. In this study, 111 out of 120 respondents indicated that managers from the personnel function were responsible for the present operations of the program.

### Shifts in Responsibility for Program Administration

When first launched, a program needs top management support and supervision. Some opposition may be encountered and important gaps in responsibility or overlaps in duties and authority may be discovered. After the program has been operating for a while, it becomes somewhat regularized. Theoretically, at least, conflicts and problems have been resolved and responsibility for keeping descriptions up to date may then devolve upon someone lower in the organization. This individual normally is connected with either personnel or compensation administration.

*Frequency of Shifts.* In most cases the program continues to be managed by the same official—that is, the manager of the program has the same title. In others, responsibility for managing the program is assigned to a different office than at its inception.

One might suppose that the older the program, the more likely a shift in responsibility for managing it. However, the 1958 AMA study showed no direct relationship between time from inception and shift in responsibility. In fact, such shifts apparently occur quite soon after the program is started—probably after the first full set of managerial descriptions is finalized. In other words, a top executive initiates the program and it is shortly thereafter turned over to a middle manager or personnel specialist.

In general, the frequency of the shifts in program managers seems to bear little or no relation to changes in the basic purpose behind the program. If its initial purpose was compensation administration and that was broadened to include other uses (or vice versa), the program apparently continues under the same personnel official (if it is already under someone from personnel) or the program shifts toward the personnel function.

*Direction of Changes.* An illuminating comparison could be made between those who originally head the programs and those who ultimately are in charge. The shifts are generally in a downward direction within the organization—that is, a lower-level official takes over after the program is well established. It seems that more compensation administrators are finally charged with sustaining the program than at the outset. Top executives almost entirely drop out of the picture. This is not to say they do not *use* the descriptions, but they do apparently cease supervising their preparation.

One interpretation of this tendency toward lower-level administration is that once a managerial position description program is written, printed, and put into use, it has already started to find its own place in the organization and does not need as much top-echelon support behind it.

*Decentralization of the Program.* Almost all managerial position description programs are centralized. In this way descriptions can be standardized and control maintained over their initiation, amendment, and revision. However, a few organizations (less than 5 percent) have decentralized their programs after they had been established for a while. Some organizations have delegated control over the program to line managers and managers of separate staff departments because it was felt that each manager should be responsible for his or her employees and because development of these descriptions is a line, not a staff, function. Other organizations have assigned authority over the program to personnel departments in each of their major divisions because they wished to shift responsibility for compensation administration from staff specialists to the operating line. Other organizations have maintained decentralized programs under the control of line managers with general staff guidance from the personnel function because line managers are responsible for the development of their subordinates, but need the expert advice of personnel specialists.

### Outside Sources of Assistance

Many organizations employ outside sources to help set up or revise their position description programs. Indeed, most organizations use some type of consulting service when initiating such programs. But many organizations use nonconsultant services—for example, advice and counsel from other organizations in the same type of operation, help from a central office of the organization, the assistance of outside speakers in introducing the program, and advice and assistance from seminars like those of the American Management Associations.

The organizations that are apparently willing to "go it alone" are those that do not intend to use position descriptions for salary administration. For example, organizations that intend to use the description program for organization design and the development of executives seldom use outside consultants. Perhaps many top managers feel compelled to keep tight control over important reorganization decisions, whereas job evaluation on the managerial level is better handled by "neutrals" and so can be turned over to an outside firm of consultants. Organizations that intend to use the descriptions solely for salary administration frequently hire management consulting firms.

*Consultants' Fees.* Some organizations make far greater use of consulting services than others. Fees vary widely depending on the scope and nature of the job. Today fees for differing amounts of service range from $1,000 to $200,000. Indeed, a larger corporation or public agency may pay even greater sums to have its program handled *completely* by an unbiased, outside party. Consultants' rates range from $200 to $300 per day as an average to as high as $500 per day. The differences in fees depend in part on a consultant's experience and background. For example, in the same consulting firm a *consultant's* services may be billed at $200 per day, an *associate's* at $300 per day, and a *vice president's* at $500 per day.

Most organizations have been willing to pay these fees during the process of initiating or revising their programs because they require and receive an external, impartial view. In some of the more costly situations, consultants have supervised the entire project from the initial announcement of the new program to all employees to the final implementation of the descriptions. Today most organizations are satisfied with the work of consultants in establishing or revising their managerial position description programs.

## RESPONSIBILITY FOR EXISTING PROGRAMS

During the past fifteen years the level of executives responsible for position description programs has dropped significantly. In 1958 approximately 28 percent of these programs were directly administered by either top or executive management. Today they directly supervise less than 5 percent of the programs (see Table 4). Almost all the programs are now administered by some middle manager. (For the titles of these positions, see the accompanying list.) Indeed, some of the programs appear to be administered at even lower levels by professionals in personnel and compensation administration with such titles as compensation analyst or personnel spe-

Table 4. Titles of executives responsible for managerial description programs.*

| | TITLES BY AREAS OF SPECIALIZATION | | | | | |
| TITLE BY LEVEL OF AUTHORITY | GENERAL MANAGEMENT | PERSONNEL AND/OR EMPLOYEE RELATIONS † | COMPENSATION ADMINISTRATION | ORGANIZATION PLANNING/ MANPOWER PLANNING | OTHER AREAS ‡ | TOTAL |
|---|---|---|---|---|---|---|
| Top Management (Chairman, President, Director, President's Office) | — | — | — | — | — | — |
| Executive Management (Group Vice President, Executive Vice President, General Manager, Deputy Director, Corporate and Division Vice Presidents) | — | 5 | 1 | — | 1 | 7 |
| Middle Management (All managers below officer and above supervisory levels) | — | 37 | 64 | 9 | 10 | 120 |
| Total | — | 42 | 65 | 9 | 11 | 127 |

* 136 organizations had job descriptions; 11 did not answer the question; 1 gave a nonspecific answer; 3 reported that the program was jointly administered by two executives.

† This classification includes industrial relations.

‡ This classification includes recruitment, management development and training, administrative services, and unspecified officers and managers of organizations.

cialist. Perhaps the programs have reached maturity and need less top management commitment and support than they did at their founding. Apparently they have proved their value.

## TITLES OF MANAGERIAL DESCRIPTION
## PROGRAM EXECUTIVES *

**Personnel Executives**

Vice President, Employee Relations
Vice President, Personnel
Executive Assistant to Vice
    President, Personnel
Assistant to Vice President,
    Employee and Labor Relations

Personnel Manager
Personnel Administrator
Personnel Officer
Manager of Personnel
Manager, Personnel Administration
Personnel or Office Manager
Manager of Employee Relations
Chief, Corporate Personnel Staff
Personnel and Organization Manager
Salaried Personnel Manager
Manager, Industrial Relations
    and Personnel
Assistant Manager of Personnel
Manager, Industrial Relations

Personnel Director
Director of Personnel
Director of Personnel and Safety
Director of Employee Relations and
    Communications
Associate Director of Personnel
Director of Corporate Human
    Resources

Personnel Supervisor
Personnel Analyst

**Compensation Administration
Executives**

Vice President, Management
    Compensation

Manager, Wage and Salary
Manager, Wage and Salary
    Administration
Manager, Wage and Salary Services
Wage and Salary Manager
Manager, Salary Administration
Manager, Management Salary
    Administration
Manager, Compensation
Manager, Compensation and Benefits
Manager of Compensation
Manager, Salary Compensation
Manager, Compensation
    Administration
Manager, Executive Compensation
Manager, Employee Compensation
Compensation and Organization
    Planning Manager
Manager, Compensation Services

Director of Wage and Salary
    Administration
Director of Compensation
Director of Compensation and
    Benefits
Director, Office of Position Evaluation
Chief, Classification Division

Wage and Salary Administrator
Corporate Salary Administrator
Salary Administrator
Compensation Administrator
Administrator of Compensation

Wage and Salary Supervisor
Supervisor of Wage and Salary
    Administration
Supervisor, Corporate Salary
    Administration

* Although titles of positions are listed, the number of citations of each title is not noted.

Classification Supervisor
Supervisor, Job Evaluation

Personnel Officer, Compensation
Salary Administration Specialist
Compensation and Benefits Specialist
Wage and Salary Analyst
Senior Job Analyst

**Organization Planning/Manpower Planning Executives**

Manager, Organization Analysis
  and Compensation
Manager, Organization and
  Manpower Planning
Manager, Organization Planning
Manager, Organization Development

Director of Organization Planning
Director of Organization Planning
  and Manpower Development

Director, Management Recruitment
  and Development
Director, Associate Relations
Administrative Officer
Director, Manpower Planning
Director, Organization Planning
Director, Organization Development

**Other Executives**

Vice President
Administrative Vice President
Assistant Secretary

Manager of Manpower Development
Manager, Employment, Training,
  and Development
Manager, Corporate Services
Assistant Manager

There has also been a significant shift in the areas of specialization of the programs' supervisors. Fifteen years ago 36 percent of the executives in charge of the programs were in personnel, while 22 percent were in wage and salary administration. Today those figures are 33 percent and 51 percent, respectively. In other words, there has been a significant shift toward placing all responsibility in the personnel function (84 percent). Indeed, if the organization and manpower planners are placed in the personnel function (as in many organizations they are), the programs are almost entirely handled by that function. Moreover, within that function, compensation administration is now handled in fully one-half of these programs as a specific subfunction of personnel.

Although the shift in responsibility for the programs has been downward, the overall involvement by top and executive management continues through the reporting points for these programs. Ten percent of the program executives still report directly to the chairman of the board of directors or the president, while 60 percent report to either top management or the executive management group at the vice-presidential level or above (see Table 5). Thus it is evident that top management still retains a significant interest in the programs through the reporting, controlling, and monitoring procedures, while daily administration of the programs continues at lower levels in the organizations. In addition, it is clear that the compensation-administration function in most organizations does report to or through the personnel function. Approximately 57 percent of the per-

Table 5. *Titles of executives to whom managerial description program executives report.**

|  | TITLES BY AREAS OF SPECIALIZATION | | | | | |
| --- | --- | --- | --- | --- | --- | --- |
| TITLE BY LEVEL OF AUTHORITY | GENERAL MANAGEMENT | PERSONNEL AND/OR EMPLOYEE RELATIONS † | COMPENSATION ADMINISTRATION | ORGANIZATION PLANNING/ MANPOWER PLANNING | OTHER AREAS ‡ | TOTAL |
| Top Management (Chairman, President, Director, President's Office) | 12 | — | — | — | — | 12 |
| Executive Management (Group Vice President, Executive Vice President, General Manager, Deputy Director, Corporate and Divisional Vice Presidents) | 10 | 29 | 1 | 2 | 11 | 53 |
| Middle Management (All managers below officer and above supervisory levels) | — | 42 | 15 | 1 | 1 | 59 |
| Total | 22 | 71 | 16 | 3 | 12 | 124 |

* 136 organizations had job descriptions; 11 did not answer the question; 2 gave nonspecific answers; 1 stated that program executives reported to two top executives.

† This classification includes industrial relations.

‡ This classification includes recruitment, management development and training, administrative services, finance, and unspecified officers and managers of organizations.

sonnel executives serve as the reporting point immediately above the program directors.

Analysis of the data on the numbers of professional staff personnel involved in description programs indicates that there is little or no relation between the size of an organization and the numbers of persons involved in the ongoing operations of these programs. Although program support personnel in manufacturing organizations vary from one exempt employee to 27 exempt employees and in nonmanufacturing organizations vary from one to 30, most programs have fewer than 8 exempt employees engaged in their operations. Indeed, the median number of exempt employees in position description programs is two in both manufacturing and nonmanufacturing organizations. Thus the number of staff support personnel in most of these programs is apparently not a serious cost consideration.

## ACCESSIBILITY OF POSITION DESCRIPTION INFORMATION

To measure the openness of the description programs, a question was asked to determine which groups of employees had access to job descriptions. Unfortunately the responses were quite mixed: 19 organizations indicated the descriptions were available to all employees, 21 indicated they were not available to all employees. However, a measure of the accessibility of position description information was obtained by analyzing other questions.

Incumbents of managerial positions have access to their position descriptions in almost all organizations. Furthermore, they have access to the job descriptions of subordinates for whom they are responsible. Ninety-eight percent of the organizations participating in this study provide managers with access to the job descriptions of subordinates. In those cases where an executive is not responsible for a given position or positions, most organizations (69 percent) provide access to descriptions. However, most of the programs can best be described as relatively "closed." For example, in only 18 percent of the organizations is everyone allowed to see every description (see Table 6). Thus any exempt or nonexempt employee has access to this information. Almost one-half of the organizations (49 percent) operate on a "need-to-know" basis—that is, employees can see other descriptions when the information they need to know is required in their own jobs. In 14 percent of the organizations employees are allowed to see only their own and subordinates' job descriptions. On the whole, most organizations can be described as having closed systems and as providing limited accessibility to managerial position descriptions.

Apparently, organizations that use position descriptions primarily for salary administration are less likely to allow all employees free access to them than are organizations in which the descriptions are not an integral part of compensation administration. In almost all organizations, production and clerical workers are not allowed to examine managerial position

Table 6. Accessibility of managerial position descriptions.*

| RESPONSE ON OPENNESS OF PROGRAM | NUMBER OF RESPONSES |
| --- | --- |
| Anyone can see any description. | 22 |
| Employees can see other descriptions on a "need-to-know" basis. | 59 |
| Employees can see other job descriptions by request, but organization cannot be described as "open." | 23 |
| Employees are allowed to see only their own and subordinates' job descriptions. | 17 |

* 136 organizations had job descriptions; 35 did not answer the question. Several organizations responded with more than one reply to the question.

descriptions or manuals except where explanations of the organization's basic structure seem to be needed. In light of the many positive uses of descriptions in the development of managers and executives, it would seem that a relatively open system would be all to the good. It may come about with the drive toward participative management.

Several observations may be made on the basis of information received from the respondents:

1. Any incumbent should have access to his or her own description.
2. Any executive should have access to descriptions of positions under his or her jurisdiction and/or within his or her own department.
3. Nonmanagerial employees need not have access to managerial descriptions. Although the descriptions may be of little value to production and clerical workers, they may have significant use in orienting new employees, particularly if the descriptions are written in easily understandable language.
4. Descriptions used exclusively or in large part for salary determination should be sharply restricted if it seems that salary adjustments will cause significant disagreements. However, if access to them will improve the situation, then managers should be given that right.
5. The number of employees allowed access to description manuals and position descriptions is roughly in inverse proportion to the importance of these descriptions in salary administration.

### PROBLEMS IN DEVELOPING POSITION DESCRIPTIONS

Thirty-eight organizations in this study indicated they were having trouble developing managerial job descriptions. Most of these responses fall into one of two categories: (1) negative managerial responses to the position description program, and (2) difficulties in implementing the program itself.

In the first case, managers have continued to resist the creation of position description programs. They offer several reasons: (1) The programs are not necessary in an institution that has such a proud, dignified record; (2) they are too confining and will not allow us to do our jobs; and (3) they will take too much time to prepare. In organizations with constantly evolving description programs, managers tend to discount the value of their own position descriptions both to themselves and to others and to resent the time it takes to develop them. For example, one respondent saw the significant problems as: "(1) difficulty in getting the immediate supervisor to sit down, develop, and prepare a position description of the job known best to him or her; (2) the tendency of managers to be subjective in describing jobs and to portray the incumbent and his or her personal characteristics rather than the existing job; and (3) difficulty in getting managers to effectively use position descriptions as a vital tool in management—delegation, review and control, motivation, and performance appraisal."

In the second category, one of the major difficulties in implementing the program is the lack of both staff and time to develop the program. In many cases, not only is the organization understaffed, but the existing staff is inadequately trained. Another problem area is the continuous battle to keep the position descriptions current. Because of constant growth and changes in organization structure, position descriptions rapidly become dated. Thus a program requires considerable coordination, monitoring, and control to keep it up to date. One company noted: "We have had an administrative problem in getting all departments to prepare and maintain current copies of job descriptions." On the other hand, another stated: "Many descriptions are prepared to describe a position as it is expected to be in several months or years in the future. We want to know what the job involves now or in the immediate future and update the description as the job grows or changes."

A common problem appears to be the difficulty in obtaining accurate, definitive data for position descriptions. Most program personnel trace this to managers who fail to provide the information, the form or format used to obtain the information, and lack of sufficient details. One organization clearly identified the problems as "identifying responsibilities in new jobs, establishing meaningful accountabilities, maintaining current descriptions, and eliminating unimportant information (incumbents want everything in)." Another stated: "Our current format tends to be awkward and forces the preparer to think, hence shortcuts are often sought. The time necessary to develop a comprehensive description is often unavailable to line management, resulting occasionally in less than a complete product."

Another difficulty arises in defining managerial jobs themselves. Since these jobs are difficult to describe briefly and tend to change with the incumbent, program directors become extremely frustrated in trying to determine whether brief or detailed descriptions are better for managers at various levels of the organization.

Finally, some organizations do have real difficulties in keeping up with shifts in organization structure. For example, one respondent listed several of his organization's primary developmental difficulties: "company acquisitions and divestitures, top realignment of business groups and departments, reassignment of company divisions from one group to another group, and departments realigning responsibilities to various individuals following organizational changes."

## PROBLEMS IN THE USE OF POSITION DESCRIPTIONS

Thirty-three organizations reported having difficulties in using managerial position descriptions. Most of these problems could be briefly classified into three categories: (1) decrease in managerial involvement in the program, (2) inflexibility of managerial position descriptions; and (3) changing job content of descriptions.

First, managers in some organizations are not using the descriptions. Apparently this is one way to continue resisting a position description program after it has been established. Some respondents felt that management must be made to see the need to use job descriptions in objectively analyzing a job's relative worth and, therefore, the need to write and maintain up-to-date descriptions. Others felt that managers must be convinced "to use descriptions and salary grades as guidelines in an open manner with employees." Obviously some respondents feel a strong need to indoctrinate or reindoctrinate managers on the importance of managerial position description programs.

Second, several organizations have complained about the inflexibility of managerial position descriptions. On one hand, some argue that they are too detailed. On the other, some claim they are too general. But most respondents agreed that most managerial position descriptions are too inflexible to serve a rapidly changing organization. One manufacturer stated: "In a growth company, position responsibility assignments tend to be fluid, that is, change rapidly. Time isn't always available to develop and maintain descriptions, nor are the descriptions realistic because of changing responsibility/organization assignments." Another said: "Ours is a changing organization with little or no indirect staffing, causing most job description formats to be too inflexible. Most managers in our company, for example, handle more functions than average." Another organization feels that it has solved this problem: "Ordinarily, job descriptions for managerial positions are too rigid. We prefer to have each manager prepare a written listing of his (her) responsibilities."

Third, respondents feel that a major problem in using position descriptions arises from changing job content. Keeping the descriptions up to date is a major concern of most program directors. In some rapidly developing organizations it is almost impossible to keep up with the changes in job content. Under such circumstances current job descriptions frequently do not adequately describe the present work of the incumbent. A second aspect of this problem is the lack of communication between managers and description program directors concerning shifts and changes in job content. Many managers are so busy that they neglect to notify the program director about these changes. As a result of this lack of communication, control over the descriptions in the program is inadequate. In such organizations, different sets of rules could be established for differing rates of change in job content in particular positions.

# 5

## *Obtaining Executive Acceptance for the Program*

In establishing a new managerial position description program or significantly revising an old one, a necessary step is introducing it to executives whose positions are to be included. To forestall rumors, the announcement of the program should be made as soon as the project has been definitely decided on. Organizations use many different methods in presenting the idea of new or revised managerial job descriptions to their executives.

### TECHNIQUES OF INTRODUCTION

In the earlier AMA study several trends became apparent. Nearly two-thirds of the organizations told their managerial personnel about the project in person (usually at a group meeting) rather than in writing (by sending a memo or letter). Of those who planned to use descriptions for several purposes besides compensation administration, approximately one-fourth believed the idea needed the fullest possible support and should be introduced by both oral and written communications.

Approximately three-fourths of the organizations introduced the new programs to their executives in groups. The remaining organizations told their executives about the new programs privately (21 percent) or through the use of both group and individual methods (5 percent). Organizations that planned to use the descriptions for both compensation and noncompensation purposes definitely tended to prefer thorough introductions using combined methods of individual interviews and group meetings.

#### Group Meetings
Some form of group meeting is by far the most popular general method of introducing executive and managerial personnel to new or revised posi-

tion description programs. Other methods include a form letter or memo (usually signed by the top executive) sent to each executive whose position is to be described and a personal explanation given individually to each program participant.

"Group meetings" vary considerably from organization to organization. For example, instead of holding one large meeting to introduce the idea of managerial job descriptions to all their executives at once, many organizations hold a series of meetings, usually working from the top down. Typical of this approach: "A series of meetings was held beginning at the top level, and each officer passed on the program to his or her subordinates through the medium of meetings." Another example: "We introduced managerial job descriptions to our executives at a series of meetings with all concerned. These meetings worked from the top level on down." The implicit advantage in this "series of meetings" arrangement is that since individual groups are smaller, it becomes possible to answer detailed questions more fully. Thus the time of the larger group is not taken up by specific questions related to only one or two parts of the organization.

Group meetings also vary in their selection of the person who will chair the gathering and address the assembled executives. Usually the president opens the meeting and, after a short introduction, turns it over to another executive. This second person may be one of a number of officials—ordinarily the program's champion, the program's organizer, or a vice president in charge of personnel, administrative planning, or administrative services, aided by a representative of a management consulting firm, if one is being used. Sometimes an enthusiastic president will feel sufficiently impressed by the importance of the project to describe the plan to the assembled executives. In either case, whether the president merely opens the meeting or goes further and explains the entire description program, the support and prestige lent to the project by the top executive's presence is highly desirable.

### Essentials of Introduction

No matter who formally introduces the project to the organization's executives, regardless of how the organization plans to use the descriptions, and whether the idea is introduced at one large gathering, at a series of smaller executive meetings, or by letter, certain points about the project should be brought out in every introduction of managerial job descriptions. Although many of these points are probably obvious, they may serve as a checklist of ideas and thoughts that should be included in the presentation.

1. Explain the organizational and individual problems and the possible inequities the project is expected to cure. Describe the anticipated positive benefits to both the executives and the organization. In general, it is better

to begin by describing the results the organization hopes to achieve (organization clarification, organization planning, a more equitable salary administration policy, and so on) and then show how the descriptions will help in achieving these ends, rather than vice versa.

2. Emphasize that the project has the full backing of top management.

3. Provide a short history of how the project originated.

4. Indicate that the objective of the program is to describe the job and that performance is not being appraised.

5. Point out that no one will lose his or her job or be obliged to take a cut in salary as a result of the program. Of course, if salary reductions and streamlining the staff *are* contemplated, it is unwise to make such statements.

6. Describe the background and experience of the consulting firm (if there is one), perhaps mentioning a few companies and agencies with which it has been especially successful.

7. Explain to the executives exactly what will be required of them and what advance preparations they should make (if no preparation is required, say so). Explain how the information will be obtained (from whom, by whom, whether by questionnaire or interview, and so on), what will become of the information (who will see and pass on it), what its final form will be, and whether the individual executive will have access to his or her completed description.

8. Ask the assembled executives for cooperation and suggestions.

9. At the conclusion of the talk, answer all questions clearly and fully, allowing plenty of time for this step and encouraging frankness. If there is insufficient time remaining or if there are more queries than anticipated, clearly designate a definite way in which questions may be submitted and answers received after the session is over.

### Examples of Memoranda Encouraging Participation in Program

Some organizations provide a statement outlining the philosophy and objectives of the program. Through a combination of sales talk and fact, such a statement attempts to elicit the participation of executives in the program. At the end of this chapter, the reader will find a statement on philosophy and objectives, a memo on the purpose and use of the position guide, a memo on a reevaluation program, and a memo on an overall performance appraisal program related to position descriptions.

### Other Approaches to Presenting Programs

In contrast to these methods of presenting managerial description plans to executive personnel, some organizations use less conventional approaches. For example, no preliminary announcement of the project is made to the executives at all. When such an approach was used in one public agency, the middle management union immediately filed an unfair labor practice charge against the agency head. In some cases organizations will even go to the extreme of never disclosing the existence of managerial descriptions to its executives. For example, one organization reported: "Descriptions were written without the incumbent's knowledge of the program. Today we are receiving requests from incumbents to review their job descriptions with them. (The grapevine has told them there is a description.)" Hopefully, this organization's executives do not have to gather much other information through such indirect and devious channels. Other firms that do not formally announce the plan may introduce the project by presenting each executive with a preliminary draft of his or her duties and responsibilities and asking for comments, corrections, and criticism. However, such a practice may be part of a trial run. In such cases the program is announced later by a major executive officer at a general management meeting.

One firm, a leader in the field of executive job descriptions, made no formal announcement of its description project. Instead, it simply presented a few executives with copies of their descriptions. It explained: "Those persons who were given guides (descriptions) soon discovered their value to them as individuals in accomplishing their duties. By word of mouth and by contact on the part of those without guides with those who had and used them, the word spread." Although this is an excellent method, it takes a long time to develop momentum. It took this firm three years to receive requests and subsequently write descriptions covering "all the principal managerial positions" in just one division.

In some instances, the president may approve a program but may not immediately announce it. Instead, he or she may set up a committee composed of executives from various departments "to study the matter." In one case the committee was placed under the direction of the executive who first proposed the idea of position descriptions to the president. Shortly thereafter the committee had reviewed the project and recommended it to the respective departments.

Some organizations have accomplished the introduction by sending selected executives to management development courses stressing such a position description program. Companies and public agencies have sent their representatives to the AMA Management Course. One company stated: "First step was in having each top executive who was a member of our organization planning committee complete the AMA Management Course. This provided a common language for understanding and expediting a complete organization planning program (which included executive and managerial position descriptions)." Another said: "Approximately sixteen of our employees have attended the AMA Management Course, which was one of the early means of introducing them to the idea of having their positions described in writing."

### Executives' Reactions to Programs

Despite the diverse ways in which managerial position description programs are presented or, in some cases, not presented, the reactions of most executives to the concept are generally favorable. However, "favorable" does not mean that all executives are wildly enthusiastic about the programs. Indeed, very few respond by saying "Thank God somebody started this" or feel that such proposals get "wholehearted top management support and participation." On the contrary, many favorable statements are qualified: "mostly favorable reactions with some grumbling about the time required," "favorable with reservations," or "generally favorable, with a few skeptics."

Even within a given organization, all executives are not likely to respond uniformly to a position description plan. Typical comments: "Very mixed —some thought the idea was good, others considered it a total waste"; "generally very favorable, but varying from overoptimism about expected results to skepticism about the project's purpose"; and "mixed responses —some favorable, some lukewarm or skeptical, but a minimum of unfavorable reaction." The last two comments serve to illustrate the point that the plan was initially greeted with skepticism by at least a few executives in nearly every organization. This skepticism may take many forms, some open and some more hidden, and may range from angry opposition ("This is not necessary; everyone knows what I do!"), through raised eyebrows, to delaying tactics ("Looks good; *we* will get at it when we have time.").

In spite of isolated skeptical reactions the large majority of executives has been willing to go along with the idea, or at least to "wait and see the results before passing judgment." In a few organizations this equanimity has been explained by such comments as "The executives knew the chairman and president wanted this" or "The entire program had top management approval," thus reiterating the importance of top management backing for the project.

In instances where new programs replace older ones or present projects are substantially revised, executives have also responded favorably. One company noted: "Managerial position evaluation was accepted . . . as we had had description and evaluation of lower-level jobs for over ten years." However, if programs are changed too often or new plans adopted too frequently, executives will become extremely skeptical and will ultimately drag their feet or not participate at all. Therefore, major alterations in plans and new projects should be studied carefully and not implemented on too short a time frame.

Few organizations report that their executives' reactions are largely negative. Even in these companies and agencies, the executives' initial negative reactions "improve with time" and "as success patterns develop."

## MEMO

[Sent to each manager of a large manufacturer of power tools explaining philosophy and objectives of program.]

### ABC's COMPENSATION PHILOSOPHY AND OBJECTIVES

You have a responsibility for management salary administration if you supervise the work of other salaried exempt employees. To carry out this responsibility you must have a thorough understanding of ABC's compensation program philosophy and objectives. You must also understand and be able to explain to your people ABC's compensation policies.

Therefore, the purpose of this Guide is to provide you with an understanding of ABC's total compensation program—its purpose and scope, its objectives, its policies, and its procedures.

#### PURPOSE AND SCOPE OF THE PROGRAM

ABC must continue to attract and retain its most valuable resource—people— to maintain its leadership position as the world's largest manufacturer of power tools, and to continue to meet its growth objectives. ABC's future growth and success will depend almost wholly on the quality of its people and their ability to work together as a team. Such future success will certainly be measured by sales and profit growth, but equally important will be the ability to effectively create, manufacture, and sell an ever broadening group of laborsaving devices in new markets throughout the world. Only with competent people can ABC expect such success.

The demand for ABC products and services has doubled in the last five years. The basic problems of designing, manufacturing, selling, and distributing these products have become increasingly complex. An effective team has been built to accomplish our objectives. The effectiveness of this team will become increasingly important in the next few years as even more challenging corporate goals are established.

ABC must be certain that its compensation program, insofar as financial rewards can do so, will help retain and attract competent people and, in so doing, will increase the overall effectiveness of this team.

In order to better evaluate performance and recognize and reward individual contributions to our Company's success, an Overall Performance Appraisal Program was implemented. To link compensation practices with the objectives of the Overall Performance Appraisal Program, this Guide updates the program for administering compensation. The purpose of this Guide is to describe the compensation policies for salaried exempt personnel, to describe the underlying rationale for these policies, and to set forth instructions for implementation.

## OBJECTIVES OF ABC'S COMPENSATION PROGRAM

ABC's compensation program is designed to accomplish *three broad goals:*
1. Stimulate all employees to give their time, thought, and energies to those activities which will, in both the short and the long term, contribute to the Company's success.
2. Encourage all employees to work together as a team to attain corporate goals, establishing constructive working relationships in solving mutual problems.
3. Provide all employees with policies and procedures so easy to use, so sound, and so realistic as to encourage confidence and belief in their fairness.

ABC has established *eight specific compensation program objectives* to accomplish these broad goals. They are:
1. To insure that individuals are paid in relation to the value of the work they perform and the results they achieve.
2. To insure that the Company receives a fair return on its compensation investment.
3. To establish and maintain a sound, competitive compensation program that attracts and retains competent people.
4. To establish and maintain equitable and consistent internal job relationships.
5. To achieve a balanced program between pay and employee benefits.
6. To provide objective performance standards and to measure individual performance systematically and periodically against these standards.
7. To provide financial incentives for employees to utilize their full capabilities:
   a. To improve performance in their present job, and
   b. To advance, through promotion, to higher levels of responsibility.
8. To establish and maintain salary ranges that afford ample latitude for managers to make equitable salary decisions.

## HOW TO USE THIS GUIDE

This Guide is to be used as a working tool by all managers in U.S. operations. The policies outlined will provide a sound basis for achieving consistency in compensation administration throughout U.S. operations. Each manager is expected to follow these policies in the day-to-day administration of salaries.

This framework of policy and procedure guidelines:

1. Establishes the responsibility within the Massco Personnel Division for overall control of compensation policy to insure equitable, consistent compensation administration.
2. Decentralizes day-to-day salary decisions to where they can best be handled—at the management level where an individual's performance is best known.
3. Allows line managers to plan and control salary expenses.

Budgets, of course, provide overall control—albeit a negative one—of salary expense. The guidelines outlined here will provide a positive means for the equitable payment of individuals and for meeting both budgetary and compensation program objectives.

Each manager is expected to:

1. Become familiar with the entire contents of this Guide in order to gain an understanding of the overall compensation program.
2. Use the Guide as a reference source to answer any questions that arise when preparing a personnel action recommendation.
3. Follow the procedures outlined in the appendixes to insure proper processing of all personnel actions. Because the Personnel Action Authorization Form (PAF) is the single source document for our management information systems, it must be prepared correctly and with adequate lead time to permit complete processing prior to the effective date of the PAF.
4. Should interpretation of the guidelines be necessary, call a representative of the Personnel Division (e.g., Plant Personnel Manager, Employee Relations Manager at Massco, or the Director of Compensation) before initiating a Personnel Action Authorization Form.

CONFIDENTIAL INFORMATION

The only confidential information contained in this Guide is the ABC Salary Structure that appears in Exhibit I. It is Company policy to inform each salaried exempt employee of the range minimum and maximum of the salary grade to which he is assigned. However, he should not be informed of the ranges for those salary grades above the one to which he is assigned.

All other policies, guidelines, and procedures contained in this Guide should be discussed openly with your salaried exempt employees. More importantly, each manager is encouraged to communicate ABC's compensation policies to his people so they may have a full understanding of exactly how their own personal compensation is administered. If a detailed interpretation of a particular policy is needed, we suggest you request assistance from a representative of the Personnel Division.

# MEMO

[Sent to all management employees of an electric and gas utilities company for use in describing purpose and use of Position Guides.]

SUBJECT: PURPOSE AND USE OF THE POSITION GUIDE

The Salary Administration Organization has been assigned the responsibility of having prepared for the Company, Position Guides for all management positions and a Results Required List, if applicable.

You will soon be requested by your supervisor to prepare a Position Guide and a Results Required List, if applicable, for your job. You will be furnished by your supervisor with the proper forms and information necessary for their preparation.

Your supervisor may prepare the Position Guide when a single Guide is used to cover a number of like positions (such as Engineer, Senior Engineer, Foreman, Watch Foreman, General Watch Foreman, Engineering Assistant, Analyst, Accountant, etc.) in the same or in different organization units and in one or several geographical locations. All employees covered by such multi-position Guides will have the opportunity to review and comment on the Guide covering their position.

A good Position Guide is of valuable use to both yourself and management.
1. It serves as an aid in accomplishing the proper assignment of functions to positions.
2. It provides the means for you to thoroughly analyze your position and to record the work to be done and the objective to be accomplished.
3. It facilitates a discussion between you and your supervisor in developing mutual understanding and agreement on the objectives to be accomplished, the scope and limits of authority and responsibility, important relationships, and the factors to be used in measuring specific results achieved.
4. It affords a basis for sound evaluation of the differences in skills and abilities required to perform acceptably the work of specific positions.
5. It may be used by management as a basis for developing a definite and clear list of skills and abilities required by incumbents of each position, so that positions can then be staffed with individuals who have been definitely appraised as able to at least meet minimum requirements for each particular position.
6. It guides decisions with candidates for positions and, incidentally, is a means for quickly informing newly appointed incumbents with respect to their positions.
7. It will be used as one of the tools in the determination of your position level.

Since it is of the utmost importance to both management and yourself that accurate Position Guides be prepared, it is requested that you prepare the Guides carefully and completely.

Any questions you may have about this program should be addressed to your immediate supervisor.

VICE PRESIDENT

## MEMO

[Sent to each managerial employee of an electric utilities company prior to talk explaining new administrative rating program.]

### REEVALUATION OF WEEKLY RATED
### SUPERVISORY, ADMINISTRATIVE, AND TECHNICAL JOBS

As most of you know, job evaluation for weekly rated employees has been in existence in our Company for several years. It was established as an outgrowth of the demand from various departments for a more uniform method of arriving at rates of pay on a companywide basis. It was also given impetus during the war years by the need for filing our pay rates with government agencies.

There are several accepted ways of evaluating jobs, and since we believed the most efficient of these was point rating, it was used to evaluate the nonexempt jobs. However, point rating is a long and exacting job, and because of the urgency during the war years to file our rates with the government—and time grew short—most exempt jobs were evaluated by a shorter method, job comparison. While we have done a lot of work on this problem since, the results have not been wholly satisfactory, and job grades have therefore been assigned on a temporary basis.

We have planned, and are now able, to review the evaluation of exempt jobs thoroughly, and have secured the services of the *ABC* Management Consultant Company for this purpose. These consultants have for many years installed job evaluation systems and are now working with one of the largest industrial companies in the United States, located in the Detroit area. They have, during the last year or two, developed a special method for evaluating supervisory, administrative, and technical positions which has worked well in several companies, and seems to be a distinct improvement over the methods we have been using so far.

This project, which will start in October of this year, requires a review of the lines of authority, responsibility, and duties included in each job, and the rewriting of occupation descriptions.

You will be assisted in writing your own occupation description, and then it will be reviewed and is subject to approval by your supervisor. The Wage and

Salary Board, with the aid of your department head and council member and with the guidance of a representative of *ABC,* will then evaluate your occupation on the basis of this description. There is no doubt that a better overall alignment of jobs will result from this plan which will make possible a more accurate appraisal of the difficulties, responsibilities, and authority involved in every job. The result will not be put into effect until the plan as a whole is completed. No individual's rate of pay will be reduced as a result of this program.

The grades ultimately assigned will be the responsibility of the Wage and Salary Board, which will be assisted in this work by the Wage Planning Division of the Personnel Planning Department and representatives of *ABC.*

The Wage and Salary Board intends to start work on this program in October. The board, through your council member and department head, will make arrangements for you to participate in this program by attendance at meetings in which the forms and methods for preparing your occupation description will be explained and the schedule for your participation will be made known to you.

PRESIDENT

## MEMO

[Used by large national manufacturing firm in introducing management-by-objectives program.]

SUBJECT: OVERALL PERFORMANCE APPRAISAL PROGRAM

Each of you, and each individual working for you, is vitally interested in knowing how well you are doing in your job. Each of you is deeply concerned about your own future and personal development—the growth of your knowledge and skills and the direction of your career. Each of you is largely dependent on the man for whom you work to tell you these things.

XYZ management is also sincerely interested in your performance and your growth. And we want to make sure that every salaried exempt employee has regularly planned opportunities to discuss these important matters with his boss. To those ends, we are establishing our new *Overall Performance Appraisal Program,* which will be described in succeeding pages.

We have carefully researched this program with outside consulting help. Various levels of our management in all divisions have reviewed it, and approved it. We are sure it is practical and sound. We know that it will provide a means of *continuing communication* between manager and individual, so necessary in any effective appraisal program.

In addition, our Overall Performance Work Sheet will provide a working tool by which our top management can communicate its corporate goals down the line to division, to department, and to you—the individual. Each individual, working with his manager, should then translate these goals into his own work targets that will contribute to achieving total corporate goals.

The entire process will take extra time and careful thought from each of you. But I can assure you, if the job is done well, our results will be rewarding to XYZ and to you.

# 6

# *The Preparation of*
# *Position Descriptions*

Most of the organizations responding to this survey believe that participation by executives is crucial to the success of a managerial position description program. In 86 percent of the responding organizations, executives whose positions are included in the program participate in preparing their own descriptions. Each executive either writes the first draft of his or her description or supplies facts to a person who writes the first draft. At the very least, the executive reviews the description after the first draft has been formulated or before the final version is formally adopted.

Thirteen organizations did not include the executive in the preparation of the position description. They have used either the executive's immediate superior or the superior's superior or both in formulating the executive's job description. Apparently these organizations do not feel that it is worthwhile to consult incumbent executives about their work when writing up the descriptions. This approach is remarkable because some of these organizations indicated in their responses that the descriptions should "describe the job as it is being done at present" (rather than as it should be done). It would seem difficult to analyze a managerial position without at least consulting the executive doing the work.

This chapter discusses the characteristics of a good position description; top management control of the program; gathering the information for and writing the first draft of a position description; reviewing, revising, and approving first drafts; writing and approving the final version; keeping the descriptions up to date; and new methods of describing jobs. A sample position description interview and a sample position description are presented.

## CHARACTERISTICS OF A GOOD POSITION DESCRIPTION

To help us to formulate a good definition of a position description, the organizations participating in this survey offered their concepts of what constitutes a good description. Based on that information, a *managerial position description* is a brief, clearly written statement of a manager's job in terms of job objectives and the scope and level of job responsibilities, accountabilities, and authority. Depending on their use, descriptions may be written as the job exists presently or as the job should exist in the future. The statements of participating organizations provide a composite definition of a good managerial position description.

1. *Brevity:* Something brief that will still adequately describe the overall function, major duties, and responsibilities, and yet something broad enough not to stifle or limit initiative. (A transportation company.)

   One or two pages of narrative style explaining the essence of the job and how it fits into the organization, defining "what" and "why" and omitting "how." (A large metropolitan bank.)
2. *Clarity:* Clarity as to what the specific responsibilities and areas of accountability are. (A concrete manufacturing company.)

   Clarity, meaningfulness to incumbent, accuracy, and completeness. (An entertainment conglomerate.)
3. *Organization objectives:* A description that can be readily understood and interpreted in meeting the organization's objectives and the purposes of the job description program. (An appliance manufacturing company.)

   A description that provides both supervisor and subordinates with the objectives of a job and an understanding of why it exists within a corporation. (A rail transportation firm.)
4. *Scope and level of job:* A description that thoroughly describes the manager's objectives, areas of responsibility, accountability, and authority. (A large public utilities company.)

   A good description is one that accurately describes the scope and level of position responsibilities, accountabilities, and relationships. (An airline company.)

   A good description meets the following criteria: (1) reflects assignment and position as understood by subject manager, his/her superior, and executive management; (2) sufficiently distinguishes function and responsibilities to eliminate organization conflict; and (3) provides a basis for applying job evaluation or measurement of position value. (An arms manufacturer.)

   One that provides the uninformed person with a good conception of job content, authority and responsibility limits, and skill requirements. (A chemicals-pharmaceutical manufacturer.)

In defining a good job description, some organizations argued that it ought to be written by the incumbent and reviewed with the incumbent and the incumbent's superior by the person in charge of the job description program. Others thought that format was extremely important. For example, a furniture manufacturer noted: "A good description covers the following: (1) title of position, (2) reports to, (3) type of authority (line or staff), (4) basic function, (5) major results expected, (6) limits of accountability, (7) basis for performance standards."

In their definitions of position descriptions, employers frequently touched on the relations of the descriptions to their use. The definitions covered such items as performance appraisal, job evaluation, manpower planning, and career development.

### Descriptive versus Prescriptive Job Descriptions

One of the significant arguments that arises in the development of managerial position descriptions is whether they should be written as the job presently exists (descriptive) or as the job should be done (prescriptive). Some organizations use the job description to define clearly what the executive is presently doing. Thus the descriptions can be used to measure performance and determine equitable salary structures. Other organizations use the descriptions to inform executives of what is expected of them, no matter what they may be actually doing when the description is written. This type of description is useful for reorganization and management-development purposes. Additionally, after all managerial positions are brought up to the standard set in the descriptions, an equitable compensation system could be worked out on the basis of the descriptions. This "as is" versus "should be" issue affects the whole nature of the description program—how the information on work is gathered, the formulation of the description, and the content.

To provide us with some light on this topic, the survey participants were asked: "Do your organization's present managerial job descriptions describe the job: (1) As it is being done at present? (2) As it should be done? (3) As it was done in the past?" Of the 122 respondents who gave 140 responses (some gave multiple answers), 80 (57 percent) said a managerial description ought to describe the job as it is being done at present, 53 (38 percent) said the description should portray the work as it should be done, 5 (4 percent) said the job should be described as it was done in the past, and 2 (1 percent) replied with a nonspecific "other" answer.

It appears that a managerial description, *when written for salary administration,* should describe the work as it is presently being done. One executive noted: "There is no purpose in paying for a job as it should be done if it is being done better or worse. Besides, if the position 'as done' is very different from the position 'as it should be done,' management should see that the position is reorganized." Another strongly declared: "We pay for 'as is,' not for 'as should be.' "

On the other hand, 53 organizations definitely stated the work should be described as it ought to be done. These organizations were primarily interested in the value of position descriptions in organization planning and in the development of individual managers. A number of executives explained that this type of description provides a goal for the manager to shoot at. Some went on to say that such a description works best when "as is" and "as should be" are not impossibly far apart and where it seems distinctly possible to reconcile existing differences within a reasonable time. Extremely idealistic descriptions run the danger of being written off as pie-in-the-sky visions that offer no real incentive for a practical manager.

More and more organizations are using descriptions for several purposes. This tends to increase the interrelations between descriptive and prescriptive concepts of managerial job descriptions. For example, three respondents offered these comments:

> Writing descriptions of how a job is done often leads to discussion as to how it should be done.

> In writing a description, (1) the analyst should try to determine what should be done, and so prepare the managerial description; (2) if this is not acceptable, he should then modify the description to cover the job in compromise fashion. The incumbent may not do the work in this way, but this is the goal to aim for.

> For the initial evaluation with the present incumbent, the job should be described as is. Later, when a different individual takes over the position's duties, the job should be described as it ought to be fulfilled.

These opinions support the idea that one natural way in which a program evolves is from wage and salary descriptions to management guides. An organization starts describing positions "as is" to establish just compensation and later goes on to write descriptions for organizational and developmental purposes.

In planning a program an organization should consider the question of "as is" versus "should be" carefully at the project's inception and should weigh which arrangement will more nearly suit the uses planned for the descriptions. These decisions should be made clear to all who have a hand in formulating descriptions and to all who use them.

This is not to say that an ordinary job evaluation program does not embody some aspects of development and organization. Certainly if a first draft of a description shows gross overlap of authority and responsibility between this and another position, something must be done about it when the problem comes to the attention of persons with authority to resolve it.

In such a situation the position can be reformulated before the final draft is completed and accepted as valid. In other words, the necessary changes can be made immediately if absolutely needed, and the final version of the description will still describe the job "as is"—after the changes have been made.

## TOP MANAGEMENT CONTROL OF THE PROGRAM

The preceding discussion introduces the idea of top management control of the description process. In certain cases it would be foolish to let the incumbent executive have sole authority to describe the position as it is currently being performed, with no check on the accuracy of the statements. An ambitious person may attempt to take more authority than the organization wishes to delegate; a person inactive in a position may understate its requirements or attempt to gloss over his or her weaknesses with euphemisms. It is also possible that an organization description specialist may misstate the position. Therefore the organization must maintain some control over the process; otherwise a description program may run away with the organization and result in a worse situation than the one that inspired the program in the first place. Describing a position usually involves several steps:

Gathering the information necessary to describe the work.
Writing the first draft.
Reviewing, revising, and approving first drafts.
Writing and approving the final version.
Keeping descriptions current.

Top management control of the program may be exercised at any step, or the organization can elect to throw primary responsibility for the development of descriptions entirely on the shoulders of those managing the program. For instance, a few organizations do not consult executives when describing their positions. Others allow the executive to formulate the first draft, and some even permit the individual to write the final version without much reference to higher authority. Most of the organizations exercise control when they are comparing and revising the first drafts of the descriptions. Since this is a very flexible process, little can really be generalized about it in a definitive way. The final, authorized version of a description may suddenly be questioned if a top executive becomes concerned with the work described. Indeed, this may happen in almost any segment of the chain of command if serious disagreements over job duties, responsibilities, accountabilities, and authority arise.

## GATHERING THE INFORMATION

Several persons collect the information necessary for writing the managerial position descriptions. These include internal organization specialists of many types, including those in personnel and compensation administration, incumbent executives, the supervisor of the executive, and the department head over the supervisor and the executive (see Table 7). These

*Table 7. Methods of gathering information for position descriptions and sources of the data.\**

| METHOD † | SOURCE | | |
| --- | --- | --- | --- |
| | EXECUTIVE | EXECUTIVE'S SUPERVISOR | EXECUTIVE'S DEPARTMENT HEAD |
| Interview with: | 83 | 85 | 55 |
| Observation of: | 34 | 12 | 6 |
| Questionnaire to: | 35 | 25 | 8 |

\* 136 organizations had job descriptions; 17 organizations did not answer the question; multiple answers were given by many organizations.

† Other methods were mentioned. 67 organizations used prior managerial position descriptions; 8 used personal knowledge of the job; 1 used knowledge of the organization; 1 used information from the American Management Associations and local and national personnel data; 1 used information from personnel directors in other divisions of the organization.

persons use many different methods to gather the information. Interviews, observations, questionnaires, and previous position descriptions are the major sources of data. Other sources include personal knowledge of the job, personal knowledge of the organization, information from professional associations like the American Management Associations, and personnel directors in other sections or divisions of an organization.

### Methods and Sources

During the past two decades there has been significant institutionalization of managerial position descriptions in companies and public agencies. In the 1958 AMA survey the use of prior descriptions was not mentioned prominently. Today, 67 organizations use previous descriptions as a starting point and an initial source of information for writing new ones and revising old ones. Moreover, standardized procedures are used for obtaining job information in approximately one-half of all the organizations writing descriptions. Many of these standardized procedures include manuals that provide step-by-step instructions for specialists in developing the total description programs as well as position description guides to aid executives to define clearly what information is needed for the descriptions. (See Part Two for brief examples of manuals.) A food processor divided its position description manual into four parts: (1) *definition of position description,* explaining what it is to be used for; (2) *preparation,* which involves a step-by-step procedure to explain the program to subordinates; (3) *procedure,* which provides a series of steps describing how the position description is to be written, using two worksheets; and (4) *final draft,* an analysis of the final description broken down into specific sections—general responsibility, organizational relationships, and specific duties.

In addition to using prior descriptions, writers still use extensive interviews with executives (83) and their superiors (85) and department heads (55). This is still the most widely used method of obtaining information. Through the use of structured interview questionnaires, much valuable information can be obtained from the interactions between the interviewer and the interviewee. Questionnaires prepared by executives without these interactions frequently do not provide all the needed information. As a result, further communications or interviews or both are still necessary with the person completing the questionnaire.

In conjunction with interviews, job description writers frequently spend time observing the executive in his or her daily operations. These observations are usually taken on a systematic or random sampling basis. Occasionally the observers will view executives on a continuing basis for some extended period of time. More than one-half of the observations are made while the executive is alone. Infrequently, the executive's supervisor is observed for potential interactions with the executive (23 percent) and his or her department head (12 percent). Such observations can be expensive, and the more that are taken the more expensive and time-consuming the method becomes.

Questionnaires may be used in conjunction with interviews or sent directly to the executive or the executive's superiors without an interview. Seldom are questionnaires about an executive's job sent to the department head. Executive position questionnaires may be written in either instructional or question form. An instructional form may use the following format for obtaining data about position activities:

1. Outline, in general order of importance, each specific responsibility or function performed. Identify or illustrate the extent and nature of decisions made with respect to each function, particularly as to authority to change policy, objective, or procedure.
2. Illustrate special or nonrecurring assignments, identifying specific projects and actions taken.

3. Indicate responsibility, if any, for each of the following including extent and degree of authority for action:
   (a) Budget planning and control.
   (b) Purchasing.
   (c) Personnel hiring, salaries, promotion, dismissal, and other changes.
   (d) Product pricing.
   (e) Product changes, additions, and eliminations.
4. Indicate the level and type of prior experience and academic training that you judge to be required or desirable to meet the responsibilities of the position.
5. Provide other information you believe will help clarify the requirements of this position.

Questionnaires may vary in length from one to ten pages. Some are highly structured and ask for definitive quantitative and qualitative data, whereas others are extremely general. In almost all cases, organizations using questionnaires provide fairly detailed instructions on how the forms should be completed. (For examples of questionnaires used in some organizations, see Part Two of this book.)

In analyzing the data in Table 7, it is clear that most of the information not gathered from previous position descriptions is obtained by interviews. Moreover, the executive is the key source of information about the job. In only 13 cases was the executive not involved in any way in formulating his or her position description. In seven of these cases the supervisor provided the information; in five, the supervisor and department head provided the data; and in one, the department head alone gave the data. Thus the executive and the executive's immediate superior are the two primary sources of information for job descriptions.

**Working Time Needed**
Four or five hours' working time usually is needed to gather the information and write a careful first draft of a managerial position description. This estimate, though very rough, is based on the replies of organizations that have had considerable experience.

The time spent to produce a first draft may be quite high when an organization is considering describing 500 positions. If the estimate is at all accurate, it would take 2,000 to 2,500 hours to complete such a task. Initial formulation takes most of the time, but in certain reorganization programs reworking first drafts to a point where they are binding can add to the working time.

Working time needed to produce a first draft may vary according to the person undertaking the task. When the first draft of every position description is written by specialists, the median time is approximately seven hours per description. In contrast, an executive or an executive's superior can write a first draft of his or her position description in a median working time of just under four hours.

One possible explanation for this might be that the specialist takes more pains with the task than an incumbent executive or executive's superior. Because specialists are specialists, they are in a better position to appreciate the varied uses of descriptions and often make a greater effort to see that all descriptions contain a similar amount of information. They have been specifically charged with the duty of describing the various positions adequately and therefore can (and feel they should) devote more attention to the task than a manager who has many other things to do. This explanation is supported by the fact that organizations in which descriptions are particuarly well written nearly always prove to be those that use specialists.

Many of the participants in this survey submitted sample position descriptions with their questionnaires; the quality of the descriptions prepared by specialists was almost without exception better than the quality of those prepared by incumbent executives or their immediate superiors. This is not to say that all incumbents and their superiors had prepared poor descriptions; some descriptions appeared to be quite adequate and even excellent. This was particularly true in organizations where all managers had received careful instructions on the preparation of position descriptions.

**Writing the First Draft**
Since 1958 there have been some significant shifts in the authority of the persons writing the first draft of a position description (see Table 8). A comparison of the data for the two AMA studies shows that internal specialists are not writing as many first drafts as they did earlier (32 percent versus 49 percent). Immediate superiors are now writing significantly more first drafts while executives themselves are writing about the same number. Although a few more consultants are writing first drafts today, the number (6) is still comparatively quite small.

The greater participation of an executive's immediate superior may be explained by the availability of prior position descriptions and the desire by the superior to change the characteristics of a subordinate's job. Perhaps a decision has been made to shift a job description from "as is" to "should be" and this gives the superior an opportunity to revise the description of the incumbent's position. Of course the incumbent usually is

*Table 8. Writers of first drafts of managerial position descriptions.*

| WRITER | CURRENT STUDY * | 1958 AMA STUDY † |
|---|---|---|
| Immediate Superior | 55 (33.5%) | 18 (10.7%) |
| Internal Specialist ‡ | 52 (31.7%) | 83 (49.1%) |
| Executive | 51 (31.1%) | 65 (38.4%) |
| External Consultant | 6 (3.7%) | 2 (1.2%) |
| Other | — | 1 (0.6%) |
| Total | 164 (100.0%) | 169 (100.0%) |

* 136 organizations had position descriptions; 13 did not answer the question; 123 provided 164 responses.

† 142 organizations had position descriptions; 3 did not answer the question; 139 provided 169 responses.

‡ This classification includes directors and managers of personnel, compensation administration, and organization development; specialists, technicians, and analysts in personnel and compensation administration; internal consultants; and officers.

contacted through interview, observation, questionnaire, or a combination of these methods for his or her thoughts about the anticipated changes.

Determining whether to assign the first draft to a specialist or to the incumbent executive or executive's superior depends on the incumbent executive's writing ability and the availability of a specialist who understands the work. A specialist offers the advantage of clearly understanding all the parameters of a position description and promising an expert description. An incumbent executive has the advantage of intimate familiarity with the particular position: its challenges, problems, duties, and responsibilities. An incumbent's superior provides the advantage of making it possible to inform subordinates in no uncertain terms of what is expected. However, other persons have been used for writing descriptions. In some cases joint or team efforts have been successful. Sometimes the first draft is written by one individual (perhaps an executive) and the final draft by another (usually a personnel or compensation specialist). In fact, this latter combination is quite common.

Although internal specialists may not be involved in writing initial drafts, they supervise the description program, assist in the detailed work flow for the descriptions, and write the final draft.

## REVIEWING, REVISING, AND APPROVING FIRST DRAFTS

Before the first draft of a managerial description is accepted, it must be read and approved or modified by one or more organization executives.

This is the point where almost all organizations apply executive control over the description program to avoid implementing or continuing arrangements that do not meet with top executive approval.

### Who Is Responsible for Review, Revision, and Approval?
Almost all organizations require that two or more executives formally review the first drafts of all positions. Such teams usually include at least one line executive and one specialist. Typical teams are the incumbent executive and a personnel specialist; the incumbent executive, the immediate supervisor, and a personnel specialist; the immediate supervisor, the supervisor's superior, and a personnel specialist; and the immediate supervisor, the supervisor's superior, a personnel specialist, and the program director. A personnel specialist may be an analyst, a specialist, or a program director, depending on the level of managerial position being described.

If approval is not obtained, the draft of the description must be reworked until it is satisfactory. In some cases the revision of first drafts results in "final" descriptions, since changes of a word or two are inserted as the review process goes along and no further rewriting is required. However, the description frequently must be rewritten from beginning to end.

In general, most managers are not asked to review the descriptions if they have taken part in their original preparation. Most organizations seem to prefer that their executives do one task or the other but not both—for the same description.

### When Conflicts in Descriptions Occur
Occasionally an executive and a colleague will see a particular job or some aspect of it in entirely different ways. To cite an example: An executive at the main plant of a manufacturing firm has been placed in charge of its purchasing activities. She assumes that a man who buys for a branch plant located at some distance from the head office is under her direction. On the other hand, the branch purchasing manager believes he is reporting to his plant manager and is supposed only to "coordinate" his work with the head office. Through restraint and courtesy—or by ignoring each other—each person has concealed his or her view from the other and from everyone else for some time. Now, however, each has written the first draft of a position description. When the two descriptions are examined, the discrepancy in views comes to light. The company, of course, is anxious to resolve this conflict in authority and thereby avoid the possibility of considerable inefficiency in its purchasing activities.

Which official is charged with the responsibility for resolving such conflicts? Answers to this question vary widely. Some answers show there is no formalized procedure. But the task is usually undertaken by the lowest-echelon executive with direct authority over both of the positions under review. Sometimes this is the president of a corporation; sometimes it is an operations vice president; occasionally it is a person on a very junior level. Some organizations turn the matter over to specialized organization planning departments.

Reorganization efforts at the executive level are usually placed under the control of very high level executives. Organizations initiating such programs may tackle the problem head on by issuing a formal statement. For example, one organization stated: "There may be instances in which lines of responsibility are not clearly defined in the minds of position occupants. That is, through misunderstanding, there may be duplication or omission, or a person may be performing a function which more logically belongs to someone else. When such situations are found, it is then wise to assemble the position occupants and their superiors so that a realignment of responsibilities may be accomplished by conference." Another organization commented: "Interviews between the incumbents, their bosses, and the superiors' superiors in which the 'draftee' (i.e., the company description specialist who has drafted the initial version of the descriptions) does *not* participate are frequently necessary to reconcile differences of opinion."

A primary reason for formulating managerial position descriptions is that the process brings out many such differences of opinion. Once these are in the open it is relatively easy to resolve them and thereby build a far stronger organization. Advance knowledge of the conflicts is far better than allowing them to become apparent in a crisis when a hasty decision is needed.

These conflicts in descriptions are much less likely to occur in maturing programs where jobs have been revised several times and have become fairly well defined, so that there is little formal overlap between positions. However, in maturing programs in rapidly changing organizations (for example, those operating in high-technology fields), conflicts inevitably appear in the system and provisions must be made to resolve them.

### WRITING AND APPROVING THE FINAL VERSION

Most of the organizations in the survey assign only one person to write the final versions of managerial descriptions. For this task, 66 percent of the organizations select a personnel specialist at the analyst, technician, specialist, or director level (see Table 9). As a position description program matures, the level of authority of the persons writing the final descriptions is pushed progressively lower in the organizational hierarchy.

Approximately 39 percent of the writers of final drafts are executives in personnel while another 26 percent are personnel analysts. Because description program staffs are usually very small, the program director frequently ends up writing the final version of the description.

*Table 9. Writers of final versions of managerial position descriptions.* *

| WRITER OF FINAL VERSION | NUMBER OF RESPONSES |
|---|---|
| Personnel Specialist | |
| Director or Manager, Personnel † | 33 |
| Director or Manager, Compensation Administration ‡ | 27 |
| Personnel Analyst § | 11 |
| Compensation Analyst ¶ | 29 |
| Executives at all levels | 39 |
| Incumbent executives | 13 |
| Total | 152 |

* 136 organizations had job descriptions; 16 did not answer the question; several organizations gave multiple answers concerning joint and/or individual writing.

† This classification includes directors of employee relations, industrial relations, organization planning, and organization development.

‡ This classification includes directors of compensation and benefits, wage and salary administration, and job evaluation.

§ This classification includes personnel technicians, manpower planners, organizational consultants, and personnel and organizational specialists.

¶ This classification includes compensation coordinators, wage and salary analysts, salary analysts, job analysts, and position analysts.

Writing the final version is apparently not as difficult or crucial as composing and reviewing the first draft. The first draft in a well-developed program should be fairly good. It is perhaps altered during its review, with suggestions and amendments from persons in top and executive management. Composition of the final version often only involves incorporating the suggestions of those with line authority to determine the actual contents of the descriptions and rewriting to assure optimum clarity and a uniform style in all the descriptions. If the program is clearly laid out at the beginning and first drafts are formulated according to a standard format, writing the final draft should not be an onerous or time-consuming task. This explains why in most organizations one man or woman does all the work.

In 13 organizations the incumbent executive writes the final version without help from others or with the assistance of his or her superior or a personnel specialist. Normally, the incumbent works on this draft after having had the benefit of review of the first draft by others.

The key to writing and approving a good final version is a thorough review of the first draft. This is the point at which basic differences should be reconciled. The final version reflects the recommendations made during the review, and little real difficulty should remain when the finished product is written. A few organizations believe it is better to have the same individual write both versions, provided that others have made a careful review of the first effort. In such a situation, the writer must write out his or her carefully considered understanding of any suggestions received during the review. Thus by writing the final version, the individual may participate more in the decisions made during the review than would have been possible if someone else had written it.

Other organizations hold exactly the opposite view, stating that they deliberately avoid using the same writer for both first draft and final version. These respondents commonly stated that first drafts are written by the incumbent or the incumbent's immediate superior and that final versions are written by the head of the description program or by organization description specialists. Either arrangement seems satisfactory, provided the review of the first draft is adequate.

Although many of the final drafts are prepared by personnel specialists, the final approval of the descriptions still rests predominantly with line managers. Seventy-two percent of the final versions are approved by line managers. Approximately one-half of those line managers are in top and executive management. Twenty-three percent of the final drafts are approved by personnel specialists. Only in a few cases (5 percent) does the incumbent executive approve the final draft of his or her own position description.

### A SAMPLE POSITION DESCRIPTION INTERVIEW AND THE RESULTING DESCRIPTION

Of all the steps in the preparation of managerial position descriptions, one of the most difficult to describe is the interview in which information on the job is gathered from the incumbent. Most students of the subject have fairly definite ideas about how such interviews should be conducted with production workers and even with salaried office personnel and first-line supervisors (though these interviews do pose special problems). Daniel Nicholas, a full-time job analyst in industry, interviewed an executive who was attending an AMA course at the Management Center in New York; to give some idea of how a managerial interview is often conducted, that interview was recorded and is reproduced below, along with the description Mr. Nicholas wrote. (The interview has been edited to about one-half its original length, but the essentials remain.)

John Carpenter (not his real name) is the manager of a brewing plant. Mr. Carpenter could not allow publication of the interview with real names (Mr. Nicholas, of course, has used his own real name) unless the resulting description were submitted to his superiors for approval. This is precisely what would have been done if the interview had been part of a real description program. Originally, Mr. Carpenter had intended to allow publication using his own and his company's name, but as the interview dug deeper into his work and certain vague areas of responsibility came into view, he discovered certain things on which there had never been absolutely clear understanding between him and his company. This is quite normal; it occurs in practically every managerial position description program, at least with one or two jobs.

Though the interview was conducted only to gather material for an earlier AMA report, it was actually very successful in that it raised questions that Mr. Carpenter felt had very real applications in his firm. If this interview had been part of a real description program, an effort would have been made to clear up any uncertain points by holding discussions with Mr. Carpenter's superiors. As it stands, this sample interview demonstrates not only technique but one of the primary purposes of a description program—the effort to encourage frank discussion between managers and their superiors to bring about greater understanding between them. At least a few job analysts will find one or two things they would have done differently if they had been conducting the interview or writing the description. This is to be expected, since each analyst prepares descriptions with a particular company and a particular situation in mind. Methods vary, and the interview presented is only one workable way to go about the task.

## THE INTERVIEW

NICHOLAS: Now, Mr. Carpenter, what I'll try to do here is to draw out some particularly interesting aspects of your position. By that I mean such things as status, responsibilities, and the broad overall objectives of the job. I've read up a little on brewing, and I've read a few descriptions for positions similar to your own. If I were actually working in your company, that's precisely what I would have done, and besides that, I would have looked at your company organization chart to get at least a fairly clear idea of where you fit in. Now that I have some basic knowledge, I'm going to try to use it as the basis for this interview, but if you discover that I'm working with unwarranted preconceptions, let me know.

CARPENTER: Yes, I have an idea of what you're trying to do. My job's never been written up before, and maybe this will give me some idea about how we should go about this work back home.

NICHOLAS: Now the first thing I'd like to investigate is the size of your business and your share in managing it. Your firm has about 1,300 employees, doesn't it?

CARPENTER: Yes, we have 1,300 employees and three plants. There's a main plant in Chicago; we have another plant in Milwaukee, where we make beer and package and deliver it in that area; and we have a third plant in St. Louis that is similar to mine. I'm manager of production at Milwaukee.

NICHOLAS: You run the one specific plant, then?

CARPENTER: Yes.

NICHOLAS: Do you yourself, then, have 1,300 employees under you?

CARPENTER: No, I have 185, and they are included in the 1,300 for the whole firm.

NICHOLAS: Would you say that your responsibilities in regard to these 185 employees are the same as a small company president would have toward his organization?

CARPENTER: Not exactly, because there are a lot of things that our main office in Chicago does which a small company president would do himself or have done for him in his own immediate organization. We have three people on the same level in Milwaukee. There's production; then there are packaging and delivering. "Delivering" is the transport of the finished product—not sales as such. We have a sales department that works apart from me altogether. We cooperate, but we have no authority over each other, and we have a public relations manager who works pretty much alone and is not responsible to either of us. But the three main divisions at Milwaukee are production, packaging, and delivering, as I said. Sales and public relations are handled pretty much from the main office in Chicago.

NICHOLAS: Does each of these three divisions have a staff—or perhaps I should say a workforce—separate from the others?

CARPENTER: Yes.

NICHOLAS: Then you are responsible for the operations staff, including the packaging and delivering people?

CARPENTER: That's about right.

NICHOLAS: Now, overall policies for your particular plant at Milwaukee—are they arrived at mutually with your managers in Milwaukee?

CARPENTER: I would say no. Overall policies are usually determined at the head office but after discussion with us. That seems to be the pattern.

NICHOLAS: Is there a formal committee that evolves policy at Chicago? Perhaps you may sit in on their sessions when they directly involve your plant.

CARPENTER: No, I receive my policies from the director of production; he would have arrived at the basic policy in a meeting in Chicago at the director level. We're consulted about it. We have a copy of any policy statement before it is printed, formalized, and signed, and we can make our comments and return them to our respective superiors.

NICHOLAS: Do these comments usually affect the formulation of policy?

CARPENTER: Yes, they're listened to.

NICHOLAS: Well, then, I think we've clarified that point. Out of these 185 people, how many would you say you have reporting directly to you?

CARPENTER: That would be around 150.

NICHOLAS: Now for a very big question: What may we call the big-picture objective of your specific job?

CARPENTER: Well, to put it as briefly as possible—.

NICHOLAS: You don't necessarily have to make it brief!

CARPENTER: No! Well, I have three important divisions or "subs." One is brewing beer. The purpose of our business is to brew beer—quality beer.

NICHOLAS: At your particular plant. In your own plant.

CARPENTER: Yes, then it's packaged. By that I mean that we bottle it, store it, and warehouse it. And I'm also in charge of the transport department, which means actually that I have charge of the chauffeurs. I'm responsible for them and for the trucks too.

NICHOLAS: Distribution of the product as well?

CARPENTER: Oh, not the distribution. On second thought, yes! Yes, I would say so—that is, to the extent that we would make the decision on whether it would go by rail or not, or whether the means of transportation would be by any common carrier. That would be my decision pretty much in cooperation with sales—very often, anyway.

NICHOLAS: With sales?

CARPENTER: They are interested, too, but the decision on type of carrier is mine, and the men of the transport department are hired by me.

NICHOLAS: Do you have a transport manager who reports to you? Does he report to you about the operation of the transport department?

CARPENTER: We have 16 trucks. It isn't a very large operation, and we call the head of it the "transport superintendent." He reports to me.

NICHOLAS: Who would you say is *your* immediate superior?

CARPENTER: The director of production in Chicago.

NICHOLAS: How often do you report to him? Is it a regular procedure? Do you send him a written report periodically or whenever the need arises?

CARPENTER: Certainly we meet once a month on budget matters. Not less than once a month. We communicate by telephone quite a bit, too. Weekly at least, and, of course, other things are done by correspondence. Some report figures go to him daily on our operations, some weekly.

NICHOLAS: Now, working back down the line, who reports directly to you?

CARPENTER: Well, the brewer reports to me. He's in charge of all brewing, and I already covered the transport superintendent.

NICHOLAS: Does the brewer have a staff?

CARPENTER: He has a quality control man and one foreman. That's all. And I also have the bottling shop foreman. He reports to me too. That's packaging as far as we're concerned.

NICHOLAS: The bottling shop foreman—how many people report to him?

CARPENTER: Do you mean employees and all? Well, on that basis, I'd say roughly 32. And, also, I should tell you that the brewer has 35 employees with him. Yes, that's 35 for brewing, and then shipping and receiving have one foreman. There are 18 people with him. Oh, I forgot a phase of it! Maintenance also reports to me. That's the brewer, the transport superintendent, the bottling shop foreman, and maintenance, too.

NICHOLAS: Ah—maintenance for your particular plant, is that it?

CARPENTER: Yes, there's a foreman for maintenance and a staff of about 14 people. And we have a boiler-room powerhouse foreman with about ten people. He reports to me too.

NICHOLAS: Oh? I think you've covered the reporting relationships pretty well.

CARPENTER: Yes, I think so.

NICHOLAS: We'll move on to something else, then. Are there any incentives or standards for your whole operations? I mean, predetermined standards or goals.

CARPENTER: Not in brewing, I would say. We go by previous experience more than anything else. Brewing's like that. It's an art. In bottling we do have incentives, but they are not monetary. It's a simple standard of comparison of activities in bottling plants in all of our breweries. It involves about ten different bottling shops, and we receive monthly reports on their efficiency. Sometimes it's measured in gallons per man-hour or in cost per gallon for bottling.

NICHOLAS: Who makes these comparisons, if I may ask?

CARPENTER: We are controlled by a parent company. It has four other brands besides the one we make. We send our information to the parent company, and it condenses it and sends each of the shops a full report on every other unit. Also, we make comparisons with Canadian plants.

NICHOLAS: Well, that covers standards for bottling, in a way. What about the brewer? You say there are no definite standards for brewing, and I can understand that. What do you have to do with him periodically?

CARPENTER: Well, as it happens, I'm a brewer, too, by training. I went through brewer's school. At the moment I *am* the brewer. Normally, the brewer would report to me. But I'm doing this particular work now myself. I have some assistance, though, through the director of production in Chicago. He comes to Milwaukee occasionally and inspects the plant and that sort of thing. We have the use of the Chicago laboratories, which are much more complete than our own for biological control.

NICHOLAS: Would the bottling shop foreman have much the same status as the brewer—that is, as the brewer would have if you had one?

CARPENTER: Yes.

NICHOLAS: And the same thing goes for all foremen—shipping, receiving, and maintenance?

CARPENTER: They are directly responsible to me. Is that what you're getting at?

NICHOLAS: Yes, that's right, but what I'm also getting at is your specific duties. They evolve from these specific departments. Do I make myself clear? Do you have regular meetings with these foremen?

CARPENTER: Yes, we do.

NICHOLAS: Well, that makes it pretty clear, I think. I've been doing a little research on this, and I looked at quite a few descriptions from the brewery business, and I put a few of them together to see if I could develop a few statements which you might go along with about your job. I'll read one that seems to be a fairly good summary. Contradict me right away if I've got the wrong impression. Here it is: "To determine minimum standards to be met by plant processes and building and equipment maintenance under his control; to set up operating practices, maintenance schedules, and inspection methods; and to see that these standards are met or bettered." Would you say that statement applies to your particular position?

CARPENTER: Yes, that would fit in.

NICHOLAS: Would you care to amplify that a little bit, or is it adequate?

CARPENTER: That's quite good. You said "standards," and that's my responsibility—to see that the standards have been met.

NICHOLAS: All right. Let's go on: "To plan, justify, and, through prescribed budgetary practices, obtain approval for expenditures for the original purchase, replacement, repair, and maintenance of the plant and machinery as this statement applies to your particular plant."

CARPENTER: Yes, yes.

NICHOLAS: I'm still working with the prepared statement: "As chief executive of the unit, to supervise all production."

CARPENTER: Yes, that fits in.

NICHOLAS: Fine! Now I'll read something that is quite broad and perhaps should be made a little more specific. If you think it should, don't hesitate to stop me: "To carry out all authorized policies and to secure observance of procedures and controls laid down by the company. More particularly, to guarantee strict adherence to the approved brewing formula."

CARPENTER: In that last respect, I think the statement is too specific already. There can be several interpretations of a brewing formula. In brewing, you can make the same product slightly differently each time. It's the result that counts, not the method. It's understood that you're to produce a beer of a certain quality that has been accepted by the people who buy it. Let's say that the sales department and the director of production in Chicago agree to a certain characteristic in the product. I must get that characteristic into the beer. It's my responsibility to make flavor that is accepted. We find it is better to allow our brewers a bit of leeway in making decisions and changing methods to a certain extent. It's usually done very cautiously in consultation with our technical people in Chicago and through flavor tests by taste panels.

NICHOLAS: Does any one person make the ultimate decision regarding what the formula will be?

CARPENTER: No, I would make the basic decision, but in consultation.

NICHOLAS: Not the brewmaster?

CARPENTER: No, a really basic formula change would have to be made by the director of production, but variations within the formula as to method are my basic responsibility since I do the brewing.

NICHOLAS: That's very interesting. It's somewhat different from the usual quality-control work in ordinary manufacturing.

CARPENTER: Yes, brewing is quite an art.

NICHOLAS: To move on again, do you have a responsibility to allocate work and supervise the activities of the various department heads that we've mentioned—that is, the bottling shop, transport, and so on—so that maximum efficiency is obtained?

CARPENTER: Yes, that's my full responsibility.

NICHOLAS: What sort of control do you exercise over these particular departments?

CARPENTER: Well, I follow them continuously and make out their budgets every month. Budgeting, and all that goes into it, amounts to control as far as I'm concerned. A good budget includes or allows for efficient use of material and labor. I review the budgets with the individual foremen, and I have to report on the total operation weekly.

NICHOLAS: Excellent. That's what I was trying to get at.

CARPENTER: Oh, we have all kinds of inventory control, payroll figures, warehouse reports, and everything of that sort. It's up to me to watch them and pass the information on. Some things are more important and are reported more frequently, of course.

NICHOLAS: Along the lines of budgetary control and that sort of thing, do you yourself have any informal criteria for applying pressure to a particular department that is not running up to par?

CARPENTER: Mostly in bottling. We have daily reports on the cost recorded in man-hours per gallon produced. I can tell if something's off with that, because bottling is a fairly measurable process. Brewing is another thing. You have so many variables, it's hard to measure. Yield up to quality or flavor standard is a thing we want, but one man can improve an operation so that he gets more gallons out of malt than another. But on a long-term basis you can tell if something's really wrong.

NICHOLAS: Now if certain technical services are required over and above those that you have readily available at your plant, what sort of arrangements can you yourself make to have these services brought in?

CARPENTER: Chemical analysis we don't do in our plant. We do mostly physical checks on the product that we're turning out, and we continuously send samples to our biological laboratory as it's in process at each stage. The lab reports back to us for light stability and for cleanliness. As far as chemical analyses are concerned, we are not equipped to do that sort of thing, beyond water analysis. But we have the services of our parent company's research laboratories to supplement the work done in our own laboratory and to undertake any special projects.

NICHOLAS: Do you specifically have the authority to call these people in when you feel it's necessary?

CARPENTER: Not by myself. I would speak to my superior about it.

NICHOLAS: I see.

CARPENTER: But I can send them any amount, practically, of work to be done as far as analysis is concerned within our routine, provided it doesn't become too cumbersome and take a man a full-time effort to do it. Any specific analysis that I want done I merely send to the laboratories, and we get the reports back. I get the report addressed to me and my superior gets a copy.

NICHOLAS: Now, what sort of status or responsibility do you have toward the purchase of new materials for production? That includes machinery as well.

CARPENTER: On large items, if of a repair nature, I am responsible and can purchase the work. It's usually done in consultation with the engineers, though, if it's a sizable repair. If it's a capital project, then it's the engineering department's responsibility and is done in consultation with me. Any project must be acceptable to me.

NICHOLAS: Is there a definite money amount in capital expenditures above which you cannot go without consulting your superiors?

CARPENTER: Not exactly. But we have a project book which describes all capital building and equipment projects for each year. That's very thoroughly discussed when capital projects are laid out. I can't expand my plant without prior approval through the project book, and that's where the projects are approved.

NICHOLAS: Do you feel that so far we're covering your job adequately?

CARPENTER: No, I don't. I feel that maybe something could be added.

NICHOLAS: Oh—we're not finished, not by a long shot. But I'm just wondering whether you feel that the subjects mentioned so far have been covered adequately.

CARPENTER: Well, I guess so, but I just don't know whether I've made them clear or not.

NICHOLAS: It's quite clear to me, anyway. We'll see how the description reads. Now the next thing I have here is scheduling of production. I'll read what I put together: "To insure that the sales department receives reliable reports of production and exact shipping dates; to determine and to supervise production and exact shipping dates; to determine and to supervise production scheduling to achieve this." Now is there anything about that statement that needs amplification? I'm sure there is quite a bit of work entailed in the planning and scheduling of production.

CARPENTER: That isn't entirely true. Small plants—plants of our size, I guess —are usually not very efficient as far as business goes today. We produce about 200,000 barrels of beer in a year. That is considered a fairly small size brewery. But this production is enough for our share of the market, and it's worth doing. We do the same production almost year round, so that the schedule is almost a routine. We have no seasonal curve in production. It remains almost constant. If a change becomes necessary for some reason, it's a short-term one, and whatever changes are made are determined in consultation with sales and operations in Chicago.

NICHOLAS: Do you have anything specifically to do with the rates of pay being paid to employees in your plant? I am thinking again of any system of incentive pay or even straight wage rates.

CARPENTER: No.

NICHOLAS: Are rates determined by Chicago?

CARPENTER: They are set in the union contract. I would have the responsibility for promoting men to lead hands, group leaders, and that sort of thing.

NICHOLAS: I was going to get into this a little bit later, but I think perhaps this would be a good time. Do you adhere to a practice of asking all production personnel to be constantly on the watch for new production equipment and more efficient production methods? I'm thinking specifically of members of your staff in shipping, bottling, and transportation.

CARPENTER: That's my responsibility. It isn't mine alone, I would think. Our people in Chicago tour the country, you see, and may find something good, and we can consult over it. It would certainly be, I feel, my responsibility to recommend that we purchase the type of equipment that would reduce costs.

NICHOLAS: Now for another personnel question. What do you have to do with the selection and hiring of personnel? I mean, all the workforce, even hourly labor.

CARPENTER: We have a small personnel department. It's a one-man operation. Because production is fairly constant, we tend to keep our men all the time. We don't have too many problems of people coming and going. There's practically no turnover. If we need a new man, it's up to the personnel department to find one. Naturally, I can veto if I want to. I select the foremen, group hands, and so forth. But it doesn't happen often. We're a steady plant.

NICHOLAS: Now how about union negotiations? Are they handled by you?

CARPENTER: Grievances are, and day-to-day routine problems that can occur between the union and the plant are handled by me.

NICHOLAS: Directly, and not through anyone else?

CARPENTER: They are my responsibility absolutely.

NICHOLAS: When contract negotiations come along, what happens?

CARPENTER: The contract is negotiated for both Chicago and Milwaukee plants at the same time. Negotiations are carried out in Chicago, at the head office.

NICHOLAS: We'll say, hypothetically, that arrangements for plant holidays and things like that are sent up directly from Chicago?

CARPENTER: Yes, from Chicago, that's right.

NICHOLAS: Is there anything else about the personnel aspect of your job that perhaps we're overlooking? Just stop and think for a minute.

CARPENTER: Well, I have assistance from the personnel department in matters of safety and prevention of truck accidents on the road. The personnel man is quite active in that sort of thing, but there again it's one of my direct responsibilities to prevent accidents.

NICHOLAS: Do you have a formal safety program in the plant?

CARPENTER: Yes, and we've developed it most recently. We have incentives, and that's one of the few places at the moment where there are incentives. They are for truck drivers. They have a special bonus at the end of the year and a plan for eliminating accidents. In the plant we have formal safety inspections, and I'm chairman of that committee.

NICHOLAS: Mr. Carpenter, do you have anything to do specifically with handling surplus or obsolete equipment at the plant?

CARPENTER: I recommend that we dispose of the equipment when it becomes obsolete or surplus, but it's sold through the purchasing department.

NICHOLAS: Do you recommend sale of such items to your immediate superior in a case of this type?

CARPENTER: Yes.

NICHOLAS: I'm not familiar with brewing, but I'm wondering if there are any by-products of brewing and, if so, whether you have anything to do with these by-products.

CARPENTER: We have two by-products, one of which we use. Yeast is a by-product, and that's fairly valuable. Then we have "spent grain," and we have a disposal problem in this spent grain. Larger plants would sell it to jobbers. We are not large enough to do this, so we sell it directly ourselves; and that is my responsibility—to see that it is sold and disposed of.

NICHOLAS: Now for just a check on budgeting. Does your plant have a production budget that is sent down by the main office?

CARPENTER: We make our own budget. Once a year we produce a master budget. We are given the figures on what the sales department expects us to produce, and we have to make our own budget. Unless there's something very, very wrong about it, it becomes the master budget on which we operate. It's done on a monthly basis, and every item is budgeted. In addition, there are some changes during the year, so every month we produce another budget for the forthcoming month. Both are reviewed at the budget meeting in Chicago and accepted or questioned there.

NICHOLAS: Excellent! And no doubt you have something to do with the formal preparation of these figures for the presentation at Chicago?

CARPENTER: We do all of it.

NICHOLAS: When you say "we," what do you mean?

CARPENTER: The Milwaukee plant, I mean. Just that. I have overall responsibility.

NICHOLAS: Fine! Now let's see about something else. Is it your responsibility to define in writing some of the responsibilities of personnel over whom you have direct authority?

CARPENTER: Yes.

NICHOLAS: Do you do that at the present time?

CARPENTER: No. That's why I was very pleased when I was invited to discuss my job with you.

NICHOLAS: That's fine! Glad to be helpful. Do you, at the present time, delegate in writing to your subordinates—well, not duties, but where their authority lies and how much?

CARPENTER: We may have been lacking there. It may have been clear in my mind, but not so clear in the minds of the foremen. We're actually working on that now. I intend to do my own job description—we're working on it now, since I'll get a copy—and then I intend to submit it for approval. If mine is accepted, then I feel my subordinates should write their own, and maybe we can develop a system. I'll review my description with my people in Chicago, and then maybe they can write their own. The whole collection probably will go back to Chicago to be put up in a standard form approved by the company.

NICHOLAS: In a manual?

CARPENTER: Probably. I might mention that, about 1942 or 1943, we did have job descriptions for some people that were quite good. After that time, our organization changed and we were merged with another company, and most of those things went out of date or were lost, although they were supposed to be still in effect. They were fairly valuable, actually.

NICHOLAS: Well, they're usually helpful, one way or another—you can't really guess how useful they are until you circulate them. Now, on this sheet that I have in front of me, I have written down what are called "important supervisory responsibilities." I'll read from this, and if you think the statements apply to your position, we'll use at least a few of them. If you feel that they don't apply, we'll know what to omit. And also, if they need some expansion, don't hesitate to enlighten me. The first is: "To determine the actual organization structure and relationships of all supervisors in the chain of authority beneath him, and maintain them, in strict accordance with the letter and spirit of the corporation's organization policies."

CARPENTER: Yes, that's about right.

NICHOLAS: I agree. From what we've talked about previously, it seems to apply quite well. The next is: "To authorize committees for specific purposes when committee members are part of the organization supervised by him."

CARPENTER: Yes, that's my responsibility.

NICHOLAS: Have you done that in the past? Set up committees of people within your jurisdiction?

CARPENTER: Not any other than safety. Only safety.

NICHOLAS: But when you did that for safety, it did work out along these lines, is that right? You appointed the committee members?

CARPENTER: That's right. We have the safety committee, and we have another committtee called the "safety inspection committee" that reports to them. There's a union man on the inspection committee, and there are a foreman and the maintenance man, as a rule. We set those things up.

NICHOLAS: Do you deem it your responsibility to see that your immediate supervisory subordinates determine the number and arrange for the procurement of employees to meet a specific and unusually heavy or light schedule of short-term duration? I'm paraphrasing one of the statements here.

CARPENTER: Of short-term duration, yes.

NICHOLAS: What about salaries? Do you review recommendations for salary changes for your immediate subordinates?

CARPENTER: I approve recommendations for increases for subordinates beneath the level of foreman.

NICHOLAS: Yourself?

CARPENTER: Yes. I make the recommendations for foremen, too, as far as that goes.

NICHOLAS: Are these usually of a specific amount?

CARPENTER: We have levels on which the ranges of salaries are divided into about five different increments.

NICHOLAS: Are they predetermined, these increments?

CARPENTER: Yes.

NICHOLAS: Now here's one fairly detailed inquiry. Do you have authority to authorize prolonged overtime on a specific project?

CARPENTER: Yes, I do.

NICHOLAS: Now another thing. Do you have direct responsibility to see that your subordinates administer the union contract properly?

CARPENTER: Yes.

NICHOLAS: I have to check just a few more things. Do you belong to any trade organizations or associations?

CARPENTER: Well, I'm a member of the Master Brewers Association of America.

NICHOLAS: Does your company pay the dues?

CARPENTER: Yes. And it pays any expenses when I attend the monthly meetings. Other civic associations, too—Chamber of Commerce and Community Chest, for instance.

NICHOLAS: Excellent! Do you maintain these contacts for any specific reason? I'm sure it's very hard to pinpoint, but what I'm thinking of is this. Do you obtain any valuable special knowledge or other benefits from being a member of these associations or organizations?

CARPENTER: Yes, I feel I do—that is, the company does. We do a certain amount of purchasing in Milwaukee. All our contracts or changes in buildings, painting, and that sort of thing are done locally, and all the contractors and tradesmen are in these associations, so it's been very valuable. It's a fairly small city, and it's important for us to know all these people. Our company considers it has public relations value as well, and managers are encouraged to take part in civic affairs.

NICHOLAS: Another question along those lines. Now what sort of contacts do you make, and at what level, outside your own organization? What sort of people do you do business with? At what level would you say they are?

CARPENTER: Oh, my contacts are mostly in buying from people there, not selling. They would be merchants or other managers in branch plants. Is that the sort of thing you mean?

NICHOLAS: Yes, exactly. Equally as large as your own plant?

CARPENTER: Yes, and larger. At about my own level, I would say.

NICHOLAS: Do you feel that your knowledge of brewing is essential to the duties you are now fulfilling?

CARPENTER: Yes, I'm the only brewer who is also manager of production in any of our three plants. Usually our brewers are brewers; they just brew beer and keg it, and that's that. It happens that I'm a brewer, so I'm directly responsible for brewing as well as the whole operation in general. I personally feel that if I had not gone up the ladder through brewing, I probably would not have reached my position. The other two operations managers on my level came through personnel administration.

NICHOLAS: Do you feel that there is a specific amount of experience necessary before one can become manager of production?

CARPENTER: Well, I feel—no, no, I don't! Frankly, I don't. There's been a lot of discussion along that line. I think anyone could be manager of production if he surrounded himself with competent people. There's some background, though, but it's hard to say. You'd have to get to know the industry and its problems, for instance.

NICHOLAS: Is it possible to pinpoint that background? I'm thinking specifically in terms of time. Would you say that a man, after perhaps 10 or 15 years in the brewing business, would be qualified? I'm sure it depends on the man, but—.

CARPENTER: Yes, ten years. Oh, ten years, I would say, at the most. I was thrown into that kind of work after about seven years. I was superintendent of the same plant. It involved nearly the same responsibility. It was wartime; I was assistant brewer and assistant superintendent. Both the brewer and the superintendent weren't there, really. The brewer was an older man who was ill most of the time; the superintendent wasn't there at all. After six years— well, we were able to go on operating. It wasn't too satisfactory, and the burden was rather rough, but we were able to get the work done.

NICHOLAS: Do you feel that there should be some formal education required to supplement the job experience?

CARPENTER: We seem to find a need in our organization for accounting skills as much as anything else, I would think. All things being equal, I would say accountancy. Of course, I may feel that this is true because I'm not much of an accountant. I was a brewer by training. I'm still a brewer, more or less.

NICHOLAS: Frankly, I can't think of anything else I'd like to ask. I think we've covered your position quite well. In fact, I have quite a bit more information than I could possibly use in a short description. You know, this is somewhat of an isolated experiment. If I were really working in your firm, as part of a managerial description program, I would not have to ask quite so many questions. There would be standard policies and practices applying to your job of which I would be perfectly conscious. But I'm going to attempt to write this description just as I would ordinarily do in a real program— assuming, more or less by intuition, that I have gained an idea of what is understood in your company from your description of the entire operation. In other words, I'm not going to make a description longer or more detailed than it would be in a real program. Do you feel yourself that we have discussed the job adequately?

CARPENTER: Yes, I feel that we have. I don't see that there's anything we could add, but I don't know how clearly I've put all this.

NICHOLAS: Well, this interview isn't final. I'm going to give you the first draft of the description; then it's up to you to make any corrections of real errors that you find. Normally, the first draft with your corrections would be finalized either by your boss or by me working with a committee, or by the committee itself. It would depend on the nature of the program, but since we have no real program in this experiment all we can do is develop a first draft with your corrections.

CARPENTER: Yes, I understand. Thank you.

NICHOLAS: If there's something you think of later on that you really believe is important, don't hesitate to give me a call. I'll be glad to discuss it further.

## THE POSITION DESCRIPTION
## PLANT MANAGER, MILWAUKEE PLANT

*Objective:*

To produce quality beer according to specifications set by the company through the operation of the plant under his control, including brewing, packaging, warehousing, and transportation to the point of sale.

*Relationships:*

Directly responsible to the director of production (Chicago). Responsible for the performance of the brewer, bottling shop foreman, transport manager, shipping and receiving, and maintenance. Cooperates with marketing to assure availability of proper quantities of beer to fulfill sales commitments and plans. Cooperates with local-plant public relations director and public relations personnel in Chicago.

*Responsibilities:*

1. Within the overall quality set by the company, to determine the exact standards to be met by plant processes in the production of beer.

2. To determine maintenance standards and schedules for buildings and equipment.

3. To institute and maintain proper inspection procedures to assure fulfillment of quality standards and maintenance standards and schedules.

4. To prepare and to recommend to his immediate superior a budget for the operations portion of the Milwaukee plant; to recommend approval of appropriations and the efficient use of material and labor through the various persons reporting to him.

5. To make arrangements for provision of necessary technical services when these are not available within the company, subject to the approval of the director of production, Chicago.

6. To approve, and in major cases obtain approval for, expenditures for the original purchase, replacement, repair, and maintenance of plant facilities under his control in accordance with prescribed budgetary procedures. To make recommendations to his superior on the broad (nonengineering) specifications of major items of new equipment or other facilities to be purchased for or installed in his plant.

7. To assure a constant search for better production equipment and more economical operation procedures on the part of all production personnel at his plant.

8. Through the personnel manager at his plant and through cooperation with the Personnel Department at Chicago, to see to it that an adequate and efficient staff is maintained.

9. To be chairman of the safety committtee; in the broadest possible sense, to assure observance of the best possible safety standards.

10. To make recommendations to the Purchasing Department on the disposal of surplus or obsolete equipment of the plant.

11. To sell spent grain and other by-products of the brewing process if possible, and to dispose of them in any other way if a commercial sale is not possible.

12. To determine the actual organization structure and relationship of all supervisors in the chain of authority beneath himself and to maintain them in strict accordance with the spirit of the organization and its

formalized policies; to recommend changes to his superior if a change in the structure appears necessary.

13. To review salary recommendations for his immediate subordinates and forward these recommendations on salaries for action by the proper departments.

14. To insure that his immediate subordinates properly administer the union contract.

## KEEPING DESCRIPTIONS UP TO DATE

Shortly after an organization has completed its first series of managerial position descriptions, the question of keeping them current inevitably arises. Unfortunately, this is no easy task. As noted earlier, one of the chief problems in developing or using descriptions is keeping them up to date.

Nevertheless, the task is essential. To be of any real value the descriptions must accurately reflect the changes constantly taking place in even the most conservative organization. If this is not done an organization may find itself in the situation of an executive who responded to an AMA survey with an apologetic letter explaining why his firm could not take part: "Organizational changes . . . in the company during the last five years have made our managerial descriptions completely out of date. About the only thing we have at present is the realization of a problem."

### Timing for Review and/or Revision of Position Descriptions

Almost all organizations operating managerial position description programs appreciate the necessity for reviewing and/or revising their descriptions. Of the 127 respondents answering the question on review and revision of job descriptions, 41 organizations make specific provisions for review and revision at regular intervals ranging from one to five years, and 118 organizations review or revise descriptions irregularly whenever (1) the job content changes, (2) the organization structure changes, (3) the incumbent executive changes jobs, or (4) a review is requested by the incumbent or the incumbent's superior (see Table 10). Although these latter organizations review and revise their descriptions irregularly, many of them have standardized procedures for these reviews.

According to Table 10, most of the organizations apparently have a fairly flexible approach to the problem, since they each listed two or more situations in which they revise or at least review the existing descriptions. Nine organizations review and revise their programs only at regular time intervals. Since these time intervals are sufficiently short, the organizations do not feel the need for going over position descriptions at irregular intervals. Thirty-two of these organizations review and revise descriptions at regular time intervals and also go over them at irregular intervals, as indicated in Table 10. The events most likely to trigger examination of the descriptions for possible revision are (1) a job content change (107 responses), (2) a change in organization structure (93 responses), and (3) a request for review or revision by either the incumbent or the incumbent's superior (82 responses). Occasionally, reviews are initiated because an incumbent executive changes jobs.

*Table 10. Timing for review and/or revision of position descriptions.**

| TIMING | NUMBER OF RESPONSES |
|---|---|
| Regular time intervals (one year, two years, etc.) | 41 |
| Irregularly, whenever: † | |
| The job content changes | 107 |
| The organization structure changes | 93 |
| The incumbent executive changes jobs | 20 |
| A review is requested by the incumbent or the incumbent's superior | 82 |
| Other ‡ | 7 |
| Total | 350 |

* 136 organizations had job descriptions; 9 did not answer the question.

† Some organizations reviewing and/or revising at regular time intervals also indicated actions taken on an irregular basis. 118 organizations noted that reviews and revisions are taken on an irregular basis. Almost all of these gave multiple answers.

‡ Included in this category: When the purpose of the position changes; when job title changes; if a revision seems required; report by managers every six months on whether there is any need for change in position; to ascertain impact of proposed or possible changes in assignments; when there are shifts in salary review process.

Reviews and/or revisions of descriptions, in some instances, could not be classified under the specific categories noted in Table 10. Among the more interesting responses under "Other" was the consideration of review or revision when managers wished to ascertain the impact of proposed or possible changes in assignment. By thoroughly examining the jobs through standardized description procedures, the impact was more easily determined. Some of the additional circumstances under which revision or review is undertaken or considered were (1) when the purpose of a position changes, (2) when the job title changes, (3) when revision seems to be required, and (4) when there are shifts in the salary review process.

## Frequency of Reviews and Revisions

Most of the organizations reviewing managerial position descriptions at regular intervals reported that their descriptions are brought up to date annually. Twenty-two organizations follow this practice. Other organizations regularly review and revise their programs at intervals ranging from two to five years (see Table 11). Most of these are on a less-than-three-year cycle. Obviously most organizations prefer a relatively short time frame for review of position descriptions.

Many organizations consider annual review as an ideal to work toward. Several respondents who review descriptions at intervals longer than a year or who initiate revisions whenever the incumbent changes or whenever it seems required (for some other reason having nothing to do with time intervals) made such comments as: "We plan to institute a regular annual review beginning this year" and "We have not been able to follow our ideal of regularly revising and/or reviewing once a year, and so we have done the job as changes have occurred in the organization."

Table 11. Frequency of regular reviews and revisions for managerial position descriptions.*

| FREQUENCY OF REVIEWS AND REVISIONS IN YEARS † | NUMBER OF RESPONSES |
|:---:|:---:|
| 1 | 22 |
| 2 | 10 |
| 3 | 7 |
| 4 | 1 |
| 5 | 1 |
| Total | 41 |

* 136 organizations had position descriptions; only 41 had regular reviews and revisions.
† No organization had reviews and revisions on less than an annual basis.

It should be noted that 32 of the organizations represented in Table 10 review descriptions at regular time intervals (usually annually) and whenever one or more of the circumstances listed in the table occur. If frequent reviews are required, and if assurances are given that all descriptions will be overhauled at least once a year, this is probably the best system. It allows for changes in descriptions whenever unusual circumstances make them necessary, and yet also provides for scrutiny of the descriptions at regular intervals.

## Revision Procedures

Most organizations (58 percent) follow essentially the same procedures when reviewing and revising their descriptions as when formulating the originals. If, for instance, the incumbent executive writes the original first draft and approval must be obtained from the program's head before it can be finalized, the same arrangement is followed when revisions are made. The incumbent drafts the necessary revision, and it is referred to the program's head for approval.

Only 13 organizations indicated that the review procedure varied among different job levels in their organizations. Four stated that reviews were much more common for middle and top management. One company indicated that reviews are more frequent for higher-level jobs to assure that each position fits into the total structure of responsibilities necessary to accomplish the company's objectives. On the other hand, several other organizations argued that lower-level positions should be reviewed more frequently. For example, one believed that "lower-level jobs are more specific, more subject to change, particularly if the group is organized." Interestingly, organizations holding this view were usually organized by one or more unions. One respondent indicated that the greatest degree of variation between levels occurs when more levels of supervision are involved in the review or job audit. Only a few organizations vary their revision procedures among different levels in the organization and no consistent pattern could be found in the various procedures.

### DIFFERENCES BETWEEN PROCEDURES
### FOR WRITING ORIGINAL DESCRIPTIONS
### AND FOR REVISING DESCRIPTIONS

Although 58 percent follow the same procedures in producing both the original and the revised version of managerial position descriptions, 42 percent follow different procedures. These different procedures cover the entire description program from gathering the information to getting final approval of the description. In many organizations the revised drafts are much simpler to write than the originals because the organizations use approved final descriptions as the starting point in the revision process. In some cases this means only correcting or changing the original. In others it means a complete rewrite including the use of questionnaires and interviews with the incumbent, the incumbent's superior, and the superior's superior. The entire organization may have been involved in initiating a description program. In revisions, only those concerned with changes are involved.

In describing its use of the original description as a starting point, one organization stated: "We generally start with an existing description and focus on key changes intended. We focus on such questions as: 'Why do we have this job? Why should this job be composed of these responsibilities? What is the objective of this job? Why do we need it?' " Most or-

ganizations "expect that each revised description will be an improvement over the original since the basic information can be better confirmed and expanded. Defining and redefining function, responsibility, authority, and other parts of the description tend to lead to better descriptions."

In some organizations the incumbent has little or nothing to say about the revisions in his or her job. For example, a manufacturing company noted: "Personnel generally initiates the first draft and submits the description to the incumbent's manager." Another noted that the "supervisor of the position is more active in description preparation." However, in other organizations where procedures in preparing the original and the revised versions of the description differ, the incumbent is clearly involved. "The incumbent prepares changes and updates the original with the aid of a job analyst if necessary. Final approval is still made by the immediate supervisor." "On revisions, the supervisor checks out the prior description with the incumbent to note changes required." "The incumbent is requested to review the description with the supervisor and with a staff specialist. Then additions, corrections, and revisions are made."

In some organizations interviews and questionnaires are frequently omitted or are used sparingly in the revision process. In these cases the incumbent, the incumbent's superior, a staff specialist, or a combination of these reviews the managerial position description and rewrites it. Incumbents are frequently asked to review and update their original job descriptions without interviews or questionnaires. If an interview is used, it probably will be much shorter because of the information already provided by the initial description. If a questionnaire is used, it, too, is much shorter than the original questionnaire used to describe the job. In most cases, "the usual procedure is to rewrite only that portion of the description that has been affected by the addition, deletion, or change in duties." In some rare instances, "the description may be amended by memo or by submitting new pages rather than rewriting the entire description."

### REVISED DESCRIPTIONS COMPARED WITH ORIGINAL VERSIONS

In general, revised descriptions, though longer or shorter than their predecessors, are more concise and sharper as to meaning. Apparently, descriptions move through several stages in being revamped over several successive periods of time. In an earlier AMA study, two executives described these stages. The first described three stages and stated that the organization was in the third stage.

1. Short outline form with some variance in sequence and presentation of material.

2. Improved organization of material, more uniformity in coverage and method of presentation, but statements possibly too long, too detailed, and too wordy.
3. Uniform organization of material and improved presentation; shorter descriptions, more concise and accurate in phrasing.

The stages cited by the second executive included:

1. Long and detailed descriptions—too long to read.
2. Shorter descriptions, but stereotyped—didn't tell anything.
3. Current descriptions that are relatively short and emphasize the "what" and "how" of each job, particularly in the middle management group.

In each of these organizations the descriptions evolved toward shorter lengths. In the following paragraphs, changes in job descriptions are discussed in terms of length, language, content, and format.

**Changes in Length**

In initially revising their descriptions, most organizations lengthen them. However, others tend to shorten them. Such differences are to be expected since managerial position descriptions vary considerably in length from organization to organization. Examination of the descriptions reproduced in this report shows that the number of words considered adequate to describe the chief executive's position in one organization would be considered entirely inadequate in another. Finding the optimum number of words and amount of detail is a process of trial and error that can apparently be mastered only after considerable experience. Some of the descriptions for fairly senior management positions presented in the third part of this report are quite extensive, whereas others are very short. The authors have seen some that are only one paragraph long and others that cover eight single-spaced typewritten pages. Either extreme may be appropriate, depending on the complexity of the work being described, but the optimum length seems to lie somewhere in the middle. Only a detailed study of a large number of descriptions and some experience in formulating them can give one a feeling for the right number of words to cover a given position.

**Changes in Language**

In most instances, as descriptions are revised, the language becomes more concise, sharper, and more explicit. In some cases organizations use standardized phraseology so that all descriptions will be written in much the same terminology. Some organizations have developed glossaries of standard terminology to be used in position descriptions. This is done "to avoid misconceptions where responsibilities are alike or parallel." Standardization of terminology has frequently made an organization's descriptions much more meaningful. Other linguistic changes occurring in revisions are shifts away from "lengthy narrative style" toward the use of "more 'action' words." Indeed, one organization has stated that the descriptions should be written "more in the vernacular of those concerned."

**Changes in Content**
With respect to changes in the content of descriptions as a result of reviewing and revising them, most organizations are concerned about the "Responsibilities" section. This is also called the "Responsibilities and Authority" section. Actually, this is the central section of the description; it outlines the real work the executive is to perform, no matter what specific heading is used to designate it. Besides this section, most descriptions also define the executive's "Relationships" and contain a section commonly titled "Function" in which a very broad statement of the entire job is made.

With respect to the responsibilities section of a job description, it is more common to shorten the section as revisions occur. However, many organizations do in fact lengthen them. Apparently, responsibilities sections increase in length as efforts are made to produce descriptions that portray the job more completely. When executives read early versions of descriptions of their work, they find that important areas of responsibility have been omitted. Often, a whole series of descriptions gathered from a file will show expansion of the responsibilities section. This may occur because the description was incomplete when first formulated. Sometimes the expansion occurs because the number of responsibilities with which the manager is charged has increased. This is very common when an organization is growing rapidly. Indeed, a series of descriptions written for the same position over the years may show that the position has grown to such an extent that the manager is obliged to delegate some of his work to subordinates. This may result in a shortening of the description, since it is no longer necessary to state the delegated work in great detail. Sometimes a different tendency sets in. The broad supervisory responsibilities of a top executive may become so complex and diffused that it requires a great many words to describe them. Probably the marked differences in opinion on this subject simply reflect the different stages in which the participating organizations find themselves.

Deliberate efforts have been made in some organizations to shorten unwieldy responsibilities sections of position descriptions. Usually this is done by listing in an organization manual a series of items that are common to all managerial positions. (Some examples of these statements of common responsibilities are reproduced in Part Three.) The relationships section of each description can also sometimes be greatly shortened by drawing clear organization charts that make some written statements unnecessary.

More and more organizations are moving toward imposing standards of performance for their executives through some type of management-by-objectives, management-by-results, or other similar program. There is a significant interaction between executive work plans initiated under such programs and formal job descriptions. Changes in formal job descriptions are frequently initiated by changes in executive work plans. Changes in responsibilities on a daily, monthly, or yearly basis ultimately are reflected in formal job descriptions. This trend toward more objective standards of performance for executives and more meaningful ways of appraising that performance will have a significant impact on managerial job descriptions in the future.

**Changes in Format**

In addition to making changes in content, language, and length of individual descriptions, a few organizations have significantly altered the format of their full set of descriptions. More recent versions of the descriptions are more carefully organized and follow more uniform patterns than earlier versions. Increasingly, standardized headings and subheadings are being used to assure inclusion of similar items in all the descriptions. Through such standardization, organization-wide descriptions can be especially important when comparisons between jobs are to be made to determine compensation levels.

## POINTERS ON RECENT NEW METHODS OF JOB DESCRIPTION

Organizations were asked in one part of the questionnaire: "Does the manner of describing these new jobs (jobs initiated during the past 5 years) differ from prior methods of job description?" Twenty-three organizations reported significant shifts in the way they are now handling the job description process. In addition to noting the usual common changes of shorter or longer descriptions, more or less detailed descriptions, and shifts in format, the organizations listed several significant modifications in their methods:

1. Length of forms for the collection of information has dropped dramatically. For example, one organization stated: "We have substituted a one-page form for the former cumbersome seven-page document."
2. Greater attention to the total environment of the executive's job.
3. Movement toward smaller numbers of key responsibilities ("rather than a longer, less important duty listing").

4. More emphasis on job accountabilities ("rather than on job duties").
5. More emphasis on upward mobility and career ladders within the organization. As an illustration, one manufacturer stressed the "incorporation of career series titles rather than single incumbent classes."

During the next decade, significant shifts in these directions should be watched by top management and compensation executives.

# 7

## *Format and Contents of Typical Descriptions*

Without a doubt, position descriptions are changing in their basic nature. With the advent of management by results and management by objectives, more and more organizations are moving toward the use of job descriptions as a means of measuring a manager's performance. Indeed, position descriptions are using terms such as "accountability objectives," "end results," "specific objectives," and "specific accountabilities." These expressions show the clear intent of top management to attain more and more measurable indicators of managerial performance throughout the organization. This chapter describes the major sections of position descriptions and the manuals used to implement description programs, and examines the differences between managerial and lower-level descriptions in an organization.

### MAJOR SECTIONS OF THE DESCRIPTION

Although many different satisfactory arrangements and styles are used in preparing managerial descriptions, the typical description is divided into three or four major sections. Today these sections are usually arranged under one or the other of two differing sets of major headings: (1) Function, Duties and/or Responsibilities, Authority, and Relationships; or (2) Accountability Objectives, Dimensions, Nature and Scope, and Specific Accountabilities. The first arrangement tends to be the most widely used; however, the second is rapidly gaining proponents as more and more top managements demand results-oriented performances from their executives. The differences between these two types of position descriptions are vividly portrayed in Part Three of this book.

The three or four major sections of managerial job descriptions are frequently supplemented by other sections (see Table 12). The data clearly show that duties and responsibilities are part of almost all job descriptions, whether these are written in a descriptive or prescriptive manner. In addition, accountabilities are noted in over one-half of the reporting organizations. More and more organizations are moving toward results-oriented position descriptions. In the following paragraphs, each of the major sections of a position description will be described.

*Table 12. Major sections of managerial position descriptions.**

| MAJOR SECTION | NUMBER OF ORGANIZATIONS |
| --- | --- |
| Duties and Responsibilities | 115 |
| Status (Reporting Relationship) | 83 |
| Basic Function | 74 |
| Summary Statement | 67 |
| Accountabilities | 67 |
| Titles of jobholders reporting to incumbent | 62 |
| Authority | 47 |
| Objective | 44 |
| Relationships | 43 |
| Job Specifications | 38 |
| Person Specifications | 21 |
| Other † | 19 |

* 136 organizations had job descriptions; 13 did not answer the question.

† This classification includes job dimensions (4), problem solving (3), scope of activities (2), succession (1), qualifications desired (1), magnitude and degree of financial impact (1), influence on business development (1), division and location (1), special or nonrecurring assignment (1), guidance available (1), and pertinent statistics (1).

*Function* (also called "Summary Statement," "Purpose," "Basic Function," "Objective," and "Mission"). This section serves as a summary of, and a general introduction to, the position under consideration by stating its basic purposes briefly and in very direct language. It should enable anyone reasonably familiar with the organization to understand the primary purpose of the position, its raison d'être, and those major factors that distinguish this post from others. Although this section of the description is often written last, it is invariably placed at the head of the final version. This is similar to the practice of many writers who find it easier to compose the introduction of their book after the main text is written. The following examples of instructions given to executives and analysts preparing job descriptions clearly delineate the purpose of this section:

> *Function:* State in one or two sentences the purpose or objective of your job—the reason for its existence—the reason requiring the performance of the duties described below. (A retail grocery chain.)

> *Primary Purpose of Job:* In this section, you should describe what the purpose of the job is in terms of the contribution it makes to our business. That is, you should answer the question: "Why do we have this job at ABC Company?" You will probably need only two or three sentences—a short paragraph at most—to describe the primary purpose of the job. (A tool manufacturer.)

The short, concise nature of such function sections in position descriptions is illustrated in these three examples:

> *Position Summary:* Planning, organizing, controlling, and establishing policies and procedures for achieving a satisfactory rate of growth in group premium income within budgetary limits. Responsibility for group sales and administration. (Vice President and Director of Group Insurance, an insurance company.)

> *Basic Function:* Controls the manufacture and distribution of XYZ products through proper management of facilities, inventories, personnel, and transportation. Plans facilities and services for present and anticipated division growth. (Vice President, Manufacturing and Distribution, a manufacturing company.)

> *Mission:* As chief executive officer, exercises responsibility for general management and coordination of all bank activities; insures that the business of the bank is conducted on a sound, realistic, profitable basis in accordance with policies laid down by the Board of Directors; provides leadership for the entire staff. (Chief Executive Officer, a major bank.)

*Accountability Objectives.* This brief, concise section is quite similar in format to the function section just discussed. Organizations using accountability objectives state that they are attempting to provide performance-oriented objectives in these statements. However, the statements frequently tend to be exactly like those under the heading of mission, purpose, summary statement, or basic function. In fact, some of them are significantly broader and less clearly defined than those noted in the function section. One manufacturer gave the following instructions to its executives:

> *Accountability Objectives:* Defines the overall objectives of the job. It is a brief, undetailed, but specific statement of the end result or results that should be accomplished by a job. It may be thought of as the topic sentence of the description.

Two other illustrations of the use of accountability objectives are:

*Accountability Objectives:* Under the guidance of the Chairman, this position is concerned with developing sound strategic plans to insure the future survival and profitable growth of the Company, and with their implementation particularly in the area of discovering and acquiring profitable enterprises to expand and diversify the product line. (Financial Vice President and Treasurer, a food manufacturer.)

*Accountability Objectives:* Under the direction of the President, this position is charged with developing and maintaining an industrial relations climate that will create and permit a stable and productive workforce; and enhancing overall employee relations through the direction and coordination of the separate personnel/industrial relations functions. (Vice President, Industrial Relations, a manufacturing company.)

*Duties and/or Responsibilities* (also called "Major," "Specific," or "Basic Duties and/or Responsibilities" and "Principal Activities"). This section enumerates the principal specific duties and responsibilities that must be met by the incumbent to fulfill his or her basic function or accountability objective as outlined in the description. The duties and responsibilities in this section are often listed in their order of importance or as a group under a series of appropriate subheadings. The most common arrangement is to divide the position's duties into (1) line and staff categories; (2) responsibilities such as organization, planning, analysis, operations, and review of operations; and (3) functional categories such as responsibilities for personnel, materials, and finance. This section generally makes up the larger part of most managerial position descriptions. Typical instructions to analysts and executives are shown in these two examples:

*Responsibilities:* You should list the *primary* responsibilities of the job in this section. This list should spell out the job functions, not the duties or tasks, for which you will hold the individual accountable. In this section, you will want to focus on the *major* job responsibilities that are the primary functions of the job. Probably you will, after some editing, end up with from three to six or seven major responsibilities. State these as completely and concisely as possible—one or two sentences per responsibility—and list them in numbered paragraphs. (A large manufacturer.)

*Primary Duties or Principal Activities to Carry Out the Function of Your Job:* Briefly list the principal specific activities in which you are engaged in the course of discharging the major functions of your job, preferably in the order of the amount of time spent on each, starting with the activity that requires the largest amount of your time. (An oil producer.)

The major duties and responsibilities of a Manager, Environmental Protection, are shown in the following section from a position description:

Within the approved limits of authority and company policy, the Manager —Environmental Protection is responsible to the Vice President—Manufacturing Services for carrying out the general management duties and responsibilities and those listed below:

1. Maintains current knowledge of all air, water, sound, soil, and other pollution control laws and regulations including local ordinances in areas where the corporation operates or intends to operate plants.
2. Monitors the corporation's performance with respect to all pollution control regulations and presents regular reports to division management.
3. Studies newest pollution control technology and equipment for applicability to the corporation's problems.
4. Works with Regional Operations Managers to develop programs that will insure full compliance with local, state, and federal control regulations at minimum cost to the company.
5. Participates, aided by the Secretary and counsel, in efforts to shape new laws by working with industry committees, testifying at hearings, lobbying, etc.
6. Makes presentations to local pollution control boards; assists plant management in personal contacts with local community leaders.

*Accountabilities* (also called "Specific Accountabilities," "Principal Accountabilities," and "Principal Results Areas"). Although most sections of this type are devoted to statements of end results, the concept of accountability varies in the field. For example, one machine manufacturer, in considering accountability, asked its executives: "(1) How independent are you from the regulation of others? (2) How do you influence company income or volume? (3) What is the general size of the area(s) primarily affected by your position? (Whenever possible, report such statistics as total sales, units of production, etc.)." The following examples illustrate other approaches:

*Principal Results Areas:* Identify the principal areas in which the incumbent of this position is accountable for achieving results. For each result area, briefly describe: (1) the end result expected, (2) what is basically involved in achieving this result, and (3) the principal challenges encountered in achieving this result. (A large bank.)

*Accountabilities:* The "why"—the end results or objectives the job is expected to achieve. It should include information on the following: (1) enumeration of end results, (2) demands for planning, and (3) what the job should accomplish. (A manufacturer.)

The "principal accountabilities" of a vice president for administration are illustrated in this extract from a position description:

1. Insure an effective organization, designed and structured to accomplish objectives within the division.
2. Insure a staff of competent personnel to best utilize individual and group capabilities by selection, developing, compensating, and motivating subordinates.

3. Develop sound plans and objectives that will optimize divisional effectiveness.
4. Insure effective financial and operational controls that protect assets.
5. Insure accurate and timely financial reports for management as a basis for sound business decisions.
6. Insure optimum efficient utilization and growth of management information systems and their application as management tools.
7. Contribute toward the availability and effective utilization of competent manpower to attain the company's objectives and goals through the conception and administration of sound personnel programs and policies.
8. Guide and direct staff departments in attaining goals and taking appropriate corrective action.
9. Foster an environment of teamwork and total commitment of personnel throughout the organization by developing and improving methods of effective communications.

*Authority* (also called "Limits of Authority" and "Key Decision Areas"). Since many organizations feel that responsibilities and authority are inextricably interdependent, the sections labeled "Duties and Responsibilities" and "Authority" are, in many descriptions, combined into one large section. In this study, few of the descriptions analyzed had separate authority sections although authority may have been mentioned in other sections. This section sets the limits to which an executive may go in performing his or her duties. It specifies the exact extent of an incumbent's power or authority insofar as this is possible. Some respondents regard this section as the "charter" or "grant of authority" under which a manager operates. One clearly defined set of instructions by a chemicals manufacturer states:

> *Key Decision Areas:* The purpose of this section is to identify your authority to make or influence decisions that commit the company to a course of action (e.g., if you are not directly involved in a decision, but your superior uses your recommendations as a basis for deciding what action to take).

In another case, an aircraft manufacturer clearly indicates the interrelatedness of responsibility and authority:

> This section is the core of the guide, and since the responsibilities and authority of a position are inextricably interdependent they have been combined. Responsibility is used in the sense of work or activities assigned to an individual. Authority is used in the sense of the right to make decisions in order to fulfill a responsibility and gives the right to require compliance with the decision by subordinates.

A district sales manager's authority was described in these terms:

> *Authority* (Describe briefly what the incumbent can do without supervisor's prior approval):

1. Operate district sales activities within Corporate and departmental policies.
2. Select and recommend hiring of subordinates.

*Dimensions.* This section is normally found only in those position descriptions oriented toward management results (i.e., in end-result and accountability-oriented descriptions). Such a section is usuallly not narrative in nature, but specifies such items as annual operating budget, annual production volume, average inventory value, value of capital assets maintained, number of operating plants supervised, and number of exempt salaried, nonexempt salaried, and nonexempt hourly employees supervised. These dimensions are directly observable and measurable, yielding figures that can be used as control mechanisms by top management. One manufacturer states in its instructions:

> *Dimensions:* The dimensions of a job are the figures that are used to indicate the size of the job. They frequently are personnel and annual dollar figures under such headings as Personnel—Exempt, Personnel—Nonexempt, Production Volume, Operating Budget, Cost Reduction Goal, Approval Authority, Sales Volume, and Project Value. They can also come under the headings Mileage Traveled, Value of Shipping, and Policies Issued. Generally the same figures are used continually in the same field. In some cases, especially in staff positions, there may not be any pertinent figures, so simply write "indeterminate."

As an illustration of a dimensions section, the position description for the senior vice president for finance of a large mining corporation has three dimensions: sales, corporate cash borrowings, and company assets. In another instance, the position description for the second vice president for group pension administration of a large insurance corporation has five dimensions: employees, payroll, operating budget, group pension premium, and group pension assets.

*Relationships.* A given position description basically contains three different types of information on relationships: (1) status of the person to whom the incumbent reports, (2) titles of jobholders reporting to the incumbent, and (3) internal and external relationships with others and with other organizations. These three relationships may be grouped together in one section of the position description or individual sections may be devoted to each of the three. For example, one set of instructions for a meat processor states:

> *Organization Relationships:* This section describes responsibility relationships and other relationships. In this section, show the position of the individual to whom the incumbent reports *directly,* and the position of the individuals who report *directly* to him. Also show the individuals, departments, divisions, etc., of the organization with which he has business relationships, but not a direct authority relationship.

Instructions for a status section in one organization reads:

*Reports to:* Put a "reports to" heading on the description and indicate to whom the job incumbent will report. If there are any unique or unusual organization relationships for the job (e.g., a dotted line or functional tie to another organization), describe them in this section.

To describe *subordinate* parts of an executive's job, a large bank issues the instruction:

Attach an organization chart and a separate sheet briefly describing for each immediate subordinate component: (1) its major function, (2) the size and nature of its staff and accountabilities, (3) areas of current emphasis, and (4) any activities requiring particular attention from this position.

A large utilities company uses sections of its job descriptions to stress *internal relationships* including full freedom of communication, supervision received, and supervision exercised; and *external relationships* covering the company's relationships with the general public, other corporations, and public agencies.

The position description for the vice president for materiel of a candy company serves as an excellent illustration of a general definition of relationships:

A. The Vice President reports to the President
B. Supervises:
    1. Director of Purchasing
    2. Director of Traffic and Distribution
    3. Assistant to the Vice President
C. Internal relationships with all executives
D. External relationships with
    1. Vendors
    2. Carriers and insurers
    3. City, state, and federal officials
    4. Subcontractors
    5. Customers
    6. Counterparts in other organizations and in trade associations
    7. Public warehouses

*Qualifications* (also known as "Job Specifications" and "Person Specifications"). Approximately one-fourth of the position descriptions in this study have a section on qualifications for a particular job. However, in almost all these cases, the sections were extremely short. In general, such sections discuss previous experience, training, and other qualifications that an individual must have to be hired for the position. One manufacturing corporation stated:

*Qualifications:* This section is optional for most job descriptions. You will want to use it only in those descriptions where you believe the position incumbent should possess unique qualifications to effectively achieve the results expected. For example, some jobs will require certain types of education or experience. Others may require an intimate knowledge of our operations; hence you would specify a certain company experience as a qualification for the job. Clearly, not all jobs will need unique or unusual qualifications. Therefore you should use this section only for those job descriptions in which you must communicate the need for such unique qualifications.

In a large foods corporation, the qualifications for the director of marketing included the following: (1) *Education:* B.A. degree in Marketing or Business Administration. (2) *Experience:* One year of field sales experience in the foods industry. Minimum of three years' experience in recognized consumer or institutional marketing department. (3) *Skills:* Must have exhibited competence in overall marketing activities, as well as demonstrated abilities in direct supervision and other management skills.

*Other Sections.* Two new sections that are beginning to appear in position descriptions are "Position Dynamics" and "Challenge." The first deals basically with the potential growth of a managerial position. For example, a chemicals manufacturer uses the following instructions:

> *Position Dynamics:* Under this section, describe any significant changes you think will occur in the content of the position, assuming ABC grows from a $300 million company to a $500 million company. Focus in particular on any new activities you think the position might entail. Be as specific as you can and do not mention normal scale-up.

Through this type of examination of position descriptions, organizations can use the innovative ideas of their employees and preplan upward mobility for its junior executives.

The challenge section is included primarily in accountability-oriented position descriptions. This section basically defines what is important or crucial in the incumbent's job. For example, the position description for a senior manufacturing engineer in a large manufacturing firm states:

> *Challenge:* The thrust of the job is to provide the necessary technical backup for the established current product lines with heavy emphasis on the anticipated influx of new product families evolving from the Research and Development section, thus enabling the quick and effective transition from laboratory, to pilot stage, to full efficient production through strong, experienced know-how.

## MANAGERIAL POSITION DESCRIPTION MANUALS

Most organizations with a position description program prepare some type of manual for these descriptions. The manuals may differ significantly in their purposes as well as in the materials each contains. Some manuals contain only instructions on how to formulate descriptions or contain the descriptions themselves, whereas others include such additional material as organization charts, job evaluation policy guides, discussions of performance appraisals and operating relationships, and statements of corporationwide limits of authority.

Sometimes the presence of such additional material, rather than the executive and managerial position descriptions themselves, determines which employee groups will have access to the manual. For example, a manual may include information that is confidential. As a result, only division heads, branch managers, and their authorized representatives may have access to it.

### Length of Descriptions

Descriptions that commonly appear in managerial position description manuals range in length from less than a page to a total of eight pages (see Table 13). Analysis of the data shows that top management and hourly workers actually have fewer job descriptions than any of the other classes of employee. As noted earlier, top managers frequently contend that their jobs are too complex and diverse to be described, while the job descriptions of hourly workers frequently are determined by union contracts. Most top management, executive management, and middle management position descriptions range from one to three pages. First-line supervisors, salaried exempt professional employees, and salaried nonexempt professional employees tend to have shorter descriptions—usually no longer than two pages. Indeed, it appears that top, executive, and middle managers tend to have longer position descriptions than lower-level managers in the organization.

### Titles of Manuals

In an earlier AMA study approximately 80 percent of the responding companies collected their completed managerial position descriptions into some type of manual or loose-leaf binder. In this study organizations were asked to indicate the title of their manual or other collection of position descriptions. Only 39 organizations responded to the question (see Table 14). Of these, three indicated that their manual had no title. The table shows clearly that there is no standard practice in naming such manuals. Their titles vary from the most common one of "Organization Manual" to such variants as "Job Description Manual," "Salary Administration Manual," and "Management Guide." Only twelve of the organizations even use the term "description" in their manual title. From examining many of the titles of the manuals listed in the table, it would be difficult to determine that position descriptions were actually involved.

*Table 13. Length of average position description, in pages, for different classes of employee.\**

| | LENGTH IN PAGES † | | | | | | | | | |
|---|---|---|---|---|---|---|---|---|---|---|
| CLASS OF EMPLOYEE | LESS THAN 1 | 1 | 2 | 3 | 4 | 5 | 6 | 7 | 8 | TOT |
| Top Management (Chairman, President, Director, President's Office) | 2 | 23 | 34 | 18 | 9 | 3 | 2 | 1 | — | 9 |
| Executive Management (Group Vice President, Executive Vice President, Senior Vice President, General Manager, Deputy Director, Corporate and Division Vice President, including both line and staff officers) | 2 | 22 | 39 | 27 | 7 | 5 | 1 | 2 | — | 10 |
| Middle Management (All managers below officer and above supervisory levels) | 3 | 32 | 53 | 22 | 5 | 4 | 1 | 1 | — | 12 |
| First-line Supervisors (First supervisory level exempt from FICA with responsibility for operating employees) | 4 | 50 | 43 | 12 | 7 | — | — | 1 | 1 | 11 |
| Salaried exempt professional employees (Engineers, chemists, technical workers, etc.) | 3 | 46 | 45 | 17 | 4 | 1 | — | 1 | — | 11 |
| Salaried nonexempt employees | 6 | 68 | 27 | 3 | 3 | 1 | — | — | — | 10 |
| Hourly workers | 9 | 58 | 9 | 2 | 1 | 1 | — | — | — | 8 |

\* 136 organizations had job descriptions; 11 did not answer the question.
† Not all organizations have position descriptions in each of the classes. Therefore the figures in each class do not add to 125.

In some organizations, descriptions are gathered into a series of manuals or binders. Each of these binders contains the managerial position descriptions for one department, division, plant, or other unit. Under this system each unit may be allowed access only to the binder containing its own managerial position descriptions, while a few top executives (usually the president and executive vice president, the head of personnel, and the description program's head) are the only managers given copies of the complete set of binders covering all positions.

**Accessibility to Manuals**
The manual containing managerial descriptions is generally distributed to members of the management group. In some organizations this includes all

*Table 14. Titles of manuals used in managerial position description programs.*

| TITLE OF POSITION DESCRIPTION MANUAL | NUMBER OF TIMES MENTIONED |
|---|---|
| Organization Manual | 9 |
| Job Description Manual | 4 |
| Job Descriptions | 3 |
| Salary Administration Manual | 3 |
| No title on manual | 3 |
| Job Specifications | 2 |
| Position Description Book | 2 |
| General Administrative Manual | 1 |
| General Management Organization Manual | 1 |
| Management Guide | 1 |
| Management Guide to Salary Administration | 1 |
| Managerial and Professional Salary Administration Plan | 1 |
| Middle Management Compensation Evaluation | 1 |
| Officer and Staff Guide | 1 |
| Organization of the Company | 1 |
| Organization Guide | 1 |
| Policies, Organization, and Procedures | 1 |
| Policy and Procedure Manual—General Administrative | 1 |
| Salary Description | 1 |
| Standard Practices | 1 |
| Total | 39 |

* 136 organizations had job descriptions; 50 did not have a position description manual; 47 did not answer the question.

executives and managerial personnel down to first-line supervisors; in others, distribution is limited to key officials.

Usually, some attempt is made to limit distribution of the manual to managers who are directly concerned with its contents. For example, if the manual has been prepared primarily for wage and salary administration, it may be better to narrow its circulation, because arguments may develop among incumbents over the organization's evaluation of the comparative worth of the different positions and the effect of that evaluation on total compensation for each job. If the descriptions are prepared primarily for organizational and developmental purposes, the distribution appears to be wider.

With the advent of newer styles of management, some organizations favor widespread distribution of descriptions so that all managers are aware of the duties and responsibilities of other managers and their contributions to the organizational objectives, know the possibilities for promotion and the career opportunities available to them, and have full information about the relative payments for different types of jobs within the organization. Basically, this position of "open disclosure" is based on the premise that the more information managers have, the better the organization will be able to meet its objectives.

## MANAGERIAL-PROFESSIONAL VERSUS NONMANAGERIAL DESCRIPTIONS

In practice, are managerial position descriptions identical with the descriptions written for nonmanagerial positions, aside from the fact that they portray more important work? In this study, similar formats were quite common for top, executive, and middle managements, first-line supervisors, and salaried exempt professional employees. Formats for salaried nonexempt employees generally differed from those of hourly employees. In some organizations the formats were similar for all employees. In most cases the contents of the descriptions differ markedly between managerial and nonmanagerial employees.

Usually the job descriptions of managerial, professional, and technical employees differ from those of salaried nonexempt and hourly employees in that: (1) managerial position descriptions stress intangibles to a greater extent, and (2) the emphasis is on results rather than on the mechanics of doing a job. For example, the job descriptions of salaried nonexempt and hourly employees stress the mechanics of "how" a man or woman goes about doing his or her work (day-to-day duties and assignments) and place little emphasis on the position's responsibilities, the contribution the work makes to the organization's welfare, and the impact of the job on the organization's operations. Managerial descriptions are usually written in more general terms and tend to give greater weight to relationships and lines of authority (how a position fits into the overall organizational scheme) and to results-oriented performance rather than to the internal, self-contained duties of a particular position.

Some organizations believe there are differences in writing styles between the two types of position descriptions and in the amount of detail contained in them. However, in most instances, there is little difference in writing styles because analysts go over all the descriptions submitted and are fairly consistent in their approach to them. With respect to the amount of detail, some organizations believe managerial-professional descriptions have more detail than the descriptions of lower-level positions, whereas others believe the reverse is true. Some obviously hold the belief that the inclusion of details in a description simply means that the entire content of a particular job is represented in a description; others take the term to mean that a great deal of written material is included. If the latter position were taken, earlier data in this chapter would support the belief that managerial positions have more detail (on the basis of length of description).

Apparently the differences between the position descriptions of salaried nonexempt and hourly employees and managerial-professional employees are a natural outgrowth of the differences between the two types of work —in their functions and scope of responsibilities and in the results expected of managers at the different levels of authority.

On the other hand, the distinctions between the two types of descriptions may reflect the different purposes for which they are used. Descriptions of lower-level jobs frequently are written primarily for wage and salary administration and so center directly around duties and day-to-day assignments, whereas descriptions of higher-level jobs are more closely related to organization planning. For this latter use, descriptions of interrelationships, overall responsibilities, and lines of authority are more vital.

# 8

## The Future of
## Managerial Position Descriptions

Managerial position descriptions will continue to be used in the future. One of the questions raised in this study was whether the respondents believed there would be any *significant* changes in position descriptions during the next five years. Twenty-nine percent of the respondents believed the changes would be significant; the remaining 71 percent believed there would be no substantive changes. This chapter examines a few methods that some organizations have found to be better than job descriptions and discusses the significant shifts in position descriptions that may be expected during the next five years.

### NEW METHODS IN POSITION DESCRIPTIONS

Eleven organizations believed they had found methods or techniques that were better than, or were complementary to, position descriptions. These can be grouped into four classes: (1) brief, unstructured, functional statements about top, executive, and middle management positions; (2) the use of a related organization chart; (3) the use of performance appraisal and development rather than position descriptions; and (4) training guides as supplements to position descriptions.

First, several organizations have moved toward briefer, less structured statements about top, executive, and middle management positions. These include *functional guides,* which briefly spell out the basic functions of a job with no additional information; *mission and business scope statements,* which include several short statements defining the overall purpose of the job; *generic job descriptions and generic organization models,* which are highly generalized statements for common sets of managers and professionals throughout the organization (within these statements, managers and professionals delineate their own jobs—for example, all directors may have a common "generic" position description, but a marketing director would define his or her own job in terms of its specific needs); and the *unstructured position concept,* which is only a short statement or two describing the expected role of the incumbent. In almost all these cases, organizations are attempting to cope with rapidly changing markets, technologies, economic conditions, and competitive organizations. Three brief statements encompassing some of these concepts are presented:

> General statements of function have been useful in higher-level management positions. (An automobile manufacturer.)

> In lieu of a job description for the general manager of our business units (divisions and subsidiaries), we prepare more detailed *Mission and Business Scope Statements.* The major sections are labeled Mission and Business Scope. The latter includes market orientation, product specialization, service specialization, technology specialization, and relationships. In lieu of job descriptions for Corporate Staff heads, we prepare more informative *Purpose and Scope Statements.* The major sections are labeled Purpose and Scope. The latter includes services to the Corporate Office, central services for the corporation, services to operating units, services to other corporate staffs, external relationships, and a general paragraph. (A high-technology manufacturer.)

> At higher levels, we occasionally prefer an unstructured position concept, which is merely a couple of paragraphs describing the expected role of the position. At lower levels, however, the job description is most suitable. (An airline.)

Second, one organization considered organization charts to be an important supplement to position descriptions. It stated:

> Equally important to the description is an attendant organization chart which includes comprehensive information *re* subordinate assignments, schedules, shifts, pending changes, retirements within five years, open employment, authorizations, special duty, levels of classification, and pertinent historical notes. (An arms manufacturer.)

Third, several organizations believed that position descriptions for managers and professionals were really unnecessary and that results based on substantive standards of performance were far better. In one case, a trucking corporation stated: "The position description is no substitute for standards of performance which are written for all salaried jobs." In another, a utilities company commented: "Appraisal and development show responsibilities better."

Fourth, one organization felt that a supplement—a detailed guide—was necessary in management development and employee training. It noted:

"For the purpose of training or 'breaking in' employees, a detailed operating outline or guide is more useful. This appears to be most practical at lower levels of the organization."

## SIGNIFICANT SHIFTS EXPECTED IN THE FUTURE

Thirty-seven organizations think there will be significant shifts in managerial position description programs in the future. As our society rapidly changes, these organizations will have to adjust to the turndown in population growth, the increasing automation of industry and public agencies, the continuing information explosion, and the changing methods of management. Practically every facet of these programs will be affected by these alterations in the internal and external environments of these organizations.

In terms of *coverage,* managerial position description programs will continue to expand upward hierarchically. Speaking about changes expected during the next five years, one organization noted: "We will have much heavier utilization of upper, middle, and lower management position descriptions." Another stated: "Probably we will include our officer level by then." Organizations presently without position description programs are moving toward adopting such programs. However, the programs may have significantly different orientations than those now in operation.

The *uses* of position descriptions probably will change substantially in the future. This study shows a definite shift toward more results-oriented or performance-oriented descriptions. With the rapid shifts occurring in managements, organizations, and environments, position descriptions must become more attuned and adaptable to these changes. Several statements that clearly illustrate this movement toward more results-oriented position descriptions are presented:

The productivity and managerial responsibility concepts will assume greater degrees of importance.

There will be more focus on our Overall Performance Appraisal (OPA) Work Sheet, and less focus on formal job descriptions because OPA tends to be more incisive and up to date.

More accountability and development of standards.

More precise indications of authority and accountability; jobs defined more from the standpoint of objectives and goals than just numerically listed duties; inclusion of quantitative factors such as numbers supervised, annual budgets controlled, volume of sales or purchases, etc.

We must address ourselves to a performance-measured orientation, probably by supplementing an improved version of position descriptions with a periodic goal-commitment document.

Career patterns will be stressed in the future because of the tremendous impact of affirmative action programs on organizations in both the public and private sectors. These career patterns will manifest themselves in position descriptions in terms of potential career ladders actually being written in the description (that is, what potential jobs does this job lead to?) and in terms of specific qualifications being incorporated in the description. These latter qualification or specification statements will have to be bona fide occupational qualifications and will have to be shown to be truly related to the job in question (commonly known as validity). Two respondents clearly indicated the impact of equal employment opportunity programs in their organizations:

> Because of certain federal laws dealing with unfair hiring practices, it will be necessary to validate all job requirements.

> Position descriptions will have revised duties because more female employees, handicapped employees, and minority group employees are qualifying for higher-skill jobs.

Through such career patterns, persons who traditionally have not been in the main line of employment opportunity will have more of a chance at managerial positions.

Organization structures have been changing radically in the past two decades. Many new forms of structure have evolved. As a result, position descriptions must be sufficiently flexible to respond to these organizational challenges. One respondent stated: "Organization structure is changing and strengthening—resulting in more emphasis on job descriptions and wage and salary administration, with the end result that a higher-trained staff is needed for the accomplishment of these programs."

With these new organizational forms and new technologies, many new managerial positions will be established during the next five years. As noted earlier, many new types of managerial and professional jobs have already been initiated during the previous five years. Some organizations are facing this plethora of new jobs with generic job descriptions and generic organization models.

Significant shifts may be expected in the procedures for *organizing* and *designing* programs. Some organizations have indicated that, with sufficient detail in the descriptions, computer programs can be established to eliminate duplication of efforts in different managerial positions. Specifically, one manufacturer stated: "Position descriptions will incorporate sufficient detail to allow for computerization, which will result in orderly and systematic analysis to eliminate or materially reduce duplication." Although computerization could be used at lower levels of the organization, it probably would be difficult to implement in managerial positions unless there really were significant amounts of detail in the descriptions.

The authors believe that modular standardization of end results or accountabilities is possible. By using well-defined components, duplications of effort could be eliminated. In fact, the computer could be used as a positive force—by adding additional challenges to jobs when needed or by deleting some when specific parts of the job have been expanded to the point where the manager is no longer able to handle all its requirements. Such use of modular components would be consonant with newer management concepts of job enrichment, job enlargement, and job redesign.

With the increasing demand by consumers and stockholders for more information on corporate activities and a greater "openness" throughout corporate structures, position descriptions probably will become more accessible not only to managers within organizations but also to internal and external pressure groups requesting access to them. This openness of communications throughout the organization again is one of the cardinal precepts of innovative managements.

Significantly more attention will be paid to the *preparation* of position descriptions because of the need for valid descriptions to meet the criteria established by equal employment opportunity agencies. This will require additional analysts. Furthermore, executives will have to be far better trained in preparing these descriptions than they have been in the past. They will have to clearly understand why it is important that valid sections of the description be prepared.

The *format* and *contents* of typical descriptions probably will change significantly in the next five years. For example, one manufacturer said:

> In order to maintain "currency" and to force use as a specific goals-results-oriented device, job descriptions may evolve into a one-page document containing three or four vital duties and three or four key events with specific goals and measurable results. A new document would be prepared during and after annual or semiannual performance-appraisal interviews.

Such a procedure would provide flexibility and a results-oriented position description, but would generate a tremendous staff load. Here again is a place for the computer—as a tool in reducing the workload of compensation specialists. By putting the descriptions on computer tape, they could easily be changed after the annual review. Thus a set of up-to-date descriptions would be available constantly. This would provide an adequate response to those who contend that position descriptions are always out of date and cannot be used.

Some organizations believe that position descriptions will become much shorter and, hopefully, more standardized. In the latter case, some organizations are hoping to implement standardized terms for such managers as director, manager, general supervisor, section supervisor, technicians, and specialists. With respect to length, the following statements certainly indicate the hopes of these organizations:

Shorter—limited to one page and with more specific information.

I think we'll key in on two or three factors.

We currently use narrative story form. We are working toward a briefer, more telegraphic format. It is easier to evaluate—better to read, not as long.

In the next five years more and more organizations will turn to some type of job specification or job qualification statement for managers. Many of these statements will be placed in the position descriptions—for example, because of the need for specific affirmative action programs within the organization. Two organizations stated:

We will add job specifications to our descriptions.

Expansion to include "person" specifications for each job in conjunction with governmental controls relating to EEOC.

## TOMORROW'S MANAGER AND TOMORROW'S POSITION DESCRIPTIONS

Tomorrow's manager will be faced with many challenges that are not yet visible. Today's manager is already faced with the prospect of increasing interactions with the society as a whole, with government agencies, and with other organizations—public, private, and nonprofit—and increasing stresses brought on by the acceleration of technological change and the new generation of workers. The manager of tomorrow will need additional skills to face these challenges and those still not discovered. Today such skills include those of the innovator, the leader, and the administrator.* Tomorrow a manager will need the additional skills of organization builder and statesman.

Futhermore, the volume of general management work is rapidly growing. Indeed, in some large organizations the workload has exceeded the capacity of the chief executive officer to handle it and executive teams have been established to share the burden. Decision making is becoming more and more involved with the choice between long-term and short-term resource commitments, unique situations never faced before by the organization, the need for advance formulation of strategies and policies, and the ability to

* H. Igor Ansoff and R. G. Brandenburg, "The General Manager of the Future," *California Management Review*, Vol. 11, No. 3 (Spring, 1969), pp. 66–68.

react quickly to different challenges facing the organization. The decision-making process will also change radically in the next decade. More and more models will be used for trial runs. More and more specialists will be needed to assist in meeting the new challenges.

All these changes in managerial skills, in managerial workload, in the nature of decisions, and in the decision-making process will be reflected in managerial position descriptions. The next decade will see major shifts in the nature and use of position descriptions.

# PART TWO

---

*A Handbook of Methods*
*for Preparing Position Descriptions*

This section shows several methods and forms used in the preparation of managerial position descriptions. Because of space limitations, all these items have been condensed. Included are:

Organizational Terminology
Position Description Manual
Managerial Questionnaires
Managerial and Analyst Interview Guides
Evaluation Sheet for the Training of Interviewers.
Overall Performance Work Sheet

# Organizational Terminology

---

I. PURPOSE

The purpose of this Instruction is to define the system of organizational terminology, including titles applying to:

A. The various parts or elements within the organization.

B. The individuals heading these elements.

II. ADVANTAGES

The Company plan of organizational terminology offers the following advantages:

A. It indicates the relationship of one part of the organization to the entire structure.

B. It indicates the inter-relationships of various elements of the organization to each other.

C. It establishes a consistency among supervisory and technical titles.

D. It assists in distinguishing between a person heading a line (or operating) element, and a person heading a staff (or functional) element.

E. It enables employees, merely by use of titles, to know just where an organization element or supervisor is classified, thereby assisting employees in performing a more intelligent job.

F. It provides a sound basis for future planning and expansion of the organization along logical and desirable lines.

III. GENERAL LEVELS OF ORGANIZATION AND TITLES

Following are general guidelines for levels of organization, and corresponding titles. "Levels" are *horizontal* terms, indicating only *who reports to whom*. All jobs at the same "level" are not necessarily the same in responsibilities and pay (for example, in the 3 levels of Division, Department and Section, a job at the Section or 3rd level might receive the same pay as one or more jobs at the Department level).

A. *Administration*. There are two "Administrations" in the Company—the General Office Administration, which is primarily staff, planning or advisory; and the Field Administration, which is primarily operating or line relating to (a) Region and Terminal Organization; (b) The

133

Line Haul and Maintenance field organization; and (c) the field organization of the Special Commodities Division.

B. *General Office Administration.* The General Office Administration has *four* general levels and titles, as listed below. There may be other titles, however, as indicated in Charts following:

| ELEMENT | TITLE |
|---|---|
| Division | Vice President |
| Department | Director |
| Section | Supervisor |
| Unit | Head |

C. *Field Administration.* The Field Administration has *four* general levels and titles, as listed below. There may be other titles, however, as indicated in Charts following:

| ELEMENT | TITLE |
|---|---|
| Region | Manager |
| Terminal, Station S.C.D. District | Manager |
| Terminal Section | Manager; Chief |
| Terminal Unit or Shift | Head, or Foreman |

IV. RULES GOVERNING TITLES

Titles shall be chosen (1) to indicate clearly the element supervised, and (2) to show, wherever possible, whether such supervision is functional (staff) or line (operating), *whether such positions exist in the General Office or Field Administration.*

A. *Functional (Staff) Titles.* Wherever possible, such terminology will show the title first and the function second. The title may be followed by (1) the preposition "of"; or (2) a dash (—). Examples:

Vice President—General Commodities
Director of General Accounting
Supervisor—License and Regulatory

B. *Line (Operating) Titles.* Wherever possible, such terminology will show the *segment/function* first and the *title* second. Examples:

Terminal Manager
Terminal Operations Manager

C. *Miscellaneous.* Following are general rules regarding use of specific titles:

1. *Vice President. Primarily* refers to first main level in General Office, reporting to President or Chairman of Board, although title is not automatic with level.

2. *Director. Primarily* a General Office (functional) title.

3. *Manager.\* Primarily* a Field (line) title.

* May also include high staff function

## SPECIFIC GUIDES TO TITLES—GENERAL OFFICE ADMINISTRATION

| ORGAN, ELEMENT | DEFINITION | TITLE |
| --- | --- | --- |
| Division | Major staff element of Company. | Vice President |
| | May have control of several departments. | Manager ** |
| Department | Standard job at this level. | Director |
| Section | Standard job at this level. Large enough to involve supervision of fair degree through immediate staff. | Supervisor |
| Listed only by identifying words "Market Research" "Methods" | If specialized job reporting to Director or Section Head, but not heavy on supervision of immediate staff. | Specific identifying title: Administrator; Engineer; Analyst; Auditor |
| Unit | Standard job at this level. Large enough to involve supervision of fair degree through immediate staff. | Head/ Unit _____ |

** Responsibility lies between Director level and Vice President level

## SPECIFIC GUIDES TO TITLES—FIELD

| ORGAN, ELEMENT | DEFINITION | TITLE |
| --- | --- | --- |
| Region | Main operating element in Field Administration. | Regional Manager |
| Terminal or S.C.D. District | Line Supervision at field location. | Terminal Manager; S.C.D. District |
| Section | First field level below Manager. | Manager; Chief |
| Unit | Second level below Manager —office or administrative employees. | Head |
| Shift | Second level below Manager —Operating employees. | Foreman |

# Position Description Manual

THE PREPARATION OF JOB DESCRIPTIONS

The purpose of this material is to impart to those charged with preparing job descriptions the type of information to be included, and the desired format for them.

The job description is a management analysis. It must be systematically developed and must deal with both the objectives and responsibilities of the job.

The job description is the formal mechanism for translating a position into factual, concise, precise and unambiguous information which will leave no doubt in the mind of the reader about the nature of the job: *what* there is to do, *how* these things are done, and *why* the job exists in terms of its component elements, and in total. If these questions are clearly answered, we have a good job description.

A job description sometimes is regarded as a more or less routine statement of duties, experience required, education, organizational relationships, etc., etc. Such a routine statement is inadequate for the sort of management position analysis which is fundamental to this assignment.

*Writing the Description*

Stress must be placed on the uniformity of the format and on the completeness and style of the content. The writer must never forget the purpose of the description; i.e., to provide the Evaluation Committee with all the necessary information essential to a fair and proper evaluation of the job. All significant facts should be included; all incidental or trivial information should be excluded. A verbose, rambling description will only confuse the reader. IT MUST BE PRECISE, CONCISE, AND WELL-ORGANIZED.

The writer's job is to sort out the most important facts about the job and to record them—*not* to reach conclusions concerning them.

The description must be written on the basis of how the job is being done *at the time of preparation;* not how the incumbent thinks it should be done or organized, nor how it was done in the past, nor how the incumbent plans to do it in the future.

THE DESCRIPTION FORMAT

The following is the type of information to be sought, and the various sections of the format:

1. BASIC FUNCTION:

What is required here is a brief, undetailed, but specific statement of the end results that should be accomplished by the job. The purpose is to gauge the over-all significance from a company viewpoint; i.e., what part of the total company objectives must be accomplished by this job, why this job exists, and what it is paid for achieving.

2. DIMENSIONS:

This section should summarize in broad terms all pertinent statistics about the job in order to give the reader a clear picture of the size of the "show" the incumbent runs, and the magnitude of the end results which are affected by his actions. In listing, be inclusive, not exclusive—"if in doubt, record it." Do not usurp the function of the Evaluation Committee, which is charged with selecting the controlling elements and judging the impact that each has on the incumbent's job content.

Magnitude is measured in terms of money on an annual basis, whether operating budget, sales volume, cost of wages and salaries, or other aspects significant to the job. To provide additional perspective, also list pertinent things other than money; e.g., number of subordinates, unit volumes, number of plants, etc.

3. NATURE AND SCOPE OF POSITION:

This is the real "meat" of a job description. If well done, it will give a person possessing a reasonable amount of sophistication the major part of what he needs to know in order to assess the job with considerable precision. It will tell the reader what the job is all about: how it fits into the total frame of company operations; what kind of subordinate staff is involved and what they do; the various organizational relationships, etc.

This section should bring out the following facets of the job:

a. How the position fits into the organization, including reference to significant organizational and outside relationships.

   To whom does the job report?
   What other jobs report to the same superior?
   What are the most frequent contacts inside and outside the company?
   What committees is the job represented on?
   Is much travel involved—where and why?

b. The general composition of supporting staff. This should include a thumbnail sketch of each major function (if any) under this position: size, scope and the reason for its existence. If any of these functions require specialization on the part of the incumbent, this fact should be brought out. It should outline briefly:

The scope of each subordinate job and the type of subordinate, e.g., whether qualification or long experience is needed.

How control is exercised over subordinate jobs.

What information for control is used.

If it is necessary for the person performing this job to have as much technical know-how and specialist knowledge as his subordinate.

c. The general nature of technical, managerial and human relations know-how required: what the basic challenges of the job are, e.g., if a marketing job, it tells what is sold, how, nature of distribution, promotion, competition, and the other main challenges of the job. It should indicate:

What specific technical training and experience are necessary.

What aspects of technical/specialized experience are most important.

If the job is more administrative or more technical.

If supervision of subordinates is direct, or motivating them to direct themselves.

d. The nature of problem solving: what are the key problems that must be solved by this job and how variable are they?

What is the job's greatest challenge?

What part of the job gives the most opportunity to its own authority; what types of problems does it refer to higher authority or consult with others?

e. The nature and source of controls on freedom to solve problems and to act, whether supervisory, procedural or because of the nature of the vocation or profession.

How often and on what type of problems does this job report to superior?

What authority is there on:
 –hire and fire
 –capital expenditure
 –current expenditure
 –setting prices
 –changing production or marketing methods
 –changing design or quality or production
 –changing salaries

What are the principal rules, regulations, precedents, or personal control within which the job operates?

4. PRINCIPAL ACCOUNTABILITIES:

This is a list of the important end results which the job exists to achieve. Some overlapping with statements made in the preceding section is permissible, but the two sections should be as mutually exclusive as is reasonable, with the emphasis here being on specific end results as opposed to the general descriptive material in the preceding section.

Since we are dealing here with action, each accountability statement should relate to an end result or objective which must be accomplished. They should bring out an accountability against which some measurement of performance can be applied. If no clear objective is accomplished by what is done, the accountability should be omitted.

The following will help ensure a complete coverage of the broad managerial areas for which a job might possibly be held accountable: organization, strategic planning, execution, review and control. Big jobs will probably have heavy accountabilities for organization, policy and planning. In smaller jobs, requirements for them will hardly exist. If the position is not significantly concerned with objectives under some of these headings, then no statement of accountability should be made.

*Organization.* These statements have to do with the degree to which the incumbent must: (a) plan the structure of his own organization; (b) man his own organization; (c) develop and maintain his own organization including recruitment, training, development and appraisal, wage and salary administration, hiring and firing, etc.

*Strategic Planning.* Strategic planning in the sense used here is planning for the long-range future, and we are concerned in this subsection with the activities which involve planning and policy making in the fullest sense.

There are many positions which are not accountable for planning of this kind and possibly many people who think they make policy and strategic plans, but in fact do not. If there is no significant accountability for strategic planning, leave it out.

As part of their planning, large jobs tend to establish policy objectives. At levels below this, jobs may be concerned with setting more limited objectives within a broad framework. In determining the accountability of a job, it must be clarified whether: The job sets output goals or targets? If so, how far ahead? The job establishes costs or pricing limits? The job determines specifications, designs or quality standards?

*Tactical Planning, Execution and Directing the Attainment of Objectives.* This section is concerned with the specific job of managing, supervising or performing activities from a day-to-day operational standpoint in order to carry out assigned functions effectively. The statements will describe end results which the job achieves either through: (a) getting the work done by others, or (b) doing things himself.

*Review and Control.* In many positions, the incumbent must review and control activities in his area of responsibility as well as supervise or perform them. The description should include what is required of the job in terms of assessing the effectiveness of the organization in achieving its objectives, i.e., what are the key controls available to the job giving the incumbent warning signals when things go wrong.

It is worth re-emphasizing here that an accountability is an end result or objective which the job exists to achieve. The end result is of such importance that the incumbent would expect his performance to be measured in terms of his effectiveness in achieving it. In contrast, a duty or responsibility, as often stated, is the means by which end results are achieved.

### OTHER USES OF JOB EVALUATION

In addition to achieving compensation objectives, job descriptions and evaluations can also be used in:
1. Management recruitment, placement and development.
2. Analyzing organization structure.
3. Relating job content values to the growth of the organization.
4. Measuring the performance of an incumbent against the stated accountabilities of the job.

### POSITION DESCRIPTION

*Title:*
*Incumbent:*                    Unit:
*Reports to:* (title)           Date:
*Prepared by:*                  Approvals: _____
                                                    (Incumbent)

                                           _____
                                                    (Supervisor)

#### BASIC FUNCTION
A brief statement of the over-all purpose or major end result the position is to achieve; essentially a "what" and "why" statement.

#### NATURE AND SCOPE
First paragraph—*organizational relationships*—subordinate positions reporting to this position.

Second paragraph—briefly identify principal function or activity of each subordinate (direct report) position.

Environment: What are the external forces which influence how this position functions, the priorities it establishes, the problems it is confronted with? Is there a uniqueness to this Division? What's happening around the position?

Major activities of the position—how and why does the incumbent spend significant chunks of his time? What background and seasoning does he require? (beer truck) What turns him on?

Restrictions on his thinking or taking action. Are the parameters procedural, policy or supervisory in nature? What can't he do? What does he refer to others? What challenges is he faced with?

Human relations—what face-to-face contacts does he have? With whom? Is he "selling" or does he carry the weight of sound technical judgment?

PRINCIPAL ACCOUNTABILITIES

These are the major, make or break consequences of the action taken by the position in which failure to achieve would seriously affect over-all performance. These include:

1. A people accountability
2. A planning accountability
3. An organizing accountability
4. Executive and review accountability

These statements should complete the statement "this position is answerable for . . . the . . . ."

These accountabilities should support the basic function statement. (To achieve the basic function he must achieve these accountabilities.)

DIMENSIONS

Dollar figures for the area or ballpark most directly affected.

Operating Budget
Sales
Value Added
Department Payroll
Number of Employees

# Managerial Questionnaires

PURPOSE

It is an objective of the Corporation to have current Position Guides for each executive position within the Company. This objective is based upon purposes which the Position Guide can serve. A few of the more important purposes may be:

—To provide a documented common understanding of the responsibilities which a person is fulfilling or expected to fulfill in an exempt position.

—To provide a basis for the successful performance of anticipated objectives or goals of a position.

—To furnish information for a meaningful evaluation of a position, establishing its Executive Level for compensation purposes.

Normally, an individual should not be hired for, or transferred into, a position until a Position Guide covering that position has been prepared or revised. The Organization Development function maintains a file of all existing Position Guides and offers assistance in their preparation to management throughout the Company.

Managers or Supervisors must assume the responsibility for reviewing Position Guides with incumbents of the positions to ensure a complete knowledge and understanding of their responsibilities and authorities. As revisions relating to changing functions and responsibilities occur, Organization Development should be advised.

The following material is presented as an aid for the preparation of Position Guides. Please read it thoroughly before beginning to write. By following these guidelines carefully, it should be possible to prepare a Position Guide with a minimum of effort and a maximum of meaningful information.

WRITING THE POSITION GUIDE

The Position Guide you are about to write is a means of presenting the content of your position. Keep in mind that Position Guides are a means of communicating to your supervisor and others what is performed in your position and even what it is hoped will be performed. Try to avoid trade or professional jargon whenever possible.

It is quite normal for a Position Guide to be rewritten three or four times in order to achieve mutual agreement within the organization.

A Position Guide has three main parts: I. General Function(s), II. Specific Responsibilities, III. Relationships. These are all explained in the following material. You should be reminded that one does not always have a multitude of General Functions in his or her position. The General Function(s) should answer why any position is in existence. The things done or performed under each General Function, when listed, become the "Specific Responsibilities" section of your Position Guide. A sample guide is included to illustrate the style and layout that we adhere to in the creation of a Position Guide.

I.    *General Function(s) of the Position*
      This should be a simple description and summary of the purpose(s) filled by having the position in existence. In effect, the General Function(s) becomes(s) the goal(s) of the position. These purpose(s) should be grouped into separate paragraphs each covering a major division of the work to which more can be added in order to be expanded into the Specific Responsibilities in II.

II.   *Specific Responsibilities*
      Restate the General Function(s) from the above section and underneath each function list those activities actually performed. It is unnecessary to show procedural steps in carrying out each responsibility. Simply enlarge on each General Function(s) as suggested in the attached sample.

The following thoughts, words or phrases are provided for your consideration in order to help you be more meaningful as you write the material for "Specific Responsibilities."

"Specific Responsibilities" can, generally, be broken down by performance relationships into four groupings:

1. Activities undertaken individually.
2. Activities performed by or with subordinates.
3. Activities undertaken with supervisor.
4. Activities undertaken with associates.

In putting down in words the things people do, it may be best to start with an appropriate verb. The following verbs or verb phrases are suggested for your use to best describe the activities within these performance relationships:

1. Activities undertaken individually:

| | | | |
|---|---|---|---|
| Administers | Calculates | Establishes | Originates |
| Allocates | Compiles | Formulates | Posts |
| Analyzes | Develops | Initiates | Reviews |
| Assembles | Distributes | Operates | Supervises |
| | | | Transfers |

2. Activities performed by or with subordinates:

| | |
|---|---|
| Approves: | Indicates authority to give final approval without the necessity of going higher in the Company. |
| Endorses: | Indicates that recommendations may be put into action as a result of endorsement, but it may be necessary to have final approval from a higher authority. |
| Counsels with: | Indicates that no formal approval is required, but that some responsibility for the decision itself is shared. |
| Ensures that: | Indicates that complete responsibility has been delegated to subordinates. |
| Directs: | Indicates that responsibility has been delegated, but that some degree of participation in the final decision is retained. |
| Advises with: | Same as "Counsels with." |
| Arranges for: | Same as "Ensures that." |

| | | |
|---|---|---|
| Discusses with | Keeps informed as to | Requests |
| Inspects | Receives from | Reviews with |
| Instructs | | |

3. Activities undertaken with supervisor:

| | |
|---|---|
| Recommends to: | Indicates endorsement, but implies the necessity for approval by superior. |

| | | |
|---|---|---|
| Confers with | Informs | Submits to |
| Consults with | Reports to | Suggests to |
| Furnishes | | |

4. Activities undertaken with associates:

| | |
|---|---|
| Decides jointly with: | Indicates equal share in responsibility and development of programs or plans. |

| | | |
|---|---|---|
| Advises | Furnishes | Requests |
| Confers with | Receives from | Reviews with |
| Consults with | | |

III. *Relationships*

These should be broken down into the following categories:

A. To what position does this position report?

B. What positions report to this position?

C. To what other positions or departments within the Company does this position relate itself and for what reason?

D. To what outside organization or individuals does this position either formally or informally relate itself and for what reasons?

# A MANUFACTURING COMPANY
POSITION DESCRIPTION AND PERFORMANCE STANDARDS

JOB IDENTIFICATION NO.

| | | |
|---|---|---|
| TITLE: (OF POSITION) | DIVISION: | DATE: |
| NAME: (INCUMBENT) | DEPARTMENT: | SECTION: |
| PREPARED BY: (Signature of Incumbent and Supervisor) | APPROVED BY: | |

| LIST HERE MAJOR SEGMENTS OF POSITION (*What individual has to do*) | WT. % | CLASS | | | LIST HERE OPPOSITE EACH SEGMENT THE STANDARDS OF PERFORMANCE (*Results expected from each segment*) |
|---|---|---|---|---|---|
| | | 1 | 2 | 3 | |

| | |
|---|---|
| Segment is a specific part or step of a total job—one element of what *is to be performed.* List here major segments of position—in order of importance. In "Wt.%" column indicate weight it bears to the total job—15%, 25%, 40%, etc. Segments should contain essentials of what is to be performed—*specific; what is the incumbent* required to do? *Avoid meaningless generalizations and details.* The great majority of jobs should not contain more than four segments. Statements should be direct and "action oriented." Use liberally such verbs as: advise, analyze, approve, conduct, determine, develop, direct, initiate, manage, negotiate, perform, recommend, review, supervise, schedule, instruct, control, plan, communicate, maintain. CLASS (Check 1, 2, or 3) indicates authority incumbent is to exercise: | List here for each segment the result or results expected. Standards should be realistic, attainable and "tied to" division, plant, area, or department goals. Standards are what the employee is being paid to accomplish. <br><br> When preparing standards, consideration must be given to the following: <br> 1. Must relate directly to the work and established goals—direct, specific, *no generalizations.* <br><br> 2. Most standards should be measurable and will refer to specific documents used to manage the business—budgets, other financial reports, schedules, annual plans, strategic plans, etc. <br><br> 3. If not measurable, standards should be so stated that it is possible to make accurate judgments regarding what was accomplished. |

| | | | | | | |
|---|---|---|---|---|---|---|
| Class 1: | Complete authority. Action taken without consulting supervisor. | | | | | Note: It is not necessary to record specific quantitative data on the Position Description which appears in a regularly used document—for example: annual budgets. |
| Class 2: | Limited authority. Supervisor informed prior to taking action. | | | | | If these three factors are understood, the work segments specific, and overall goals are established, it is possible to have standards that have direct meaning to the employee. If a standard does not meet these criteria, don't use it. The employee must have a complete understanding of what results are expected—both supervisor and employee must agree that standards are realistic. |
| Class 3: | No authority. Action taken after consulting supervisor and at his direction. | | | | | |
| Example: (Gen. Mgr.) | 1. Manages all plant operations—direction, control, and coordination of major functions. | 60 | X | | | 1.a. Budgets are submitted on schedule—approved budget goals are met. |
| Example: (Prod. Eng'ng. Mgr.) | 1. Supervises design and/or redesign work re: modifications, new applications, etc. of present products | 25 | | X | | 1.a. Product specifications and design factors are accurately and completely established. |
| Example: | 1. Supervises all area service operations and area meter repair facility. | 10 | X | | | 1.a. Service calls meet customer requirements and time schedules. |

The position description has three main uses: (1) Defines the position and the basis for any performance appraisal; (2) Job specification in terms of function and requirements (education, experience, abilities) for good selection (hiring or promotion); (3) Job evaluation or value of the job in salary dollars.

After completing the identification section of form 40R-31B (Title, Name, Division, Department, Date, etc.) the following information should be put on the first page of each description for easy reference. Every effort should be made to record this information in *concise and specific terms*. For example: Function should be a one sentence statement that precisely identifies the need for the job and in what functional area; Job Requirements should be specific re: what education, experience, and abilities you believe the incumbent should have to satisfactorily perform.

FUNCTION:

(One sentence statement that describes basic function of this position.) Examples:

General Manager—Manages and directs all operations of (location) plant.

Div. Staff Director Manufacturing—Administers and performs activities required to develop and recommend division manufacturing, financial and strategic plans and goals.

Product Engineering Manager—Manages and directs all product engineering activities at the (location) plant.

ORGANIZATIONAL RELATIONSHIPS:

Reports to: Title of person to whom incumbent of this position reports.
Supervises: Number and title of people supervised by incumbent.

| | |
|---|---|
| (No.) | (Title) |

JOB REQUIREMENTS:

Education experience and abilities required for job. Be specific re: requirements needed to perform.

*Examples:*

Degree in Engineering (ME or IE) or Industrial Management. (Gen. Mgr.)

High school education with courses in Advanced Short Hand and General Business-Office Practices. (Secretary)

10 years of combined, successful and progressive experience in at least two major functions—manufacturing, manufacturing engineering, materials, accounting, engineering—which includes at least four years as successful manager of a plant function. (Gen. Mgr.)

3 to 4 years successful experience as stenographer which includes taking shorthand, transcribing and typing accurately, and filing. (Secretary)

Proven ability to manage and develop key subordinates, do effective planning and implement approved plans. (Gen. Mgr.)

Ability to type accurately at 55/wpm and take shorthand at 90/wpm. (Secretary)

ACCOUNTABILITY (DIRECT ☐ INDIRECT ☐) IN $ _____

This applies to *Management Plan* positions *only*. Depending on the position, this figure can be the amount of money budgeted to operate a plant, department, etc. (material, labor, services, etc.), a Sales Quota, the amount of purchases for which a Buyer is responsible, or other dollar amounts for which a position incumbent is responsible. Direct Accountability means incumbent has direct responsibility for control of budgeted dollars to operate his operations or other dollar amounts for which he is responsible. Indirect Accountability means incumbent has an impact or influence on budgeted dollars, quotas, etc. See more complete explanation and examples in Corporate Compensation Manual.

Any change in Accountability dollars can be submitted on a PIRS Audit Report when returned for performance appraisal updating.

The preparation of a Position Description can be and probably should be a joint effort of the supervisor and the employee, with the exception of a new employee or a new position. There definitely must be basic agreement between supervisor and employee re: what is to be performed and what results are expected—Standards of Performance.

---

## MCDONNELL DOUGLAS CORPORATION
### POSITION GUIDE

*Organization:* Name of Affected Organization
*Position:* TITLE OF POSITION IN CAPITAL LETTERS

BASIC FUNCTION:   Provide a succinct generalized summary of the primary and unique features of tasks for which the incumbent is responsible. It may include major functional area and basic objectives of the position, cause of action, objective or purpose of the position, and may identify the particular position so as to distinguish it from all others and indicate its size and scope.

REPORTS TO:   Title of Supervisor

RESPONSIBILITY
& AUTHORITY:

1. The first paragraph should state: Fulfills the requirements of the "Common Responsibilities of Director Level or Higher," General Instruction, Corporate Organization Manual.
2. This section is the core of the guide and since the responsibilities and authority of a position are inextricably interdependent they have been combined. Responsibility is used in the sense of work or activities assigned to an individual. Authority is used in the sense of the right to make decisions in order to fulfill a responsibility and gives the right to require compliance with the decision by subordinates.
   a. State in more detail the responsibilities and authority

vested in the position and define the specific duties and tasks of the position.

b. State specific authorities vested in the position, including extent, which fully support and make possible the fulfillment of the responsibility (e.g., levels, areas, approvals, decisions, organization changes, salary adjustments, expenditures, scheduling, management powers, etc.).

c. Enumerate the significant activities which must be accomplished to discharge assigned duties and provide the responsibility and authority to take or initiate action.

d. Describe the sum of the vested rights to enable performance of assigned tasks, fulfilling of delegated responsibilities, and the authority to make decisions or take action.

e. A definition of appropriate authority of a position must be included if the incumbent is to understand and be held accountable for the manner in which he fulfills his responsibilities.

| (Signature) | (Signature) |
|---|---|
| Typed Name and Title of Signature Authority | Typed Name and Title of Signature Authority |

# *Managerial and Analyst Interview Guides*

A FOOD CHAIN
POSITION DESCRIPTION
INTERVIEW GUIDE

I. TITLE
    A. Is this descriptive of the job being performed?
    B. Other suggested titles.

II. ORGANIZATION
    A. Who is your immediate supervisor?
    B. What is his title?
    C. Do you supervise or provide work direction to others?
    D. If so, what are their titles and names?

III. FUNCTION
State in one or two sentences the purpose or objective of your job—the reason for its existence—the reason requiring the performance of the duties described below.

IV. DUTIES AND RESPONSIBILITIES
    A. What type of work do you perform? Describe the things you do.
    B. What is the nature of responsibility for the work you perform?
    C. Describe your responsibility for assets and operations in terms of your direct or indirect accountability for income production, sales development, safeguarding of assets or effecting cost savings.
    D. Describe your activity and responsibility for generating, approving, securing and analyzing records and reports. Where does information come from, what do you do with it, where does it go?
    E. What types of work contacts do you have in departments other than your own?

        1. Purpose        3. Level
        2. Frequency    4. Require tact or persuasion

    F. What types of work contacts do you have with persons, companies, or agencies outside____Food Stores?

        1. Purpose        3. Level
        2. Frequency    4. Require tact or persuasion

G. Are you required to exercise supervisory or work direction responsibilities?

| | |
|---|---|
| 1. Number | 3. Training, Hire, Set Standards |
| 2. Types of Jobs | 4. Employee Relations—Time Off, Schedule, Discipline |

H. What types of decisions do you make?
   1. Are they reviewed?
   2. What can be the consequence of a poor decision?
      a. Loss of sale or asset. (Gain)
      b. Loss of good will. (Gain)
      c. Additional expense.
      d. Influence upon production or quality.
 I. Describe your responsibility for developing, revising, approving or installing policies, procedures and methods.
      a. Influence on your area.
      b. Influence outside your area.
      c. Reviewed by whom?
 J. In what areas of short and long range planning are you involved?

V. KNOWLEDGE
   A. What types of knowledge must you possess in order to perform your job?
      1. Products, procedures, organization.
      2. Special technical or professional fields of knowledge.
   B. What is the source of this knowledge?
      1. Formal education—How much?
      2. Specialized Training—What type?
      3. Work experience—How long?
      4. Combination
   C. How do you use this knowledge in carrying out your job duties?

VI. OPPORTUNITIES
   A. What job or jobs is your present activity preparing you to perform within____Food Stores?
      1. How much preparation do you feel is needed?
      2. What special skills are needed?
   B. Is additional training needed?
      1. Experience (O.J.T.)
      2. Formal Training

# Evaluation Sheet for Training Interviewers

(Check "yes" or "no" as you listen to the practice interview.)

| YES | NO | |
|---|---|---|
| | | *Accountability Objective:* Did the interviewer determine: |
| — | — | a summary of the end results that should be accomplished by the job? |
| | | *Dimensions:* Did the interviewer determine: |
| — | — | the "size" of the job's impact on Company operation? |
| — | — | the volume in $? |
| — | — | non-money measures of magnitude? |
| | | *Nature and Scope:* Did the interviewer determine: |
| — | — | where the position fits into the organization? |
| — | — | reporting relationships—above/below? |
| — | — | subordinate functions and/or personnel? |
| — | — | budget controls? |
| — | — | what products or services he provides? |
| — | — | challenges of the job? |
| — | — | the nature and source of controls on freedom to act? |
| — | — | degree of creativity job provides? |
| — | — | specific assignments of the job? |
| — | — | nature of outside contacts on behalf of the Company? |
| — | — | skills, technical knowledge, and general abilities of the job? |
| — | — | human relations skills required in this job? |
| | | *Principal Accountabilities:* Did the interviewer determine: |
| — | — | the Manpower and Organizational development accountabilities? |
| — | — | the job's Communication accountabilities? |
| — | — | the demands of the job for Planning? |
| — | — | what the present job holder thinks should be accomplished in the job? |
| | | *General Interviewing Techniques:* Did the interviewer: |
| — | — | explain the program? |
| — | — | get data to fill in the heading of the Job Description? |
| — | — | put the interviewee at ease? |
| — | — | ask specific questions to get the interview started? |
| — | — | use more conversational techniques later in the interview? |
| — | — | avoid dominating the interview? |
| — | — | maintain control of the interview? |

# *Overall Performance Work Sheet*

## *Black & Decker®* OVERALL PERFORMANCE WORK SHEET

Fiscal Year 19 _____
Grade _____
Age _____
Years With Company _____
Years in Present Job _____

### GENERAL INSTRUCTIONS

**OBJECTIVES**

The four objectives of this Program are to:

1. Help the individual to improve his knowledge and skill.

2. Assure continuing two-way communications between the individual and his immediate supervisor.

3. Convert Black & Decker's goals into targets for the individual.

4. Realistically appraise the individual's performance.

**TARGET SETTING PROCEDURES**

1. The manager of each division, department or section should meet with his subordinates in a briefing session to discuss the overall targets of the group. Also, the manager should discuss how the group's targets can be converted to targets for each individual.

2. After the briefing session, each individual should review the group's targets and determine what his own targets should be to help the group achieve its overall targets. Then the individual should prepare the first three elements of the Work Sheet, Parts A through C. Each manager should do the same for each individual reporting to him.

3. Finally, the individual should again meet with his manager and mutually agree on his personal and job targets and principal job responsibilities for the next year.

NOTE: Both the manager and the individual will have a copy of the Work Sheet. The individual's copy is his working copy to be used throughout the year. The manager's copy is his working copy and becomes the permanent file copy at the end of the year.

**REVIEW AND APPRAISAL**

During the year the manager should hold periodic meetings with the individual to review target progress, discuss any help or assistance needed to achieve a target and make any target changes necessary.

At year-end the manager completes Parts A through E, evaluating how well the individual performed. Then he should meet with the individual to discuss the overall performance appraisal.

WHAT IS THE PURPOSE OF THIS JOB IN TERMS OF THE CONTRIBUTION IT SHOULD MAKE TO THE BUSINESS?

_____
_____
_____

## A | Instructions

### A. PERSONAL DEVELOPMENT

1. Describe, as specifically as possible, the type of work this individual desires in the near future (2-3 years) and in the long range.

1. Career Aspirations: _____
_____
_____

2. List the individual's personal and professional strengths on which he can build to achieve his future aspirations.

2. Areas of Greatest Strengths: _____
_____
_____
_____

3. Indicate those personal and professional areas where he needs further development.

3. Areas Requiring Further Development: _____
_____
_____
_____

4. Discuss personal development with the individual and together develop a plan to attempt to attain his objectives. Then select a few personal targets which will increase his present knowledge, skills and potential to help him achieve his career aspirations.

NOTE: These targets should largely be determined by the factors that affected the individual's performance last year.... see Part D.

| 4. Personal Targets for the Year | How Well Were Targets Accomplished? |
|---|---|
|  |  |
|  |  |
|  |  |
|  |  |
|  |  |
|  |  |

**B. PRINCIPAL JOB RESPONSIBILITIES**

Suggestions:

Review the individual's job responsibilities to develop a current list of all his functions and responsibilities. These are job functions for which the individual is held accountable.

Next, select and list only the major job responsibilities which are the PRIMARY functions of the individual's job.

At the year-end review the manager should analyze the individual's overall performance on the primary responsibilities, write his appraisal in the space provided and then discuss it with the individual.

**C** | Instructions |

**C. SPECIFIC JOB TARGETS**   1st Quarter R

Select the specific job targets (Projects, programs, assignments) the individual is expected to accomplish. The targets should be specific, mutually understood and agreed upon. Also, to the extent possible, indicate priorities, completion times, and results expected. If a target is complex or requires a prolonged period for completion, break it into separate phases showing when certain elements or parts will be completed.

During the year, the manager should meet at least quarterly with the individual to:

1. Review his progress towards target completion.

2. Discuss any help or assistance he needs to achieve the targets.

3. Make any changes necessary to current targets; add new targets if workload permits.

Also, the manager should indicate in the space provided, what action was taken on each target.

At year-end, the manager should evaluate the results accomplished in the column provided, noting the quality and quantity of the work done. This should then be discussed with the individual.

**D** | Instructions |

**D. OTHER FACTORS AFFECTING JOB PERFORMANCE**

This part is to be completed at the year-end review. This section is not to be completed in advance.

The manager should:

1. Analyze the other critical factors which in your judgment have interfered with the individual's performance through the year, e.g., knowledge the man brings to the job, technical and managerial skills, and personal characteristics.

2. Select those factors which have MOST adversely affected his performance last year, describe and give examples in the space provided.

3. These factors should be considered when the individual's personal targets (Part A, #3 and #4) are established next year.

## HOW WELL DID HE PERFORM?

_____
_____
_____
_____
_____
_____
_____
_____
_____

| d Quarter Review | 3rd Quarter Review | 4th Quarter Review | Results |
|---|---|---|---|
| | | | |
| | | | |
| | | | |
| | | | |
| | | | |
| | | | |
| | | | |
| | | | |
| | | | |
| | | | |
| | | | |
| | | | |
| | | | |
| | | | |

## DESCRIBE AND GIVE EXAMPLES

_____
_____
_____
_____
_____
_____
_____
_____
_____
_____
_____

**E** | Instructions

# E. OVERALL PERFORMANCE SUMMARY

To be completed by
the manager:

1. Check the statement
which best describes
the individual's over-
all job performance.

1. HOW WELL DID HE MEET STANDARDS OF JOB PERFORMANCE?

_____FAR EXCEEDS: Outstanding Performance in Present Assignment in <u>practically every</u> respect.

_____EXCEEDS: Above Average Perfomance in Present Assignment in <u>most</u> respects.

*baseline performance level*

_____MEETS NORMAL REQUIREMENTS: Average or Satisfactory Performance in PRIMARY
FUNCTIONS, JOB TASKS and MANNER.

*baseline performance level*

_____MEETS MINIMUM REQUIREMENTS: Acceptable but does not meet average performance
in the majority of primary functions, job tasks and
manner.

2. EXPLAIN IN DETAIL:

2. Then support this
performance rating by
giving a word picture
of the individual's
performance.

3. Review the individ-
ual's career aspira-
tions on page one.
Then, based on pres-
ent performance and
overall growth poten-
tial, recommend a
career path or future
jobs you feel the in-
dividual is capable of
achieving. It will be
helpful to consult with
other managers in oth-
er divisions for their
opinions about the in-
dividual's performance
and potential.

3. CAREER PATH RECOMMENDATIONS:

NOTE:
All factors in this
overall performance
appraisal should be
considered when pre-
paring next year's tar-
gets for the individual.

If the individual or the
rater's superior would
like to comment on this
appraisal, attach his
statement to the com-
pleted Work Sheet.

SIGNATURES:

Individual Rated_____ Date_____

Rater_____ Date_____

Rater's Superior_____ Date_____

☐ SEE ATTACHED STATEMENT

Form No. 2283

# PART THREE

*A Handbook of Position Descriptions*

# *Statements of Common Responsibility for All Managers*

Some organizations supplement their position descriptions of individual managers with descriptions of responsibilities common to groups of managers and supervisors. This practice has a distinct advantage: common responsibilities need not be repeated in each individual's description. It is enough merely to refer to the common list.

---

A PUBLIC UTILITY
CHARACTERISTICS OF
ALL MANAGEMENT POSITIONS

OBJECTIVES

Efficient and effective response to the needs of our customers and stockholders and the general public, with due regard for the rights of employees.

FUNCTIONS

1. Interpret and follow established objectives, policies and procedures.
2. Plan assignments and establish priorities.
3. Achieve maximum production at practical economic minimums.
4. Secure or provide staff services and/or support as required.
5. Analyze and appraise results and develop innovations to improve performance.
6. Initiate corrective action within limits of delegated authority or secure approval of necessary action to achieve positive results.
7. Keep informed of current developments, trends and practices in his field.
8. Support and secure acceptance of Company's integrity, reputation, product and service.

INTERNAL RELATIONSHIPS

1. Secure or provide service, total cooperation and appropriate functional authority to achieve objectives through accurate and complete information and freedom of communication.

2. Supervision received:
   a. Receive outline of policies, procedures and objectives.
   b. Communicate on matters where supervisor's accountability is involved.
   c. Receive training, counsel and appraisal of performance.

3. Supervision exercised: (if part of assigned functions)
   a. Establish objectives, standards, policies and procedures.
   b. Make work assignments and provide resources.
   c. Delegate authority to act with adequate controls.
   d. Lead, guide and direct activities to secure positive results.
   e. Appraise results, plan necessary changes and authorize action.
   f. Maintain programs to develop individuals for greater responsibilities.
   g. Recommend the selection, promotion, corrective discipline and appropriate wage and salary changes of subordinates.

EXTERNAL RELATIONSHIPS
1. Enhance the Company's image in each private, public or business contact.
2. Secure or provide appropriate information or services in accordance with Company policies.
3. Maintain compliance with applicable laws, regulations and agreements.

QUALIFICATIONS
1. Knowledge of:
   a. Technical and/or professional processes, Company practices and current trends related to assigned functions.
   b. Government regulations and legal commitments affecting assigned function.
   c. Management philosophy, key personnel and relationship of functions as they contribute toward achievement of corporate objectives.
   d. Fundamentals of management, leadership and human relations.

2. Ability to:
   a. Train, lead, guide and inspire subordinates to achieve objectives.
   b. Work harmoniously with people at all levels.
   c. Analyze and evaluate situations, make decisions and develop alternatives.
   d. Endure high mental and physical frustrations.
   e. Sustain an authentic and favorable Company image.

## ORGANIZATION LEVELS AND THEIR BASIC OBJECTIVES AND FUNCTIONS

The following organization levels and their distinctive characteristics apply to both line and staff management groups as they direct and integrate their functions to accomplish the overall objectives of the Company.

A. EXECUTIVE MANAGEMENT POSITIONS
   (*President & Vice-Presidents*)
   Objective:   To manage the business and property of the Company in a responsible, ethical and profitable manner with due regard to social responsibilities.
   Function:    Establishes overall, long-range corporate objectives, policies, philosophy, structure and standards of performance.

B. ADMINISTRATIVE MANAGEMENT POSITIONS
   Objective:   To insure the effective management of a corporate function or major geographical division.
   Function:    Interprets and administers objectives, policies, philosophy and standards of production within the guidelines set by executive management.

C. OPERATING MANAGEMENT POSITIONS

   1. SUB-DIVISION MANAGERS
      (*Dist. Mgrs., Supts. and Section Mgrs.*)
      Objective:   To assure effective management of immediate business activities.
      Function:    Directs and/or supervises the day-to-day operation of closely related activities in a specialized section or area within the framework of administrative policies and procedures.

   2. UNIT MANAGERS
      Objective:   To accomplish immediate results through the work of other people.
      Function:    Supervises subordinates and directs use of equipment and materials in completing work assigned according to established policies, practices and procedures.

D. STAFF MANAGEMENT POSITIONS
   (*Scientists, Engineers, Analysts & Coordinators*)
   Objective:   To assure complete and innovative staff support as a reliable basis for management decisions.
   Function:    Develops and provides expert, specialized information, advice, guidance and detailed studies and plans.

# SPECTOR FREIGHT SYSTEM, INC.
## MANAGEMENT RESPONSIBILITIES
## OF THE SUPERVISOR

I. PURPOSE AND SCOPE

The following Sections contain descriptions of *specific* responsibilities in each key management position in the Company. The purpose of this Instruction is to define management responsibilities which are common to *all* of these positions. Meeting these responsibilities, together with the responsibilities of his specific job description, becomes each man's obligation in fulfilling his part of his "contract" with the Company.

II. MANAGEMENT RESPONSIBILITY OF THE SUPERVISOR

A. To attain profit as set up in budget and/or to control expenditures to conform to budget; to prepare or assist in preparing budgets, review costs and number of people needed to carry out assigned functions, and to take corrective action as necessary; to direct the maintenance of appropriate records covering quality and quantity of work; and to assume full leadership in cost reduction and participate with other organizational units in cost reduction.

B. To meet Standards of Performance, as established.

C. To program and plan work systematically, organizing the various jobs under his supervision, determining the organization structure needed, developing organization charts, and assigning and delegating specific duties, authority and responsibilities to each individual, on the premise that the supervisor's purpose is to "obtain results through people"; to check and control to see that plans are being followed.

D. To know the extent of his authority for each of his responsibilities and to use this authority wisely in carrying out his responsibilities.

E. To think and perform like a member of management:
1. To deal honestly with people and to make no promise he cannot keep.
2. To report to his own supervisor the feelings and attitudes of his staff; to report also concerning progress, deficiencies, irregularities and other significant factors affecting his assigned responsibility, being forthright in dealing with these matters.
3. To help each employee understand and meet his obligations to the Company.
4. To establish and maintain productive working relationships with his immediate supervisor and other superiors, and to coordinate the activities of his organizational unit with those of other units.

5. To set a high example by his own conduct; to be "Spector" to his employees and not just the supervisor of his unit. To fight for the rights of his employees, but to remember that he is one supervisor among many, that employees of other supervisors have similar rights, and that his responsibility in enforcing general rules may restrict his own actions and feelings; to obtain knowledge of related functions of the Company to understand better the relationship of his own job to the over-all operation of the Company.

F. To seek constantly to simplify and improve methods of performing all jobs and projects under his supervision and to maintain all established standards of performance in his work area; to keep informed and up-to-date on all matters, methods, research or equipment which might contribute to efficiency, increased production and progress in his specialized field and in the general fields of operations and management.

G. To utilize modern techniques of job training and individual training and to counsel his employees regarding outside training and development possibilities.

H. To select qualified new employees to fill vacancies; to make the final decision regarding the selection and to be responsible for the success or failure of that selection.

I. To evaluate the performance of his employees and advise of ways to improve their areas of weakness and to praise his employees when work accomplishments warrant it; to complete and discuss with them their Development Reviews or Performance Ratings, and to recommend or withhold salary increases according to the employee's rate of development and the salary range of his job; to avoid allowing personalities to sway his judgment either for or against individual employees.

J. To recommend employees for transfer, reassignment or promotion.

K. To win the confidence and respect of his employees, so that they will communicate freely; to interpret policies and procedures to employees, and to give his full support to such policies and procedures, expressing constructive criticism, if he deems it necessary, at the proper time and to the appropriate superior; to keep his employees informed, advising them in advance of changes which will affect them; to conduct periodic meetings to discuss matters of general interest, such as work progress, work plans, new policies, etc.

L. To determine resources in terms of equipment, tools and machinery necessary to get the job done; to assume full responsibility for proper maintenance and good housekeeping of machines, equipment, and any physical facilities for which he is responsible.

M. To make decisions promptly and competently and to be accountable for such decisions.

N. To maintain discipline and morale and teamwork at a high standard and to motivate employees to carry out their work in the most effective manner.

O. To discipline employees, including issuance of letters of warning where required, suspension and discharge.

P. To anticipate grievances whenever possible and to settle problems of his employees promptly, thoroughly and fairly and to foster cooperation and team spirit at the highest possible level.

Q. To prepare himself for additional responsibilities and for promotion by training an understudy for his own position, thereby opening the way for possible promotion for himself.

R. To keep clean, healthy and safe facilities and procedures; to keep accidents and personal injuries at a minimum.

S. To perform any additional duties as assigned (although not described in this Manual).

T. To remember that the customer is the final judge of his efficient performance as a supervisor.

---

# MCDONNELL DOUGLAS CORPORATION
## ALL SUPERVISORS AND MANAGERS

RESPONSIBLE TO: NEXT HIGHER MANAGEMENT LEVEL.

PRIMARY FUNCTION:

To plan, organize, motivate, and control resources (viz., personnel, equipment, facilities and materials) placed at his disposal to accomplish the responsibilities assigned to him.

TYPICAL DUTIES:

1. *Policies, procedures, and practices:*
   a. Develops and implements plans and controls for discharging assignments.
   b. Interprets, adapts and recommends policies/procedures, plans objectives and implements controls established at higher management levels.
   c. Develops, authorizes, implements, coordinates and continually appraises policies, procedures, plans, objectives and controls for all activities under his jurisdiction and ensures that they are consistent with management objectives.

2. *Personnel and Facilities:*
   a. Determines personnel requirements and selects qualified personnel to fill established openings.

  b. Provides or arranges for training as required.

  c. Sets performance standards and develops subordinates for promotion.

  d. Assigns work, follows up and evaluates completed work.

  e. Determines merit of recommendations submitted by subordinates.

  f. Rates performance of personnel reporting to him directly and assists subordinates in evaluating those reporting indirectly.

  g. Recommends promotions, compensation changes and/or employee status changes.

  h. Initiates or recommends disciplinary action such as termination, layoff, demotion or other action.

  i. Hears and acts upon employee complaints and grievances.

  j. Provides or arranges for required equipment, space, supplies, material, etc.

 3. *Costs:*

  a. Plans and continues a program of operational improvement, modernization and cost reduction.

  b. Prepares budget estimates and ensures compliance with budget limitations.

 4. Informs supervision of problems and seeks advice when necessary; resolves problems submitted by subordinates.

 5. Participates with other managers in analyzing and discussing operating programs/problems, in ensuring coordination and integration of activities, and in exchanging information, counsel, and guidance.

SUPERVISION EXERCISED: Directly 2  Indirectly 0

NORMAL BACKGROUND AND EXPERIENCE REQUIREMENTS:

Requires a formal educational background consistent with the requirements of the specific field of supervision or equivalent practical experience normally gained through progressively greater responsibilities within the field or through applicable experience acquired outside MDC. Must be capable of efficiently organizing the resources provided for the discharge of assigned responsibilities and must be cognizant of the interrelationships existing between this area of responsibility and that of contacted areas. Experience requirements for satisfactory performance are dependent on the level of supervisory responsibility, the nature of the judgments required and the complexity of the field involved.

# Limits of Authority Statement

[*Contained in the introductory section of the Koppers Organization Manual.*]

"Authority" is defined as the power of an individual to carry out his assigned duties and responsibilities. Therefore, every person to whom duties and responsibilities have been given possesses certain implied authority. It is necessary, however, for management to exercise a certain measure of control over the use of authority by a large number of individuals, in order that adherence to policy and plans may be obtained, and in order to protect the company's assets from improper use.

"Limits of Authority" are designed to produce the control required by management. They may exist either through general rules of conduct or through definite statements of specific limits. As an example of the former, the basic relationship of staff to line is a limit of authority. While the staff is responsible for the manner in which certain functions are performed throughout the company, it possesses no line authority over other units. This type of limitation is covered in the individual job specification for each position.

As to definite statements of specific limits, there will be found in the portion of [the Koppers Organization] manual for each unit a schedule of limitations covering some of the more common ways in which authority is exercised. The exercise of authority within the limits indicated for each position, or within other limitations specified by management, is further confined to the activities, functions, and supervisory scope of the individual position. Where authority is absent or limited, the matter at hand should be referred to the immediate supervisor. Where the duties and responsibilities of an assistant specify that he will manage the unit in the absence of his superior, he will act with the authority of his superior at such times, except as specifically prohibited by the "Limits of Authority."

The limits of authority set forth in the manual are not all-inclusive and should not be confused with certain administrative controls which are considered desirable in individual units of the company. For example, the District Sales Manager may have full authority to approve traveling expense incurred by his salesmen. Yet administrative controls may require *all* expense reports to clear through the Finance Department Manager before reimbursement is made. In such an example the District Sales Manager exercises authority to approve, and the Finance Department Manager performs a routine administrative control action.

Amplified definitions of the specific authorities for which limits are indicated follow:

*Personnel Administration*
1. Hiring Additional Employees
   Hiring salary or hourly paid employees considered necessary to conduct assigned operations, except replacements, and within salary or wage approval authority.
2. Discharging Employees
   Release of salary or hourly paid employees, with or without cause.
3. Transferring or Promoting Employees
   Reassignment or promotion of employees under supervision of the individual position involved, whether or not entailing immediate change in rating or compensation, except elective officers of the company.
4. Approving Salary Rates of Employees Covered by the Job Evaluation Plan
   Determining the rate of compensation of a salary employee in connection with initial hiring, transfer, or promotion to a new position, or within a specific position, covered by the company's job evaluation plan and subject to the limitations of existing salary schedules and policies. (Limits shown are on an annual basis.)
5. Approving Salary Rates of Employees Not Covered by the Job Evaluation Plan
   Determining the rate of compensation of a salary employee in connection with initial hiring, transfer, or promotion to a new position, or within a specific position not covered by the company's job evaluation plan. (Limits shown are on an annual basis.)
6. Fixing or Adjusting Hourly Wages
   Determining the wage rate of hourly employees or adjustments thereto within the limitations of existing wage schedules, except where specified by an existing labor contract or labor agreement.
7. Executing Labor Agreements
   Ratification of labor contracts, wage agreements, or settlements of other labor negotiations, by written approval or consent.
8. Authorizing Paid Overtime
   Authorizing work schedules which will involve overtime compensation to salary or hourly paid employees.
9. Approving Excused Leave
   Approving absence of employees from their duties, whether or not regular compensation will be paid for the period of absence.

*Administrative Expenses*
10. Authorizing Travel
    Authorizing travel of employees in connection with the performance of company business and the payment of travel advances.

11. Approving Travel Expense
    Approving expense reports of employees for reimbursement or credit against travel advances, covering authorized travel in connection with the performance of company business.
12. Approving Entertainment Expense
    Approving expense reports of employees for reimbursement or credit against advance, or other charges for entertaining or otherwise promoting goodwill in connection with company business.
13. Approving Moving Expense
    Committing for or approving payment of expenses incurred in the temporary or permanent relocation of employees (including employees being originally hired), including moving of dependents, household goods, etc.
14. Approving Employee Activities Expense
    Committing the company to bear or share the cost of employee outings, sports participation, and similar group activities. (Limits refer to total per year per unit.)
15. Approving Social Membership Dues
    Purchasing or maintaining membership in clubs or other organizations primarily of a social nature, to be used in connection with company business and at company expense. This authority is restricted to the Office of the President.
16. Approving Trade Membership Dues
    Purchasing or maintaining membership in professional societies, trade associations, civic groups, etc., in connection with company business and at company expense.
17. Approving Advances to Employees
    Approving advances to employees against future earnings or other types of loans to employees, involving company funds.
18. Approving Donations or Gifts
    Committing for or making donations or gifts of company funds to charitable, civic, or other organizations. (Limits refer to an individual donation or gift. The total of such donations or gifts must be within the limitations of annual programs approved by the Board of Directors.) This authority is delegated to division general managers and staff department managers only, and cannot be redelegated.

*Sales*
19. Setting or Approving Sales Prices
    Setting or approving sales prices for products ordinarily sold under fixed price lists and discount schedules.
20. Making or Approving Price Quotations
    Making or approving price quotations on products ordinarily sold on an estimate and quotation basis, except as may be specifically authorized by the Board of Directors.

21. Accepting Sales Orders
   Accepting or approving sales orders or contracts obligating the company to manufacture and/or deliver goods or services.
22. Approving Credit Arrangements
   Extending or approving credit to customers in connection with sales transactions.
23. Approving Advertising and Public Relations Commitments
   Committing or approving expenditures for product or institutional advertising, or for other public relations activities.

*Operating and Capital Expenses*
24. Approving Petty Cash Items
   Approving requisitions for petty cash funds for reimbursement of miscellaneous minor expenses in connection with company business. (Limits refer to one individual item.)
25. Approving Purchase Commitments
   Approving requisitions, purchase orders, contracts, or other actions which involve committing the company to purchase materials, supplies, services, and any other items required for assigned operations (except those covered by separate authority delegation). This authority includes approving commitments for capital items and real property, but only after approval of capital appropriations by the Board of Directors or within the limits of authority as delegated to managers and general managers for the acquisition of capital items. (Limits refer to an individual item.)
26. Approving Transportation Contracts
   Purchasing or contracting for transportation services such as trucking, barge shipments, ship loadings, etc. (Limits refer to an individual contract.)
27. Employing Professional Services
   Committing for or approving the expense of professional business services, such as management counsel, business surveys of company operations, and organization studies or procedure studies by outside consultants. These limitations do not apply to professional services required in engineering, technical, legal, auditing, medical, and similar functional fields. This authority is restricted to the Office of the President.
28. Acquiring Capital Equipment
   Purchase or approval to purchase or construct machinery, equipment (including office equipment), and other forms of capital property. (Limits refer to an individual item.) Purchase or approval to purchase real property is restricted to the Board of Directors, except for timberlands (see Authority No. 34).
29. Selling Capital Equipment
   Disposal of capital equipment or real property which is worn out, obsolete, or otherwise unusable for future operations. (Limits refer to selling price

or book value of an individual item.) This authority is delegated only to division general managers and the Manager, Traffic and Transportation Department, and cannot be redelegated.

30. Leasing Property or Equipment

Renting or approval to rent plants, machinery, equipment, buildings, land, office space, or other capital property to be used on a permanent or semi-permanent basis in company operations. This authority is delegated to division general managers and staff department managers only, and cannot be redelegated.

31. Acquiring Expensed Equipment

Purchase or approval to purchase or construct equipment, tools, and other items, the cost of which will be charged to operating expense rather than capitalized. (Limits refer to an individual approval.)

32. Approving Maintenance and Repair

Approving maintenance and repair expenditures for work on buildings, machinery, equipment, land, and other property. (Limits refer to an individual project.)

33. Approving Disposal of Surplus Material

Approving sale or disposal of operating materials and supplies or excess construction materials not required for operations or contract performance.

34. Approving Purchases and Sales of Timber and Timberlands

Approving the acquisition or sale of standing timber and/or timberlands. This authority is delegated to the General Manager, Wood Preserving Division only.

# Descriptions of Individual Positions

The descriptions in the following pages are arranged by *type of organization* and by *managerial level* within the organization. The first classification includes the following: manufacturing; non-manufacturing which incorporates airlines, railroads, utilities, hotels, restaurants, retail trade, and wholesale trade; banking and insurance; public agencies at municipal and county levels; and hospitals. Few position descriptions were obtained from the insurance industry and educational institutions. These latter two classes are discussed by showing typical descriptions from one insurance company and one public university.

The second classification breaks out managerial position descriptions by different hierarchical level. In manufacturing, separate sections are devoted to the officers of the corporation or organization (including chairman, president, and executive vice-president), operations and related functions, finance, marketing, personnel and industrial relations, research and development, administration, and management information systems. In non-manufacturing, banking, insurance, public agencies, and hospitals, the managerial descriptions are listed in hierarchical form from the top down. Some specialized professional position descriptions have also been included at several points in the organizational classifications.

## Manufacturing—Officers and The Board of Directors

### A HOLDING COMPANY
#### CHAIRMAN OF THE BOARD AND CHIEF EXECUTIVE OFFICER

*Organization Unit:* Office of the Chief Executive
*Reports to:* Board of Directors

ACCOUNTABILITY OBJECTIVE
To obtain maximum profitability and growth for the parent company and the member companies which comprise it.

DIMENSIONS
   Personnel:
   Total Revenues: $ _____
   Annual Growth Objective:

NATURE AND SCOPE

This is a holding company with three major organizational groupings: the Office of the Chief Executive, the corporate staff, and the operating Companies.

The Office of the Chief Executive consists of this position and the President.

The parent company's staff reports to the Office of the Chief Executive and consists of the Vice President of Finance, Vice President and General Counsel, Vice President—Governmental Affairs, Vice President of Real Estate, Vice President of Public Relations, Vice President and Secretary, and Director of Manpower Resources.

There are five major groups of operating Companies: manufacturing, transportation, real estate, consumer products and financial services. Within each of these groupings is a number of operating Companies, each headed by a Chairman or President who reports directly to the parent company's Office of the Chief Executive.

The parent company has total revenues of approximately $ _____ and some 34,000 employees. By the four major groupings, these figures are respectively: manufacturing, $ _____ and 14,000; transportation, $ _____ and 14,800; real estate, $ _____ and 100; and consumer products, $ _____ and 4,700. Revenue does not include financial services group, which is considered "other income."

As the Senior Official, the Chairman and Chief Executive Officer has the ultimate accountability for the success of the parent company and its affiliated operating Companies.

To direct an organization as large and diversified as a holding company, the incumbent established the three part organization structure of the Office of the Chief Executive, the parent company's staff, and operating Companies ("profit centers").

The Office of the Chief Executive (OCE) functions in a manner similar to a Board of Directors for each of the Companies in the profit centers. The OCE concerns itself with those matters which would concern an active, aggressive, competent, and inquisitive Board which held large blocks of stock.

To assist the OCE perform in that manner, a second group was established: the specialists of the parent company's staff. It is their function to draw up detailed procedures as to how policy (established by the OCE and the Board) is to be implemented and, further, to consolidate information from the profit centers for the Office of the Chief Executive.

The third group is the profit centers themselves. They operate as autonomous operating units within the policy established by the OCE, reporting information on their operations to the OCE, using the report formats and procedures published by the parent company's staff.

Within the Office of the Chief Executive itself, authority is exercised in this fashion: the Chairman's *primary* (but not exclusive) orientation is outward and toward the unique; he is primarily concerned with the parent company's relations with the financial community, other business and industrial concerns, the shareholders, and American society in general. Within the parent company and its Companies, he is primarily concerned with the unique, novel, or non-recurring situation which by its uniqueness or magnitude requires his attention. The President's role in the Office of the Chief Executive is to function in such a manner that the Chairman and Chief Executive Officer may operate in that fashion.

The President, thus, has a *primary* inward orientation. He is primarily concerned with the continuing and on-going functions of the parent company's staff and of the operating Companies. He provides continuing direction to these groups in their operations. In addition, he also provides executive leadership to the planning and acquisition function. The President brings to the Chairman and Chief Executive Officer's attention both those unique or non-recurring situations of large magnitude, as well as acquisition opportunities for evaluation, information, and/or decision.

PRINCIPAL ACCOUNTABILITIES
1. Establish broad policy guidelines to the end that operating Companies may operate autonomously while still maintaining effective, centralized control.
2. Develop sound plans and tactics to achieve maximum profit realization consistent with long-range growth objectives.
3. Direct and motivate a competent staff of executives, organized to optimize individual and group capabilities and to ensure continuity of management.
4. Lead the parent company into new areas of operations by actively pursuing acquisitions of profitable new ventures which enhance overall performance.
5. Cause changes in tactics and emphasis as needed to meet unexpected problems or to take advantage of opportunities as they arise.
6. Represent the holding company to the financial community, other business and industrial concerns, the shareholders, and the public in general to the end that it is perceived as a profitable, well-managed, vital organization, aware of its place in the business community and in society in general.

# A MACHINERY MANUFACTURER
## MEMBER OF THE BOARD OF DIRECTORS

*Basic Function*
Responsible to the stockholders of the Company for considering and approving matters of policy, objectives, plans, programs, investments, disposal or transfer of assets, methods of financing, and other matters affecting the broad aspects of Company operations; and for electing officers of the Company, establishing By-Laws, and establishing such other regulations as are considered advisable for proper control of Company operations.

*Basic Objective*
To exercise prudent business judgment in guiding the affairs of the Company, to the end that the interests and rights of the stockholders and other creditors shall be properly protected.

*Major Duties and Responsibilities*
1. To attend Board meetings; and carry out his functions as prescribed in the By-Laws of the Company.
2. To review and appraise, jointly with other members of the Board, management's performance, future plans, and programs; and in joint action:
    *a.* Approve them.
    *b.* Revise them, after appropriate consideration has been given to recommendations of special committees of the vice chairmen assigned to study specific projects.
    *c.* Recommend specific actions to be taken by general management in the form of orders and resolutions of the Board.

*Limits of Authority*
1. Specific authorities of this position are covered in the By-Laws of the Company.
2. Through consideration and decision on basic matters of Company policy, organization, and use of funds, and through election of Company officers, each member of the Board exercises, in conjunction with other members, complete authority over all aspects of the Company's operations.
3. No line authority over general or divisional management except through orders and resolutions of the Board.

*Relations with Others*
Responsible to the stockholders of the Company for the performance of above duties.

*Measurement of Performance*
The performance of the member of the Board of Directors will be measured by the degree of effectiveness with which he assists the Board in guiding the affairs of the Company and the degree to which he satisfies the stockholders of the Company with the performance of his duties.

# A MANUFACTURING COMPANY
## EXECUTIVE VICE PRESIDENT

ORGANIZATIONAL RELATIONSHIPS

Reports to:   President

Supervises:   1.  President and Division Manager—Valves
2.  President and Division Manager—Gas
3.  President and Division Manager—Power Tools
4.  President and Division Manager—M&U
5.  President and Division Manager—Sterling
6.  Division Manager—LFM Foundry
7.  Division Manager—Engines

JOB REQUIREMENTS

Broad and continued education (Bachelor's Degree or equivalent) in Industrial Management, Engineering, Business Administration, Marketing, etc.

Successful management experience including management of a division or a major corporate function—manufacturing, marketing, finance, engineering, etc.

Complete knowledge of corporate line and staff organization, also the ability to develop key subordinates and make sound, timely decisions effecting corporate goals and growth.

| LIST HERE MAJOR SEGMENTS OF POSITION | WT. | CLASS | | | LIST HERE OPPOSITE EACH SEGMENT THE STANDARDS OF PERFORMANCE (*Conditions which will exist when each segment is performed satisfactorily*) |
|---|---|---|---|---|---|
| (*What individual has to do*) | % | 1 | 2 | 3 | |
| *Basic Functions:*<br>1. Responsible for providing positive and aggressive leadership to operating divisions consistent with policies and objectives established by the President.<br><br>a. Direct the establishment of sound and achievable division financial goals and programs.<br><br>b. Accountable for achieving results in line with established goals and objectives | 55 | x | | | 1.a. Annual budgets and programs for each division are approved by the President.<br><br>b. Approved division operating budgets are met, and approved programs are carried out and projected results achieved.<br><br>c. If general economic or industry specifics prevent attainment of budgeted orders and shipments, then quick response in develop- |

for each operating division.

c. Policies and practices have a positive impact on sales, product development, manufacturing costs and profits.

d. Operating policies are effective as guides and controls yet provide division management necessary freedom to act.

e. Communications and coordination of line operations are effectively maintained in a work atmosphere of mutual trust and respect.

ing "profit protection" programs is taken and execution results in meeting targeted program goals.

d. Divisions are managed in a manner which reflects understanding of accountability for results.

e. Operating policies, plans and strategies are understood by subordinates, and assist them in achieving desired operating results.

| | | | |
|---|---|---|---|
| 2. Consults with corporate staff officers with respect to division programs. Sees to it that staff assistance is directed to various divisions' needs for maximization of profit and ROCE. | 20 | x | 2. Staff departments are consulted regularly and their efforts directed to maximize profits. Divisions are treated fairly with respect to allocation of staff assistance. Division management coordinates with staff departments to insure staff assistance and support as required. |
| 3. Continuously develop an organization capable of achieving division and corporate goals and objectives.<br><br>a. Initiate and implement organization changes necessary to meet changing needs and business trends and to insure maximum utilization and development of manager capabilities.<br><br>b. Compensate personnel commensurate with their responsibilities and performance. | 15 | x | 3.a. Understanding and agreement is achieved by incumbent and his subordinates concerning their responsibilities, authority and the required performance of their position—as evidenced by an approved "Position Description & Performance Standards" for each position.<br><br>b. Subordinates meet or exceed performance standards for their position.<br><br>c. Organization structure meets the current and immediate future needs of the business. |

| | | | |
|---|---|---|---|
| | | | d. Performance appraisals and salary reviews are conducted in accordance with established policy and practice. |
| 4. Provide guidance and direction to long-range planning to insure the continued economic growth of each division consistent with overall corporate objectives. | 10 | x | 4. Long-range economic growth goals are developed and action plans established for obtaining results. |

# A FOOD COMPANY
## GROUP VICE PRESIDENT

### I. BASIC FUNCTION

Responsible to the President of the Corporation for the effective management of the Profit Centers currently reporting to him. This also involves the continual evaluation and development of each of these Profit Centers, or the recommendation for the elimination of a Profit Center that shows less than desired potential.

### II. RESPONSIBILITIES AND AUTHORITY

Within the limits of authorized Corporation policies, procedures, programs, and budgets he is responsible for and has commensurate authority to accomplish the duties set forth below:

1. Formulates long-range objectives, plans, and programs for the markets and business areas served by the Profit Centers assigned to him; and works with the President and other members of the Corporate staff to integrate these into overall Corporation objectives, plans, and programs.

2. Reviews and authorizes the short- and long-term objectives and major plans and programs of each of the Profit Centers assigned to him, making sure that they are in harmony with and in furtherance of Corporation objectives, plans and programs.

3. Insures that authorized plans and programs of his Profit Centers are properly executed, and that both he and the President are kept informed on the over-all conditions and trends in each division and on all important activities affecting them.

4. Provides for maintenance in his office of long-range forecasts of the operations of his Profit Centers as to volume, market position, intro-

duction of new products, major development expense, financial requirements, personnel needs, organization plans, inventory and facility requirements and the projected effect of all of these on investment and earnings.

5. Develops and authorizes specific performance standards for each of his Profit Centers in such key result areas as marketing, utilization and development of people, operating efficiency, innovation, physical and financial resources, public responsibility, and profitability; evaluates the performance of his Profit Centers against these standards; and coaches and assists the Profit Center heads in improving their planning and performance.

6. Sees that each Profit Center assigned to him maintains and uses a plan of organization which suits the objectives and particular problems of the Profit Center, and authorizes major internal additions, eliminations, or alteration in these plans.

7. Provides for optimum utilization of managers in the Profit Centers assigned to him. To this end sees that his Profit Centers are staffed with competent people, that they are delegated authority and are compensated commensurate with their responsibilities; that necessary reservations of authority are defined and understood; and that managers are continually being developed so that qualified successors are available for key positions when needed.

8. Recommends the appointment, promotion, retirement, or release within his Profit Centers of major members of management in cases requiring action by the President; and authorizes such actions in cases where he has been delegated final authority. He directly administers the activities of the Profit Centers reporting to him in case of a temporary unfilled position at the head of a Profit Center.

9. Within the overall Corporate policy he sees that appropriate salary and wage structures are developed and their use properly controlled in the Profit Centers assigned to him; authorizes installation of specific salary and wage plans for each Profit Center within annual Corporate policy.

10. Sees that his Profit Centers maintain effective relationships with labor organizations, and that commitments in contracts with unions are consistent with basic Corporation policies and objectives. Authorizes union contract provisions where action by his office is required.

11. Initiates and/or reviews proposals for entry into or departure from specific businesses of his Profit Centers and the transfer of businesses or functions in or out of his group or from one Profit Center to another in his group, and recommends appropriate action to the President.

12. Makes sure that his Profit Centers evaluate the need for and effectiveness of proposed corporation-wide policies; and recommends appropriate action on establishment of Corporation policy.

13. Reviews major contracts and commitments, from or affecting the Profit Centers assigned to him, and takes appropriate action.

14. Reviews capital expenditure requests and appropriations and requests for condemnation of capital assets, requiring authorization by the Board of Directors, and takes appropriate action within the authority assigned to him.

15. Sees that the authorized budgetary procedure is properly used in the Profit Centers assigned to him; recommends policies and basic procedures governing budgets and financial controls; assists the President and the Comptroller in preparing and presenting consolidated Corporation budgets, and in securing authorization of the annual budgets of the Profit Centers assigned to him.

16. Sees that all funds, physical assets, and other property assigned to his Profit Centers are properly safeguarded and administered.

17. As necessary, coordinates the operations and the policies of the Profit Centers assigned to him, both with each other and with other Profit Centers of the Corporation.

18. Recommends specific acquisitions that will enhance the development and/or the profitability of the Profit Centers reporting to him.

19. Sees that appropriate facilities and conditions are provided for the maximum motivation and utilization of the abilities of the managers within their Profit Centers.

20. Sees that appropriate formal programs of profit improvement, vacation scheduling, counseling, management by objectives, hours control, incentives and safety are instituted and followed through in each of the Profit Centers reporting to him.

21. He is a member of the Corporation Advisory Management Committee and routinely participates in by-weekly meetings concerning Corporate progress and planning.

22. Specifically coordinates the full integration of the ABC Company into the subsidiary, DEF Company.

23. Executes such others of the general responsibilities common to all executive positions of the Corporation as are not specified above.

III. RELATIONSHIPS

He observes and conducts the following relationships:

1. The President of the Corporation
   a. He is accountable to this executive for proper interpretation and fulfillment of his functions, responsibilities and authority, and relationships.
   b. As delegated in this job description or elsewhere in writing, he exercises the authority of the President in relation to the Profit Centers assigned to him, and keeps the President informed as to his use of these delegated authorities.

2. Heads of Operating Profit Centers Assigned to Him
   He directs, guides and coordinates the operations and activities of these executives; guides them in effectively utilizing the knowledge and assis-

tance available from the Corporate staff; secures their advice in formulating Corporation objectives, plans, and programs affecting their businesses; and stands ready at all times to render them advice, support and directions.

3. Corporate Staff
   a. He promotes effective communication between these executives and their staffs and the Profit Centers assigned to him, to the end that his Profit Centers secure appropriate guidance on the handling of all matters within the functional responsibility of the Corporate staff departments.
   b. He advises the Corporate staff heads as to the effect on his divisions of proposed Corporation policies.
   c. He secures the advice and assistance of the Corporate staff heads and their subordinates in formulating long-range corporate objectives, plans, and programs for the markets and business areas served by the Profit Centers assigned to him.

4. Other Members of Management
   He consults with and encourages other members of management as he deems advisable, and stands ready at all times to assist them in areas where he is qualified.

5. Industry and Trade Associations
   He conducts such relationships with industry and trade associations as are necessary or desirable in the best interests of the Corporation.

6. Government, Labor, Public Service Organizations, Customers, and Vendors
   a. He conducts such relationships with representatives of government, with various public service organizations, and with customers and vendors as are necessary or desirable in the best interests of the Corporation.
   b. He engages in such other outside activities as are advantageous toward fulfilling the obligations of the Corporation as a member of industry and the community.

7. Outside Assistance
   Sees that specialized assistance is brought in from outside the Company where it is essential and not available within the Company.

8. Coordinates with Other Profit Centers
   He coordinates the activities of the Profit Centers reporting to him with other Profit Centers within the Corporation as appropriate.

9. Others
   He will conduct such other relationships as the President may from time to time specify.

# Manufacturing—Operations and Related Functions

## ANDERSON, CLAYTON & CO.
### VICE PRESIDENT MANUFACTURING AND DISTRIBUTION

BASIC FUNCTION

Controls the manufacture and distribution of Anderson Clayton Foods products through proper management of facilities, inventories, personnel and transportation. Plans facilities and services for present and anticipated division growth.

PRINCIPAL ACCOUNTABILITIES

1. Assures continuity of manufacturing operations of the division through constant appraisal and assessment of the output of his organization in relation to the needs dictated by customers, existing quality standards, and division cost structure.

2. Develops long range planning for manpower and facilities which will allow the division to produce existing and new product lines.

3. Ensures through his managers appropriate distribution of the goods manufactured by the division with a minimum inventory investment.

4. Plans the structure of his organization in order to achieve established goals and selects, trains, and motivates competent managers to assure a high level of performance within his organization.

5. Recommends enactment of new or modified policy relating to engineering, manufacturing, distribution, manpower planning, and regulatory authorities.

6. Ensures through his managers optimum freight costs for the pick up of raw materials and delivery of finished products within prescribed lead times.

7. Develops guidelines for labor contract negotiations which will insure continuity of operations and competitive labor rates.

8. Reviews performance standards and develops the operating segment of the profit plan.

NATURE AND SCOPE

The incumbent directs all manufacturing and distribution activities for Anderson Clayton Foods and reports to the Division President. Close communication must be maintained with the Director, Management Information Systems; the Personnel Director; and the Vice President—Administration on various administrative matters. The Industrial Sales Department also is frequently contacted when dealing with various sales contracts and bid prices. Closely related to this would be the interchange necessary with the Oil Trading and Purchasing groups on raw materials and supplies procurement. Technical and quality matters are discussed with the Vice President—Technical Research and his staff. The corporate engineering department is contacted along with corporate technical service group on facilities planning and improvement. The incumbent also represents the company in the National Association of Margarine Manufacturers, the American Oil Chemists' Society, and the Institute of Shortening and Edible Oil Manufactures—each a responsible industry organization. Extensive travel is necessitated by the efforts required to coordinate the many activities under the incumbent's control.

The incumbent has five functional areas over which he exercises control. These are:

1. Manufacturing—Three manufacturing facilities, widely dispersed geographically, are each controlled by a Plant Manager who is responsible for carrying out the processing and packaging activities at his facility.
2. Distribution—Headed by a Distribution Manager, this responsibility includes customer service, orders processing, warehouse and inventory control, and production planning for the division.
3. Traffic—The Traffic Manager leads this group and has the responsibility for providing all transportation needs for raw materials, supplies, ingredients, and finished products for the division.
4. Process Engineering—The Section Head, Process Engineering controls this area and works on projects in this field for the division.
5. Project Engineering—One individual functions in this capacity working on specified activities set out by the incumbent in his field for the division.

The technical nature of the incumbent's position requires a technical degree background along with specific experience in manufacturing management; operations analysis; information systems computer application; chemistry of food products; and engineering application of processing, packaging, utility, and similar equipment. A major problem he encounters is in motivating people who work for him (and some who do not) which requires an ability to get along well with all levels of people. He must also have working background in the fundamentals of cost accounting and control; labor relations; and federal, state, and local regulations. He is required to choose among alternative capital requests, analyze budget variances and sales plans to determine areas needing attention, and aid M.I.S. in the automation of reports and analyses.

The incumbent's activities are regulated somewhat by the needs of the sales departments and their deadline dates, by the Food and Drug Administration, the Meat Inspection Division regulations, various state and local regulations, industry standards, and customer's specifications within the framework of the existing and/or proposed division facilities. He has the responsibility for training and maintaining his own staff primarily through his managers. He has authority to recommend salary changes, make additions to or deletions from the work force, and recommend changes in existing facilities, though a portion of these actions must be approved by a higher authority. Within the framework of existing policy and facilities he may accomplish his objectives in the manner he deems most expeditious.

DIMENSIONS
    Annual Operating Budget:
        Manufacturing $ _____
        Distribution $ _____
        General & Administrative Manufacturing Services $ _____
    Annual Production Volume: _____ pounds of Finished Product
    Average Inventory Value: $ _____
    Value of Capital Assets Maintained: $ _____
    Operating Plants: _____
    Exempt Salaried Employees: _____
    Non-Exempt Salaried Employees: _____
    Non-Exempt Hourly Employees: _____

# MODINE MANUFACTURING COMPANY
## OPERATIONS MANAGER

ACCOUNTABILITY OBJECTIVE
Achieve the highest level of profitability in aluminum products manufacturing facilities by directing plant manufacturing facilities toward optimum efficiency in high quality production to meet company and division objectives and customer requirements.

DIMENSIONS
    Number of plants directed:    4
    Personnel directed:    4 plant managers
    Sales volume generated:

NATURE AND SCOPE
Under the guidance of the divisional manager of operations, this position is charged with the responsibility for coordination of the total manufacturing operations of the aluminum plants of the A&I Division. The incumbent is responsible for determining total plant production capacity as well as the current level of production at each individual plant. He compares future production requirements to plant capabilities and recommends the acceptability of additional business volume to top management.

Much of the incumbent's work is involved in tactical planning covering individual plant and total radiator plant production. This includes planning for modification of existing facilities and recommendations for expansion of present plant capacities. He establishes and interprets operating guidelines for plant managers, setting attainment levels for production to satisfy division objectives and requirements for customer's orders.

Reporting at the same level is the operations manager for radiator plants, the manager of manufacturing engineering, the chief industrial engineer and the manager of claims and warranties. The incumbent works with them in the integration of their functions with the production and products of his plants. Where staff manufacturing or industrial engineers are assigned to his plants, the incumbent keeps tabs on progress of their efforts to assure solution to the problem. Similarly, the incumbent keeps current with studies done by costing or accounting personnel as they affect his plants.

In addition, the incumbent assists division product managers, account representatives and quality control personnel in the solution of customer-related problems. This may involve inspecting with a prospective customer the production facility where his products will be produced.

The incumbent assists in labor contract negotiations, providing consultative assistance to the plant managers, plant personnel managers and corporate industrial relations personnel in developing limits for bargaining. He sits in on all decision-making meetings on labor contract provisions.

The overall responsibility of the position is one of ensuring company management of the continuing effectiveness of the aluminum plants toward a profitable business experience and of actions taking place to improve the profitability of operations. The incumbent constantly reviews reports and analyzes information on manpower, shipments, scrap, cost, labor utilization, workmen's compensation, quality control, insurance, salaries and many others.

SPECIFIC ACCOUNTABILITIES
1. Direct each plant manager in the attainment of production and manufacturing objectives.
2. Ensure profitability of manufacturing operations and performance against budget, by individual plant and total plants.
3. Review and recommend status changes of plant personnel (salary increases, transfers, promotions, et. al.)

# THE LEISURE GROUP, INC.
## OPERATIONS MANAGER

*Basic Function*

The operations manager is responsible for the performance of all manufacturing and engineering activities. It is his responsibility to see that quality products are produced in accordance with acceptable schedule requirements and at budgeted cost or better.

*Reporting Relationships*

|  |  |
|---|---|
| Reports to: | Division General Manager |
| Directly Supervises: | four to eight |
| Type: | Materials Control Manager |
|  | Plant Accountant |
|  | Production Foreman |
|  | Traffic Manager |
|  | Engineering Manager |
|  | Production Manager |
|  | Quality Control Manager |
|  | Personnel Manager |

*Specific Duties*

1. Directs the manufacturing and engineering activities toward the accomplishment of division and plant objectives as specified in annual operating and business plan. Develops and recommends manufacturing and engineering department operating policy.
2. Defines and recommends manufacturing objectives; develops specific short-term and long-range plans and programs together with supporting budget requests and financial estimates.
3. Directs the manufacture of all plant products at lowest cost consistent with established specifications as to quality and quantity. Provides for adequate staffing of organization and sees that staff personnel are properly trained.
4. As required, participates at plant levels in Union contract matters and negotiations in a manner which is consistent with corporate policy and procedure.
5. Supervises installation and maintenance of all processing equipment used in manufacturing.
6. Provides for preparation of cost control reports, cost estimates, manpower and facility requirement forecasts, production and inventory control reports, delivery estimates, etc.
7. Insures prompt and economical receipt of needed materials and supplies and delivery of finished product to customers.
8. Directs the preparation of specifications for purchase as to quality, quan-

tity, delivery and service required for purchase of plant equipment, supplies, and materials to meet production schedules.

9. Sees that adequate inventory controls and levels to conform with budgets and forecasts are maintained to assure satisfactory customer service and delivery at acceptable costs.

10. Formulates and installs standard practices based on comparative studies of methods, costs and production figures.

11. Provides for an adequate control program to assure that finished product consistently meets or exceeds required standards.

12. Establishes and maintains an engineering activity which is adequately staffed with sufficient skills and talents to cope with plant and product engineering and design matters. Provides engineering collaboration to marketing and product management in matters of product engineering and design.

---

# SUNDSTRAND CORPORATION
## MANAGER, MATERIEL

GENERAL STATEMENT

Plans, directs and controls activities relating to purchase, production scheduling, movement and storage of materials used in manufacture of Division products. Develops and installs policies and procedures to assure efficient operation of areas supervised, and works with other department managers to resolve problems affecting production schedules and delivery commitments. Responsible for operating within the scope of company policies, and according to budgetary limitations. Works toward continued improvement of operations, and keeps immediate supervisor informed of progress in meeting schedules and overall goals.

Reports to: Plant Manager

DUTIES AND RESPONSIBILITIES

1. Plans and organizes activities having to do with acquisition, distribution, movement and storage of material; exercises control over departments such as Purchasing, Production Planning and Control, Material Handling, Stockrooms and Shipping and Receiving.

2. Directs and authorizes preparation of production master schedules to reflect manufacturing capacities, available manpower, delivery dates, etc., and assures coordination of the purchasing function with this activity.

3. Develops and maintains methods of communication on schedule fulfillment, delays, and changes.

4. Responsible for inventory control consistent with Division requirements, and to assure preparation for periods of high and low product demand.

5. Meets periodically with Division management personnel to discuss and resolve problems involving production scheduling, engineering, manufacturing, shipping, labor relations, etc.

6. Assures that materials, supplies, parts and assemblies are transported and stored in an efficient manner within the plant, and that shipments are prepared in accordance with customer requirements.

7. Establishes and/or approves budgets for departments supervised and implements controls necessary to keep expenditures within such budgetary limitations. Reviews various reports from subordinates to determine expenditures as related to budgetary allowances.

8. Prepares periodic reports or other data for presentation to immediate supervisor indicating record of achievement on established goals, recommended improvements, projected personnel requirements, etc.

9. Directs continuing effort toward cost reduction and control in areas of authority. Stimulates development of ideas, programs and new approaches among subordinates.

10. Periodically reviews performance of subordinates and recommends salary adjustments accordingly. Also recommends or makes determinations on such matters as promotions, transfers, hiring, disciplinary action, etc.

11. Provides for and authorizes training programs to assure a high level of skill and proficiency among employees supervised.

12. Remains familiar with provisions of the Labor Agreement as they affect areas of responsibility, resolves legitimate complaints or grievances and assures equitable treatment of all employees.

13. Performs related miscellaneous duties or other assignments as directed.

---

# A MANUFACTURING COMPANY
## PRODUCTION MANAGER

FUNCTION

Under administrative guidance of General Manager, manages production, maintenance, warehousing, and engineering functions, and is responsible for the over-all performance of factory operations.

DUTIES

1. Establishes policies and objectives for plant manufacturing operations within Division guidelines with the General Manager, and implements programs and procedures to make them effective.

2. Communicates policies and objectives to supervisors and subordinates and gives general direction in organization, controls, and procedures to carry out policies and achieve objectives.
3. Monitors manufacturing expenses, costs, waste and various other performance measures, evaluates performance to identify problems, and takes corrective action as necessary.
4. Sees that effective programs are operating in the following areas: quality control, waste control, safety, production incentives, preventive maintenance, purchasing, employment, housekeeping, employee training, and inventory control.
5. Establishes appropriate local policy and procedures for selection, hiring, training, compensation, appraisal, counsel, discipline, and termination of all supervisory, engineering, and factory personnel.
6. Develops plans for improvement and/or expansion of plant facilities and equipment and recommends to General Manager.
7. Sees that an effective labor relations program is implemented and assists in the negotiation of collective bargaining agreements.
8. Reviews the performance of Superintendent and Industrial Engineer; and counsels with them to achieve effective performance.

RELATIONSHIPS
1. Accountable to the plant General Manager for the fulfillment of his function.
2. Provides leadership for all manufacturing employees and is the direct supervisor of the Superintendent and Industrial Engineer.
3. Coordinates total plant efforts with Office Manager and the Sales Office Staff.
4. Frequent contact with customers, suppliers, and service agencies in the performance of his function.
5. Maintains functional relationships with Division Production and Engineering staff.
6. Maintains production counseling relationship with sheet plant superintendent.

---

U. S. BORAX
MANAGER OF PRODUCTION PLANNING

STATEMENT OF JOB
Responsible to the Materials Manager for overall planning and scheduling of production and inventory of borate products to meet Company sales requirements generated by the Marketing Department; plan and direct the operation of the bulk shipping program; provide a primary channel of communication and coordination between the Production, Marketing, and Technical Departments relative to matters of product supply, customer specifications, service, and com-

plaints; ensure coordination of the marketing, distribution, inventory, and production objectives, represent the Production Department on the Specifications and Bag Specification Committees.

DUTIES OF JOB

1. Direct the development of annual and monthly production and inventory plans which will optimize production and inventory costs and insure finished product availability to meet sales requirements generated by the Marketing Department; determine both inventory levels and warehouse locations, except for potash products, to meet this objective.
2. Oversee the coordination of production, distribution, and inventory objectives to ensure consistency with marketing objectives. Oversee the establishment of economic product runs and optimum inventory levels for products.
3. Advise the Marketing Department of the physical and economic capabilities and limitations of production and distribution so that they may establish optimum customer service objectives.
4. Insure that product and inventory plans are understood and followed by the individual plants insofar as possible; analyze actual sales trends in comparison with budgets and production capacities; when necessary, coordinate with plant personnel in adjusting production and inventory plans to meet production and cost contingencies.
5. Distribute production requirements between plants as it is necessary to achieve production, distribution, and inventory efficiency.
6. Direct the operation of the bulk shipping program, scheduling shipments in such a way as to optimize costs, including shipping charges, product mix (bulk and bags), inventory levels in silo, use of supplemental barge storage, etc., establish long-term plans for the program.
7. Coordinate with interests outside the Company relative to the bulk shipping program including BCL/BNV, and others as necessary; coordinate with the Manager of Distribution concerning contract provisions relative to the bulk shipping program.
8. Analyze or assist in analyzing delivery expenses, and develop recommendations to improve distribution costs. Analyze long-range sales projections and compare these with existing and planned plant capacities; cooperate with other departments in production capacity and capability relative to product quality and cost reduction.
9. Establish production scheduling priorities when products are in short supply and coordinate with the Distribution section in all matters of mutual interest, such as railroad car availability, rates, lease tracks, etc., supplement the direct communication between the Distribution section and the Production plants, assisting as necessary in solving any shipping or scheduling problems.
10. Coordinate, either personally or through the Production coordinators, Production section activities with the Marketing Department on all non-routine matters, including product quality, customer complaints, loading and pack-

aging problems, ability to produce, promotions of 20 Mule Team Products, cost information, and general sales needs.

11. Review and summarize overall quality complaint trends, suggesting remedies as indicated; analyze and develop comparisons of Company and competitor product quality trends; direct the development of data for the Product Specifications Committee; represent the Production Department on the Committee, recommending acceptance or rejection of specification changes according to the best interest of the Company.

12. Participate in the solution of questions of quality involving shipment of "questionable" products, and ship-hold conditions; when necessary, render final decisions in the bulk shipping program on whether to ship material.

13. Coordinate packaging studies to establish optimum cost package/container; bag specifications; analyze finished product material handling and shipping methods; oversee determination of customer needs and costs for special types of packs.

14. Keep abreast of packaging development and recommend new equipment, material, and procedures; maintain close liaison with Purchasing personnel concerning bags, packages, and containers; serve as Chairman of the Packaging Committee.

15. Coordinate with the Technical Department relative to new product formulations or processing procedures to improve quality and/or reduce costs; recommend installation of capital facilities when needed for capacity, product quality, and cost reduction.

16. Maintain records of sales and production statistics, summarizing information to facilitate analysis and interpretation.

17. Review various product and cost reports to identify potential areas for cost reduction efforts; perform cost studies as requested.

The statements made on these pages are primarily for purposes of job classification and are not intended as a complete description of all work requirements that may be inherent in the job. Minor changes in work assignment will not necessitate revision hereof.

---

## STAUFFER CHEMICAL COMPANY
### PLANT MANAGER

FUNCTION

The Plant Manager is responsible to the Production Manager for the operation of the plant in the manufacture of carbon tetrachloride, chlorine, caustic soda, and other chemicals.

RESPONSIBILITIES

1. Plan, direct, and control plant operations including production, process development, engineering, cost and quality control, maintenance, safety and loss control, employee relations and ancillary functions such as traffic and inventory.
2. As directed by the Production Manager, coordinate and implement construction and start-up of special plant projects in conjunction with Engineering and Research and Development Departments.
3. Direct investigation of customer complaints and take necessary corrective action.
4. Advise and assist Area Employee Relations Manager in negotiating agreements with employee groups and labor unions and administer agreements as approved.
5. Prepare budget and capital expenditure forecasts and initiate and approve appropriation requests and other expenditures within company approval limits.
6. Provide for and review reports pertaining to production, inventories, scheduling, quality control, costs, efficiencies, safety, plant security and personnel, and take corrective action, as indicated, informing and consulting with the Production Manager and divisional staffs, as necessary.
7. Establish and maintain relationship with community officials, other organizations, regulatory authorities, other plant managers, divisional and staff personnel as necessary to manage the plant.

POSITION REQUIREMENTS

A. *Knowledge and Experience*
College degree or equivalent in chemical engineering, chemistry, or related field.

Expert working knowledge of appropriate plant production processes and equipment; management skills; thorough working knowledge of plant engineering and quality control; background knowledge in traffic, purchasing, accounting, and general office functions.

Ten to fifteen years' experience in chemical plant production processes, methods and techniques with emphasis on the manufacture of carbon tetrachloride, chlorine, and caustic soda, or other industrial chemicals, including approximately seven years in managing production activities.

B. *Supervision:* Direct

| | |
|---|---|
| 1 Production Superintendent | 1 Plant Engineer |
| 1 Maintenance Supervisor | 1 Office Manager |

C. *Supervision:* Indirect

| | |
|---|---|
| 2 Production Supervisors | 1 Plant Accountant |
| 8–10 Production Foremen | 1 Plant Chemist |

2 Maintenance Foremen            2 Lab Technicians
2 Production Engineers           5–7 Clerical personnel
2 Process Engineers              100–125 Hourly personnel

TOTAL Direct and Indirect 129–158

D. *Accountability*

Cost of Annual Production $ _____        Total Number of Products _____

Plant Replacement Value $ _____

May approve expenditures, without *specific* prior approval, up to a maximum of _____.

---

# A CONSUMER PRODUCTS MANUFACTURER
## PLANT MANAGER

STATEMENT OF THE JOB

Under the direction of the Vice President, Manufacturing, directs, supervises, coordinates and controls all plant activities. Produces all manufactured products in accordance with established quality standards and at economical costs. Maintains all plant facilities and equipment and assures a clean and orderly manufacturing environment.

DUTIES OF THE JOB

1. To manufacture products to meet the requirements of approved production plans at minimum cost, within quality limits and consistent with F.D.A. Good Manufacturing Practices.

2. To manufacture all products according to written product-quality standards and specifications.

3. To direct the maintenance of an approved system of control reports to permit responsible individuals to exercise control over costs, product quality, production and other critical factors.

4. To analyze results of plant operations and determine variances from standard. To correct the conditions causing the variances, informing the Vice President, Manufacturing of the action taken.

5. To prepare the capital budgets for improvement, re-equipment and expansion of the plant and offices.

6. To administer the expenditure of funds to carry on plant operations.

7. To arrange for the procurement of raw materials, packaging materials and operating supplies to meet local production requirements. To supervise the procurement of maintenance equipment and supplies according to policy.

8. To develop improved manufacturing methods, layouts, equipment and techniques and submit recommendations to the Vice President, Manufac-

turing for their adoption. These recommendations must include the necessary justification.

9. To conduct a continuous cost-reduction program throughout the entire plant.
10. To administer personnel policy in accordance with corporate policy, using the advice and counsel of the Director of Personnel.
11. To administer a program for safety, hygiene and fire protection to safeguard the health and welfare of the personnel and preserve the plant facilities.
12. To maintain the plant building, equipment and grounds in good operating condition and appearance.
13. To recruit, train and develop the necessary personnel to staff the plant for the forecast level of operations.

# REXNORD
## SUPERINTENDENT, HEAVY MACHINERY FABRICATION AND ASSEMBLY OPERATIONS

### I. GENERAL RESPONSIBILITY

Direct, supervise and coordinate all areas of production and related services through subordinate General Foreman and Foreman to achieve timely production of quality products at the most economical costs and in the proper quantities. This includes Process Equipment and Conveyor product lines applicable to the Heavy Machinery manufacturing facility. Also the manufacture of Heavy Machinery related products for Construction Machinery. The manufacture of these product lines includes piece parts, welding, assembly, and shipping.

### II. AUTHORITY RELATIONSHIPS

Acts under direct line authority from the Heavy Machinery Factory Manager.

### III. SPECIFIC RESPONSIBILITIES

A. Supervises directly General Foreman with respect to departmental personnel, cost, delivery schedules, and operation.
B. To supervise the efficient utilization of plant facilities and personnel.
C. To maintain and develop both a facility and work force capable of meeting manufacturing requirements in the present and future to accomplish objectives in accordance with production and delivery schedules.

    D. Maintain a facility which meets the company's goals in the area of safety and good working conditions.

    E. Act as liaison between management and the work force to keep plant supervision informed, avoid breach of contract, and maintain highest possible level of employer-employee relationship.

    F. To develop an operating budget plan for each department. Then initiate action to operate within those fiscal plans.

REPORTS TO:

Factory Manager, Heavy Machinery Operations

DIRECT SUPERVISORY RESPONSIBILITY FOR:

    5 General Foremen
    16 Foremen
    335 Production Shop Employees

MONETARY RESPONSIBILITY

(Expressed on an annual basis in terms of departmental budget, sales volume, sales quota, payroll, goods purchased, value added in manufacturing, etc.)

$x$ Million Dollars — Factory budgets (including direct labor)
$x$ Million Dollars — (Construction Machinery Sales Volume)
                            (Process Equipment Sales Volume)
                            (Conveyor Sales Volume)

PRACTICAL SPECIALIZED OR TECHNICAL KNOW-HOW

(What does the incumbent have to know to function in the job?)

    A. To interpret and administer company policies, work rules, regulations and union contract.

    B. Detailed knowledge of plant equipment functions and applications to manufacturing processes.

    C. Basic knowledge of departmental activities as related to the manufacturing organization. These departments include Sales, Engineering, Methods and Production.

    D. A general engineering background related to plant facilities and product lines, gained by either formal education or experience.

    E. A sound understanding of financial matters such as budgeting, costing as related to factory cost, and capital equipment.

HUMAN RELATIONS KNOW-HOW

(What does the incumbent have to do with or about people which indicates the qualitative skills in human relations required by the job?)

    1. Develop and maintain an effective working relationship with representatives of the bargaining unit in order to implement significant changes beneficial to the company and to assist in the settlement of contract problems and grievances.

    2. Supervise and train supervisory personnel by directing their activities, and through them the activities of the entire work force under his responsibility.

3. Develop a rapport with staff department personnel such as engineering, sales, personnel, methods and production in order to efficiently maintain operations.

MANAGERIAL KNOW-HOW

(What does the incumbent have to do about managing, i.e., integrating and coordinating diverse activities, contributions to planning and policy formulation?)

1. Through motivating techniques, delegation of authority and responsibility to subordinates, coordinate diverse activities such as actual manufacturing, staffing, training, and employee relations.
2. Formulate operating policies for Plants 3 and 4 within the guidelines of overall company policies and union contract rules.
3. Plan the use of facilities, equipment and personnel to meet current and future manufacturing requirements. This includes using departmental budgets as guidelines, plant layout and improvement, and capital expenditure programs.

PROBLEM SOLVING

(What are the job's requirements for original thinking, i.e., analyzing, reasoning, developing new methods, policies, products, ideas, etc.?)

1. To solve problems involving work flow, utilization of personnel skills, machines and facility to assure an efficient and expedient manufacturing process.
2. Maintain sound labor relations in order to obtain significant solutions beneficial to the company, especially those involving interpretation of union contract and settlement of grievances.

# THE MAYTAG COMPANY
## CHIEF METHODS ENGINEER

*Reports to:*   Manager, Production Engineering

**I** *Character of the Job* (Nature and Scope)

This position exists to manage the Methods Engineering Department which is responsible for the evaluation, development and improvement of manufacturing methods, layouts and material handling equipment. This department is also responsible for providing cost estimates on all types of existing or proposed manufacturing methods and for systematic planning and expediting progress of major engineering projects. The incumbent is guided by general directions from Manager, Production Engineering. The position involves considerable investigation and development of highly coordinated long range plans which result in efficient manufacturing methods being completed on schedule.

The position requires a seasoned background in mechanical engineering; knowledge of Maytag production facilities, methods, handling equipment and manufacturing goals; keeping current on new methods available; ability to plan and coordinate involved projects including efforts from many Maytag departments and vendors; and using management and administrative skills in directing staff.

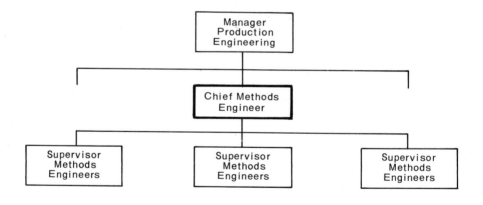

**II** *Statistical Data*

Staff of three supervisors and 20–25 engineers, draftsmen, technicians and clerks. Budget is $ _____. Annual cost of manufacturing: $ _____.

**III** *Accountabilities* (End Results)

1. Comprehensive evaluation of layouts, manufacturing methods and material handling equipment. This involves:

a. Assuring the maintenance of records and preparation of reports to measure the effectiveness of existing facilities and methods.
b. Evaluating effectiveness of facilities and methods for current and projected manufacturing schedules.
c. Appraising technological developments in this field and investigating feasibility of new equipment and techniques for application at Maytag.
d. Assuring that dependable cost estimates are prepared to guide management in evaluating alternate proposals.

2. Provision of systematic planning and coordination service to achieve orderly and timely completion of major projects involving various engineering and line staffs, vendors and contractors. This involves:
   a. Participating with top management in the development of long range plans for major layout changes, preparing for manufacture of new products, incorporation of new processes or equipment, etc.
   b. Directing staff in the use of systematic planning techniques to plan integrated steps, estimate progress schedules, and identify problem areas.
   c. Coordinating efforts of various Maytag departments, vendors and contractors to assure timely progress in completing major projects.
   d. Expediting segments of project to avoid costly delays.

3. Provision of efficient manufacturing layouts and production operation methods. This involves:
   a. Assuring thorough analysis of factors and planning and proficient designing by staff.
   b. Reviewing and approving proposals to assure efficient production methods, flow of work and utilization of space.
   c. Guiding staff in obtaining approvals, expediting progress and resolving problems encountered.
   d. Following completed projects to assure that anticipated benefits are achieved.

4. Provision of effective material handling equipment such as conveyors, containers and trucks. This involves:
   a. Assuring that staff proposals include factors such as efficiency, dependability, quality and safety.
   b. Evaluating bids for equipment and services and recommending selection of vendors and contractors.
   c. Assuring that equipment and installation service meets specifications and time schedules.
   d. Resolving problems previous to final payment for equipment and services, and release of facilities for production.
   e. Directing the fabrication and refinement of mechanical handling working models previous to authorizing installation in production areas.

5. Provision of effective cost analysis work for manufacturing division. This involves:
   a. Assuring that staff utilizes efficient and consistent methods of gathering and analyzing cost data.
   b. Providing interpretation and evaluation of cost analyses to other manufacturing management personnel.
   c. Assuring prompt handling of requests for cost analysis work and cooperation between departments involved.

6. Proficient management of staff and equipment in area of accountability. This involves:
   a. Selecting and developing subordinates, evaluating performance of individuals and recommending salary adjustments, promotions and manpower rebalancing.
   b. Establishing priorities, delegating areas of responsibility, assigning projects, coordinating activities and expediting progress.
   c. Administering company policies and rules related to various personnel situations.
   d. Providing written and verbal reports regarding status of projects, performance of material handling equipment, etc.
   e. Controlling department expenditures and recommending cost reduction ideas for any area of manufacturing.

---

# NORTON COMPANY
## (*Industrial Ceramics Division*)
### SENIOR MANUFACTURING ENGINEER

*Reports to:*    Superintendent, Ceramic Components

ACCOUNTABILITY OBJECTIVE

To develop and design new processes for production and to improve present processes in order to achieve better quality and lower costs, to provide general technical support for the Ceramic Components unit, act as technical advisor to Manufacturing Engineers and Production Supervisors, especially in new product areas.

DIMENSIONS
Sales Volume Support:    $ _____
                         Personnel: One Technical Assistant

NATURE AND SCOPE

*Organization and Relationships*
The Senior Manufacturing Engineer reports to the Superintendent of Ceramic

Components along with production foreman, production engineers and manufacturing engineers. He is the recognized technical manufacturing authority for the product lines involved and advises other manufacturing engineers in their projects and daily problem solving. His technical assistant performs various tests, inspections, trials, oversees new items in production, maintains records and assists with problems of production.

PRODUCT AND PROCESS DESCRIPTION

Wear resistant products occupy a limited but important part in industry, particularly heavy industry for sand blasting, and its composition boron carbide exhibits unique properties in thermal neutron capture and as control rod material for reactor control in nuclear applications. Although basically of one chemical composition, its molded form comes in an almost infinite variety of shapes, many of which pose unusual problems in mold design and fabrication. Density requirements demand values close to theoretical having uniform microstructure. Appurtenant support processes are milling, treatment and impurity removal and performing.

Since the hot pressing technique is fundamental to the emerging new product technologies, a well-grounded professional background complemented by a broad experience is vital in these areas where the state of the art is still imperfectly understood.

FUNCTIONS

The Senior Manufacturing Engineer determines his own programs to control and improve manufacturing processes and product quality based on his evaluation of existing problems and conditions and the state of the art within and without the company. He develops projects and accepts assignments recommended by others subject to the approval of the Superintendent of Ceramic Components.

He maintains an engineering data log book on details of each project and reports verbally and in writing at key points in quarterly progress reports and upon the conclusion of each project. He meets with the Superintendent of Ceramic Components regularly to review progress and to re-establish priorities.

The incumbent serves as a consultant to other manufacturing engineers and to the Research and Development section. He suggests possible solutions and methods of approach to these problems. Based on his experience and knowledge, he helps them analyze findings and recommends solutions or alternative paths toward solutions.

The incumbent spends the major portion of his time pursuing major projects aimed at substantial improvements in cost and quality. He evaluates and investigates new equipment and processes on the market. He works with plant engineers in designing special purpose machinery and equipment for the product lines. This involves visits to other installations, vendor plants and customers to observe equipment, product use and methods in order to determine our production needs.

Other projects involve the study of the characteristics of basic raw materials to improve product quality. This involves physical, chemical, x-ray and size analysis determination and the effects of these on our processes and quality.

The Senior Manufacturing Engineer works closely with research engineers in developing and testing new products before they are introduced into production. The development of a new product may require new methods of production including new equipment and different materials. Based on the results of research and their recommended specifications, he designs the process flow and specifies the equipment and the operations. He is responsible for the major installation of new products and processes.

He is a member of the Product Management team and assists the cost reduction committee.

### KNOW-HOW REQUIRED
The Senior Manufacturing Engineer requires extensive experience and expertise in ceramic engineering, chemical engineering, mechanical engineering, product use, materials, processes, testing and evaluation techniques. He must have good planning ability, a strong analytical sense and sound engineering approaches. Human relations skills are needed to train, persuade, influence and motivate others such as engineers, foremen, and staff and production personnel.

### ACTIVITIES
The Senior Manufacturing Engineer spends most of his time on long range projects with other time devoted to consulting, daily production problems and competitive evaluations. In the pursuit of his projects he has regular contact with customers, vendors, supervision, other engineers, plant engineers, accountants, and research engineers. Other contacts are with product engineers, purchasing, buyers and production people. He has frequent contact with Division Management.

### CHALLENGE
The thrust of the job is to provide the necessary technical back up for the established current product lines with heavy emphasis on the anticipated influx of new product families evolving from the Research and Development section, thus enabling the transition from laboratory, to pilot stage, to full efficient production, to take place quickly and effectively through strong experienced technical know-how.

### SPECIFIC ACCOUNTABILITIES
1. Oversee and advise technical control for all phases of production.
2. Periodically examine unit processes for up-dating techniques, quality and overall efficiency.
3. Institute meaningful cost reduction programs in the same areas.

4. Recommend and specify new materials and/or equipment when desirable.
5. Give functional guidance to technical assistant and other manufacturing engineers as needed.
6. Work closely with Research and Development groups to implement emerging new product lines into production.
7. Write complete manufacturing instructions as new products are approved for production.
8. Carry out special assignments and projects in broad areas upon request of the Superintendent of Ceramic Components.
9. Provide general and specific technical knowledge where needed to achieve the stated goals of management by objective.

---

# MCDONNELL DOUGLAS CORPORATION
## MANAGER, PLANT DESIGN AND MAINTENANCE ENGINEERING

*Responsible to:* Director, Plant Engineering, MCAIR

PRIMARY FUNCTION

To plan, organize and manage the activities of all personnel engaged in plant design and maintenance engineering activities and provide liaison support to maintenance and construction functions.

*See also MCDONNELL Position Description*
*"All Supervisors & Managers"*

TYPICAL DUTIES
1. Monitors the:
   a. Design, development and implementation of plant structural, mechanical and electrical components for proposed plant construction and/or modification of existing facilities.
   b. Preparation of technical information/reports required by management to evaluate need, cost and/or expenditures of proposed Plant Engineering projects.
   c. Preparation and review of preliminary design studies to eliminate major changes or redesign after drawing completion.
2. Develops and monitors engineering procedures and drafting room practices to simplify drawings, and expedite the completion of designs.
3. Provides consulting services, engineering studies, etc., required by management to develop utility systems, equipment installations and facility requirements.

4. Reviews design drawings for adequacy and completeness, for application of sound design and drafting practices and for compliance with company/department/governmental standards and/or requirements.
5. Evaluates existing and proposed facilities to improve operating and maintenance efficiency or to ensure economical design and construction.
6. Ensures the development of a maintenance engineering program designed to establish maintenance material standards and specifications, lubrication requirements, standard maintenance procedures and maintenance methods studies/improvements.
7. Represents Plant Design and Maintenance Engineering at management, other company, municipal, federal/state/local and other meetings as required.

SUPERVISION EXERCISED:   Directly 5–7; Indirectly 50–80

NORMAL BACKGROUND AND EXPERIENCE REQUIREMENTS
Requires a Bachelor's degree in Industrial, Civil, Structural, Architectural or Electrical Engineering or equivalent design/maintenance engineering experience. Must have a thorough knowledge of company organization, policies and administrative procedures. Ten or more years of Plant Design and Maintenance or related experience is normally required for satisfactory performance.

---

# THE MAYTAG COMPANY
## PURCHASING AGENT (METALS)

*Reports to:*   Director of Purchases

I *Character of the Job* (Nature and Scope)
This position exists primarily to buy all the various types of metal needed by The Maytag Company in conformance to established policies and delivery schedules; position also includes purchasing of other miscellaneous assigned items. The position involves spending a major portion of time buying metal and devoting a lesser portion of time in supervising a subordinate buyer and two clerks. Incumbent is expected to carry out delegated responsibilities with limited supervision, but Director of Purchases is available to provide guidance in handling unusual or critical problems.

The position requires considerable metal-buying experience; knowledge of Maytag purchasing policies and procedures, characteristics and production requirements of metals used at Maytag, available sources of supply and current trends in supply market; ability to supervise small staff; and exercising human relations skills in dealing with vendor representatives and Maytag personnel. The position requires prompt response to situations such as defective lots of material, labor or transportation strikes and major production level changes.

II *Statistical Data*
Annual metal-buying volume is approximately $ _____.

III *Accountabilities* (End Results)
1. Selection and development of reliable vendors that effectively fulfill the needs of Maytag at minimum cost. This involves:
   a. Interviewing vendor representatives, verifying financial ratings of firms and visiting plants to appraise proposed vendor's capability of supplying material to Maytag.
   b. Negotiating terms of purchase agreements and buying contracts with vendor representatives, and recommending vendors and terms to superior.
   c. Informing vendors of Maytag policies, quality requirements, delivery schedules, etc.
   d. Developing cooperative business relationships between vendors and Maytag.
2. Assuring that vendor performance conforms to Maytag terms for quality and delivery schedules. This involves:
   a. Appraising quality of purchased material through reports from inspection and engineering departments, and working with vendors and Maytag departments to resolve quality problems.
   b. Collaborating with inventory control, traffic and vendors to resolve problems related to shipping damage, delayed arrivals, deviations in size of shipments, identification of metal, etc.
3. Effective control of metal inventories in conformance to company guide lines, condition of stock on hand, and status of vendors' production ability. This involves:
   a. Analyzing weekly sheet metal register (prepared by data processing) to assess status of various types of stock.

    b. Taking appropriate action to avoid shortages, balance inventories, correct record discrepancies, etc.

    c. Working with scheduling personnel to resolve discrepancies in records, assure proper disposition of reject material, accumulate data for processing of freight claims, etc.

4. Prompt and accurate processing of requisitions, purchase orders, invoices, etc. related to area of accountability. This involves:

    a. Reviewing and approving requisitions, purchase orders and invoices, correcting discrepancies; and expediting flow of paper work.

    b. Assuring that pertinent reports and records are prepared, analyzed and maintained.

5. Perceptive appraisal of business, material and labor trends and planning of purchasing functions to assure continuing production. This involves:

    a. Keeping current on developments such as potential strikes, vendor performance changes, new vendors entering market, production changes, etc.

    b. Anticipating effect of above changes on Maytag sources of supply and transportation industry and developing strategy which allows Maytag to effectively respond to adverse or changing conditions.

6. Effective disposition of metal scrap generated from production operations. This involves:

    a. Reviewing records of scrap available for sale.

    b. Communicating with prospective buyers to secure best price.

    c. Resolving problems as to quality of scrap, discrepancies in weights, etc.

7. Significant contribution to control and reduction of material and other manufacturing costs. This involves:

    a. Assuring competitive price bidding from two or more reputable vendors.

    b. Initiating ideas for cost reduction and soliciting ideas from subordinates.

    c. Collaborating with other departments such as engineering, accounting and traffic to develop and evaluate proposed improvements.

    d. Implementing the incorporation of changes such as buy to make at Maytag, adding or cancelling a vendor and use of different materials.

8. Effective supervision and development of subordinate buyer and clerks. This involves:

    a. Planning subordinate staff requirements and delegation of functions, and recommending changes to superior.

    b. Training, evaluating performance, motivating and recommending salary adjustments and promotions for subordinates.

    c. Administering company policies and rules as they relate to supervision of subordinates.

d. Advising superior of unusual or critical problems and soliciting his guidance as required.

9. Presenting company image of integrity in contacts with vendors, carriers and public. This involves:
   a. Conducting transactions in a courteous and ethical manner.
   b. Assuring that selection of vendors is determined without prejudice and results in greatest benefit to Maytag.
   c. Building a mutual respect and confidence between vendors and Maytag Company.

## *Manufacturing—Finance*

# AN OIL COMPANY
## TREASURER

### FUNCTION
Serves as the chief custodial officer of Company funds (24 separate corporations), administers and assumes responsibility for (1) management of Company funds and investments, (2) custody and safekeeping of all Company funds, securities and other written evidences of indebtedness, (3) general credit and collection operations, (4) insuring Company properties and personnel against loss and liability, (5) maintaining bank relationships.

Participates in contract negotiations, financing arrangements on purchase and sales transactions, and initiation of other similar business relationships with outside parties.

Advises and consults on divisional operations and other corporate matters. Sets company policy with respect to the activities under his jurisdiction.

### GUIDANCE RECEIVED
Under the general direction of the Vice President, Finance and Planning.

### NATURE OF POSITION
The activities of this position are grouped under three major functions:

### 1. TREASURER
In this capacity this position is concerned with managing and directing the handling of Company funds to:
   a. accelerate collections and arrange for depository bank facilities.

   b. retain payments as long as possible without losing discounts or damaging credit rating.

   c. ensure adequacy of bank balances and maintain bank relationships.

   d. invest excess cash in short-term securities.

   e. measure risk, liquidity, and marketability of short-term investments and select appropriate securities to maximize income.

   f. issue commercial paper or borrow under revolving credit agreement as required.

   g. advise Manager, Financial Planning and superior regarding possible level of participation of various banks in loan agreements and assist in securing bank participation as requested.

   h. carry out legal requirements of debt obligations incurred through issuance of debentures, notes, and credit agreements.

   i. negotiate contracts for Brinks, Inc. and armored car service.

   j. negotiate contracts with collection attorney and similar collection agencies.

   k. safekeep certificates of stock and notes receivable.

2. DIVISION MANAGER

Directs operation of the Treasurer's Division of the Finance and Planning Department which includes:

*Treasurer's Administrative Group* (8 F.T.E. employees) General administration of control function, external communications with banking community and staff work for policy decisions.

*Cash Unit* (Approximately 19 F.T.E. employees) Control of cash receipts, disbursements, cash balances, and investments under supervision of Assistant Treasurer.

*Credit and Collection Unit* (6 F.T.E. employees) Control of general credit policies of credit and collection operation and supplying staff counsel and guidance on all credit activities.

*Insurance and Claims Unit* (7 F.T.E. employees) Execution of Company risk and liability insurance. Handling of claims work, workmen's compensation, bonding of employees, contracts, etc.

3. STAFF MEMBER OF CORPORATE MANAGEMENT

In this capacity the Treasurer is concerned with internal and external relationships:

*External Relationships:*

Acts and speaks on behalf of the corporation in public, civic, industry, and government affairs when delegated to do so by senior officers.

Serves on boards and fund raising committees when it is in the interest and within objectives of the corporation to promote eleemosynary endeavors.

Maintains relationships with finance companies with respect to commercial paper issuance or purchase.

Maintains relationships with banks and receives bank officers to discuss Company banking matters.

*Internal Relationships:*
Counsels and advises corporate management with respect to forecasting banking, credits, collections, insurance, and cash reporting.
Serves as alternate member of S.E.I.P. Committee.
Cooperates with Vice President and Controller, to ensure establishment of appropriate accounting and financial controls.
Coordinates his efforts with other corporate executives in furtherance of Company objectives.
Advises and counsels division, region and general managers on treasury matters.
Authorizes investigation and prosecution or disciplining of Company employees in embezzlement cases.

The following are illustrative of the activities of this position:

1. Directs the study, analysis and forecasting of the Company's daily cash flow.
2. Assists in developing financing plans for lease, short-term funds, bank loans and promissory note flotation.
3. Signs tax returns and assumes general corporate officer's responsibility for accuracy thereof.
4. Appraises economic conditions of money market for most profitable timing of investments in purchase and sale of short-term securities.
5. Controls allocation of cash disbursements; coordinates payments for payrolls, taxes, dividends, interest, sinking fund, etc.
6. Establishes organization structures for assigned activities with approval of superior; defines functional responsibilities of supervisors; selects key personnel; advises on the selection and placement and development of nonsupervisory personnel; appraises performance of supervisors; approves salary recognition within delegated limits.
7. Directs record keeping and procedures to account for receipts and disbursements; arranges for adequate banking facilities for field collection and transmission of funds; investigates most efficient way to handle bank funds received in field offices; maintains custody of security investments, notes and loans and arranges for their safekeeping by approved financial institutions.
8. Directs company insurance and claims activity, reviewing experience, costs and claims, and confers with the Manager, Insurance and Credit, on plans and proposals for new, improved and revised programs.
9. Supplies staff counsel and assistance on credit and collection activities to the operating departments; reviews current credit conditions and proposed credit policies and procedures. Retains custody of debtor (distributor) collateral pledged for securing accounts.
10. Sees that proper Company relations are maintained with about 800 banks (1187 bank accounts) to open accounts, authorize signatures and

    secure adequate service at minimum cost; arranges for foreign exchange and banking facilities for foreign operations.

11. Submits reports to superior and Board of Directors on cash position, analysis of investments, investment inventory and other figures for financial planning or forecasting.

12. Recommends and advises the Manager, Financial Planning, and superior on bank loans and agreements when additional funds are needed to finance corporate objectives, goals and projects.

13. Speaks on treasury matters before employee groups when requested by department.

ACCOUNTABILITY

This position is accountable for providing for the safe and efficient receipt, custody, and disbursement of funds; the profitable investment of surplus cash; the protection of Company interests through an adequate program of property and casualty insurance; and the staff assistance to ensure sound extension of credit for 24 corporations and three affiliates, of which the parent Company Treasurer is a similar officer in such subsidiaries and affiliates.

| | |
|---|---|
| Annual cash receipts | $ _____ |
| Annual cash disbursements | $ _____ |
| Daily average cash and securities controlled | $ _____ |
| Commercial notes sold in market | $ _____ |
| Revolving bank credit | $ _____ |
| Bank term loan | $ _____ |
| Short-term investments purchased | $ _____ |
| Short-term investment income | $ _____ |
| Liability coverage | $ _____ |
| Property protection coverage | $ _____ |
| Liability and property protection premiums | $ _____ |
| Annual expense budget | $ _____ |
| Annual capital budget | $ _____ |

# U. S. BORAX
## CONTROLLER

STATEMENT OF JOB

Reports directly to the Senior Vice President, Finance. Exercises responsibility as the Corporation's chief financial control officer and directs corporate accounting, financial planning and budgeting activities.

Duties of Job

1. Formulate, recommend, and implement financial control policy for the Corporation. Advise the Senior Vice President on all matters affecting financial control policy. Provide liaison with the Corporation's independent auditors.

2. Assure that: (a) books of legal requirement are properly kept and retained for the Corporation and for its U.S. subsidiaries; (b) all recording and reporting requirements are met for management, stockholders, and regulatory agencies as required by law; and (c) accounting operations are effectively and efficiently performed.

3. Maintain effective financial control over the assets and liabilities, income, and disbursements of the company, including land and property, capital expenditures, inventories, etc.; coordinate with the Production Department in the taking and pricing of physical inventories.

4. Prepare periodic financial, analytical, and interpretive reports for management; provide statistical and analytical services to departments; assist the Marketing Department in the formulation of pricing policy and provide information for pricing review and analysis.

5. Set high standards of professional, technical, and business conduct and competence for department personnel; coordinate staffing and allocation of department resources as appropriate to accomplish objectives of individual managers.

6. Coordinate with other Financial Department managers and with all departments or functional areas of the company in maintaining proper financial control.

7. Direct a comprehensive budgetary program.

8. Through continuing contact with responsible departments in the Corporation, keep abreast of operating plans which have significant effect on financial projections including manning, capital expenditures, operating programs, product development, pricing, etc.

9. Prepare for U.S. BORAX and for RTZ U.S.A. group companies, the annual and five-year financial forecasts of operating results including profit and loss, cash flow, capital expenditures and appropriate narrative discussion of the economic and operating environment.

10. Prepare periodic financial plans and five-year forecasts including evaluation of financial prospects for existing operations and new projects, products, and product lines, both stand-alone and in combination with existing operations. The primary objective is to provide a financial perspective of long-range plans and of alternative strategies under consideration by corporate and operating management.

11. Maintain a continuing review of factors affecting future prospects for profitability and cash flow of the companies for which responsibilities are assigned.

12. Review product sales forecasts with departments responsible for planning and with the Technical and Production Departments as a basic element in capacity studies.

13. Ensure compliance with U.S. Government price control regulations. Together with marketing and production management, determine those alternative pricing actions that will result in greatest corporate earnings within the regulations.

The statements made on this/these pages(s) are primarily for purposes of job classification and are not intended as a complete description of all work requirements that may be inherent in the job. Minor changes in work assignment will not necessitate revision hereof.

# A LARGE MINING AND MANUFACTURING COMPANY
## MANAGER OF INTERNAL AUDITING

*Position Reports to:*   Corporate Comptroller

### SUMMARY STATEMENTS

Assists management in achieving the most effective administration of the organization by furnishing an independent and objective review, appraisal, evaluation and verification of accounting, financial and other operating controls and procedures established to safeguard the company assets against fraud and waste and by furnishing recommendations for improvement on existing policies and procedures, as well as recommendations for establishing new policies and procedures which appear to be appropriate as disclosed by audits performed.

### DIMENSIONS

| | |
|---|---|
| Sales: | $ _____ |
| Departmental Personnel: | _____ |
| Departmental Budget: | $ _____ |
| Operations Audited: | _____ |
| Number of Audits Performed: | _____ |
| Territory: | United States and Canada |

### NATURE AND SCOPE

This position reports to the Corporate Comptroller, as do the Director-Financial Controls, the Director of Taxes, the Manager of Corporate Accounting and Consolidating and the Manager-Profit-Planning. Reporting to the incumbent is a professional staff of twelve auditors, consisting of one Audit Supervisor, three Senior Auditors, three Auditors and five Assistant Auditors.

The audit function is a centralized responsibility of the Corporate Headquarters, within the Corporate Comptroller's function. No divisions have separate auditing staffs. Operational activities examined by the audit staff consist of the activities of various corporate headquarters, the fabrication and distribution of copper, brass, and aluminum products, the mining, smelting, and refining operations relating to nonferrous metals, as well as other company related operations, such as railroad operations, lumber operations, retail store operations, and geological operations.

The Internal Auditing Department of the corporate office functions as an independent appraisal activity within the company established to perform a service to management by furnishing an independent and objective review, appraisal, evaluation and verification of accounting, financial and other operating controls, and furnishing recommendations for improvement on existing policies and procedures, as well as recommendations for new policies and procedures which appear to be appropriate as disclosed by activities reviewed. The aforementioned objective is carried-out by (1) reviewing, appraising, evaluating, and verifying the soundness, adequacy, and application of accounting, financial, and other operating controls and procedures, (2) ascertaining at all operating units examined, the extent of compliance with accounting, financial, and other operating policies and procedures prescribed by the company, (3) ascertaining the extent to which the assets of the company are safeguarded against fraud and waste, (4) verifying the reliability of accounting and other financial data developed within the company. The results of examinations carried-out within the framework of the aforementioned activities are reported to management through the issuance of a report on audit which contains recommendations for corrective action when appropriate.

The incumbent in this position (1) is the expert on auditing within the corporation, and in his capacity fills an advisory role with top management, and (2) directs all auditing activities to be carried-out within the company.

This position is responsible for formulating, establishing, and implementing such auditing and administrative policies and procedures as are necessary to effectively carry-out the objectives of the auditing function, to assure consistent high standards of quality performance, and to meet departmental objectives at an optimum cost to the company.

The incumbent monitors the effectiveness of the auditing function by (1) continually reviewing audit programs and audit workpapers to assure that the work of his subordinates is being performed in accordance with generally accepted auditing standards and procedures, that auditing objectives, as well as all departmental objectives, are being met, and that costs to audit are optimized, and (2) developing and implementing such procedures and methods as are necessary to effectively control the actual performance of audits being conducted at operating units of the company to ensure that the work is performed on a timely basis.

The incumbent coordinates the work of the department with the company's independent accountants to assure that all operating units located in the United States and Canada are audited on a regular basis, that duplication of audit coverage is minimized, and that the work performed by his subordinates conforms with accounting and reporting requirements imposed by legal requirements of outside authorities. The incumbent reviews, edits, approves, and issues reports of audit findings and makes appropriate recommendations in such a manner that management may evaluate the matters covered in the report and take appropriate corrective action.

The manager of internal auditing develops such procedures as are necessary to provide that reports on audit are followed up, and keeps management informed of the corrective action, or lack of corrective action, taken on the recommendation contained in the report on audit.

The manager of internal auditing develops and maintains a highly professional staff of auditors to meet the needs of the auditing function. To accomplish this, the incumbent hires, trains, disciplines, and dismisses members of the staff under his supervision. Furthermore, the incumbent is responsible for developing a sound professional development program for his staff to enable the staff to perform at maximum effectiveness, as well as preparing them to take on greater responsibilities within the company.

The incumbent is responsible for (1) establishing and maintaining a cooperative relationship with both corporate and divisional management directed toward a full understanding, acceptance, and utilization of the internal auditing function, and (2) providing audit assistance to both corporate and divisional management with respect to any requests made through the corporate comptroller for conducting such special audits as deemed appropriate.

This position contributes to the over-all profitability of the company by providing a service to the company at an optimal cost and by making such cost improvement recommendations as are appropriate as disclosed by auditing activities.

To insure that the work of the department is carried out efficiently and effectively, the incumbent keeps abreast of latest developments in the field of auditing procedures and techniques and accounting procedures and practices by reference to authoritative publications and attending meetings and conferences relating to this subject matter.

PRINCIPAL ACCOUNTABILITIES
1. Policies and procedures for the most effective organization and direction of the auditing function of the company.
2. Safeguarding the assets of the company against fraud and waste through an effective and efficient program for auditing all operating units of the company located in the United States and Canada, as well as such other units located outside the continental limits of the United States and Canada as deemed appropriate by the company.
3. Verifying that operating units of the company comply with accounting, financial, and other operating controls and procedures prescribed by the company, as well as checking on the reliability of the accounting and re-

porting system of the company, through effective auditing of the afore-mentioned units.

4. Recommendations for establishing new or making improvements on exist-ing financial, accounting and other operating policies and procedures as disclosed through auditing activities, and reporting to management on the corrective action, or lack of corrective action, taken on the recom-mendations.

5. Effective training, development, and motivation of subordinates to insure a dynamic organization of professional personnel, capable of carrying-out the audit requirements of the company and meeting requirements for more responsible positions within the company.

---

# A MANUFACTURING COMPANY
## CREDIT MANAGER

ACCOUNTABILITY OBJECTIVE

Under the general direction of the Company Treasurer, this position (1) estab-lishes and regulates open account credit for the company's customers and (2) works to recover for the Company money that is due and (3) advises Com-pany Management and Sales Departments on economic trends as they affect credit.

DIMENSIONS

Personnel Supervised: 4 (non-exempt)
Annual Department Budget: $ _____
Annual Company Sales: $ _____

NATURE AND SCOPE

Activities of the position can be categorized into three phases: credit phase, collection phase, and supervisory-advisory phase.

In the credit phase, incumbent determines whether and how much credit can be granted a new customer through an analysis of the customer's status from in-formation compiled from trade reports, telephone and mail contact with other suppliers, and an analysis of the customer's financial status. Continuing credit is granted to old accounts based on past performance and trade reports. To establish a basis for credit, incumbent must make judgments to determine if the customer's financial status is sufficient to permit repayment of credit, how other suppliers view this customer, performance of customer's management, and how long customer has been in business. Incumbent establishes credit bases for companies ranging in size from major customers to the building con-tractor who may buy only one or two heating units.

The collection phase involves working with customers who fall into three categories: companies whose unpaid invoices are oversights and need only a call to make payment; companies who are usually good payers but will be slow when finances become pressed; and companies who are habitually delinquent in payment. Collection may be complicated by customers claiming inferior material. This requires investigation of the problem by the incumbent and then working out a solution with sales and with claims and adjustments.

Collections are accomplished through mailings of form letters, telephone calls, and, in cooperation with the legal department, bringing legal action to bear when necessary. The extent and manner in which collection pressure is applied in each case is determined by the incumbent based on past experience with the customer, and nature of the problem causing delay in payment. Decisions by the incumbent are usually final, but may occasionally be reviewed by the Company Treasurer.

Phase three, supervisory-advisory, requires incumbent to determine what guidelines are to be used in granting credit. He must be continually aware of current economic conditions and how they affect sales. Monthly cash forecasts are prepared by the position and submitted to management showing amount of cash yield from present accounts receivable and amount of cash return from the current month's sales. Position must be constantly aware of the fluctuation of credit outstanding as related to sales to determine the amount of effort to be put on collections. This position advises the Sales departments on the credit rating of old and new customers. It has direct contact with people inside and outside the company, the latter primarily by telephone and letter. Incumbent has, on rare occasions, been required to make a personal call on a customer. Tact in dealing with reluctant people while being firm with them is essential to the position.

SPECIFIC ACCOUNTABILITIES

1. Select, train and develop a subordinate staff sufficient to maintain the functions of the department, including necessary clerical and accounting knowledge.

2. Investigate financial status of potential new customers and from this decide if credit should be granted and how much.

3. Keep a continuing surveillance on the credit status of existing customers to be aware of any changes in credit standing that would affect Company relations with them and to take appropriate action.

4. Take whatever actions are required, up to and including requests for legal process to collect overdue accounts.

5. Investigate claims of inferior and faulty materials that prevent prompt collections and, with the Sales and the Claims and Adjustments departments, work out a solution to the problem.

6. Determine clerical, accounting and bookkeeping procedures for efficient collection of accounts.

7. Advise Treasurer's office and Sales departments about changes in the economic climate that have an effect on the credit status of customers and the Company's working relationship with them.

---

# MCDONNELL DOUGLAS CORPORATION
## (*Contracts and Pricing Division*)
### DIRECTOR, CONTRACT ADMINISTRATION

BASIC FUNCTION

Responsible for policy direction and coordination or administrative control of all Corporate contractual activities.

REPORTS TO

Corporate Vice President, Contracts and Pricing

RESPONSIBILITY AND AUTHORITY

1. Fulfill the requirements of the "Common Responsibilities of Director Level or Higher," General Instruction, Corporate Organization Manual.
2. Coordinate, review and approve major proposals in accordance with MDC HQ policy before submission to customers.
3. Approve the negotiation of contracts or amendments to contracts which deviate in substantial respect from a proposal, Operating Plan or other documents previously reviewed by MDC HQ or which depart from MDC HQ policy.
4. Responsible for MDC HQ coordination and control and proper execution of major contract documents as required by MDC HQ policy.
5. Prescribe the basic terms and conditions to be used in contracts including, but not limited to, type of contract, payment terms, warranty provisions and rights granted or obtained.
6. Provide for the formulation, interpretation and direction of the policies under which components of the Corporation submit proposals and enter into and administer contracts with the government or with other companies or individuals.
7. Provide a focal point for Corporate Office review of key business documents submitted for MDC HQ approval by MDC components, e.g., teaming agreements, selected Make-or-Buy decisions, selected inter-/intra-Corporate transactions, etc.

8. Direct and negotiation and administration of corporatewide agreements, e.g., IRAD, Bid and Proposal, Basic Agreements, etc.
9. Responsible for negotiation and administration of all licensing activity relating to research and development spin-off technology and major systems and components of the Corporation's prime products.
10. Review and comment on the Operating and Long Range Plans.
11. Direct the coordination of industry association activity as it may relate to contractual activity (AIA-P&F Committee, etc.).
12. Maintain liaison with such governmental agencies as necessary in order to ensure compliance with local, state and federal regulations relative to contracts and licenses.
13. Perform general administrative tasks and other special assignments as assigned by the Vice President Customer Contracts.

---

# AN AUTOMOBILE MANUFACTURER
## MANAGER, PROFIT AND INVESTMENT ANALYSIS

1. Develop and administer a system for developing and presenting long-range operating and financial plans which include forward profit plans and which are based on marketing plans, product/volume plans, cash/capital allocation plans, manufacturing plans and associated management programs. Consolidate and present the long-range plans or prepare them for presentation to the Long-Range Plan Committee. Coordinate divisional presentations.
2. Develop and administer a system for the review, approval, authorization and control of proposed program/project/investment and disposal actions. Coordinate the technical, financial, and operational reviews of all program, project or disposal requests received from originating divisions. Reconcile conflicting recommendations. Prepare final summaries and recommendations to appropriate corporate officers. After approval by appropriate corporate officers and the Comptroller, prepare agenda of projects to be submitted to the Administrative Committee, and, if required, prepare agenda for the Board of Directors and/or its committees.
3. Develop and recommend control volume levels for future years consistent with sales planning volumes and corporate volume plans.
4. Consolidate, review and evaluate financial plans, investment proposals and budgets submitted by groups and divisions; recommend their acceptance, amendment or rejection to corporate management.
5. Develop corporate-wide manufacturing expense budgetary control and general and administrative expense budgetary control programs; prepare implementing procedures.

6. Develop corporate-wide programs and implementing procedures for reporting actual performance against approved budgets and profit plans. Consolidate profit plan, capital plan and budget performance reports for corporate management review. Prepare quarterly reviews, comparing actual performance with approved plans. Recommend areas for corrective action.
7. Review and evaluate the profitability of proposed automotive production schedules; make recommendations to Executive Scheduling Committee.
8. Coordinate the development of and evaluate long-range and annual capital plans. Consolidate data for inclusion in corporate presentations.
9. Develop criteria for evaluating and ranking investment proposals. Provide assistance to corporate officers and other management in evaluating and recommending project expenditure proposals for approval. Issue formal program, project, and disposal authorization notices. Coordinate and administer a system for post-project evaluations.
10. Prepare special financial studies concerning Source and Application of Funds, Forecast Balance Sheets, Minimum Cash Requirements, and the like.
11. Perform special assignments relating to project expenditures as directed by the Assistant Comptroller, Financial Control and Analysis.
12. Develop and publish burden rates for use in establishing standard costs.
13. Carry out cost reduction studies and surveys in the manufacturing and nonmanufacturing cost areas. Perform related special assignments as requested.

---

# A MANUFACTURING COMPANY
## MANAGER, FINANCIAL PLANNING

FUNCTION

Administers and determines requirements for Division financial analysis and planning activities—ROCE, profit projections, costs, pricing, cash flow, financial reporting systems.

ORGANIZATIONAL RELATIONSHIPS

*Reports to:*   Vice President and Division Manager (may take direction from VP Marketing, VP Manufacturing on special projects)

*Supervises:*   None

JOB REQUIREMENTS

1. Degree in Business Administration with major in finance-accounting; graduate level courses in financial planning and systems is desirable.
2. 6–8 years successful and progressive experience in general accounting, auditing, financial analysis, and financial planning.

3. Thorough knowledge of corporate financial and controlling functions particularly as applied to Manufacturing, Marketing, and Engineering functions—financial reporting systems and practices, interpretation of financial data as related to effective business operations and planning.

4. Ability to recognize, assimilate, and interpret significant financial aspects of operating problems and projects—also to provide sound recommendations *or* alternatives as a basis for sound management decisions.

5. Ability to present information to management thoroughly and objectively.

6. Ability to deal effectively with all levels of management.

Accountability: (Indirect) $ _____

| LIST HERE MAJOR SEGMENTS OF POSITION<br><br>(*What individual has to do*) | WT.<br><br>% | CLASS | | | LIST HERE OPPOSITE EACH SEGMENT THE STANDARDS OF PERFORMANCE<br>(*Results expected from each segment*) |
|---|---|---|---|---|---|
| | | 1 | 2 | 3 | |
| 1. Develops and recommends sound financial plans—required analyses, collecting and presenting specific data, may participate in decision making related to division (domestic and international) manufacturing and marketing operations which involve annual and projected goals. This will include:<br><br>  a. Effective utilization and application of Discounted Cash Flow to manufacturing operations.<br><br>  b. Comprehensive division financial systems and reporting procedures related to improved management by exception and management by objectives—budgets, other financial reports.<br><br>  c. Coordinates activities between division and corporate financial planning.<br><br>  d. Accurate standard costing.<br><br>  e. Inventory levels.<br><br>  f. Correlates annual plans with projected plans (3 | 60 | X | | | 1.a. Division management has at all times pertinent financial data and reporting systems to effectively control operations and make sound decisions.<br><br>  (1) All reports, data, analyses, etc. are accurate and submitted on date scheduled.<br><br>  (2) Permanent financial reports and systems are reviewed at least semi-annually re: use, application, need, etc. and necessary revisions made. |

| | | | |
|---|---|---|---|
| yrs. or more) re: DCF, ROCE, profits, growth rates, new markets, etc. | | | |

2. Develops, as directed, supporting data and plans re: division strategic planning, participates in decisions. This will include:

  a. Acquisition (also leasing and partnership) studies—feasibility and recommendations.

  b. Divestiture studies—feasibility and recommendations.

  c. ROCE and profit objectives.

  d. Market growth and expansion—evaluation and analysis of trends, economic conditions, competitors' strategies, pricing, earnings.

  e. New product introduction —projections re: ROCE, profits, etc.

  f. Capital expenditures—projections re: ROCE, payouts, etc.

**25    X**

2.a. Division management has available, on date required, all necessary financial data to prepare and recommend specific strategic plans to corporate management.

  (1) Required controls and systems are established and maintained to effectively evaluate the implementation of approved strategic plans at least semi-annually.

3. As directed, provides financial analyses for Gas Products Marketing. This can involve:

  a. Product line price and cost comparisons.

  b. Using marginal income concepts, evaluate products and lower end of life cycle re: feasibility of redesign.

  c. Financial evaluation of proposals re: effectiveness of specific marketing strategies—advertising, freight policy, discounts, etc.

  d. Evaluation and coordination of present marketing

**15    X**

3.a. Division management can make marketing decisions on the basis of considering all division financial aspects —profitability, cash flow, ROI.

statistics and other financial data re: sound comparisons, use and application to decision making.

4. Provide and maintain a continuous financial evaluation of division research and engineering projects—applicable also to plant engineering projects. This will involve:

    a. System for reviewing all costs and expenditures.

      (1) Detect and report any variances—particularly those affecting ROI projections of a project.

4.a. All financial aspects of engineering projects—costs, profit projections, ROI, etc. —can be evaluated prior to approval.

    (1) Engineering projects' costs will be reviewed monthly—if projected goals are not being met, projects will be discontinued or necessary corrective action will be taken immediately.

---

# A MINING COMPANY
## CORPORATE TAX DIRECTOR

*Position Reports to:*    Comptroller

SUMMARY STATEMENT

Directs and coordinates the Corporate Tax function to: determine the Company's responsibilities under federal, foreign, state and local tax laws and regulations and insure compliance therewith; and provide analytical and evaluative information to management and others on all tax matters and their impact on Corporate planning and policy making.

DIMENSIONS

*Annual Tax Expenditures*
Federal:    $ _____
State and Local:    $ _____
Foreign:    $ _____

*Departmental Budget:*    $ _____

*Personnel:*    Total 10
Exempt    8
Nonexempt    2

NATURE AND SCOPE

This position reports to the Corporate Comptroller as do the Director of Financial Controls and the Managers of: Profit Planning, Auditing and Corporate Accounting. Reporting to the incumbent is the Tax Manager.

The corporation consists of five major operating entities and a vast array of interests within and outside the U.S. involving partial ownerships, joint ventures, relationships with owners of mining rights, etc. The major divisions or companies operate relatively independently, often with sizable operations in the same state and with resulting complex tax requirements. The incumbent is responsible for coordinating, reviewing and approving all tax planning and compliance activities on a worldwide basis with special emphasis on federal, state, foreign and local taxes. Although certain tax matters are handled locally by the operating entity (Company or division), the incumbent's review and approval are necessary before major tax returns, payments, or other commitments are made or tax plans implemented.

The incumbent operates as the Company's principal tax counsel on all major tax matters. The reporting Tax Manager operates as an alter ego. The Tax Department consists of eight exempt personnel, including the incumbent and Tax Manager with three individuals concerned chiefly with tax planning and three with compliance. These two activities include the following:

*Tax Planning:* Study and maintain familiarity with existing and proposed tax laws and regulations in any way affecting the Company; recommend to management means to minimize tax impact and otherwise to protect the Company's interest; analyze tax problems, conduct tax research, devise courses of action to produce optimum tax results and take implementing action as authorized; coordinate all tax planning matters among major operating entities.

*Tax Compliance:* Determine tax liabilities of the Company; prepare and file tax returns, approve tax payments; negotiate with appropriate tax authorities regarding problems in respect to determination of taxes; conduct tax audits and prepare and process tax refund claims, protests, and administrative appeals; coordinate all tax compliance matters among major operating entities.

The incumbent has a heavy Corporate advisory role both in the Accounting-Control Division and with other top managers such as Treasury and Legal, in his capacity as the Company's principal tax advisor.

PRINCIPAL ACCOUNTABILITIES

1. Direct or coordinate compliance with all federal, state, local and foreign tax laws and regulations to which the Company and its principal operating divisions or subsidiaries are subject, including preparation or review of tax return and payments; conducting and supervising major tax audits, administrative hearings and tax litigation; requesting major tax rulings and conducting negotiations with taxing authorities.

2. Direct or coordinate all tax planning functions of the Company and its principal operating divisions or subsidiaries, including reviewing and recommending courses of action to produce optimum tax results with

respect to major business transactions or arrangements, forms of organization or reorganization, and major business policies and practices.

3. Advise top management and others of the impact on the Company's activities of all tax laws, decisions, regulations, rulings and proposed legislation, and maintain continued awareness through research and analysis of a wide variety of tax and tax-related matters in order to identify and suggest solutions with respect to principal problem areas.

4. Provide functional guidance and direction to division and subsidiary personnel to ensure the Company's interest is protected in all tax matters.

5. Perform for the Tax Department the managerial functions of setting objectives, planning, staffing, integrating activities, motivating and developing personnel, as well as assuring compliance with overall Company policies and procedures.

6. Collaborate with various governmental and public bodies and taxing authorities to improve tax systems and their administration in jurisdictions to which the Company and its principal operating divisions are subject.

## *Manufacturing—Marketing*

# A CONSUMER PRODUCTS MANUFACTURER
## SENIOR VICE PRESIDENT, MARKETING

STATEMENT OF THE JOB

Under the direction of the President, develops objectives, policies and programs for marketing activities of the Corporation. Plans, directs and coordinates the efforts of Marketing personnel toward the accomplishment of Corporate objectives. Maintains and constantly strives to improve the Corporation's competitive position. Insures maximum sales volume at minimum cost.

DUTIES OF THE JOB

1. Directs and coordinates activities of the Marketing operation in accomplishing Corporate objectives, policies and defined sales goals.

2. Insures that consolidated sales forecasts are prepared; recommends short- and long-term sales goals. Makes certain assigned sales volume and profit goals are achieved.

3. Directs sales planning which includes an analysis of competitive products and selling techniques, consumer research, marketing legislation, sales budgets and quotas.

4. Makes recommendations to achieve product modifications or improvements derived from Market research or technical service work.
5. Decides pricing policies including quantities, terms and conditions of sales. Approves delegation of pricing authority and individual pricing questions which have policy implications.
6. Directs the administration of all advertising, sales promotion and market research activities and approves the selection of advertising agencies and services.
7. Directs sales service activities and develops and maintains favorable relations with customers and sees that satisfactory customer service is provided.
8. Administers Marketing Division budget preparation and consults with the Controller on budget recommendations. Responsible for the Marketing Division performance against approved budget objectives.
9. Initiates and recommends personnel requirements for the Division. Coordinates with the Personnel Department in employee relations activities. Insures that all Division personnel are trained to perform their jobs effectively.
10. Conducts searches for Companies to acquire and negotiates contracts for this purpose. Also conducts negotiations on licensing purchase of products.
11. Coordinates Product Development Department with Research and Development Division and other Divisions of the Company to insure the flow of profitable new products.
12. Performs special assignments as directed by the President.

SPECIAL DUTIES
1. Serves as Officer of the Company, when elected by the Board of Directors.
2. Serves as a Director of the Company, when elected by the stockholders.
3. Serves on the Profit Sharing Trust Committee.

---

# ANDERSON, CLAYTON & CO.
## VICE PRESIDENT, GROCERY PRODUCTS MARKETING

BASIC FUNCTION
This position is accountable for planning, developing, implementing and directing short and long-term marketing objectives, strategies, and policies to achieve both profit objectives and a long-term profitable growth for branded grocery products.

PRINCIPAL ACCOUNTABILITIES
1. Ensure increased sales volume and market share through establishment of market objectives and direction and approval of advertising and sales promotion plans and strategies to achieve these objectives.

2. Ensure attainment of profit objectives through the formulation, recommendation, and direction of marketing policies, procedures, and methods related to production forecasting, pricing, terms of sale, new product line extensions, and new or improved packaging.
3. Ensure sound departmental fiscal operation through development, measurement, and adherence to budgets and post-evaluation and justification of expenditures of effort and dollars.
4. Develop a sound overall marketing plan, both long and short-term approaches, and establish methods of measuring its impact and contribution.
5. Exploitation of changing market opportunities and response to competitor's strategies and tactics by modifying and adjusting the marketing plan and its components.
6. Stimulation, direction, and implementation of feasible and profitable new, different, or improved products, packaging, advertising, and promotions.
7. Ensure effective advertising programs through outside agency direction and evaluation of agency effectiveness.
8. Ensure an effective organization, designed and structured to accomplish departmental objectives.
9. Ensure a staff of competent personnel to best utilize individual and group capabilities by selecting, training, compensating, and motivating subordinates.

NATURE AND SCOPE OF POSITION
Under the guidance and direction of the President, Anderson Clayton Foods, this position has the mandate of developing and implementing the total marketing function of Chiffon, Seven Seas and New Grocery Products. The position is accountable for ensuring total Grocery Products' profitability, before overhead allocation and taxes. To accomplish the department's objectives, the incumbent is currently structured as follows:

*General Sales Manager (27 employees)*—responsible for directing overall sales operations to attain sales volume objectives in accordance with approved marketing plans and budgets. The sales organization is national in scope with the sales force deployed through four Regional Sales Managers and sixteen District Sales Managers who, in turn, directly supervise a total of 77 independent food broker organizations.

*Manager, New Grocery Products (2 employees)*—responsible for the identification and development of potentially profitable new grocery products.

*Two Product Managers (3 employees each)*—responsible for recommending plans and initiating action to market effectively their respective brands —Chiffon or Seven Seas. Overall product coordination encompasses recommending market objectives and strategies for the product, pricing, packaging, consumer and trade promotion, creative and media advertising, consumer research, expense budgets, and cost savings programs.

*Marketing Information Coordinator*—responsible for maintaining and distributing essential decision-making background information on Anderson Clayton Foods and competitive marketing activities.

The emphasis in this position is to deliver profits through the effective integration and direction of the component units of the Grocery Products Department.

This position is accountable for allocating and controlling a budget of several millions of dollars to advertising media and sales promotions with the informal concurrence of the President, Anderson Clayton Foods, to guide and evaluate the efforts of outside advertising agencies; sponsoring product or package development or improvement research, involving expenditures above and beyond the direct marketing budget, in the W. L. Clayton Research Center and to set research objectives for such projects; and authorizing trade deals with independent food brokers. The President's review and approval is required for decisions regarding the initial overall marketing plan and its components and product price changes. While formal approval is not necessary for many of the incumbent's major decisions, those decisions are frequently made in consultation with the President.

The continuing major challenge of this position is developing and maintaining the initiative for Branded Grocery Products, working under the pressures of a very competitive environment. It requires the development of creative and innovative marketing techniques. It requires the assignment of priorities and timely coordination and completion of a multitude of different projects and plans, and to do so in ways that result in the achievement of sales, volume, profit and market share objectives. Another major challenge is inherent in the perishable nature of the product. As a result of its limited "shelf life," accurate market forecasts are imperative. Inaccurate forecasts result in higher unit production costs, loss of sales, returned merchandise, and excessive storage and freight costs.

DIMENSIONS

    Seven Seas Sales Volume:   $ _____

    Chiffon Sales Volume:   $ _____

    Estimated Branded Grocery
       Products Volume:   _____ lbs.

    Gross Anderson Clayton Foods
       Sales Volume:   $ _____

    Estimated Anderson Clayton Foods
       Volume:   _____ lbs.

    Direct Branded Grocery Products
       Marketing Budget:   $ _____

    Estimated Technical Research:   $ _____

# UNIVERSAL FOODS CORPORATION
## DIRECTOR OF MARKETING

*Reports to:* Vice President, Sales and Marketing

### PURPOSE OF POSITION

To organize and develop the Marketing Department, whose function is to develop and execute marketing plans that will contribute to corporate profit and growth objectives.

### DUTIES AND RESPONSIBILITIES

#### SELF-PERFORMED

1. Prepare effective advertising and merchandising programs to accomplish volume objectives.
2. Analyze and control gross profit by product line.
3. Analyze sales to determine where to advertise and promote.
4. Prepare and maintain files on advertising and promotional programs, objectives, results, etc.
5. Work with public relations firm on product publicity and promotion tied in with over-all marketing objectives and strategy.
6. Spend necessary time with field sales personnel to have a good grasp of the customers' needs in the markets we serve.
7. Prepare, administer, and control all advertising and product promotion budgets.
8. Select and purchase consumer and trade premiums.
9. Prepare all printed matter related to advertising and promotion, and control these budgets.
10. Analyze and study competitive advertising.
11. Supervise all activities of the advertising agency.
12. Work with Sales Departments to prepare trade show and convention exhibits.
13. Fully utilize Home Service Department to benefit all product lines.
14. Coordinate all package design changes and package size and type modifications, working with Sales and Manufacturing.
15. Be responsible for all new labels, private labels, label changes, etc.
16. Handle market research projects as directed by Vice President, Sales and Marketing.

#### DELEGATED

1. Responsibility for certain of the above items on assigned products with predetermined and agreed-upon limitations.
2. Operation of Home Service Department.

AUTHORITY

(Describe briefly what the incumbent can do without supervisor's prior approval.)

1. Commit advertising and promotional funds within budget limitations.

TITLES OF SALARIED EMPLOYEES DIRECTLY REPORTING TO INCUMBENT:

1. Product Manager
2. Manager of Advertising and Sales Promotion

KNOWLEDGE AND EXPERIENCE

1. *Education:* B.A. degree in Marketing or Business Administration.
2. *Experience:* One year of field sales experience in the food industry. Minimum of three years' experience in recognized consumer or institutional marketing department.
3. *Skills:* Must have exhibited competence in over-all marketing activities, as well as demonstrated abilities in direct supervision and other management skills.

---

# A. O. SMITH CORPORATION
## DIRECTOR, INTERNATIONAL MARKETING

*Position Reports to:* Vice President, Marketing
*Supervision Exercised:* 1 Coord., International Marketing
1 Sec. Steno., Marketing

PRIMARY FUNCTION

Guides and audits the product divisions in the marketing function involved in the sale of company products in international markets. Responsible for recommending policies covering direct and indirect international sales and service and possible imports for U.S. sale, including pricing, promotion and credit. Under the Vice President of Marketing administers corporate policy as it pertains to international operations. Develops and determines new opportunities for export of corporate products and the import of products for sale by domestic product divisions. Investigates new foreign ideas applicable to A. O. Smith present lines and possibility of new product lines. Acts as coordinator and advisor in the negotiation of licensing and joint venture arrangements for foreign manufacture of A. O. Smith products.

DUTIES AND RESPONSIBILITIES

1. Develops, installs and administers the methods, procedures and facilities required to accomplish objectives and programs.

2. Audits international sales and marketing activities and possible import activities involving products for resale.
3. Directs international market surveys to assist product divisions in determining international market potential.
4. Develops and determines new opportunities for export of corporate products.
5. Develops international sources for products required by product divisions to fill out product line for sale in the U.S.
6. Investigates new foreign ideas applicable to A. O. Smith's present lines and possibly new product lines.
7. Acts as coordinator and adviser to the product divisions in the negotiation of licensing and joint venture arrangements with foreign manufacturers.
8. Administers foreign licensing agreements involving products not associated with A. O. Smith product divisions.
9. Arranges for visits of international business visitors interested in discussions regarding A. O. Smith products.
10. Makes periodic visits to major international markets to assess the business conditions and to enhance A. O. Smith's international business.
11. Participates in various international trade association activities so as to keep abreast of social and economic conditions abroad, new techniques, customer requirements and business opportunities.
12. Keeps abreast of all the corporation's products and research, international industry development as to customers, competitors, products, processes and applications.
13. Recommends changes in international and corporate policies to keep them attuned to international market conditions.

This description covers the most significant duties performed, but does not exclude other occasional work assignments not mentioned, the inclusion of which would be in conformity with the other duties assigned to this job.

---

# A CLOTHING MANUFACTURER
## MANAGER, ADVERTISING AND SALES PROMOTION

BASIC FUNCTION

He is responsible to the Vice President and General Sales Manager for the overall national sales promotion of division products. He will develop and direct individual in-store promotions and in particular set up specific promotions for target accounts. He is to maintain a close operating liaison with the merchandising and sales departments of the division. Through frequent traveling with salesmen, he will help develop sales volume and set up and execute promotions. Is responsible for planning and executing all advertising activities of the Division; to promote brand name acceptance, increase sales, and co-ordinate work of advertising agency and manufacturers of display items.

The following individuals report directly to this position:

Assistant Sales Promotion Manager    Advertising Stockman
Assistant Advertising Manager    Secretary

## RESPONSIBILITIES

A. *Sales Promotion*

1. Develop, recommend, and administer the sales promotion plans for the division products.
2. Develop and administer the budget for:
   a. Fixtures
   b. Cooperative advertising
   c. Mats
   d. Radio-TV cooperative advertising
   e. Statement stuffers
   f. Brochures
   g. Selling aids
   h. Display materials
   i. Store promotions
   j. Publicity
3. Contact large department stores in key territories for the purpose of
   a. Institutional promotions
   b. Target in-store promotions
   c. Special merchandise promotions
   d. Price promotions
4. Develop sales promotion, advertising and merchandising ideas at store level.
5. Assist salesmen in elevating our position in the Men's and Boys' furnishings and sportswear classifications with the retail stores.
6. Build a fashion and quality image and increase the prestige for our line in the accounts that we are now selling.
7. Maintain a rapport between buyers, merchandise managers, and executives of our key accounts.
8. Develop promotional mailings periodically to regular accounts.
9. Correspond on a regular basis with key account executives that have been contacted on sales promotion trips and in the apparel market.
10. Develop individual store promotion brochures to include
    a. National ad tie-ins
    b. Local advertising
    c. Publicity
    d. Basic stock merchandising plans
11. Develop and set up controls for the distribution of fixtures.
12. Recommend for development point of sale aids.
    a. Sales kits
13. Recommend for development counter displays and window displays for retail stores.
14. Recommend for development dealer aids.

15. Assist in the developing and recommendations of premiums.
16. Allocate and administer all cooperative advertising money
    a. Newspaper
    b. Catalog agreements
    c. Radio
    d. Television
17. Develop advertising campaign tie-in promotional plans.
18. Contact and develop a rapport with the New York Resident Buying Offices.
19. Suggest ideas for
    a. Enclosures
    b. Mailers
    c. Mats
    d. Suggested ads
20. Communicate the sales promotional ideas to the salesmen through the weekly sales bulletin.
21. Develop and obtain publicity with magazines, newspapers and trade journals.

B. *Advertising*
1. National and trade advertising
    a. Recommends the selection of advertising agency to the Vice-President and General Sales Manager.
    b. Directs the development of advertising programs and coordinates these programs with the merchandise and sales departments.
    c. Directs and approves advertising media, themes, art displays and copy.
2. Directs and approves product package, label and hang bag design.
3. Directs the selection, creation and protection of brand names and designs.
4. Publicity
    a. Prepares and supervises the preparation and release of publicity and product and divisional activities.
    b. Supervises the administration of gratis garment distribution.
    c. Supervises the administration of the professional golfer accounts.
    d. Actively participates in tournaments, shows and exhibits for product and corporate publicity.
5. Prepares the advertising budget and submits it with appropriate recommendations to the Vice-President and General Sales Manager for approval; administers and controls budget distribution and expenditures.

C. *Sales*
1. Study and make recommendations on all phases of the division's marketing efforts.
2. Travel with salesmen calling on accounts throughout the country. To work with the retail buyers and merchandise managers at na-

tional and regional Men's and Boys' apparel markets to develop sales volume for all division products.

3. Develop sales aids in the way of fact sheets and promotional brochures.
4. Develop store clinics for our salesmen to conduct with retail sales personnel.

D. *Participation in Regional and National Sales Meetings*
1. Assist in the programming and the agenda of the sales meetings.
2. Present the promotional plans for the underwear and sportswear line to the salesmen.

E. *Assist the Vice-President and General Sales Manager as follows:*
1. Develop programs for new accounts.
2. Build a stronger acceptance for our line.
3. Increase sales volume in target accounts.
4. Improve salesmen morale.
5. Information regarding new ideas, competitive price ranges, competitive quality, etc.

F. *Company Relationships*
He is responsible to the Vice-President and General Sales Manager of the division for the development, recommendations, and administration of sales promotion functions in accordance with approved company objectives, policies, and procedures. He is to assist in the coordination of all efforts on matters affecting the sale of the division's products.
1. The sales force in connection with sales promotion and development of sales volume.
2. Merchandising in connection with needed product development and merchandising ideas.
3. Advertising in connection with the development of promotional elements and tie-ins.
4. Customer service department in relation to shipments covering specific store promotions.
5. Administrative department in relation to cooperative advertising expenditure.

G. *Non-company Relationships*
1. The advertising agency in connection with the development and administration of sales promotional programs and materials.
2. Retail buyers, merchandise managers and executives in connection with the sales and promotion of division products.
3. Resident buyers and merchandise managers in connection with the sales and promotion of division products.
4. Fashion magazine, trade paper, and newspaper personnel in connection with editorials and publicity for division products and promotions.
5. Suppliers of fixtures, point of sale aids, display pieces, packaging and promotional pieces and related items.

# AN AUTOMOTIVE ACCESSORIES MANUFACTURER
## MANAGER, RETAIL ADVERTISING

*Title of Immediate Supervisor:* Assistant Advertising Manager
*Duties* (List by major captions and show estimated percentage of time for each. Include principal contacts outside dept.)

ADMINISTRATIVE—40%
1. Initiation of plans and action for creation of new or modification of existing programs and policies pertaining to Retail Advertising. Finalization of same through individual and conference contacts with Home Office and Division Office Management—Sales, Legal, Development, and other Department personnel.
2. Coordination:
   a. Between advertising agency and Creative Advertising Department for compatible national-retail programs.
   b. Between divisions of Creative Advertising Department for uniform advertising message in all retail media.
   c. Between Creative Advertising and Production Departments to insure balanced work flow, proper attention to priority projects and meeting advertising deadlines.
3. Review and evaluation of all advertising proposals, requisitions and projects to determine most effective and economical ways to develop and produce.
4. Organization, direction and recapitulation of results of field tests on proposed tire promotions. Conducting weekly surveys by telephone or teletype on results of current tire promotions.
5. Interviewing job applicants. Organizing and directing indoctrination programs for department trainees.
6. Developing and delivering Sales Class Advertising Presentations for dealer and store personnel and college trainees. Preparation and delivery of special advertising presentations to Home Office Departments and district staffs.

SUPERVISORY—40%
1. Assignment of all advertising projects to appropriate Department Managers. Follow through at every stage to see that each project is being handled as requested. This entails review and evaluation of all layouts and final art, and proofreading and editing of all copy.
2. Evaluating and taking necessary action (through correspondence, telephone, teletype and field trips) on all vital retail advertising information received. Basic sources of such information are newspaper linage reports, monthly advertising schedules, newspaper tear sheets, and Market Research reports.
3. Preparation of special studies and presentations to meet localized situations at the district, dealer and store level. Reviewing and processing of special advertising requests for individual markets.

CREATIVE—20%
Preparation of wires, letters, special announcement bulletins and brochures, related to advertising and promotion primarily directed to our field sales organization and dealers.
*Formal Education Required:* College graduate
*Previous Experience Required:* Newspaper and catalog copywriting 5 years (minimum 2 years as Mgr. newspaper adv.). Sales promotion activity 5 years (minimum 2 years as Sales Promotion Manager).
*Positions Supervised:* Adv. Dept. Mgrs.: Sales Promotion, Newspaper, Truck & Farm Tire, Technical Data, Packaging and Labeling, Tire Promotions, Coast Division Adv. Rep., Store Identification Supervisor, Secretary
*Number of Employees Supervised:* Directly 3 Indirectly 17
*Title of Next Promotional Level:* Assistant Advertising Manager

---

# A CONSUMER PRODUCTS MANUFACTURER
## DIRECTOR, CORPORATE MARKETING RESEARCH

*Reports to:* Corporate Vice President, Planning
*Supervises:* Senior Marketing Research Analyst (4)
Assistant Marketing Research Analyst
Warranty Card Editor

BASIC FUNCTION
Provide the timely and accurate information regarding market characteristics, competitive strengths, consumer preferences, product acceptance levels and general economic conditions to form a sound basis for making product and marketing decisions. Director of Corporate Marketing Research is responsible for coordinating inter-group research projects providing business economic analysis and performing market and industry information in support of the Corporate Planning procedure.

PRIMARY DUTIES AND RESPONSIBILITIES
1. Provide marketing research services on request, for several operating divisions including: Consumer Products Group, Communications Group, Schools Group, Audio-Visual Division. Other Groups, domestic and international, on request.
2. Select and engage the services of marketing research suppliers.
3. Direct the design, conduct and analysis of product concept and product acceptance research.
4. Prepare recommendations for Product Line Directors regarding the initiation, continuance, modification or cancellation of individual products or product lines.

5. Advise Sales Management on the selection of distribution channels, the effectiveness of sales programs and the establishment of sales territories.
6. Monitor and evaluate the receipt of consumer warranty card data.
7. Assists in the preparation of Group or Divisional Annual Marketing Plans by completing those portions of the plan dealing with the market situation and by providing long range projections which suggest the direction of future marketing and product line effort.
8. Responsible for department personnel, including selection, compensation, promotion and termination in accordance with established policies and procedures.
9. Responsible for coordination of inter-group marketing research projects.
10. Supports Corporate Planning by development of industry, competitive, and other market data showing trends and forecasts.
11. Assists in Corporate and/or Group acquisition studies providing estimates of market potential and product market liability.

---

# U. S. BORAX
## MANAGER, NEW PRODUCTS

STATEMENT OF JOB

Reporting to the Vice President, 20 MULE TEAM Department, the Manager of New Products is responsible for developing and recommending department goals and criteria for the identification, screening, development and marketing of new products and concepts. He is responsible for evaluating, planning, implementing and assessing product test markets and for managing all aspects of product development to the point of commercial reality. He is responsible for recommending expense levels and staff requirements to achieve assigned responsibilities. In all of these activities, he maintains a continuing liaison with the department vice president, market research, USBRC and other functional groups.

>               Reporting to him:   Project Leaders
>                                   Assistant Product Manager
>                                   Staff (as required)

DUTIES OF JOB

1. Develop and recommend for approval criteria and guidelines to define primary areas of opportunities for new products commensurate with department goals.
2. Collaborate with the marketing staff, including sales and product managers, in the identification and definition of opportunities in new product areas and with relation to present product lines.

3. Establish a formal identification and appraisal system for new product ideas emanating from sources both within and outside of the department. Establish criteria to appraise new product opportunities and assign priorities.

4. Assess new product ideas from a marketing point of view to determine feasibility. This assessment will include:
   - Analysis of market size and trends.
   - Gathering and appraisal of all available information on competitive products.
   - Preparation of product description.
   - Price characteristics necessary to compete effectively in the market.
   - Estimates of sales and profit potential.
   - Description of initial marketing plans and requirements.
   - Manufacturing and technical feasibility and capital investment requirements, if any.
   - Insure product performance from a consumer standpoint.
   - Preparation of initial budget estimates for marketing tests and programs, including package tests, advertising, publicity and test marketing.
   - Preparation of a written summary report on each new product idea for review with management.

5. Review and seek approval of new product business proposals with the department vice president.

6. Develop and recommend the marketing test programs for each new product in close cooperation with the agency, market research and sales management.
   - Prepare budgets and plans for preliminary test market or screening tests, including package design, brand name, advertising, promotion and prices.
   - Develop plans for measurement and projection of marketing tests to expanded distribution.
   - Complete the market test plans, including budgets, timing, location and promotional schedule.
   - Plan and develop the necessary supporting advertising and promotional material and work with the field sales organization to carry out the test market programs.
   - Monitor the test market and recommend appropriate action based on its results.

7. Establish and control all advertising, merchandising and test market expenditures which are made against approved budget.

8. Provide direction and counsel to assigned advertising agencies and other outside support groups in the preparation of advertising materials or other programs for the marketing tests.

9. Recommend to management the final disposition of new products in terms of abandonment, modification, further development and/or testing or commercial marketing.

10. Manage the new product budget and periodically report to management on expenditures versus plan.

11. Transfer responsibility for sales and profit performance on new products to the appropriate managers when test marketing has been successfully completed.

12. Maintain an up-to-date knowledge of trends and developments in new products and processes in the industry, maintain liaison with research and product development groups, and participate in marketing and management seminars and associations.

PRINCIPAL WORKING RELATIONSHIPS

1. Collaborate with the department vice president and other corporate executives in defining and establishing new product goals and direction to guide the new product development effort.

2. Work with the product managers and staff to obtain new product ideas and select project leaders for specific projects to utilize their expertise in the evaluation and development of marketing test plans and results.

3. Collaborate with the Research Corporation in the development and/or modification of research objectives based upon product concepts as defined in the product description.

4. Work with sales management to obtain field sales and broker support for test markets and to obtain information of trade reaction and acceptance of new products and promotional programs.

5. Work with market research in the design, administration and evaluation of research projects.

6. Work with the advertising agencies and other support groups to solicit and evaluate new product ideas and to plan and develop test markets and materials.

7. Work closely with manufacturing, cost accounting, procurement and other corporate functional groups on matters related to the development, production and marketing of new products.

8. Supervise, train and evaluate personnel reporting to him.

The statements made on this/these page(s) are primarily for purposes of job classification and are not intended as a complete description of all work requirements that may be inherent in the job. Minor changes in work assignment will not necessitate revision hereof.

---

# A FOOD COMPANY
## SENIOR PRODUCT MANAGER

*Reports to:*   Product Group Manager

BASIC FUNCTION

To manage the short- and long-term profit growth of the business.

NATURE AND SCOPE

The product line generates the second largest sales volume and dollar profit in the _____ Division.

This is one of our most successful new product entries and it has virtually a 100% share of the seasoned coating mix category which it created. Future growth opportunities are excellent considering the product now coats only 2% of domestic chicken servings and a smaller percentage of fish and pork servings.

The Product Manager on the product reports to the Group Product Manager on _____ Products and works with all Division functional areas (Sales, Operations, Market Research, Finance, Promotion Planning, and Technical Development). He also works closely with the advertising agency in the development and execution of the Brand's marketing plans, especially in the area of advertising copy and media.

Deals with Corporate Advertising Services in media planning and execution and for counsel on advertising and promotion development.

Works with the Kitchens on product testing and development, advertising, publicity, and consumer correspondence.

Deals with Corporate Purchasing on package design and development and on point-of-sale and related display material.

Works with the Law Department on advertising, promotion, and package development and seeks their guidance on matters relating to State and Federal laws and on the protection of existing trademarks and copyrights.

Utilizes Corporate Market Research as a counselor and advisor on special projects and unusual business problems.

PRINCIPAL ACCOUNTABILITY

Develops, recommends, and gains Management approval of the annual Marketing Plan including volume and profit goals. Supervises the execution of the approved Marketing Plan or, as necessary, recommends changes in the plan.

Consistent with the Brand's Marketing Plan, establishes volume and consumption goals and continually measures progress toward these goals.

Meets monthly with Operations to review marketing plans and changing market conditions as they relate to production requirements. Works to optimize inventories by accurate sales forecasting and careful communication of any changes affecting raw and packaging material supplies.

Works closely with the advertising agency to insure a clear understanding of the Brand's marketing objectives and needs. Provides leadership for the agency in the areas of copy development and media planning. Supervises the execution of the advertising plan to insure the efficient and effective uses of the Brand's advertising funds.

In conjunction with Sales and Promotion Planning, develops, gains approval, and executes promotion programs consistent with the Brand's marketing strategy. Administers the expenditure of the Brand's promotion funds to insure they are employed effectively and efficiently.

Works with the Market Research Department to identify the Brand's research needs and to establish programs designed to satisfy these needs.

Provides direction for Technical Research in the areas of product improvement and new product development.

Continually reviews the Brand's packaging and, when indicated, initiates projects to improve the graphic or structural design.

Reviews and analyzes the Brand's pricing structure and recommends pricing action when indicated.

Participates in the selection and training of personnel. Establishes programs to develop subordinates for positions of increased responsibility.

Insures concise and timely communications across functional areas. Keeps Management apprised of matters substantially affecting the business.

DIMENSIONS

> Advertising and Promotion Budget:
> Unit Sales (12 packages):
> Gross Sales:
> PBT:
>
> Advertising Agency:
>
> *Staff:*
> One Associate Product Manager
> Two Assistant Product Managers
> Two Secretaries

---

# A MANUFACTURING COMPANY
## MANAGER, MARKETING SERVICES

*Position Reports To:* Executive Director, Market Support

*Scope of Supervision*
List by title all exempt positions reporting directly to this position:
> Market Research Manager
> Sales Performance Manager
> Field Information Manager
> Customer Visits Supervisor

Number hourly employees directly supervised: 1
Total number exempt and hourly employees reporting through this position: 22

*Purpose of Position*
Directs the initiation, development, and distribution of marketing information for worldwide use by all levels of the marketing organization; the function includes market research, demand volume projections, analysis of market data and trends, preparation of annual and five-year forecasts, compilation of marketing manuals. Also responsible for the Customer Visits function.

*Specific Functions*
1. Directs the activities of the worldwide Market Research function.
2. Directs special studies to determine current, historical, and projected market penetration to provide Management with guidelines for action to increase sales.
3. Directs the studies and research programs related to all affiliate contracts.
4. Maintains all records of affiliate operations and prepares reports on the performance of affiliates, including problems to be resolved and action to be taken.
5. Directs and initiates the development of sales volumes for all products in all markets for the Corporate Five-Year Business Plan.
6. Directs the development of yearly sales goals for engines, parts, and components for the Corporate Annual Operating Plan.
7. Directs the preparation and participates in the presentation of special reviews as required by Corporate Management.
8. Directs the preparation and publication of periodic and special sales statistical reports for Management information.
9. Directs the analysis of sales data to provide guidelines for Marketing Management.
10. Initiates and directs the compilation of comprehensive sales, policies, and procedures manuals.
11. Directs the gathering, coordination, and dissemination of written material to the Field Marketing staff.
12. Directs the coordination of arrangements for worldwide Marketing Customer Visits.

I *Position Requirements:* the minimum education, skills, experience, and special background required to perform the duties satisfactorily; possible sources of experience and special skills inside and/or outside the Company.
Bachelor's degree in marketing, business economics or finance. Minimum of 4–6 years experience in administrative, planning, finance, or marketing functions.

II *Judgment Exercised:* the need for applying knowledge and making decisions; the amount of supervision or direction received; the extent to which decisions and actions are subject to review; the requirement for analytical ability and creative or original thinking.

Requires a great deal of judgment in the analyses of sales data and marketing trends. The findings and recommendations provided by this function will play a substantial role in important decisions by Marketing and Corporate Management. Requires creative abilities to improve methods used in analyses and statistics.

III *Relationships Responsibility:* the nature, scope, and importance of required relationships.

Works closely with all levels of Management. Frequent contact with top members of affiliates. Dealing with middle Management on a day-to-day basis.

IV *Demand and Working Conditions:* the extent of unusual pressures and deadlines; any unusual working conditions to show percent of travel and exposure to dirt, noise, and/or hazards.

Constant pressure to meet urgent deadlines on all reports and projects. Travel estimated at 10–20%, partly overseas.

---

## A LOCK MANUFACTURER
### GENERAL SALES MANAGER

SUMMARY

Directs the Sales Division, co-ordinating the promotion and sale of company products to achieve maximum market penetration and to attain short and long-range objectives for company sales growth.

| Reports to: | General Manager | *Degree of Supervision* |
|---|---|---|
| Supervises: | National Sales Manager, Residential | General Direction |
| | National Sales Manager, Commercial | |
| | Sales Co-ordinator | |
| | Advertising Supervisor | |
| | Sales Secretary | Direct Supervision |

RESPONSIBILITIES

1. Plans and establishes divisional organization and policies for effective attainment of the division's objectives.
2. Provides guidance to subordinates as required in carrying out responsibilities for selection, development and motivation of personnel under direction.
3. Develops additions or revisions to company sales policies and strategy and submits to the General Manager for approval.

4. Reviews recommendations submitted by National Sales Managers and finalizes development of company sales forecasts.
5. Reviews field information and analyzes market trends to develop long-range company sales plans.
6. On receipt of annual company sales objectives from General Manager, establishes annual sales quotas for each district and territory; reviews actual sales results to determine variance from plan; takes corrective action as required.
7. Finalizes sales expense budgets; reviews actual results to determine variance from plan; takes corrective action as required.
8. Oversees application of sales policies in the field; approves recommendations for discounts or special services to customers when in accordance with established policy; refers recommendations outside of policy guidelines to General Manager for approval.
9. Recommends establishment of or revisions of selling prices to General Manager for approval.
10. Oversees the development and implementation of programs for the transmission of product knowledge to dealers and distributors.
11. Participates in the development of and approves advertising and product promotion programs.

DUTIES

1. Makes periodic trips to the field to keep fully informed of conditions in each territory and to provide assistance to field personnel as required.
2. Contacts key accounts and prospects personally when desirable.
3. Keeps informed of competitors' activities through review of information from the field or from other sources.
4. Keeps General Manager informed of any problems or important matters relative to his division.
5. Maintains control on salary and performance reviews for salaried personnel within the division; coordinates administration of the sales incentive program; recommends to General Manager candidates for promotion in the division.

| RELATIONSHIPS | CONTACT | NATURE OF CONTACT |
|---|---|---|
| Internal | Management personnel in all company departments | receipt and transmittal of information relative to sales |
| External | Customers, present and potential | contact with senior representatives on matters relative to sales |
| | Divisional Head Office counterpart | co-ordinates exchange of information on sales matters. |

# UNIVERSAL FOODS CORPORATION
## DISTRICT SALES MANAGER

*Reports To:*   Vice President, Bakery Sales

*Purpose of Position*
To administer the Bakery sales program within the district to produce annual budgeted sales and profits in keeping with the department goals.

## DUTIES AND RESPONSIBILITIES

SELF-PERFORMED
1. Direct all administrative and sales activities, service operations, and employee training programs within the district in compliance with existing company policies and procedures.
   A. *Administrative Duties*
       1. Hire, train, and supervise Area Sales Managers, Service Technicians and, in some instances, Supervisors.
       2. Supervise and review credit and collection policy, making every effort—with the cooperation of all sales personnel—to maintain accounts receivable on a current basis.
       3. Actively participate in principal trade association meetings, conventions, etc.
       4. Preserve and promote the Corporate image in all trade relations and with all company personnel contacts.
       5. Maintain an adequate staff of competent and qualified personnel throughout the district.
       6. Keep current on all pertinent aspects of the baking industry, including competitive and allied trade activities.
       7. Make full use of company facilities to help service accounts, such as technical service, advertising and sales promotion, public relations, and visits by appropriate company officers.
       8. Analyze market potential.
       9. Administer work program.
       10. Submit all required reports to Home Office.
   B. *Sales Duties*
       1. Prepare, review, and accept responsibility for attainment of district sales and expense budgets.
       2. Make regular sales development contacts with all major customers and prospects.
       3. Establish a planned, selective coverage of all trade within the district.
       4. Establish account responsibility for each possible sales outlet.
       5. Review activity reports, expense reports, and sales statistics.
       6. Assist Area Managers in keeping a working sales record of their

accounts, both customers and prospects; also assist in maintaining condition and adequate inventories of products in branches.

7. Assume responsibility for carrying out advertising-merchandising programs and survey assignments.
8. Provide proper delivery service consistent with prudent economics to trade in the district.
9. Investigate the possibilities of distributor distribution wherever such a move will be more profitable for the Corporation. Determine in advance that the distributor complies with the principles and policies of Bakery sales, and that the ultimate potential is great enough to warrant appointment.
10. When a distributor has been appointed, arrange for and assign the necessary personnel to assist in the sale of Bakery products by continuing sales meetings, product education, distribution of sales aids, and planned sales coverage.
11. Work closely with the Director of Technical Sales in order to fully utilize the talents of Technical Sales Representatives.

C. *Service Operation Activities*
Schedule technical service assignments, in conjunction with sales personnel, in a manner that will effectively establish and support the business in the district.

D. *Employee Training Programs*
Develop an adequate training program to improve sales techniques and product knowledge, and to impart complete information regarding company policies.

DELEGATED
1. Certain account sales responsibilities.
2. Route supervision.

AUTHORITY
(Describe briefly what the incumbent can do without supervisor's prior approval):
1. Operate district sales activities within Corporate and departmental policies.
2. Select and recommend hiring of subordinates.

*Titles of Salaried Employees Directly Reporting to Incumbent*
1. Area Sales Manager
2. Technical Sales Representative

*Knowledge and Experience*
1. *Education:* College graduate or equivalent.
2. *Experience:* Minimum of five years' experience in sales of bulk or specialty products to commercial bakeries. Should have sound trade knowledge.
3. *Skills:* Must have demonstrated supervisory and organizational skills, as well as personal sales ability.

# A FOOD COMPANY
## SALES REPRESENTATIVE

*Reports to:* Sales Supervisor

### PURPOSE

To assist the District Sales Manager in the development of agreed upon distribution and to attain maximum levels of support from assigned store managers and other decision makers in order to achieve quarterly budgets, improve annual trends, and develop the _____ franchise.

### NATURE AND SCOPE

For administrative purposes, the Sales Representative in most cases reports directly to a Sales Supervisor who provides direction, training and development, and evaluation of performance. There may be instances, however, when a Sales Representative is assigned to an Account Manager or Area Manager for geographic reasons or for the purpose of customer vertical deployment.

The Sales Representative concentrates primarily on assigned high-volume retail stores that contribute significantly to the growth of Direct Accounts in the district. Under certain circumstances a Sales Representative can be given Direct Account responsibilities that are consistent with his geographic area, and commensurate with his ability or need to further his managerial progress. Generally, the total volume contributions of these accounts is less than 7% of the district's volume.

The number of Direct Accounts, Supervisor contacts and retail calls assigned will depend upon store classifications, point of decision, frequency pattern and the geographic area involved. The Sales Representative function relies heavily on being kept well informed by the District Office, Sales Supervisor, Account Managers and other Sales Representatives in the marketplace in order to properly plan his daily contacts and to establish productive objectives. Likewise, he must be a good communicator to other members of the team, as well as providing accurate and prompt reporting on his results to his Supervisor.

The Sales Representative must know how to carefully analyze his customers, the market, competitive situations and then develop a sales strategy on a store-by-store basis that will result in increased volume and in the development of the [product] position at the point of sale. In following this planning procedure, the Sales Representative will establish customer objectives, set priorities, arrive at a deployment pattern, and finally review all elements with his Supervisor for assurance that the programs are co-ordinated with other activities transpiring in the district.

Specifically, the Sales Representative must be knowledgeable about the policies, procedures and plans of the _____ Division and be able to co-ordinate and present these programs to customers in his area. He must be able to create strong sales plans and presentations directed to the problems and opportunities on brand and size distribution, competitive pricing, favorable shelf exposure and maximum promotional support on our products.

The Sales Representative must assure adequate inventories at all levels of customer organizations to reduce out-of-stock conditions to an absolute minimum, as well as making certain that damaged or out-dated merchandise is handled within the guidelines of the _____ Division.

To meet established goals, the Sales Representative is required to develop the necessary controls that will lead to successful accomplishments as planned.

When these goals or objectives are not met, it is his responsibility to prepare specific recommendations that will lead to corrective actions. The Sales Representative must constantly evaluate his activities and take steps to improve in areas that will lead to the achievement of greater results.

The Sales Representative must be a high-level professional, who must utilize good record-keeping and depth-planning techniques, as well as directing his time and talents toward building volume and developing the over-all Division franchise.

### PRINCIPAL ACCOUNTABILITIES

1. Secures and maintains agreed upon district distribution objectives of the product line for each account. Influences customer to maintain salable inventory to meet consumer needs at all times. Each direct account and retail store stocks Division products and sizes as determined by Management.
2. Sells to the account promotion plans, both headquarters and self-developed, that include features, point of purchase materials, displays and tie-ins, which are designed to increase consumer purchases. Level of performance for specific merchandising activities will be determined by management.
3. Implements Division shelving program which includes installation of planned shelving, overseeing maintenance of planned shelves, improving shelving where no planned shelf can or should be installed. Shelving plans for each retail store direct account, and store supervisor, as determined by the Sales Representative and/or Supervisor are realized.
4. Performs necessary analysis and planning to assure that objectives and priorities for each call are established and met within time limits, recommends coverage plan and related work activities necessary to accomplish agreed upon responsibilities. Current plans include the district's current priorities. Objectives for each call are realistically based on past performance of the account and current product and/or promotion objectives.
5. Develops a satisfactory proprietary relationship with all customer personnel who materially influence our business such that there are no justifiable complaints about the salesman's services by the customer.
6. Checks pricing levels to assure they reflect current competitive conditions, corrects out of standard prices via agreed upon procedures. The out of

standard pricing situations found in making store checks are within the limits determined by management.

7. Performs necessary verbal and written presentations to effectively accomplish agreed upon responsibilities. Sales presentations are given in an effective and acceptable manner. Attains desired results.

8. Works with others so that the total job responsibilities are met in a satisfactory manner, and contributes to the district sales team as a whole. Effects cooperation, integrity, tact and consideration with superior, customers, and peers. Contributes to the over-all "team" effort and single intent of the district's plans and programs. Exercises sound business ethics.

9. Accomplishes those activities necessary to keep management informed on all planning, analysis, work performed, and results achieved. All records required by management are complete and accurate, up-to-date and submitted on time. Records are in such condition that they are meaningful to anyone who might use them, and be readily accessible.

10. Exercises proper care and judgment in the use of all assigned company assets. Company equipment and other property maintained in good condition and trust fund can be accounted for at any time.

DIMENSIONS

Number of stores assigned:
Share of District Budget, if applicable:
Sales Volume, if applicable:
Geographical area covered, if applicable:

*Manufacturing—Personnel
and Industrial Relations*

# A MANUFACTURING COMPANY
## VICE PRESIDENT, INDUSTRIAL RELATIONS

ACCOUNTABILITY OBJECTIVES

Under the direction of the President, this position is charged with developing and maintaining an industrial relations climate that will create and permit a stable and productive work force; and enhancing overall employee relations through the direction and coordination of the separate personnel/industrial relations functions.

DIMENSIONS

Personnel Supervised: 8 exempt plus 6 clerical departmental employees; functional over 10 plant personnel managers.

Department Budget:

NATURE AND SCOPE

The VP, Industrial Relations reports to the President and is responsible for embodying the philosophy of the corporate objectives in all areas of employee relations. The position is a member of the Management Committee and Long Range Planning Committee, along with corporate officers and appointed top executives.

The position is primarily responsible for labor relations and directs and coordinates the development of the various labor contracts between the Company and the recognized collective bargaining agents. It determines the broad parameters within which contract provisions will take place, and establishes bargaining limits that may be used for negotiation between the Company plant management representatives and the local bargaining units. It works closely with the Company's labor counsel in developing strategy and planning for labor negotiations. When necessary and when called upon, the position gives direct assistance to the plant managers and personnel managers in the conduct of negotiations.

The position is responsible for the direction and coordination of all other functions of industrial relations including corporate employment, psychological testing and management development and training, employee benefits, wage and salary administration, manpower planning, and employee communications. The position operates directly in sub-functions such as conducting of management executive recruitment, and search efforts, engagement of industrial consultants, supplemental compensation consideration, scheduling executive physical examinations, etc., and administers other functions through staff managers. The position also functionally advises plant personnel managers on day-to-day handling of plant problems of contract administration, discipline, grievances, et al.

The position is responsible for generating policy on personnel administration and for the development of policy statements for top management approval that will reflect the Company's thinking regarding employee benefits, practices and procedures. It keeps top management advised of trends in labor negotiations, patterns of settlements or changes in employee benefits, or other areas that may require the attention of top management.

SPECIFIC ACCOUNTABILITIES

1. Select, train, develop, and organize a subordinate staff to effectively use to maximum advantage the group and individual capabilities.
2. Provide counsel in the preparation for and conduct of contract negotiations to arrive at fair and reasonable labor agreements.

3. Provide leadership in the establishment and maintenance of industrial relations that will assist in attracting and retaining a desirable and productive labor force.
4. Advise top management of significant matters pertaining to labor difficulties, manpower shortages and future needs, imminent rate or benefit changes, etc.
5. Counsel employees and supervisors on personnel problems.
6. Support the divisional general managers and other top-level executives in the achievement of their operational purposes by providing his direct assistance or that of his staff functions or personnel.
7. Develop personnel policy to ensure consistent treatment of employees within the framework of the Company philosophy.

---

# A MINING COMPANY
## DIRECTOR, CORPORATE HUMAN RESOURCES

*Position Reports to:*   Senior Vice President, Administration

### SUMMARY STATEMENT
Sufficient numbers of qualified, well-placed, effectively motivated people in all elements of the Corporation by functional guidance and direct implementation (where required) in all matters of organization and manpower development and compensation.

### DIMENSIONS
Total Corporate Salaried Payroll:

Cost of Employee Program:

Budget:

### NATURE AND SCOPE
This position reports to the Senior Vice President, Administration, as do the General Counsel; Director, Corporate Management Systems; Vice President, Corporate Relations; and Director, Labor Relations. This group of corporate administrative functions provides highly professional policy development, consultative advice and counsel and specialized problem solving services, corporate-wide.

Each of the two principal functions reporting to this position is concerned with the planning and policy development, consultative services, required operational administration and functional review of Division operations in the following two broad areas of Human Resources activities:

The *Manager of Compensation and Benefits* is concerned with total compensation (cash, near-cash, and noncash) including position structure and evaluation systems for the exempt and nonexempt employee population.

The *Manager of Manpower Planning and Development* is concerned with manpower forecasting, planning, recruiting, employment, assessment, development and training systems and services.

This position retains direct accountability for organization planning and development.

The incumbent is responsible for providing those reporting to him with the necessary strategies and corporate planning direction so they can direct their functional activities toward achievement of specified objectives. To achieve this, he meets regularly with them singly or jointly to assist them in establishing goals, provide guidance in planning functional objectives, review and direct progress toward achievement of objectives and provide coordination among the functions.

Inherent in this position is the requirement upon it to provide professional guidance and counsel on all human resource matters to all members of top management of the Corporation. Long-range strategy and planning of the Corporation's Human Resources requirements and policies is the key element of this position. This calls for close coordination with the Corporation planning functions and the Operating Divisions regarding human resource matters.

The incumbent is appointed by the Board of Directors as a member of the Corporate Pension Committee and the Corporate Retirement Committee. He also carries out special studies as assigned by the President.

PRINCIPAL ACCOUNTABILITIES

1. Counseling key corporate management in establishing corporate objectives bearing on Human Resource requirements that will facilitate achievement of corporate plans and objectives.
2. Short-term objectives and long-term goals of Human Resources that will complement and facilitate achievement of corporate plans and objectives.
3. The organization structure within which necessary policies, practices and techniques as a professional Human Resources function can occur and serving as the prime motivator in implementing these on a corporate-wide basis.
4. Staffing and motivating key management within this function to insure professionalism and to achieve functional continuity.
5. Regular review and assessment of the broad quality, content and economy of Operating Division personnel groups and recommendations of corrective action as necessary.
6. Personal professionalism in Human Resources management.
7. Tactical guidance and direction of all activities reporting to this position toward maximizing the quality of concept, policy and service within reasonable economy of operation.

# PPG INDUSTRIES
## DIRECTOR, COMPENSATION AND BENEFITS

*Reports to:*   Vice President, Employee Relations   *Division:*   Staff
*Department:*   Corporate Employee Relations   *Location:*   General Office

ACCOUNTABILITY OBJECTIVE
Plan, design and recommend a balanced system of compensation and benefits for all categories of employees in all domestic, subsidiary and international operations which provides for an economical expenditure of Company funds and at the same time provides for compensation and benefits that will attract, retain and motivate the necessary human resources; evaluate continually the effectiveness of current programs and recommend timely change; and communicate to employees current and revised programs to ensure proper understanding and acceptance.

DIMENSIONS

    Total 1972 Payroll & Benefits  $ _____
    Total PPG Employment   38,000

    Personnel: 5 Professionals—Manager, Benefits Planning; Benefits Analyst; Compensation Coordinator; Compensation Specialist; and Compensation Analyst
           1 Clerical

NATURE AND SCOPE
The incumbent reports to the Vice President, Employee Relations, along with the Director, Management & Organization Development; Director, Professional Personnel; Director, Labor Relations; Director, Safety and Security; Medical Director; Director, Equal Employment Opportunity Program; and Manager, Psychological Services.

The incumbent directs two inter-related programs broadly defined as compensation and benefits. He is responsible for providing a properly balanced total compensation package that will meet employee needs, be competitive, and be motivating to the point that the costs affect earnings in a positive manner. In directing these programs, he must relate closely with the Management Committee, Employee Welfare Board, Finance Department, Law Department and other sections of Employee Relations in developing and recommending plans and policy; and additionally with the four divisions, staff departments and subsidiary companies to determine their needs and to advise them on the implementation of the policies, rules, procedures, and programs which have been approved.

In the period since the last review of this position, several significant changes have occurred in terms of job enlargement. The incumbent has been assigned the accountability for the design and recommendation of intermediate and long range capital income programs and the responsibility for their communication following approval. Secondly, he has been designated to assist in the design of sales incentive programs and under the direction of the Vice President, Finance, to control administration to Management Committee Guidelines. Other forms of compensation, such as job perquisites, are now determined and recommended by the incumbent.

The incumbent is responsible for the analysis, evaluation, plan design and recommendation, coordination and communication of a comprehensive compensation and benefit program throughout the entire Company including subsidiary companies and international operations. While the direct administration of these programs is not currently a function of the incumbent, coordinating and servicing of compensation and benefit programs is an on-going responsibility.

The need for sound, well thought out programs encompassing the short range problems of this year and next year requires the incumbent to continually analyze and evaluate existing compensation and benefit programs to determine if they continue to meet the objectives for which they were designed and are sufficiently adequate to meet rapidly changing requirements in the marketplace.

Equally as important, however, is the development of long range planning to recommend specific objectives for future compensation and benefit programs. Such programs are broad based and with respect to compensation include: base compensation as well as all forms of extra compensation such as incentive compensation, sales bonus plans, profit sharing, stock option plans, and the like. Benefit programs encompass almost every conceivable type of program outside direct pay for time worked including such considerations as pension programs, life insurance, long-term disability, salary continuance, savings plans, severance pay, as well as many other forms of employee benefits.

In the design of compensation and benefits programs, the incumbent must be cognizant of government regulations, Cost of Living Council, Federal Wage and Hour, and Social Security laws, SEC and IRS regulations and controls. It is imperative that he be able to interpret the impact they have on the various programs and the cost to both the Company and the employee. He plans with pending legislation in mind, and through proper channels makes the Company's position known to government officials.

He has the responsibility for designing and recommending compensation and benefits programs for subsidiary and international operations. Planning, developing and monitoring Canadian and other foreign incentive, pension, thrift and other plans requires knowledge of new type work habits and business conditions, and involves interpretation of international laws, monetary systems and political situations.

The Director of Compensation and Benefits is responsible for annually developing, documenting and preparing recommendations concerning adjustments to salary schedules and size of merit budgets to be presented to the Management Committee. After adoption, he assists divisional management in the determination and implementation of their merit budgets and salary schedules.

The incumbent provides an information function on compensation and benefit matters. Compensation and benefit plans of other relevant industrial concerns affecting all categories of employees are analyzed and management is informed by the incumbent. Additionally, the incumbent has the responsibility for communicating to all levels of management new programs, policies and procedures and to provide not only the necessary training to insure understanding and acceptance, but also advice and counsel to enable appropriate management to carry out their responsibility in an adequate manner. Still another important role concerning information involves the dissemination of information relating to federal, state, and local laws as they apply in the compensation and benefit area.

The Director, Compensation and Benefits ensures, through auditing procedures, as well as advice and counsel, that administration of compensation plans conforms to established policy and practices by reviewing administration, and training divisional and plant employee relations personnel in the principles and techniques of sound wage and salary administration.

The incumbent assists management with the classification of all jobs up to the officer level. In this connection, the incumbent provides a review and recommendation function for all jobs outside General Office in jobs below the Executive Level. For those in General Office and in Executive Level positions, the incumbent assists in the review and recommendation of appropriate classifications along with a salary committee and the assistance of the Manager, General Office Salary and Payroll Administration. The incumbent is responsible for assisting the Law Department and Division Employee Relations Departments in determining the status of jobs under applicable federal laws and in justifying those determinations to regulatory agencies, and for assisting the Law Department in arbitration or other hearings involving wage or salary administration practices.

During labor negotiations, the incumbent is responsible for providing support by recommending appropriate changes in compensation and benefit programs and by providing company negotiators with cost data on compensation and benefit programs existing in PPG, those proposed by PPG or unions, and those existing in the industry generally.

ACCOUNTABILITY OBJECTIVES
1. Direct the design, development and recommendation of a full range of cash and non-cash compensation programs, both short and long range, for all categories of employees in all domestic, subsidiary and foreign operations of the Company and assist management in their implementation.

2. Develop and recommend compensation and benefit policy, rules and administrative procedures to effectively carry out the administration and understanding of the PPG total compensation program and assist management in their implementation through educational programs and other appropriate communications vehicles.

3. Develop and present on a continuing basis informational programs on compensation and benefits which communicate to all levels of management current and new programs, policies, procedures and governmental laws and regulations; and communicate to all employees through manuals, letters and educational meetings current and revised compensation and benefits programs.

4. Develop, document and recommend adjustments to salary schedules and size of merit budgets and assist divisional management in the determination and implementation of merit budgets and salary schedules. In conjunction with the recommendation of merit budgets recommend annual changes in benefits which provide with salary adjustments a well-balanced total compensation recommendation.

5. Provide a continuing program of evaluation and analysis of compensation and benefits from the standpoint of internal and external equity and keep management advised of developments for planning and decision purposes.

6. Assist management in the classification of all positions up to the officer level and coordinate Company classification systems across the Corporation to maintain equity and balance. With respect to the Hay Evaluation System, direct and coordinate the evaluation of Phase II and Phase III positions.

7. Conduct a continuing analysis of state and federal legislation, whether pending or enacted, relative to compensation and benefit matters and recommend appropriate courses of action to management in response to such legislation or laws. Additionally, provide advise, counsel and assistance in dealing with regulatory agencies.

8. Provide labor negotiations support by recommending changes in compensation and benefit programs, providing cost data, developing plan language, and assisting in framing pre-negotiation policy.

9. Develop and maintain a staff of key subordinates who are capable of providing the expertise and assistance to all levels of management and who can communicate and gain acceptance in all areas relating to compensation and benefit matters.

# CASTLE & COOKE, INC.
## LABOR RELATIONS MANAGER

I. PURPOSE

Write a brief statement of the overall purpose and functions of your position.

Recommend policy, develop programs and coordinate activities concerning the Company's relations with labor unions. Advise and assist local management in labor relations matters.

II. RESPONSIBILITY FOR EMPLOYEES

a. State the number of employees directly supervised:
b. State the number of employees indirectly supervised:
c. List the names and job titles of all employees who report directly to you. Write "None" if no employee reports directly to you.

*Primary Responsibilities—Labor Relations*

1. Formulate labor relations policies and procedures.
2. Make recommendations and provide information and guidance to operating units. Advise units during union recognition proceedings.
3. Assist operating units while contract negotiations are in progress and maintain close liaison between units and the Vice President—Industrial Relations.
4. When directed, act as negotiator or assist in negotiations at the operating unit level.
5. Assist the Vice President—Industrial Relations as required in Hawaii negotiations and other labor relations matters.
6. Assist managers with the administration of labor contracts and handling of grievances and establishing good labor union relationships.
7. Recommend as to whether grievance cases appealed to the arbitration stage should be settled voluntarily or heard by the arbitrator, and assist in the preparation and presentation of such cases.
8. Evaluate and report on significant labor relations developments of interest or value to the conduct of industrial relations programs, including labor agreements of other companies, and legislative proposals.
9. Maintain the official file of company labor agreements.
10. Establish an operative procedure for ensuring timely compliance with notice, reporting, or similar obligations under agreements with labor organizations, ensuring that all personnel with a need to know are kept properly informed of the provisions of labor agreements.
11. Keep informed on strikes, slowdowns, etc. Provide advice and assistance.
12. Assist in the development of personnel who are assigned labor relations responsibilities in the operating units.

*Other Duties*

1. Represent the company by giving speeches, participating on panels, and attending meetings, particularly where such activities require someone in the IR field.
2. Perform other such duties and special studies as the Vice President—Industrial Relations may direct.

---

# REXNORD
## DIRECTOR OF MANAGEMENT DEVELOPMENT

I. GENERAL RESPONSIBILITY

Planning, implementation and administration of corporate programs to ensure the continuing availability and development of management employees for higher levels of responsibility.

II. AUTHORITY RELATIONSHIPS

A. *Line*

Acts under direct line authority from the Vice President of Industrial Relations.

Direct supervisory responsibility for:

    1—Exempt employees
    2—Nonexempt employees

B. *Functional*

Has functional authority over key employees throughout the company in coordinating corporate management development programs and administration of the Graduate Training Program.

III. SPECIFIC RESPONSIBILITIES

A. Administration of basic corporate management development programs for Exempt-level employees:
1. Management by Objectives
2. Manpower Planning
3. Manpower Reviews
4. Personal Development Program
5. MIDAS (Computerized data retrieval system)

B. Operation of the Graduate Training Program including:
1. Curriculum administration
2. Recruiting and selection procedures
3. Campus relations

C. Personnel-type services to all line and corporate staff units including:
1. Assistance in placing promotable, surplus or misplaced Exempt personnel.
2. Internal searches to fill Exempt job openings.
3. Recruiting to meet emergency needs.
4. Evaluation of candidates for employment.
5. Psychological testing (and feedback of results).
6. Assistance in dealing with "problem employees."
7. Development of training resources (internal or external) to meet specific needs.
8. Training Sessions (MBO, Problem-Solving and Decision-Making, Supervisory Techniques, Communications, Human Relations).

D. Periodic analysis of all ongoing programs and/or activities so as to evaluate progress and/or improve results.

E. Continuing investigation of new methods and techniques and/or recommendations to improve corporate management development programs and services.

F. General assistance to the Vice President of Industrial Relations in projects and problems of personnel policies or programs—and other departmental activities on a special assignment basis.

---

# AN AUTOMOBILE MANUFACTURER
## MANAGER, PERSONNEL RESEARCH, PLANNING, AND SYSTEMS

1. PRIMARY PURPOSE OF POSITION

Direct the Personnel Research, Planning, and Systems functions. Directs the development of major studies and proposals regarding the labor economics and labor matters of the corporation. Serves as the principal Labor Economist of the corporation. Meets with industry and governmental representatives to obtain information, formulate positions and otherwise represent the corporation.

2. MAJOR DUTIES OF POSITION
1. Direct Personnel Research and Planning studies and investigations relating to all aspects of personnel relations in the corporation with principal emphasis on matters involving labor economics and analysis. Develops major labor proposals involving new or revised concepts and coordinates the required company, industry and governmental review of such plans.
2. Serves as the principal corporate Labor Economist. Meets with industry and national agencies concerned with labor economics to represent the corporation and to obtain data and views that permit the formulation of

a suitable corporate position. Supervises the preparation and reporting of data to the Department of Labor and other government agencies.

3. Directs and coordinates the Personnel Office planning for major contract negotiations. Insures labor cost aspects are defined and that major position papers are prepared. Supervises the preparation and publication of contract language and documentation.

4. Meets in national bargaining sessions with the major unions to present proposals, explain concepts and to hear and rebut union demands.

5. Supervises the Personnel Systems function responsible for the development of personnel data and information systems and the coordination of information processing with the computer operations activity. Develop and implement Administrative Personnel systems and procedures.

6. Prepare and coordinate personnel statistical reports and coordinate personnel forms control activity in conjunction with other affected corporate components.

7. Develop and coordinate long range planning and budgeting for the Personnel Office; review financial projects and other management documents from corporate staffs having general personnel research questions or implications.

8. Conduct personnel studies and surveys required to support corporate recommendations on location of facilities and operations; review for concurrence new or proposed changes in plant or group personnel office layouts.

9. Supervises the activities that: develop and administer international industrial relations research and personnel data systems programs; develop and establish methods for obtaining and analyzing data on labor costs for contract negotiations at international locations; and counsel and develop recommendations for International Operations and Corporate Personnel management on the implications of broad international labor developments.

3. KNOWLEDGE AND SKILL REQUIREMENTS
Must be a thoroughly trained Labor Economist. Normally must possess a Master's or Ph.D. in Labor Economics.

Generally must have a minimum of ten (10) years' experience in industry or government as a Labor Economist.

Must have the ability to negotiate and to represent a major corporation before industry and government groups.

4. SUPERVISION
Immediate Supervisor: Vice President, Personnel
Employees Supervised: Supv.—Labor Econ. and Research
                      Supv.—Pers. Reports and Admin.
                      Supv.—Pers. Systems
                      Spec.—Intl. Pers. Research
                      Secretary

Total number of employees directly and indirectly supervised: 17
*Annual* payroll of employees directly and indirectly supervised (use mid-point of salary range in computing) $ _____

5. FUNCTIONAL GUIDANCE AND CONTROL
   [Not given.]

## *Manufacturing—Research and Development*

### ANDERSON, CLAYTON & CO.
#### VICE PRESIDENT, TECHNICAL RESEARCH

BASIC FUNCTION
Direct and achieve timely research and development leading to new and/or improved products, processes, and packaging in support of the division's marketing and manufacturing efforts and assure the development and maintenance of adequate product specifications and quality standards for all division products.

PRINCIPAL ACCOUNTABILITIES
1. Develop and recommend an organization structure for the Technical Research Department which can effectively fulfill the objectives it is assigned, permits the clear definition of the accountabilities of key jobs, and has the flexibility to react swiftly to the division's needs.
2. Develop a team of managers and specialists which in quality, technical competence and depth assures excellent current performance and management continuity, and permits the division to introduce and maintain profitable and high quality products.
3. Within the policies of the Foods Division and the company, formulate and provide understanding of divisional technical policies and objectives which establish clearly the nature and the role of the product development activities and which also establish a constructive and creative environment to support profitable growth for the division.
4. Participate with the marketing groups in the identification of new product opportunities and provide guidance as to their technical and economic feasibility.

5. Contribute to the fulfillment of the division's need for new and improved products and processes through the development of the improved operational techniques.
6. Develop and recommend annually objectives, plans, and budgets for research and product development activities which identify the long- and short-term factors affecting product development within the division, and recommend a course of action to be followed in the development and servicing of products.
   a. Establish and maintain adequate records of technical information, formulas, process methods and standards.
   b. Develop, direct and maintain a project system for long- and short-range research and development programming and the related economic evaluations.
7. Appraise Technical Research accomplishments against objectives, assuring or directing the proper shifts in approach and emphasis when needed.
8. Assure the maintenance of adequate records to support patent action, and cooperate with patent counsel in obtaining patent protection for the division's unique processes and products.
9. Work with legal counsel to assure that all ingredient statements, product formulation, etc. comply with Federal and state government regulations and standards. Keep abreast of new and changing technical legal requirements for all types of products manufactured and sold by the ACCO Foods Division.

NATURE AND SCOPE OF POSITION
The incumbent heads the research and development activity of the Foods Division reporting directly to the Division President. Reporting to the incumbent are key functional heads, each accountable for a core activity:

*Director of Product Development, Grocery Products.*
This group is responsible to the needs of consumer marketing in the research and development of new product lines, product line extensions, and modification of existing products to assure maximum thrust and profitability. This incumbent is accountable for product research, development, environmental product testing and initial consumer testing programs.

*Director of Quality Assurance and Industrial Product Development.*
Establishes product specifications and quality control methods for all products produced by the division. In addition, this department is accountable for the final approval of the shipment of products that vary from established product specifications. This group acts in an advisory capacity to plant quality control functions and to the other core groups requiring analytical lab analysis and other technical information. The microbiological lab acts in response to requests from other research and plant groups of the division and to intercompany requests for analysis.

As many industrial products are manufactured to customer specifications, this activity is concerned with the development of processes to meet these at the lowest possible cost. The department is also active in the development of new products for the industrial market which carry a substantially higher profit margin than bulk commodity items.

*Director of Protein Research.*
In response to the needs of protein marketing, this group performs benchwork related to the development of protein isolates as a less expensive or better substitute for existing products.

*Director of Exploratory and Applied Research.*
Conducts both need and discover orientated chemical research in the solution of current problems and longer term in the development of a body fundamental chemical knowledge which may be applied to process and product improvement and/or new product development.

*Director of Packaging Development.*
Investigates and recommends packaging designs and equipment to economically meet the division's marketing objectives and maintains manufacturing specifications for all approved packaging materials.

In addition, the Office Manager and the Plant Engineer, who are responsible for various administration duties and physical plant maintenance, respectively, report to the incumbent.

The incumbent is responsible for the overall direction of the division's research and development laboratories in Richardson and Sherman, Texas, with an operation budget in excess of $1.4 million.

DIMENSIONS
R&D Budget:        $ _____
# of Employees:      _____

*Manufacturing—Administration*

---

## ANDERSON, CLAYTON & CO.
### VICE PRESIDENT, ADMINISTRATION

BASIC FUNCTION
This position is accountable for contributing to the overall growth and profitability of Anderson Clayton Foods through effectively planning, coordinating and providing direction and guidance to the administrative staff departments in the achievement of their respective goals and objectives.

PRINCIPAL ACCOUNTABILITIES

1. Ensure an effective organization, designed and structured to accomplish objectives within the division.
2. Ensure a staff of competent personnel to best utilize individual and group capabilities by selecting, developing, compensating, and motivating subordinates.
3. Develop sound plans and objectives that will optimize divisional effectiveness.
4. Ensure effective financial and operational controls that protect assets.
5. Ensure accurate and timely financial reports for management as a basis for sound business decisions.
6. Ensure optimum efficient utilization and growth of management information systems and their application as management tools.
7. Contribute toward the availability and effective utilization of competent manpower to attain Anderson Clayton Foods' objectives and goals through the conception and administration of sound personnel programs and policies.
8. Guide and direct staff departments in attainment of goals and taking appropriate corrective action.
9. Fostering an environment of teamwork and commitment of total personnel throughout the organization by developing and improving methods of effective communications.

NATURE AND SCOPE OF POSITION

This position is one of six Vice Presidents reporting to the President, Anderson Clayton Foods. As head of the Administrative Division, the incumbent guides and directs five staff departments which support the line functions of Anderson Clayton Foods, a rather autonomous operating division of Anderson, Clayton and Company.

Organizationally, the Administrative Division is structured as follows:

*Controller (15 employees)*
This department is accountable for the protection of ACF assets. Although corporate standards are established to facilitate outside auditing, policies, procedures, and control techniques are formulated and tailored to meet ACF's specific needs. Two sets of books are maintained—one for SEC reporting and one for internal management and responsibility control. Reporting to the Controller are—a Supervisor of Audits and Cost Accounting and a Supervisor of General Accounting. Plant Controllers report to the Controller on a functional basis. The Vice President—Administration provides overall direction to the control function, ensures the accurate and timely reporting of financial information, and interprets appropriate information to top management.

*Budget and Profit Planning (6 employees)*
Headed by a Director, this department ensures that budgets and annual plans for the divisions of ACF are sound and project a desirable level of profitability. Throughout the year, the Director must work closely with other departments to determine what effect various actions might have on profitability. Within this

department rests the accountability for planning and monitoring the capital budget, evaluating return on investments, and devising financial simulation models. Although not a large department, it performs a vital function in planning, analyzing, and reporting Anderson Clayton Foods' progress as it relates to achieving profit objectives.

*Banking and Credit (24 employees)*
This department, under the direction of a Manager, is accountable for providing various office services (switchboard, mail, reception area) and more importantly ensuring sound and effective banking and credit operations. Although Anderson Clayton Foods may borrow funds only through corporate channels, the Manager is accountable for maximizing the float and maintaining local banking contacts and relationships. He is also responsible for administering the plant insurance coverage program, assisting in trademark registrations, and formulating and administering Anderson Clayton Foods credit policies.

*Management Information Systems (28 employees)*
Headed by a Director, this department's overall goal is to integrate management science and systems so as to utilize common data banks. The general ledger system and provision of the computer and computer time are generally the only corporate controls over ACF systems operations. Within ACF, data processing is utilized for plant inventory control, order processing and billing, and accounting. New systems or simulation models are being developed as management tools in the future. A steering committee is comprised of ACF Vice Presidents who establish project priorities and appoint project leaders. An ultimate objective is to get total involvement of people to understand and optimize capabilities of management information systems.

*Personnel (9 employees)*
Under the direction of a Director, this department contributes toward recruiting, developing, and retaining qualified human resources to attain ACF goals and objectives. The department implements established corporate policy and develops and administers ACF policies, which cover most personnel activities other than certain employee benefit and exempt compensation programs. Major activity areas within the department include labor relations, employment, wage and salary administration, and management development and training, and payroll. The Vice President—Administration provides guidance in undefined policy areas, approves and forwards to the President recommendations for policy changes, and renders counsel and advice of personnel matters of an unusual nature.

The incumbent is accountable for ensuring a sound and effective organization to provide support to the total organization. He works with his Department Managers in developing their budgets and goals, provides guidance and direction in the attainment of these objectives, and evaluates departmental performance.

A major challenge of the incumbent is to develop and ensure total communications, involvement, and commitment within the Administrative Division and between other divisions of Anderson Clayton Foods.

He participates with other Vice Presidents, under the guidance of the President, to plan, evaluate, and recommend overall strategies for Anderson Clayton Foods to attain its goals and objectives as an organization.

*Dimensions*

| | |
|---|---|
| Sales Volume: | $ _____ |
| Budget—Administrative Division: | |
| Employees: | 86 |

# MCDONNELL DOUGLAS CORPORATION
## MANAGER, FACILITIES ADMINISTRATION

*Responsible to:* Staff Vice President, Properties and Facilities

PRIMARY FUNCTION

To manage administration activities for Corporate Properties and Facilities and to administer the acquisition and disposition of real property.

See also MCDONNELL Position Description
"All Supervisors & Managers"

TYPICAL DUTIES

1. Ascertains the availability of external facilities required to meet Operating Plans.
2. Participates in negotiations for the purchase or sale of real property.
3. Negotiates real property leases for St. Louis based components.
4. Prepares financial analyses and develops alternate methods for acquiring and disposing of real property.
5. Manages the preparation of engineering data and drawings for the acquisition and disposition of real property.
6. Prepares instruments for acquisition and disposition of real property and the necessary closing statements.
7. Reviews Authority for Expenditure (AFE) and Capital Expenditure Requests (CER) for new or leased facilities and coordinates with appropriate personnel for approvals.
8. Reviews Government Facilities Use Agreements and participates in negotiations for new or modified agreements.
9. Conducts studies and evaluations on various aspects of facilities administration for improved operational effectiveness and/or reduced costs; applies electronic data processing techniques where applicable.

SUPERVISION EXERCISED:    Directly 2–4 Indirectly 4–6

NORMAL BACKGROUND AND EXPERIENCE REQUIREMENTS
Requires a Bachelor's degree in Business Administration or any technical field or equivalent business or facilities-related administration experience. Requires a thorough knowledge of company facilities coupled with a good knowledge of Government Facilities Use Agreements. Eight or more years of Industrial Engineering or related experience is normally required for satisfactory performance.

---

# ANDERSON, CLAYTON & CO.
## MANAGER, DIVISION PLANNING

BASIC FUNCTION

Develop and formalize the ACF approach to long-range planning; provide professional guidance and advice on administration and coordination of the operational and strategic planning process throughout the division; formulate recommendations that will facilitate the effectiveness of this planning process; assist in developing the criteria necessary to identify and analyze acquisition candidates that may fit into ACF's overall long-range plan; and oversee ACF's consumer research function.

PRINCIPAL ACCOUNTABILITIES
1. Develop and formalize ACF approach to long-range planning and recommend how this function should be administered as well as coordinated among all the Profit and Expense Centers.
2. Contribute to the Division's profitability by determining priorities for the allocation of resources between our present business, product line extensions, new product development, and acquisitions.
3. Through independent research and evaluation and liaison with the various operating groups, contribute to the identification and formulation of long-term divisional goals and the annual refinement of long-range plans.
4. Facilitate managerial decisions regarding external growth by identifying and analyzing acquisition candidates that meet our standards.
5. Contribute to the achievement of division goals by planning for and helping coordinate the orderly integration of acquisitions into ACF.
6. Facilitate division management decision-making by overseeing ACF's consumer research function.
7. Structure, staff and assure the development of the Planning Department staff to gain optimum efficiency and effectiveness within the present and future planning functions.

NATURE AND SCOPE OF POSITION

The incumbent will report to the President of ACF and is primarily accountable for providing professional guidance and assistance in establishing division objectives and goals, including the establishment of priorities and degree of planning emphasis for present profit and/or expense centers, new product development areas, and acquisition candidates. He will work with the managers in the various profit and expense centers to assist as necessary in the development and refinement of the five-year plan. He will become actively involved in the identification and evaluation of acquisition candidates that might contribute to the attainment of overall division goals. He will work closely with the President and Vice Presidents to determine priorities for the investment of resources in the areas of: Improved Internal Operations, Present Products, Line Extensions, New Products and other outside acquisitions.

He will be responsible for administration of the Consumer Research Function.

There are several continuing challenges in this position. For example, the incumbent constantly attempts to improve the quality of the conclusions and recommendations yielded by studies (e.g., what should be the major directions, objectives and plans of the division). The business implications of these conclusions and recommendations can be critical to the achievement of ACF goals. Another related challenge stems from the small size of the Planning staff and the resultant necessity of efficiently and economically mobilizing other division resources on a need basis.

In order to fulfill the requirements of this position, it is highly desirable for the incumbent to: Have 10–15 years of business experience with at least five years experience in a profit-planning and execution type of management position; have the ability to translate abstract planning concepts and terminology into concrete, understandable policies; and possess an analytical approach to problem identification and problem solving.

*Dimensions*

Company Size:   $ _____

Annual Departmental Budget (estimated):   $ _____

Average Annual Division Planning Expenditures (estimated):

$ _____

Average Annual Dollar Volume of Acquisitions (estimated):

$ _____

Personnel Supervised (estimated):

# SWIFT AND COMPANY
## DIRECTOR OF PUBLIC RESPONSIBILITY

*Reports to:*   Executive Vice President, Food Group

*Supervises:*   None

BASIC FUNCTION

Directs, administers and coordinates the Corporation's policy, action and public posture in the general area known as Nutrition, Consumerism and Environmental Affairs.

WORKING RELATIONSHIPS

*Internal.* Works closely with corporate and company executives, Marketing and Legal personnel, Research & Development, and Public Relations.

*External.* Works directly or through other Swift employees with the various professional people and organizations, government agencies, industry representatives with comparable responsibility, and the consuming public.

DUTIES AND RESPONSIBILITIES

1. Acts as a central source of information on nutritional, consumer and environmental activities. Directs implementation of Swift and Company's corporate policies on agreed public and internal activities in these areas.
2. Keeps appropriate executives apprised of and acts as a central source for consumerism trends in unit pricing, product dating, and package labeling of contents of products and other areas of consumer concern. Suggests necessary action and programs to follow.
3. Keeps appropriate executives advised and acts as a central source for environmental affairs such as pollution and other ecological involvements.
4. Maintains contacts with or through other Swift employees with the industry sources, professional organizations, governmental and consumer agencies for trends in nutritional, environmental and consumer activities.
5. Maintains continuing contacts with the nutrition, consumer and environmental community, both public and private.
6. May act or will secure a corporate spokesman or representative for conferences and symposia where nutritional, consumer or environmental activities are involved, discussed or promulgated.
7. In conjunction with the Legal Department may act as or secure a corporate representative for fact-finding groups, both public and private.
8. Provides analytical and imaginative direction in the total consumerism, nutritional and environmental areas.
9. Alert Public Relations Department on all matters that may require corporate Public Relations posture in the nutrition, consumerism or environmental fields.

PERSONAL CHARACTERISTICS

1. Education—advanced degree in Food Nutrition, Food Technology, or related disciplines desired.
2. Sensitive to public information needs of the corporation and the proper approach to achieving the corporation's public image relative to the areas of Nutrition, Consumerism and Environmental Affairs.
3. Good writer and speaker.
4. Able to work effectively with a team of executives to accomplish corporate objectives.
5. Diplomatic and persuasive.
6. Able to work effectively with corporate executives, public relations, government and public sector personnel.
7. Knowledgeable as to sources of nutrition and ecological education as it applies to a variety of professionals including doctors, dentists, teachers, home economists and the general public.
8. Motivated to provide a leadership role in nutritional consumerism and ecological involvement as it affects the corporation, its products, and customers.

# U.S. BORAX
## MANAGER OF ENVIRONMENTAL AFFAIRS

STATEMENT OF JOB

Responsible directly to the President for the development, implementation and coordination of Corporate policy on pollution control activities at all company locations. Advise Management on all facets of pollution control activities, including steps to be taken to reduce pollution at all operations, interpretation of existing or proposed legislation and regulations. Represent Company at hearings conducted by government regulatory agencies, and in activities of trade associations directly connected with environmental matters. Direct the activities of the Public Relations Department through the Manager of Public Relations.

DUTIES OF JOB

1. Develop and recommend Corporate policy in the area of pollution abatement and environmental matters.
2. Coordinate overall implementation of approved policies with plant management and other involved departments.
3. Review capital projects to determine if pollution control considerations are adequate.
4. Review with appropriate Departments the pollution aspects of existing operations and new capital projects with the objective of achieving maximum cost effectiveness in relation to all expenditures undertaken.

5. Recommend and coordinate activities of outside consultants, whose retention is deemed necessary to assist in solving specific problems.
6. Represent the Company before, and in its communications with, governmental air and water pollution control agencies.
7. Assist in developing and recommending appropriate positions for the Company to take with any regulatory body.
8. Prepare reports as required for all regulatory agencies or operating units of the Company.
9. Forecast anticipated problems relating to pollution, evaluate their significance and recommend possible Corporate action.
10. Represent the Company with and before trade associations in matters concerning pollution.
11. Work closely with other staff groups, such as the Legal and Technical Departments in control programs and in promoting a favorable image of the Company.
12. Keep informed of competitive activities as related to abatement policies and practices.
13. Direct the activities of the Public Relations Department.
14. Special projects, reports, etc., as assigned by the President.

The statements made on this/these pages(s) are primarily for purposes of job classification and are not intended as a complete description of all work requirements that may be inherent in the job. Minor changes in work assignment will not necessitate revision hereof.

*Manufacturing—*
*Management Information Systems*

## A FOOD COMPANY
### VICE PRESIDENT, INFORMATION SERVICES

Reporting to the Vice Chairman of the Board, this position is responsible for initiating and directing the design and installation of business systems and procedures to provide for coordinated and economical administration and operations within and between department, division and subsidiary organizations of the company, profit centers and corporate executives. It is also responsible for the efficient use, maintenance and establishment of office facilities and services in the areas of printing, customer redemptions and other centralized services activities.

RESPONSIBILITY AND AUTHORITY

1. Establishes and develops an effective organization directed toward analysis, design and implementation of effective coordinated business systems within and between organizational entities.
2. Develops directors and staff through training and assignment to assure successful performance on current duties, projects and maximum use of their talent and ability short and long range.
3. Develops a detailed understanding of policies and goals of the company and defines organization and objectives to provide systems which direct action toward achievement of goals through information direction.
4. Determines the technical economic and operational feasibility of proposed projects in the area of systems and office services relative to the state of the art and internal capabilities.
5. Develops and maintains a long range plan of analysis design and installation of information systems to meet the needs of operating and staff divisions to maintain a competitive position.
6. Defines imaginative objectives in the area of using complex quantitative decision making models such as profit oriented optimization.
7. Appraises short and long range company plans and proposals to assure that the policies, procedures and systems plan provide for coordinated and economical administration and adequate control of operations and funds through information flow and definitive analysis.
8. Assures profitable performance of division by measurement of expected results and expected costs and through a program of post audit to assure results were achieved.
9. Recommends new or changed policy, organization or procedure to management when the analysis of operations indicates an improvement in profit, costs or coordination would be effected by such a change.
10. Determines long range computer and communication needs to provide hardware support for analysis and design of information systems.
11. Establishes and conducts a planned program of maintenance and improvement in office facilities to enhance the welfare and productivity of employees.
12. Assures all service functions maintain low costs and are more than competitive with outside services or liquidates unprofitable internal service function.

RELATIONSHIPS

A. Outside the Company
1. Conducts relationships with vendors and customers to provide adequate information support internally and to provide support of the sales effort.
2. Develops relationships with leaders in various industries associated with profit centers and outside these industries to make new information developments available to the company.

3. Maintains working relationships with university faculty to make available the advances in information technology.

B. Within the Company

1. Reports and recommends action to the Vice Chairman of the Board.
2. Maintains a close working relationship with corporate executives and profit center management to develop an adequate information program and keep management informed on purposes and progress.
3. Directs and coordinates the activities of directors in carrying out long range plans and project work, office facility, printing operations, and customer redemption services.

DIMENSIONS

1. Principal Areas of Impact:
Accurate management information to provide management the tools to manage:

$ _____ million in sales.
$ _____ million in capital expense per year.
$ _____ million in operating expenses.

2. Total Budget Controlled:
In excess of $ _____
3. Other Areas of Impact:
a. Building of information and models which provide increasingly accurate allocation of resources within consequent improved productivity.
b. Providing models which allow management coordination and optimization of functional organization.
c. Good utilization of office and printing facilities.
d. Review of capital expenditures on office facility and grounds.

# THE MAYTAG COMPANY
## MANAGER, EDP OPERATIONS

*Reports to:*   Assistant Controller

I CHARACTER OF THE JOB (Nature and Scope)
This position is accountable for the timely and accurate production of data processing reports for the company utilizing the systems and programs as designed and prepared for the Systems and Programming Department. This involves the controlling of incoming source data; the processing of information through various stages utilizing key punch and verifying equipment, unit record

equipment and 360 IBM computer and the audit and final distribution of completed reports.

Accomplishment of above accountability requires a close and constant coordination with the Systems and Programming Department in the testing, modification and trouble shooting of new, revised or current systems and programs. Also a close and effective relationship must be developed and maintained between this group and the various areas throughout the company who are feeding in the source data and receiving reports.

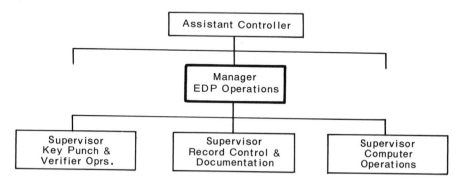

## II STATISTICAL DATA

Annual budget about $ _____ which includes manpower, equipment rental and repair costs, supplies, etc. This department contributes to management acceptance of EDP systems by promptly and accurately providing requested reports.

Staff includes 30–35 personnel.

## III ACCOUNTABILITIES (End Results)

1. Accurate and timely production of statistical information in accordance with established EDP systems and programs. This involves:
    a. Effective scheduling and follow-up to assure an accurate and smooth flow of information into, through and out of department in accordance with the time requirements of the users.
    b. Normal flow of material includes initial receiving of source data and its audit and coding, key punch and verifying of data in punched card, processing of cards through a sequence of unit record equipment and computers for the inclusion of data into storage, the print out of reports, the audit of reports against controls and finally the distribution of the reports.
    c. In case of extended computer downtime, recommending use of hardware in other firms, making necessary arrangements and determining which jobs to run based on Maytag priority and operating system utilized by other firm.

2. Effective absorption of a continual flow of new, additional and/or revised systems and programs. This involves:
   a. Working with Systems and Programming Department in the testing and installation of new systems and programs.
   b. Working out details of new systems and programs related to flow of data, controls, coding, operating procedures and methods, material retention, documentation, etc.
   c. Advising systems and programming group of apparent deficiencies in systems and programs and assisting in arriving at best solutions.

3. Attainment of maximum economy in the utilization of EDP equipment and operations personnel in relation to planned needs. This involves:
   a. Attainment of maximum possible utilization of EDP equipment through operations scheduling.
   b. Effective utilization of personnel to attain highest possible output.
   c. Advising and recommending necessary addition or deletion of equipment.
   d. Effective control of general operating expenses.

4. Effective development and preservation of EDP operational techniques, procedures and accumulated base information. This involves:
   a. Development and meticulous maintenance of department methods and procedures; files and records, documentation of operational procedures, etc.
   b. Protection of information against loss by fire, theft, accidental or purposeful destruction, etc.

5. Effective development and management of organization. This involves:
   a. Planning organization, delegation of responsibility and manpower needs and recommending changes.
   b. Selecting, developing, motivating and appraising performance of staff and recommending salary adjustments and promotions.
   c. Administering company policies related to various personnel activities.
   d. Assuring proper coordination within department and with all other Maytag departments and vendors.

---

## A CONSUMER PRODUCTS MANUFACTURER
### EDP PROJECT LEADER

BASIC FUNCTION

Analyze company business problems with responsibility for definition of information requirements and operational needs providing task-by-task assistance, guidance and direction to project team. Prepare formal presentation and written reports for review purposes on specific project direction for which responsibility exists. Participates in the organization, scheduling and estimating of individual projects and is in direct liaison with the management and personnel of user departments.

PRIMARY RESPONSIBILITIES

1. Assist in scope and objectives definition of systems studies and in preparation of detail work plans resulting in specific project. Control single project using detail work plan with responsibility for all project assigned personnel. Develop effective "audit trails" to verify correctness and/or completeness of particular project approving completed or altered programs for operational status.

2. Analyze present manual and/or EDP systems and procedures and design improved approaches working within project scope and objectives. Document problems, solutions and recommendations.

3. Define design criteria and design detail of new systems or systems improvements, participating in their development as a working team member. Evaluates system feasibility, selects appropriate analytical approaches, defines system logic and hardware requirements and directs improvements and/or corrections of existing systems.

4. Develop and analyze cost statistical data in preparation of economic comparisons associated with various alternatives to project development including cost evaluation of current system.

5. Coordinates the design of data processing logic and procedures, establishes operating parameters, selects appropriate equipment. Controls the organization, preparation and maintenance of systems documentation at all levels assisting in its creation as a working team member.

6. Present systems proposals and recommendations to data processing or management groups.

7. Recommend staff requirements for implementation. Direct the project implementation efforts in preparation of systems test data, parallel processing, project training and education, conversion schedules and user training, etc.

8. Develops and documents anticipated system volumes, data storage needs, and projected equipment utilization to assist in the planning for EDP equipment acquisition.

9. Review and report on systems proposals and their economics after implementation and design procedures and schedules for supplementary recommendations.

10. Participate in the indoctrination and training of new personnel in all System Development areas.

11. Participate in the development and implementation of internal and external departmental standards.

DECISION-MAKING RESPONSIBILITY
Independently review, analyze, document and report on current systems in

accordance with project scope and departmental standards. Define design approaches, equipment requirements, program language, input/output characteristics, operational consideration, etc. associated with design of a new system. Recommend the design of the total system. Create all aspects of systems documentation, direct and control systems analysts during the project implementation.

COMMENTS

Applicants for this position are evaluated for continued growth and development in the systems and EDP environment leading into assignments requiring increased amounts of technical knowledge, business exposure and supervision responsibility.

Applicant must be able to communicate both in writing and orally in addition to presenting a professional image of both EDP and Bell & Howell. It is essential to remain current and informed of any new technical or applications-oriented information.

This position serves as the stepping stone into the management functions within EDP and is the point at which supervisory exposure becomes a major factor in continued growth.

---

# NORTON COMPANY
## (*Computer Systems & Services*)
### SENIOR SYSTEMS ANALYST

*Reports to:* Manager of Systems (Worc)

ACCOUNTABILITY OBJECTIVE

Examine, identify and quantify the information needs of corporate or divisional management; recommend new systems to corporate or divisional management for the purpose of improving existing systems or providing new information or capabilities where none existed before; participate in the organization and scheduling of corporate and/or divisional projects whose aim is the identification and solution of various business systems inefficiencies and problems; provide direction and control within the specifications of the project schedule.

NATURE AND SCOPE

This position, along with two systems analysts and a variable number of non-CS project leaders, reports to the Manager of Systems.

The position of Senior Systems Analyst is essentially that of a higher level systems analyst with project but not administrative responsibilities. Incumbent is assigned to systems projects to provide direction and control within the specifications of the project schedule. As project leader, he participates in the project organization and scheduling and is in direct liaison with management and personnel of the user department.

Most importantly, the Incumbent, in the course of his daily activities, remains alert for other actual and potential trouble spots which might become the subject of future study. The Incumbent summarizes the problem's characteristics, defines its information requirements and analyzes possible cost savings, describes possible procedural and operating improvements and defines possible data processing support.

Incumbent conducts studies of existing manual and automated systems to determine the feasibility of converting them to new or improved data processing systems. This involves a complete investigation of the system to establish how it functions, what type of data it generates, what other systems and inputs are involved, and what the associated costs are. He then designs a complete system which includes not only the design of programs for the specific function under consideration but also the integration of the new system with all relative and/or associated systems. Incumbent then determines the probable cost savings and submits documented recommendations on each study to the Manager of Systems; he may also be required to oversee the implementation of his recommendations.

He is available on call to all corporate and divisional units for assistance and consultation on problems concerning virtually any aspect of business systems analysis.

If the Incumbent is called upon to implement a given system, he performs the major functions of systems development which are: application selection, systems survey, data gathering, data analysis, detailed design, programming, system test, training, conversion, evaluation, maintenance and documentation. He brings his additional training and experience to bear upon a problem, applying in detail all the general concepts which form the basis for his recommendations.

This position requires an extensive knowledge of business and business administration problems, a good background in accounting and/or financial areas and a sound understanding of mathematics, management science techniques, state of the art computer hardware, data management techniques and general business systems.

Incumbent may travel to any plant or division to set up or verify input and procedures, usually consulting with local management, or he may travel to any of a number of conferences, seminars or classes to remain abreast of the latest developments in various fields.

Incumbent functions with a minimum of supervision. His relationship with his supervisor involves keeping him informed as to the design, development and scheduling status of projects. In some cases, he requests the assistance of his supervisor to resolve organizational differences, make use of resources of other departments or for technical or analytical consultation.

SPECIFIC ACCOUNTABILITIES

1. Analyze present systems and procedures for possible improvement.
2. Determine the feasibility of converting existing manual and automated systems to new or improved data processing systems and design such systems upon approval.
3. Design improved approaches to operating situations.
4. Analyze cost statistics and prepare economic comparison of alternatives.
5. Organize and prepare systems documentation.
6. Organize and direct the execution of systems analysis and design tasks performed by systems analysts.
7. Design procedures and schedules for supplementary recommendations.
8. Consult and advise all divisional and corporate units on any aspect of business systems analysis, as requested.

---

# THE MAYTAG COMPANY
## SENIOR SYSTEMS PROGRAMMER

*Reports to:*  Manager, Systems and Programming

I CHARACTER OF THE JOB (Nature and Scope)

This position exists to provide software technical support to systems, programming and EDP operations staffs, and serves as the link between IBM and other vendor software specialists and Maytag personnel responsible for the development and maintenance of the operating system. The position involves constant evaluation of developments in the field of computer software and the implementation of appropriate methods and techniques to attain the most effective utilization of the computer used at Maytag. The incumbent must also keep abreast of developments in hardware characteristics and programming techniques.

Management relies heavily on the technical judgments of the incumbent regarding recommended changes in the operating system since he is the software specialist at Maytag.

The position requires thorough knowledge of computer operating characteristics, programming techniques and Maytag EDP systems and programs; ability to analyze highly technical information and to translate appropriate improvements into operating practice; and exercising verbal and written communication skills in contacts with Maytag and IBM personnel and other companies who use hardware and operating systems similar to Maytag. The position requires close coordination between IBM specialists and various Maytag EDP personnel.

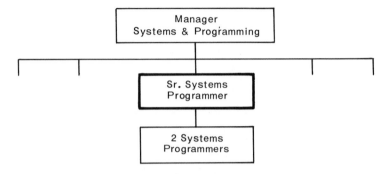

II STATISTICAL DATA

Annual computer rental is about $ _____.

III ACCOUNTABILITIES (End Results)

1. Development of effective operating systems and techniques required to attain maximum utilization from computer. This involves:

    a. Appraising latest developments and improvements in the field of software by studying literature, attending schools and communicating with members of software specialist association.

    b. Evaluating feasibility of IBM releases and other vendor software packages for use at Maytag, and recommending application, modification or rejection of specific releases or packages.

    c. Providing technical information and advice to superiors who finally determine which software and hardware changes shall be installed.

    d. Assuring that required hardware changes are made in order to use new operating system features and techniques.

    e. Developing system generation for approved changes and testing to assure proper results (operates computer as necessary).

    f. Coordinating programming and operations functions to achieve orderly implementation of operating system changes.

    g. Working with IBM field engineers to diagnose operating system problems or determine if problems are caused by hardware rather than software; implementing corrective actions after diagnosing is completed.

2. Effective documentation and maintenance of operating system. This involves:

    a. Assuring maintenance of records such as log of fixes, operating system manuals and files, literature library, master card decks and tapes and sample programs.

   b. Preparing procedural instructions and distributing and filing.
   c. Maintenance of current records related to operating system data stored in computer and systems listings.
   d. Recording operating systems problems encountered and corrective action employed.

3. Provision of software knowledge and problem solving support to programming staff. This involves:
   a. Establishing standards of job control techniques used by programmers.
   b. Developing training aids and courses, and presenting to groups or individuals involved in the use of job control and other operating system techniques.
   c. Assisting systems designers and programmers to incorporate techniques best suited to Maytag operating system.
   d. Maintaining library of programming test packs.
   e. Writing new programs or selecting and modifying available utility programs; instructing application programmers to properly use utility programs.
   f. Assisting programmers to test new user programs, particularly if new operating system techniques are being used.
   g. Providing detailed documentation for new programming techniques or canned programs.
   h. Assisting application programmers in solving specific job blow-offs by analyzing dump print-outs and determining cause and corrective action.
   i. Writing, testing and installing approved computer access methods.
   j. Providing technical support in the development and implementation of major projects such as multi-programming, conversion, recovery routines, use of new program languages and tele-processing.

4. Effective assistance to EDP operations personnel in the proper application of job control and other operating system techniques. This involves:
   a. Assuring the proper maintenance of disk file organization and space allocations.
   b. Planning and preparing written instructions to guide computer operations personnel in the use of operating system procedures.
   c. Conducting group or individual instruction sessions and demonstrating proper application on computer.
   d. Trouble shooting operating problems which may be caused by operating system procedures or techniques.
   e. Recommending changes to operating system to correct problems and improve efficiency.
   f. Working with IBM specialists, EDP operations management and programming supervisor to arrange for alternate computer source when Maytag computer is down for excessive periods of time or additional time is required for testing.

g. Assisting operating management in the planning of methods and schedules to gain most benefit from hardware and operating system.

5. Effective coordination of software packages requested and utilized by any of system design groups. This involves:
   a. Analyzing requests for purchase or installation of new software packages for feasibility, and recommending application of best packages to serve needs.
   b. Cooperating with systems designers and using departments to implement approved projects.
   c. Providing hardware and software technical assistance to engineering departments in the use of computer for research, planning and problem solving applications.

6. Effective development and supervision of subordinate systems programmers. This involves:
   a. Training and evaluating performance of subordinates.
   b. Assigning projects, auditing progress and resolving problems encountered by subordinates.
   c. Administering company policies related to personnel activity.

## *Nonmanufacturing—Officers*

### AN AIRLINE COMPANY
#### CHAIRMAN OF THE BOARD
#### AND CHIEF EXECUTIVE OFFICER

*Immediate Supervisor:* Board of Directors

PURPOSE OF POSITION

*Concisely summarize the basic function of the position.*

Serves as the Corporation's chief executive officer, responsible for directing the business in a way which will produce maximum profit and return on invested capital consistent with the balanced best interests of passengers, employees, stockholders and the general public; establishes current and long-range objectives, plans and policies; interprets and applies the policies of the Board of Directors and presides at its meetings; and controls, coordinates and maintains the various functions and operations of the Corporation.

## MAJOR DUTIES

*In order of significance, list responsibilities and tasks which will require the major portion of the position's attention. Use action verbs: e.g., analyze, interpret, develop, recommend, etc. (Attach extra sheet if necessary.)*

1. Establishes service and financial objectives of the Corporation and plans for their accomplishment, including expense and capital budgets, submitting these to the Board of Directors for approval.

2. Establishes major policies governing the Corporation's operations.

3. Reviews the major objectives, plans for their accomplishment and policies of all major line and staff departments, and ensures conformance with overall Corporate objectives, plans and policies.

4. Plans for the development of personnel resources within the Corporation and maintains programs which will ensure successful future management of the Corporation.

5. Determines the over-all structure of organization of the Corporation, the assignment of major functions, the staffing of key executive positions and major personnel actions concerning these positions, seeking the approval of the Board of Directors as appropriate.

6. In conjunction with appropriate functional executives, borrows money, contracts debts, executes deeds, leases, contracts and instruments of conveyance and appoints and discharges agents; signs certificates of stock, checks, drafts, notes and orders for payment of money as provided in the Corporation's By-laws.

7. Presides as chairman of stockholder meetings and administers the Corporation stockholder relationships, including the handling of official Corporate correspondence, and presides at meetings of the Board of Directors. Serves as member of various Board committees.

8. Controls and coordinates the Corporation's use of retained Legal Counsel.

9. Responsible for membership and project assignment to Management committees.

## CONTACT RELATIONSHIPS

*Indicate the primary positions inside or outside the company with which this position has regular contact and the reasons for this contact.*

Members of the Board of Directors and other members of management on matters concerning the Corporation's objectives, development plans, policies and performance generally. In his role as the Corporation's principal representative, maintains appropriate relationships with customers, suppliers, competitors, bankers and other financial institutions, service organizations, legal counsel, government agencies, industry associations, stockholders and the general public.

Basic title of highest level subordinate: President. Number of individuals directly supervised at this level: 1; number of individuals directly supervised, but at

lower levels: 2; total number of individuals directly and indirectly supervised: Total Corporation.

## Nonmanufacturing—Finance

---

## EASTERN AIRLINES
### EXECUTIVE VICE PRESIDENT,
### FINANCE AND ADMINISTRATION

*Reports to:* Chairman of the Board and Chief Executive Officer

BASIC FUNCTIONS
- Serves as the Company's Executive Vice President, Finance and Adminis-
tration.
- Directs the development and execution of major financial policies, plans,
procedures and controls.
- Ensures the provision of such financial services to the Company as
    accounting
    financial planning and control
    audits
    properties administration
    real estate activities
    administrative methods and procedures
    purchasing and equipment sales
    treasury
    financial public relations
- Directs the procurement and leasing of flight equipment
  —approves the contracted sale of obsolete equipment
  —approves leasing of surplus aircraft
- Directs financial analysis of and participates in the negotiations for
mergers.
- Directs financial analysis of and participates in acquisition negotiations
and internal development programs on a project basis.
- Furnishes Corporate direction to the subsidiary operations of the Company (hotels and other non-airline subsidiary corporations) in accordance
with approved plans and policies
  —reviews financial results and makes recommendations accordingly
- Maintains a Company management information system responsive to

—needs of the Chairman of the Board and Chief Executive Officer for effective control and direction of the Company
—needs of the President and Chief Operating Officer for effective management of airline operation
—needs of the other organizational units of the Company for decision-making and direction and control of their respective activities
- Serves as a member of the Executive Policy Committee and as a member of that Committee
—recommends major objectives and strategies concerning the Company's activities
—reviews and recommends action to be taken on major policies and plans
—evaluates total Company performance
- Serves as a member of the Board of Directors of National Distribution Services, Inc., and as President and Chief Executive Officer of
Dorado Beach Estates, Inc.
Dorado Beach Development, Inc.
Dorado Beach Hotel Corporation

## RESPONSIBILITIES

### PLANNING AND POLICY RESPONSIBILITIES

- Reviews and recommends overall financial objectives, strategies and policies of the Company consistent with approved Corporate objectives and goals.
- Ensures the development of financial and administrative policies, including those related to accounting, auditing, budgeting, treasury, purchasing and administrative services, based on the overall objectives of the Company.
- Provides financial assistance and guidance to the President and Chief Operating Officer in the development of major objectives and policies, in the review of plans and budgets for the operating divisions and staff departments reporting to him, and in the development of appropriate financial controls and reports.
- Furnishes executive management guidance on the Company's financial capability for expansion and growth; ensures that funds are provided for anticipated operating and capital expenditures to meet established requirements.
- Develops and recommends the long-range organization plans for those elements of the organization under his direction, with the guidance and assistance of the Vice President-Corporate Development.
- Participates with the Chairman of the Board and Chief Executive Officer, President and Chief Operating Officer, and Vice President-Corporate Development in the formulation of major objectives and strategies of the Company.

PROCEDURAL RESPONSIBLIITIES

- Establishes and recommends procedures governing
  —the financial activities of the Company such as those related to
    - recording, monitoring and evaluating its financial performance
    - cost and revenue allocation
    - the protection and conservation of Company assets
    - budgeting
    - reporting of financial results
    - receipt and disbursement of funds
    - short and long-term cash forecasting
  —purchasing and contracting
  —maintenance and publication of the Standard Practice Manuals System
  —tax and insurance planning and administration
- Ensures the establishment of procedures for capital and expense authority levels and monitors commitment performance based on authorizations.
- Develops procedures governing the financial activities of the Company.
- Approves major administrative and operating procedures submitted by the Officers who report directly to him.

OTHER RESPONSIBILITIES

- Assists the Chairman of the Board and Chief Executive Officer in the Company's major external relationships
  —contributes to the external image of the Company through public statements and participation in external affairs
- Ensures that approved policies, plans and procedures are implemented for assigned areas of responsibility.
- Approves capital and operating expenditures within budgets and the limits of his authority.
- Reviews and accepts policies and programs of staff departments for implementation by those elements of the organization under his direction
  —monitors staff services and support to see that they are consistent with departmental needs
- Reviews and recommends the organization plans and succession plans, both short and long range for those elements of the organization under his direction.
- Directs the development of performance standards for all elements of the organization under his direction.
- Implements, with the counsel and support of the Senior Vice President-Industrial and Personnel Relations, approved personnel programs, and takes all necessary actions to ensure maximum productivity of employees under his direction.
- Ensures that all appropriate Company and departmental objectives, policies, plans, programs, procedures, progress reports and related background information are communicated and explained to all employees under his direction.

- Serves as a member of the Board of Directors, Executive Policy Committee, and Corporate Staff Committee, and Chairman of the Finance Committee.
- Directs and participates in the negotiations with commercial banks, investment bankers, insurance companies, securities brokers and other financial agencies designed to provide for the capital requirements of the Company.
- Presents to, and interprets financial statements and reports for, the Chairman of the Board and Chief Executive Officer, the Board of Directors, the President and Chief Operating Officer, and the Executive Policy Committee
  —provides counsel and guidance on financial matters as appropriate
- Directs the sale of obsolete equipment and material.
- Exercises functional authority over the control of costs and expenses and the discharge of accounting and treasury functions throughout the Company.
- Recommends the independent public accountants to be retained as auditors of the Company's accounts.

## RELATIONSHIPS

### INTERNAL
- Confers with the President and Chief Operating Officer on
  —opportunities for securing optimum profits
  —the financial analysis of operating performance, budgets and appropriations
  —the maintenance of effective financial control
- Confers with the Senior Vice President-Industrial and Personnel Relations regarding recruitment, compensation, management development and training, employee relations and related matters.
- Confers with the Senior Vice President-Legal Affairs on those legal aspects of activities under his direction.
- Confers with the Senior Vice President-Public Affairs on governmental matters.
- Confers with the Senior Vice President-Public Relations on those activities dealing with financial relations.
- Confers with the Vice President-Corporate Development on the Company's diversification program, organization change and other related matters.

### EXTERNAL
- Represents the Company in appropriate relationships with major elements of the financial community, customers, the press, suppliers, competitors, industry associations, and government agencies.

## SUPERVISION
- The Executive Vice President-Finance and Administration delegates re-

sponsibilities to, and supervises the activities of, personnel in the following positions:

Vice President and Controller
Vice President and Treasurer
Vice President-Computer Sciences
Staff Vice President-Purchasing
Staff Vice President-Real Estate Development
Staff Vice President-Properties
Director-Corporate Investments
Director-Financial Analysis and Development, Finance
Executive Assistant to the Executive Vice President, Finance and Administration

## DEFINITION OF SATISFACTORY PERFORMANCE

NOTE: The following points state in general terms what is a satisfactory level of performance. They are not intended to be "standards of performance" which are specific, predetermined measures of performance.

• The performance of the Executive Vice President-Finance and Administration is satisfactory when
—the Company's long-range capitalization program is responsive to Company objectives
  adequate funds for established requirements are provided in a timely manner at a cost consistent with prevailing conditions and in keeping with the capitalization program
—the Company's profit objectives are well-defined, and areas for potential improvement identified
—inspirational leadership is provided to the organization, and the Company's image and objectives are effectively communicated to employees
—financial and statistical data analyses and reports provide meaningful and complete information for effective review and control of the Company's operations in a timely manner
—the Company's operations receive the benefit of automated and electronic data processing and computer capabilities to the fullest extent consistent with technical development and economic results
—counsel and assistance provided to management promote timely action and contribute to the attainment of financial and operating objectives
—operating and capital plans realistically reflect Company capabilities and requirements, effectively coordinate all financial aspects of Company operations, are well supported and justified by pertinent analysis, receive the endorsement of the officers responsible for their implementation and fully meet requirements established by the Company
—plans are developed which identify realistic growth and profit opportunities, facilitate the accomplishment of objectives and policies, and contribute to the achievement of the maximum allowable return on investment by the Company

—negotiations concluded for mergers or acquisitions reflect the best possible terms for the Company and are in line with the objectives established

—the Company's relationships with employees, stockholders, the financial community, the government, the industry and the general public are harmonious and constructive

## *Nonmanufacturing—Marketing*

# A GAS HOLDING COMPANY
## VICE PRESIDENT, MARKETING

PRINCIPAL OBJECTIVE

Integrates all phases of the company's retail marketing activities and coordinates a balanced marketing, market research, sales forecasting and advertising program.

KNOW-HOW (Illustrated by Activities)

The retail marketing functions of the company are managed by the Groups, and are divided into three sections: Industrial Sales, Business Promotion (promotion of gas and gas consuming appliances for residences, apartments, restaurants, and other commercial consumers) and Area Development. The company supplies roughly ____% of all the gas consumers in the United States.

The incumbent reports to the President. His organization includes a Director of Advertising, who is assisted by an Advertising Manager; and a Director of Market Research, who is assisted by a Sales Research Analyst and a Market Research Analyst. This core group has the mission of unifying the marketing activities of the four Groups and of their individual sections, of providing single source negotiation with manufacturers of gas appliances and equipment, of forecasting for Group and other facilities planning purposes overall long- and short-range usage demands and patterns, of developing advertising programs and of conducting appropriate market research.

The Vice President played a major role in helping develop good gas-fueled air conditioners, an important gas consuming appliance which tends to balance out light summer demand. Incumbent guided development of and obtaining Management approval for a method of "packaging" appliances so that the company can compete with similar "complete sets" of electrical household appliances offered in the new building market for residential and apartment projects. His office assists the Groups to secure approval for financing of the gas appliances and equipment for large projects.

1. *Coordinates* a unified domestic sales promotion effort by the Groups, recommends credit and financing strategies to promote sales of gas-using appliances, arranges sources of appliances, oversees preparation of advertising material for radio, television, newspapers, dealer sales pamphlets and direct mail campaigns.

2. *Reinforces* the industrial sales negotiations and efforts of the Groups by helping provide sound marketing strategy. Conducts studies to determine desirability of prospective customers and of the load and financial arrangement under which services can be established.

3. *Provides,* in collaboration with Groups and Planning Department, company-wide analyses of gas usage patterns and forecasts of long- and short-term requirements.

4. *Coordinates* and recommends policy in periods of gas shortage toward all users, residential, commercial and industrial.

5. *Authoritatively informs* top management on marketing matters. Investigates and recommends marketing policy changes.

6. *Arranges* annual or biennial three-day, company-wide seminars to acquaint approximately 300 industrial and business promotion personnel from the Groups with marketing matters.

7. *Guides* development of advertising and promotion programs.

8. *Supervises* market research including an annual survey of customer preferences, requirements and plans. This reveals year to year trends.

9. *Communicates* with Group marketing managements by frequent visits, correspondence, periodic issuance of Bulletin, and issuance of monthly statistics on business activity.

10. *Represents* company on various industry marketing committees of A.G.A., *Upgrade, Uprange,* National Association of Home Builders and others.

PROBLEM SOLVING

The major challenges are found in implementing measures to maintain gas's share of market, to optimize profitable sales results by developing residential and commercial base loads and industrial process loads to improve overall load factor and air conditioning load to fill the summer valley.

ACCOUNTABILITY

Insures that the company has a coherent and appropriate marketing program, supported by market research and advertising programs; provides authoritative reports of marketing results and usage forecasts for company's guidance. The company has about 1,800,000 customers; sales revenues exceed $ _____; sales have increased ____ % in the past ten years.

*Nonmanufacturing—Personnel
and Labor Relations*

## A DIVERSIFIED COMPANY
### VICE PRESIDENT, MANAGEMENT RESOURCES

GENERAL FUNCTIONS AND SPECIFIC RESPONSIBILITIES

The Vice President, Management Resources is responsible to the President for:

A. Providing counsel and guidance to the President and management of the Corporation, its Divisions, Departments and Subsidiaries in organizing, acquiring, developing and maintaining its Management Resources through the design and recommendation of compatible organization structures, through the procurement and development of operational and long-range manpower capability, skills, and continuity, through the design and implementation of viable compensation and benefits programs, through effective Labor, Minority and Employee Relations, and through a system of comprehensive personnel administration so as to assist the management achieve the goals and business objectives of the Company.

   1. Analyzes Corporate and managerial objectives and initiates design, development and recommendations for the implementation of organization structures and catalytic business environments that will integrate Company and individual objectives so as to produce optimal results.

   2. Identifies the conditions that are necessary for change to take place and those other conditions that will facilitate the change process.

   3. Provides through organization development assistance to Corporate and Divisional management in translating personalized organizational philosophies into viable managerial systems and techniques; defining specific responsibilities and authorities, providing flexibility control, coordination and two-way communications necessary to achieve Division and Corporate objectives.

   4. Directs the implementation of a continuous management resources process that identifies and projects Division and Departmental needs with regard to organization patterns, executive manpower requirements, management development needs and departmental action plans to meet those needs.

   5. Directs the design, formulation establishment and maintenance of sound compensation policies and procedures throughout the Company, ensuring corporate-wide administrative maintenance and seeing that Corporate structures remain competitive and correlate directly to operational objectives.

   6. Directs the development, recommendation, establishment and maintenance of benefit plans, policies and appropriate procedures for the administration of those insured Company benefits programs to include:

pensions, profit sharing, savings, life insurance, major medical insurance, and travel accident insurance.

7. Fosters and ensures, through appropriate guidelines and direction, the negotiation of equitable policies and agreements, continuous and harmonious working relationships between employees, the unions, and the management of the Company.

8. Identifies, designs, and directs the development of positive affirmative action programs in response to opportunities or to preclude inadequacies in minority employment, development or compensation within the Company.

9. Directs the formulation and implementation of Personnel policy and administration so as to ensure the provision of integrated Personnel Services to all Divisions and Departments within the Company.

B. Developing and directing the maintenance of a competent and adequate organization, recommending and maintaining budget; developing and implementing appropriate plans and projects; developing, recommending, administrating and maintaining policies and procedures; establishing standards of quality and performance and evaluating his department against those standards.

1. Directs the organization of his department so as to accomplish established objectives, recommending and establishing effective lines of authority, responsibility and communications.

2. Selects, develops, motivates, counsels and evaluates the personnel reporting to him.

3. Directs the development and compilation of total departmental budget and maintains approved budget.

4. Develops and establishes performance standards for his department and evaluates his personnel against these standards.

RELATIONSHIPS

A. The Vice President, Management Resources reports to the President.

B. Supervises:
1. Director, Compensation and Benefits
2. Director, Minority Relations
3. Director, Organization Development
4. Director, Labor Relations
5. Vice President, Personnel Operations

C. Maintains internal relationships with:
1. Executive management, Corporate Staff, Department and Division Staffs and managements as required.

D. Maintains external relationships with:
1. Manpower agencies
2. Consultants

3. Federal, state and local officials
4. Minority leaders
5. Labor leaders and associations
6. Executives in similar positions
7. Professional associations

# A RAILROAD

## MANAGER, ORGANIZATION PLANNING AND EMPLOYMENT

*Reports to:*  Director—Personnel

### POSITION PURPOSE

To infuse the company with new professional and managerial level employees, and to assist all departments in the manpower planning relating thereto.

### DIMENSIONS

Indeterminate

### NATURE AND SCOPE

This position reports to the Director-Personnel as do the following positions: Personnel Assistant, Salary Administrator, Manager of Training and Development, and seven Division Personnel Officers. The Personnel Specialist reports to the incumbent.

The incumbent is responsible for the interviewing, screening, and recruitment of candidates for professional and managerial positions within the company. Meeting this requirement the incumbent must coordinate closely with various departments within the company on manpower planning and staffing needs. He must work with departments in analyzing present and proposed organizational structure, recommending the creation or formation of new or revised positions as appropriate. He works with various departments to determine what qualifications are required in an area where a professional position vacancy exists, and in what way the qualifications and characteristics needed can best be found. This function includes advising departments with staffing needs of the existing labor market conditions, appropriate salary levels to be consistent with other areas within the company (coordinating with the Salary Administrator to maintain the integrity of the Salary Administration Program), and competition from other firms. The incumbent also advises departments of the availability of specific educational backgrounds and qualifications from various sources.

The position requires expert and in depth knowledge of all sources of potential professional employees. This includes maintaining recruiting schedules with various colleges and universities in the Western United States, coordinating the recruiting activities with Division Personnel Officers, making campus recruiting visits, and conducting campus interviews. The incumbent works with university placement officials between recruiting visits so that their graduates can be screened for particular vacancies, or for a certain set of skills or background. The incumbent insures that the various placement offices are supplied with information about the company and about career opportunities within the company that might be available to graduates. This includes the preparation and distribution of literature about career opportunities.

In addition to campus sources, the incumbent is required to prepare and run advertisements to fill vacancies requiring experience or skills not normally found on campuses. The incumbent also serves as the preliminary interviewing and screening agent for candidates who are being considered for the Officer Development Program. These candidates are evaluated by the incumbent with follow-up interviews then being arranged for recommended candidates, so that they may be further evaluated by other company officers. In addition to the screening activity the incumbent is also involved in actively seeking the best possible candidates for these positions.

The position requires considerable independent judgment and professional knowledge. Given a staffing requirement, incumbent must devise a scheme of action leading to the successful placement of a qualified individual. This is often extremely difficult, inasmuch as individuals with specialized skills, specific education, and narrowly defined experience may be requested. A wide variety of labor market sources must be used.

The incumbent is responsible for screening and answering all mail inquiries about possible employment. These resumes are reviewed with prospects being contacted and interviewed, and information on these individuals passed along to other departments for their consideration.

The incumbent also represents the company at such activities as Veterans Job Fair, the Chamber of Commerce Christmas Holiday Job Fair, and college and high school career days where there is both a possibility of finding qualified employees, and of dispensing information about the company. The incumbent is responsible for arranging interviews in Omaha with potential candidates who are of interest to a particular department, and then taking follow-up action in terms of writing a job offer or a negative response after the headquarters interview.

The incumbent must also work on the continuous development of company organization charts, and is responsible for periodic updates. This is a necessary prelude to organizational planning and development looking toward better organizational structure, clearer lines of responsibility, and designing career paths. The incumbent must be an expert on manpower planning and organizational structure. He must work with Company Departments to best structure and organize new positions as well as existing positions.

The incumbent works with Management Information Services coordinating the needs of the Personnel Department for automated systems support and the construction of these systems by MIS. The incumbent works with MIS on the Personnel Information Systems (PINS) Project to supply the Personnel Department, and company management, with basic information on: personnel data, authorized work force, skills inventory, and salary administration. Presently the incumbent is working with an MIS task force researching for the design of the segment of PINS to furnish basic personnel data. The work includes determining needed data for reports, dates of reports, input documents, and the information output desired and its format.

The incumbent handles any other specific tasks assigned by the Director-Personnel.

PRINCIPAL ACCOUNTABILITIES

1. To work with other departments in the company helping with their manpower planning and staffing needs for professional and managerial positions.
2. To seek qualified employees for the company to fill professional vacancies using various sources including a regular scheduled campus recruiting program. This includes both departmental vacancies and positions in the Officer Development Program.
3. To manage the company college recruiting program, and insure good college relations.
4. To examine and document the organizational structure of the company and work with other departments in organization planning and staffing.
5. To handle resumes and employment inquiries by mail or in person arranging appropriate disposition and arranging departmental interviews where deemed appropriate.
6. To insure proper systems support from MIS by coordinating the needs of the Personnel Department with the planning and construction of computer support systems for the Personnel Department.

## Banking and Insurance

---

# SEATTLE–FIRST NATIONAL BANK
## CHIEF EXECUTIVE OFFICER

MISSION

As chief executive officer, exercises responsibility for the general management and coordination of all bank activities; ensures that the business of the bank is conducted on a sound, realistic, profitable basis in accordance with policies laid down by the Board of Directors; provides leadership for the entire staff.

SUPERVISES:
President
Manager, Washington Banking Group
Manager, U.S. and International Banking Group
Manager, Administration and Control Group
Manager, Bank-Related Businesses Division
Corporate Secretary

PRIME RESPONSIBILITIES

Recommends to the Board of Directors broad objectives and changes in basic overall policies.

Reviews and approves short- and long-range plans that will best meet the bank's objectives for growth and profit.

Recommends to the Board of Directors major changes in employment of the bank's resources (knowledge, skills, physical facilities, reputation and good will, as well as monetary assets) and, when necessary, recommends means for meeting the bank's capital needs.

Ensures that objectives, policies, plans, and programs for the bank as a whole are communicated to and understood by all officers, and encourages an upward flow of communication throughout the bank.

Interprets and reports periodically to the Board of Directors, stockholders and staff the results of the bank's operations and its financial condition.

Presides at all meetings of the Board of Directors and stockholders.

Serves as Chairman of the Senior Management Committee and of the Interim Committee. Presents recommendations of the latter committee, as appropriate, to the Executive Committee and the Board of Directors.

Sees that the bank's business development plans are consistent with the bank's objectives and that they are being carried out vigorously and effectively.

Ensures that the bank's profit centers (branches and Head Office departments) are being operated in a coordinated, aggressive manner that will develop maximum business at minimum cost.

Sees that staff divisions and departments are providing effective support to the line operations.

Recommends at least annually to the Compensation Committee of the Board salary adjustments for officers of Grade 10 and above. Reviews with the Committee salary policies and salary administration concerning officers generally. Approves adjustments, as per the Senior Officer Salary Approval Authorities, not subject to Committee review, or otherwise as necessary, between meetings of the Committee.

Sees that all S-FNB prsonnel policies and procedures are applied equally to all staff, with special emphasis on the bank's Affirmative Action Program and goals.

Exercises authority to hire suitable personnel and to relieve from duty those officers and employees not meeting bank standards. Recommends official terminations to the Board of Directors but, in case of urgency, takes necessary action at own discretion.

Proposes to the Board of Directors changes in official titles. Approves official promotions and transfers not involving changes in corporate title or, as he deems appropriate, recommends such changes to the Board.

Ensures that the bank's manpower planning and development programs are providing adequately for the bank's needs, both short and long term.

Maintains a continuous review of the bank's basic organization plan and institutes changes as necessary to make it fully and continuously effective.

Develops the managing abilities of subordinates through a combination of goal setting, delegation, training, counseling and performance reviews. Ensures that their objectives are challenging yet realistic, are being met, and that in appraising total job performance, accomplishments in relation to goals are recognized. Similarly, ensures that they are developing the management abilities of their subordinates and properly administering the Management by Objectives program in regard to them.

Represents the bank to the public, participating within reasonable time limitations in such activities and attending such conventions and other events as will enable him to most effectively promote the bank's image.

Obtains outside professional advice and counsel when appropriate.

---

# NORTHWEST BANCORPORATION
## SENIOR VICE PRESIDENT AND SECRETARY

*Immediate Supervisor:* President

POSITION SUMMARY
Contribute to the general management of Banco with specific responsibility for the investigation and negotiation of acquisitions; the relationship with regulatory authorities; and the credit and examination function.

DIMENSIONS
Total Corporate Assets: $ _____
Total Corporate Income: $ _____

NATURE AND SCOPE

This position reports to the President of the Northwest Bancorporation and, in his absence, the incumbent presides at meetings of directors and stockholders. Reporting to this position are the Chief Examiner, who reports to the Board of Directors, and the Vice President-Credit. The scope of this position is illustrated by a description of these reporting departments.

The *Chief Examiner* appointed by the Board and subject to removal only by them, conducts examinations of all affiliate banks and trust departments. He makes his own plans and schedules; reviews and prepares reports. Six Examiners conduct the examinations and report to the Chief Examiner. The incumbent provides a point where he can take up matters with management but provides only general guidance in the conduct of this position.

The *Credit Department,* managed by a Vice President, analyzes and reviews selected larger loans made by affiliates, assists the banks on individual credit problems, and communicates to the Bank Relations Officers observations regarding credit capabilities or deficiencies of affiliate banks. This Department is a very highly regarded training ground for credit and loaning officers. A formal training program of 18 to 24 months duration is conducted for a small group of young men, who, during training, will make exhaustive credit analyses and often present them to the Credit Committee. The incumbent meets with the Vice President-Credit on an informal basis and gives him general guidance in credit matters. Together, they formulate credit advice and guidance to be communicated through the Bank Relation Officers.

The incumbent maintains relationships and particularly good rapport with local, regional and national officials of various supervisory agencies. These include the F.D.I.C., Federal Reserve, Comptroller of the Currency and Supervisors of banks in seven states, visiting them as needed to discuss current matters. This activity is carried on in conjunction with the Vice President-Public Affairs, and may involve gaining approval of a complicated or controversial merger, or obtaining a green light to proceed with the acquisition of a company, such as Iowa Securities Real Estate, within statutory and regulatory limits.

The incumbent is charged with investigating, evaluating and negotiating possible acquisitions and assisting affiliates with mergers and related matters. In this role, he must carefully evaluate candidates for merger or acquisition in light of the stringent regulations and prohibitions of Federal and State laws, and be cognizant of the approvals necessary from both the Federal Reserve and the Justice Department. Important also are availability, cost of ownership and business implications of Banco becoming the owner. These acquisitions and mergers often involve meetings and close coordination with the Treasurer and other members of the Banco corporate staff.

The incumbent is currently caretaker of the position of Secretary. This position, when filled, will report to him and will be involved in providing support mainly in mergers and acquisitions.

The President delegates heavily to the incumbent in the above areas, and relies on the Senior Vice President to speak for him in his absence. The incumbent participates in several internal committees and the President may ask him to be a sounding board on certain matters. Other members of the staff may ask the Senior Vice President for his reaction to proposals and ideas, to gain insights before meeting with the President.

The incumbent participates in the deliberations of the Credit Advisory Committee and of the Investment Advisory Committee, whose membership represents Banco affiliated banks.

In addition the incumbent serves on the Boards of all the nonaffiliated companies except Iowa Securities and the Northwest Computer Services Company; is President of Union Investment Company and President of Northwest Agricultural Credit Company. He is Vice President of Northwest International Bank and of Northwestern Mortgage Company, and serves on the Board of Northwest Growth Fund.

PRINCIPAL ACCOUNTABILITIES
1. Assess potential candidates for acquisition or merger to assure all opportunities for growth are carefully considered and consummated when appropriate.
2. Direct the development and implementation of Banco's Examination and Credit policies to ensure continuity and long-term effectiveness.
3. Contribute to the development of Banco's policy and relations with regulatory agencies to ensure the development and retention of a good public image and a fair and equitable hearing for all issues.
4. Selects, develops, and directs a staff competent and motivated to meet current and ongoing commitments and adequate to ensure management continuity.
5. Represent Banco internally and externally to contribute to the enhancement of its image, the betterment of the community and the development of affiliate banks' business.
6. Represent the President of Banco in his absence in an effective manner to ensure continuity and efficiency in operation.

---

# LIFE INSURANCE COMPANY
## VICE PRESIDENT, DIRECTOR OF GROUP INSURANCE

*Title of Immediate Supervisor:* Executive Vice President

I POSITION SUMMARY
Planning, organizing, controlling and establishing policies and procedures for

achieving a satisfactory rate of growth in group premium income within budgetary limits. Responsibility for group sales and administration.

## II RESPONSIBILITIES

### PRINCIPAL POSITION DUTIES

1. General management of the Group Division consisting of sales and administration.
2. Setting goals for production and profit both on a short and long term basis and responsibility for their achievement.
3. Establishing marketing policies based on evaluation of performance by office, product line, case size, and by broker.
4. Prepare and submit annual Group Division budget and responsible for operating within it.
5. Prepare and submit personnel evaluations and salary recommendations.
6. Assignment and transfer of all Division personnel.
7. Supervision of Home Office accounts and six regional Group offices and liaison with General Agency Regional Managers.

### PLANNING, PROBLEM SOLVING, ANALYSIS, CREATIVE ACTIVITY

1. Develops plans for expansion into new territories including identification of priority locations, evaluation of potential brokers, determination of time and money required to reach profitable operation.
2. Coordinates new product development and marketing.
3. Analyzes annual and quarterly statements for Group Division and institutes corrective action where indicated.

### DECISION MAKING

1. Assignment of personnel.
2. Establishment of sales quotas.

## III SCOPE AND IMPACT

*Operating Budget for Area:*    $ _____
*Other Operating Responsibilities:*
1. General management of Division with $ _____ premium income, $ _____ group life in force.
2. New premium income approximately $ _____ annually.

*Personnel Supervised*
   6 Regional Managers
   Manager, Group Administration
   Executive Secretary

## IV EDUCATION, EXPERIENCE AND SKILLS REQUIRED

### SPECIALIZED KNOWLEDGE

Bachelor's level college degree, 10 years experience in group insurance, including a minimum of 5 years in group insurance field sales and good general management knowledge and skills.

OTHER KNOWLEDGE OR SKILL
1. Have knowledge to be able to make supportable decisions for Company and Division when in the field away from Home Office assistance.
2. Ability to plan, organize, sell, negotiate, persuade, administer.
3. Communicate effectively both orally and in writing.

---

# FIRST PENNSYLVANIA BANK
## ASSISTANT VICE PRESIDENT, TRUST

BASIC FUNCTION

Efficient, cost-saving management of the General Securities area (Vault, Collection, Capital Changes/Claims, Safekeeping, Trust Securities, Files, Corporate Custody, Journal Preparation)

ORGANIZATIONAL RELATIONSHIPS

| | |
|---|---|
| Reports to: | Sr. Vice President |
| Who reports to: | Vice Chairman |
| Supervises: | 3 officers and through them 8 Supervisors, 1 O/A and 82 clerks |
| Internal Relationships: | Trust/Investment Management Officers; Trust Operations Officers; EDP Officers and personnel |
| External Relationships: | Security brokers; other banks; occasionally Trust customers |

PRINCIPAL ACCOUNTABILITIES

1. Develop, review, maintain the most efficient operating procedures for the handling and protection of close to $4 billion of trust assets, and timely collection of the income on these assets, with minimum cost.
2. Analyze procedures and develop improved methods to achieve goals.
3. Direct an efficient, effective, flexible staff to provide quality service in spite of the ever demanding and challenging security market, and extreme pressures caused by deadlines.
4. Ensure coordination of division's operations with other areas of the bank, such as EDP, Financial, and related Trust areas.
5. Effective participation in policy and fact finding committee meetings to ensure accurate representation of department's function.
6. Efficient, prompt handling of special studies and projects.

DIMENSIONS: (Securities Operations)
    Budget:
    Expenses:

Salaries:
Other:
Exp. Credits:
Total Assets:
Income:
No. of accounts:

KNOW-HOW

*Technical:* Complete knowledge of securities and security markets, bank operations, trust accounting, acquired through on-the-job training and formal education.

*Managerial:* Developing good lines of communication with managers and supervisors, and setting goals and clear definition of responsibilities.

*Human Relations:* Effective communications with administrators, brokers, other banks; developing a high spirit of teamwork.

AUTHORITY

Within department policy, has complete freedom to manage division; major decisions concerning Trust and Investment Managers are referred to Sr. Vice President; policy committee and control meetings held regularly to maintain an open line of communication with Sr. V.P.

CRITICAL PROBLEM

Continuous review and analysis of current procedures to develop new or improve existing procedures, to keep "in tune" with an ever-changing industry.

---

## FIRST PENNSYLVANIA BANK
### ASSISTANT VICE PRESIDENT,
### CENTRAL CASH–DOMESTIC COLLECTIONS

BASIC FUNCTION
Manage the Central Cash–Domestic Collection Division.

DIMENSIONS
Total Annual Expense Budget:
Total Salaries:
Total Value of Equipment:
Daily average value of negotiable coupons and payments:
Average daily cash on hand:
Monthly average cash received on deposit:

Monthly average cash paid out:
Total Staff: 1 officer, 60 non-officers.

NATURE AND SCOPE

Incumbent reports to Sr. Vice President, Funds Processing, who reports to Executive Vice President.

The Money Processing Section, under the direction of the Administrative Officer, consists of 44 non-officer employees handling all cash deposits received, cash orders and payrolls, pre-packaging currency, proving coin, wrapping coin, etc., for storage, return to Federal Reserve, or delivery to branches, large customers, correspondent banks; operates teller windows for Operations Center employees and a drive-in window for customers.

The Administrative Officer makes majority of decisions, keeping incumbent informed on activities, problems, decisions, discussing with or referring to incumbent such matters as unusual or continuing shortages, serious security or personnel problems, continuing problems with equipment, pick up and delivery schedules, etc.

Domestic Collection, under the supervision of an Officer's Assistant, is staffed by 15 non-officer employees, and is responsible for processing and securing payment on coupons, matured and called bonds, and all negotiable instruments requiring special handling or advice (checks, drafts, letters of credit, promissory notes, commercial paper, trade acceptances, certificates of deposit, photocopies of lost or destroyed checks, etc.) from customers, correspondent banks, bank departments and branches.

While the Officer's Assistant in this area sees to the day-by-day operation of the Section, signs as authorized signature on entries, advices and portions of the Section's correspondence, incumbent makes decisions of a major nature and counsels Officer's Assistant from a management standpoint.

Incumbent sees that large currency deposits by either Section and withdrawals which affect Funds position of bank are reported immediately to Money Transfer Division.

He has frequent dealings with various National Division and Public Funds officers regarding details and arrangements for handling new or existing large commercial accounts.

He is also in frequent contact with Brinks Protective Motor Service and Arhnold's Armored Car Services regarding scheduling, extra service, etc., and with various correspondent banks and large commercial customers regarding pick up and delivery of currency and coin, differences, status of collection items, items lost in transit, reasons for non-payment of items, etc.

Considerable planning is involved in order to anticipate and prepare for meeting peak volume periods throughout the year, as well as in preparation of the divisional budgets.

PRINCIPAL ACCOUNTABILITIES
1. See to prompt, accurate handling of cash flowing through Money Processing Section.
2. See to prompt, accurate collection or payment of all types of negotiable instruments.
3. Develop improved operating procedures, additional controls and safeguards wherever possible.
4. Provide utmost in security of assets (human and monetary).

KNOW-HOW
*Technical:* Position requires thorough understanding and application of negotiable instrument laws, Bank's entries and accounting procedures in relation to assets, liabilities, due to and due from accounts, as well as understanding and application of currency and coin handling problems, scheduling, etc.

*Managerial:* Position requires ability to motivate and deal effectively through officers and line supervisors to achieve maximum performance of goals.

*Human Relations:* Ability to deal effectively with corporate customers, correspondent banks, outside vendors and suppliers of protective services.

AUTHORITY
Incumbent has full authority to hire, terminate, promote and transfer within his Division, recommend salary increases and transfers out of Division.

A CRITICAL PROBLEM
To maintain a constant watch and prepare for all contingencies to see that coin and currency are made available to branches, correspondent banks and many large corporate customers in spite of sickness, weather, disasters, strikes, etc., and to provide maximum security for both money and people under same circumstances.

## SEATTLE–FIRST NATIONAL BANK
### MANAGER, BANK PROPERTIES

MISSION: To direct the management of the bank's real property.

REPORTS TO: President

SUPERVISES: Manager, Building Management
Manager, Realty Control
Manager, Head Office Building

PRIME RESPONSIBILITIES

Works with his department managers in developing property policies and recommends new or changed policies to the President or to the Building Committee, as appropriate.

Coordinates the determination of branch sites, working with Branch Banking and Marketing Planning in developing appropriate recommendations.

Reviews recommendations for purchases, leases, and sales of bank real property, approves those involving a total of $25,000 or less and endorses those over $25,000 to the Building Committee.

Oversees the bank building and remodeling program. Approves projects of $50,000 or less and sets priorities for these, working with Manager, Branch Banking. Sees that projects over $50,000 are initiated according to priorities established by the Capital Budgeting process and follows through on architecture, planning, contracts, construction and accounting to ensure satisfactory quarters at minimum cost and within approved dollar figures.

Ensures maximum return from bank properties available for rental throughout the state, with particular attention to overseeing the Head Office Building and maintaining its standing as the prime office location in Seattle.

Sees that the bank's building maintenance program provides efficiently for quality quarters, conducive to desirable working conditions, enhancement of the bank image and preservation of the bank's investment in its buildings.

Oversees the purchase of furniture and fixtures for banking quarters statewide at minimum cost, but in keeping with quality and esthetic standards appropriate to the bank's image and needs. Sees that a program for maximizing utilization of excess equipment is followed.

Sees that the bank Stockroom, Print Shop and Machine Repair Shop are providing efficiently for bankwide needs. Works with the Manager, Administration and Control, to see that these operations and the purchasing operation are coordinating their efforts toward minimizing bank outlays for forms, stationery, office supplies and office machines.

Sees that residences acquired by the bank in connection with transfers of staff members are disposed of expeditiously and with best possible return to the bank, while minimizing problems for the staff members.

Ensures that assessments of bank properties by county officials are fair and that tax bills are in order before they are approved for payment.

Keeps alert to labor relations situations resulting from bank membership in building and other trade associations and consults with the Personnel Director as to proper bank position and/or action.

Develops the managing abilities of his subordinates through a combination of goal setting, delegation, training, counseling, and performance reviews. Ensures that their objectives are challenging yet realistic, are being met, and that salary recommendations are based on their accomplishments in relation to goals. Similarly, ensures that they are developing the management abilities of their subordinates and properly administering the Management by Objectives program in regard to them.

Exercises the following basic managerial responsibilities:

Implements bankwide policies and programs.

Develops short and long range plans for his division so as to effectively implement overall bank goals.

Develops productive inter-relationships with managers of other divisions and major departments and coordinates with them in programs and activities of an inter-divisional nature.

Utilizes and/or provides staff services across division lines.

Sees that bank responsibilities under the labor contract are understood and fulfilled throughout his division.

Encourages and participates in upward communication.

## SEATTLE–FIRST NATIONAL BANK
### MANAGER, BRANCH BANKING

MISSION:       To direct and coordinate Branch Banking activities.

REPORTS TO:   Chairman of Executive Committee

SUPERVISES:   Regional Vice Presidents
Administrative Operations Officer, Branch Banking
Administrative Personnel Officer, Branch Banking
Loan Administrator, Branch Banking
Manager, Firstbank Card
Marketing Manager, Branch Banking
President, Firstbank Leasing Corporation

PRIME RESPONSIBILITIES

Directs and coordinates activities of his regional vice presidents to ensure a positive and systemwide uniformity in applying bank policies and to maximize growth and profit at all branches.

Develops the management abilities of regional vice presidents and staff assistants through a combination of goal setting, delegation, training, counseling and performance reviews. Ensures that their goals are challenging yet realistic and in conformance with overall bank goals. Sees that objectives and managerial performance standards are being met and that salary recommendations are based thereon. Ensures that regional vice presidents are similarly developing the managing abilities of their branch managers.

Approves or endorses recommendations of regional vice presidents concerning hiring, firing, transfers and promotions of branch officers and the staffs of the regional officers, except as delegated to Administrative Personnel Officer, Branch Banking. Approves or endorses salary recommendations concerning branch and regional officers per Personnel Decision Guidelines for officer salary increases.

Keeps informed of the division's long- and short-range manpower needs and ensures that hiring and development programs are being pursued so as to eliminate present and potential manpower gaps. Sees that the best candidates systemwide are considered for filling official openings throughout the division.

Sees that management decisions and policy are communicated to regional vice presidents and guides them in application thereof; communicates developments in branches and regions to key officers in other divisions and to Chairman of Executive Committee.

Sees that the interests of branch and regional managers are represented and that support from other divisions is secured so as to enable them to exploit opportunities and out-do competing banks.

Reviews and endorses recommendations for new branches, for purchases of property to be used as branch sites and for new buildings and major remodeling projects, except as delegated to Administrative Operations Officer, Branch Banking. Recommends or endorses building and remodeling priorities to the Building Committee. Ensures that a continuing review is made of branch physical facilities as to public image, adequacy for customer service and satisfactory working conditions and sees that Administrative Operations Officer works with Manager, Bank Properties Division, in correcting deficiencies.

Approves or delegates authority to approve all loans and lines within policy guidelines and not in excess of limit established by the Chairman of Executive Committee. Recommends loan limits and referral levels for regional vice presidents to Chairman of Executive Committee and approves loan and reporting limits for branches as recommended by regional vice presidents.

Recommends loan policy changes to Manager, Loan Services Division or to Loan Review and Policy Committee, as appropriate.

Provides consultation to Chairman of Executive Committee in regard to changes in the bank's prime rate.

Works directly or through Branch Banking Loan Administration with Manager, Loan Services Division and managers of other lending divisions, as appropriate, in arriving at consensus concerning changes in interest rate guidelines.

Jointly with Manager, Bank Investment Division, decides on changes in Time CD rates.

Works with Manager, Marketing Planning Division, in developing recommendations to Resource/Asset Policy Committee concerning all other time deposit rates.

Sees that regions implement approved loan, operations, personnel and business development programs.

Exercises the following basic managerial responsibilities:
Implements bankwide policies and programs.
Develops short- and long-range plans for his division so as to effectively implement overall bank plans.
Develops productive inter-relationships with managers of other divisions and major departments and coordinates with them in programs and activities of an inter-divisional nature.
Utilizes and/or provides staff services across division lines.
Sees that bank responsibilities under the labor contract are understood and fulfilled throughout his division.
Encourages and participates in upward and downward communication.

# SEATTLE–FIRST NATIONAL BANK
## REGIONAL MANAGER

MISSION: To provide leadership, support and guidance to branches within his region and to develop competent, responsible, aggressive branch managers.

REPORTS TO: Manager, Branch Banking

SUPERVISES: Branch Managers
Staff Assistants

### PRIME RESPONSIBILITIES

Coordinates activities of branches in his region to ensure understanding of bank goals, uniformity in applying bank policies, and the maximizing of growth and profits of all branches.

Develops short and long range plans for his region that will effectively implement overall Branch Banking plans and coordinates branch planning efforts so that they properly support regional plans.

Develops the managing abilities of his branch managers and staff assistants through a combination of goal setting, delegation, training, counseling, and performance reviews. Ensures that their objectives are challenging yet realistic, are being met, and that salary recommendations are based on their accomplishments in relation to goals. Similarly, ensures that branch managers are developing the management abilities of their subordinates and properly administering the Management by Objectives program in regard to them.

Ensures that each branch manager periodically analyzes training and development needs of his staff and that plans are implemented to take care of these needs.

Recommends promotions, transfers, demotions and salary changes for branch managers and regional staff officers. Makes sure that deserving officers under his supervision are considered for promotions elsewhere in the bank when similar opportunity is not available in his own region.

Reviews and endorses recommendations by branch managers concerning salary adjustments for officers reporting to them.

Approves, or delegates authority to his loan supervisor to approve, all loans and lines within policy guidelines and not in excess of limits established by Manager, Branch Banking.

Recommends to Deputy Manager, Branch Banking, loans and lines over regional limits and branch requests for policy loan decisions.

Periodically reviews branch managers' lending limits and recommends changes to Deputy Manager, Branch Banking.

Assists branch managers in liquidating problem credits.

Makes sure branch managers are carrying out business development programs energetically.

Sees that his branches are operating efficiently and that the Work Management program is being fully utilized.

Reviews continually work of his staff officers to make sure that they are effectively assisting branch officers in improving credit, business development and operating abilities.

Ensures that branch managers get proper and necessary support in all ways from Head Office staff divisions and departments.

Advises Branch Banking of branch managers' suggestions for improvements in bank and branch policies, programs and operations. Encourages and participates in upward communications generally.

Sees that bank responsibilities under the labor contract are understood and fulfilled throughout his region.

Reports annually on overall regional performance to the Executive Committee.

---

## SEATTLE–FIRST NATIONAL BANK
### BRANCH MANAGER

MISSION:    To act as key representative of the bank in the trading area served by his branch and to manage the branch so as to fulfill local banking needs and achieve branch profit and other goals.

REPORTS TO:    Regional Manager

SUPERVISES:    All branch personnel, directly or indirectly.

## PRIME RESPONSIBILITIES

### BRANCH ADMINISTRATION

Provides leadership for all subordinates: Explains their jobs and what is expected of them; keeps them informed of changes that will affect them; delegates to subordinates not only enough authority to do the job, but enough to challenge their capabilities; tells subordinates when they have excelled and when and how they can improve; rewards superior performance appropriately; sees that inferior performance is raised to satisfactory levels; ensures that subordinates receive deserved pay and promotions.

Leads the branch's planning efforts, both short and long range, and organizes the branch to best achieve quarterly and annual profit goals under the bank's planning system. Sees that controllable expenses are minimized and particularly that staff is held to recommended figures as agreed upon with the Regional Operations and Personnel Officer.

Encourages good staff morale by example and by utilizing all avenues of communication (e.g., staff meetings, person-to-person contacts) to keep the staff fully informed concerning policies, goals. and programs and to permit an upward flow of ideas, opinions, suggestions, etc. (Holds general staff meetings at least monthly; officer meetings daily.)

Personally supervises management trainees under the guidance of the Training Department and regional office; ensures that trainees achieve the level of knowledge or skill required in each assigned position and within the prescribed time period; evaluates trainee performance.

Sees that branch goals are established under the bank's Affirmative Action program and that plans to attain the goals are being positively implemented.

Sees that responsibilities under the bank's labor contract are understood and fulfilled in regard to all bargaining unit employees of his branch, either directly or through the branch Operations and Personnel Officer.

Recommends salary increases, promotions, transfers, salary grade changes and requests for personnel to the Regional office.

Sees that internal auditing controls, as specified by the General Auditor, are maintained.

Ensures that all bank and customer assets are safeguarded.

Submits required reports concerning branch operations and personnel promptly and accurately.

### BUSINESS DEVELOPMENT

Keeps alert, and trains his staff to keep alert, to competitive moves and to all opportunities (e.g., prospective customers, unfilled financial needs, new uses for bank services, etc.) for expanding and making branch business more profitable.

Plans and takes necessary action in regard to business development opportunities so as to meet or exceed quarterly and annual goals.

Ensures that the branch call program is carried out fully and effectively, working with the Regional Business Development Officer for ideas and guidance.

Coordinates branch business development efforts with overall bank plans and with special programs instituted through the Regional Business Development Officer.

Ensures that customers receive prompt and courteous treatment from the entire staff.

Keeps his staff informed concerning available services and sees that the staff sells them effectively to customers.

Identifies prospective trust customers and assists in arranging contacts with Trust Division representatives.

Ensures that he and his staff are creating a favorable image to the community so as to uphold the stature of the bank and maximize public confidence in this bank and banking in general.

Leads and participates in community activities aimed at improving economic and social conditions within the branch's trade area; encourages his staff to share fully in this responsibility.

Sees that marketing and business development ideas originated in the branch are transmitted to the Regional Business Development Officer; supplies local marketing information and data on request.

CREDIT

Exercises responsibility for the total branch lending function; commercial, real estate and installment credit.

Approves loans and lines within his limit, recommends those above his limit and those of a policy nature to the regional manager.

Delegates appropriate lending authority to his assistants and sees that they are trained to handle increasing responsibility of this type.

Ensures that appropriate interest rates within policy guidelines are established when loans are made or renewed and that scheduled fees are collected.

Sees that all loans are properly documented and that adequate and current credit files are maintained.

Initiates prompt and complete follow-up on all problem or potential problem loans, whether or not listed in reports of examination, and keeps the regional office informed of progress.

Submits required reports concerning branch loans promptly and accurately.

Ensures proper review and control of overdrafts and return checks.

# SEATTLE–FIRST NATIONAL BANK
## MANAGER, MARKET RESEARCH

MISSION:     To provide the bank and its subsidiaries with continuing market research counseling and current market information, contributing data essential for the profitable growth of the bank.

REPORTS TO:   Manager, Research, Planning and Development

SUPERVISES:   Market Research Officers and non-official staff

PRIME RESPONSIBILITIES

Originates, coordinates and completes research programs designed to provide bank management with the information necessary for profitable marketing decisions. Analyzes data relating to services, customer service, facilities and staff of the total bank and presents findings and appropriate recommendations to bank management.

Determines research priorities as necessary, ensuring that marketing research resources are allocated according to total bank needs.

Coordinates with potential research users in identifying research requirements and proposing methods for meeting them. Working with Planning and Development and other marketing departments, assists research users in developing strategies for implementing research findings.

Determines utilization of outside market research firms and consultants; serves as project director, coordinating efforts on behalf of the bank.

Maintains information on recent developments in the marketing research field through seminars, conferences and individual research.

Develops and maintains informative working relationships with market research personnel at other banks and industries.

Ensures the efficient and profitable operation of the department through utilization of management skills with direction and support of Manager, Research, Planning and Development.

Develops and recommends departmental plans, both short- and long-range, in support of the bank's goals and objectives.

Utilizes and applies all S-FNB personnel policies equally to all staff.

Develops the management abilities of subordinates through a combination of goal setting, delegation, training, counseling and performance reviews. Ensures that their objectives are both challenging and realistic and that salary recommendations are based on accomplishments in relation to goals.

# SEATTLE–FIRST NATIONAL BANK
## MANAGER, ELECTRONIC DATA PROCESSING SERVICES

MISSION:   Directs the Bank's electronic data processing efforts, centralized operational support services, check processing services, and automated customer service in an efficient, economical, and timely manner.

REPORTS TO:   Manager, Administration and Control

SUPERVISES:   Manager, EDP General Services
Manager, EDP Operations
Manager, EDP Systems and Programming
Manager, EDP Technical Planning and Support
Manager, EDP Personnel

PRIME RESPONSIBILITIES

Directs the Bank's statewide EDP, operational support services, and customer services in a manner which ensures that they function efficiently, promptly, economically, and meet the needs of all departments within the Bank and desires of banking customers.

Directs feasibility studies of suggested automated applications as approved and prioritized by the Operations Committee; ensures that user departments participate in such studies; submits the results of such studies to the committee, together with recommended action.

Ensures that the check processing system is operational in a manner which keeps the Bank cost competitive; maximizes Bankwide investment opportunity by making available deposits and investment capital through efficient management of system-wide float.

Ensures that automated customer services (Lock Box, Payroll, Correspondent Bank Processing, ARP, etc.) are price competitive, efficient, and of a quality in keeping with the Bank's reputation.

Ensures that EDP systems are written to Bank quality standards in such a way as to keep developmental and operational costs at reasonable levels. Monitors developmental progress on new computer applications and reports promptly major problems or variances in either time or cost forecasts to Manager, Administration and Control. Sees that existing systems are reviewed periodically and recommends rewrite or obsolete or unnecessarily costly system to the Operations Committee.

Ensures that technical staff is of the highest quality possible and their skills maintained and enhanced through internal and outside training, as available and appropriate. Constantly upgrades own technical knowledge so as to function as the Bank's top-level consultant to Senior Management on EDP and Bank operational support matters.

Provides for continued contact with regions, branches, and all divisions within the Bank to resolve operating, EDP, and customer problems to ensure satisfactory service to all Bank customers.

Develop both short and long range EDP and operational support systems and hardware plan which are responsive to Bankwide problems and opportunities.

Constantly monitors hardware system and personnel to ensure quality of end product, performance levels, and capacity limits.

Represents the Bank to vendors in matters involving automation and operational support systems to ensure that the Bank receives the products and level of service which it has purchased.

Directs EDP personnel to ensure that Bank responsibilities under the labor contract are understood and fulfilled by department managers; that goals are established under the Bank's Affirmative Action Program; and that plans to attain the goals are being positively implemented.

Develops the managing abilities of subordinates through a combination of goal setting, delegation, training, counseling, and performance reviews. Ensures that their objectives are challenging yet realistic, are being met, and that salary recommendations are based on their accomplishments in relation to goals. Similarly, ensures that they are developing the management abilities of their subordinates and properly administering the Management by Objectives program in regard to them.

## FIRST PENNSYLVANIA BANK
### INVESTMENT OFFICER

BASIC FUNCTION
Efficient supervision of one of three research sections; effectively analyze and recommend, for investment purposes, securities of companies and industries within assigned area of responsibility.

ORGANIZATIONAL RELATIONSHIPS

| | |
|---|---|
| Reports to: | Vice President |
| Who reports to: | Executive Vice President |
| Supervises: | 2 or more Inv. Analysts (7019) and Trainees |
| Internal Relationships: | Executive Management; Branches; Legal Division; Inv. Mgmt., Vestaur, etc. |
| External Relationships: | Corporate executives; brokers; financial analysts |

PRINCIPAL ACCOUNTABILITIES

1. Efficient supervision of one of three research sections in division; develop an efficient staff of 2 or more Investment Analysts engaged in conducting industry studies.
2. Effectively analyze and recommend, for investment purposes, securities of companies within assigned area of responsibility (consumer, technology, or cyclical and transportation); specific functions analyzed—present economic condition of company; ownership and management personnel; past history; internal operations; growth potential; industry characteristics, etc., plus trends in profit margin, per share growth earnings, dividend and other investment criteria.
3. Develop and maintain effective internal and external sources of information necessary for investment analysis purposes.
4. Provide accurate information to Investment Management and other areas of the bank, and make sound recommendations regarding security issues of companies within assigned industries, new investment opportunities, mergers, acquisitions, rights, etc.; allocation of brokers' commissions; additions/deletions to security list.
5. Contribute sound investment recommendations through participation in Investment Management Committees.
6. Keep current on developments and trends in investment field and characteristics of companies and industries in assigned area, as well as relationship of economic, political and social happenings in the world to assigned areas.
7. Represent Vice President on various bank committees; prepare special reports; complete surveys, etc.

DIMENSIONS

Responsible for analyses of about 6 industries, covering from 100 to 150 major companies. Trust holdings in assigned industries.

KNOW-HOW

*Technical:* College degree, master's preferred; background in Finance, Economics, Accounting; wide cultural background with varied interests, knowledge of various state, tax, etc. laws and regulations governing assigned industries.

*Managerial:* Direct responsibility for training and supervising 2 or more Investment Analysts and Trainees.

*Human Relations:* Working with all levels of management within the bank, as well as corporate executives, brokers, analysts of other companies.

AUTHORITY

Complete responsibility for accurate research, analysis and interpretation of information contained in own industry studies, as well as those prepared by subordinates.

CRITICAL PROBLEM

Detecting pertinent developments or trends which would affect the investment performance in assigned areas which, if not detected, could result in considerable monetary loss and embarrassment to bank; making sound investment recommendations and at the same time maintaining bank's holdings at a prescribed level.

---

# FIRST PENNSYLVANIA CORPORATION
## GENERAL AUDITOR

BASIC FUNCTION

Direct financial and operational audit functions of First Pennsylvania Corporation's subsidiaries.

DIMENSIONS (Annual)
    Expense Budget:
        Salaries:
        Other:
    Man-hours:
    No. of audits:

NATURE AND SCOPE

Incumbent reports to Director of Accounting and Audit, who reports to President, First Pennsylvania Corporation.

As General Auditor, the incumbent is charged with accomplishing the objectives of the audit program, which he achieves through the direction of 8 officers, and through them 50 Auditors (various levels), who are involved in: scheduling audits, reviewing audit reports, making recommendations for improvement in the system of internal controls, making operational audits and recommending measures to reduce expenses and otherwise improve profitability.

He appraises the soundness, adequacy and application of financial and operating controls and the extent to which management policies and procedures are carried out.

He evaluates all audit reports prepared and released by subordinates and ensures recommendations are implemented. Inadequacies which are not corrected on a timely basis are pursued through higher authority.

He attends all meetings of the Audit Committee of the Board and independently presents matters for their consideration.

He ensures the proper development of Management Trainees through an effective training program, after which they are eligible for permanent placement in any of the corporation's subsidiaries.

He has frequent contact with all levels of management, daily contact with subordinates, plus some contact with auditors of other banks, bank holding companies, State and Federal Bank Examiners, FBI agents, and occasional customers.

PRINCIPAL ACCOUNTABILITIES
1. Accomplish the objectives of the Audit Program.
2. Make sound recommendations to correct weaknesses in controls.
3. Ensure the proper instruction of Management Trainees.
4. Attend and present matters to all meetings of the Audit Committee of the Board.
5. Keep informed of new thinking in the auditing/accounting fields.

KNOW-HOW
*Technical:* College degree; experience in auditing; thorough knowledge of auditing principles and internal control standards; Chartered Bank Auditor designation, acquired by experience, study and examination, would be desirable.

*Managerial:* Directing and coordinating the activities of a professional staff.

*Human Relations:* Tactful, diplomatic dealings with management.

AUTHORITY
Authorized to audit all the affairs of the corporation's subsidiaries, maintain a continuous audit control of all property for which company has responsibility, and of company's liabilities, income and expense; gain access to all the books and records of whatever nature and appraise and report on the soundness, adequacy and application of financial and operating controls; review all proposed changes in operational procedures before they are put into effect to ensure the continuance of adequate audit controls and to ascertain the extent of compliance with established management policies and procedures. As General Auditor, delegates on-premises auditing assignments to subordinates.

CRITICAL PROBLEM
Studying the overall exposure of the corporation's subsidiaries to consequences of employee infidelity and dishonesty and developing an effective audit program incorporating appropriate audit frequency and scope in all areas of audit effort (accounts, operations, functions); coordinating the audit effort so that all requirements under the programs are met by year end; making recommendations to correct weaknesses in controls and to make operational and financial type audits to improve operating efficiency, reduce expense and/or otherwise improve profitability.

*Public Agencies—Administrative*

---

## FORT WORTH, TEXAS
### CITY ATTORNEY

**DISTINGUISHING FEATURES OF THE CLASS**
This is administrative and legal work of a highly difficult and responsible professional nature in providing counsel for the general administrative affairs of the city. The work includes the directing and coordinating of activities of the legal department. The City Attorney advises department heads and the City Manager in matters of a legal nature. The City Attorney works under the general direction of the City Manager.

**EXAMPLES OF WORK** (Illustrative only)
• Directs the activities of the legal department with responsibility for the proper and efficient handling of the legal affairs, suits, pleas, and litigations in which the city is interested.
• Provides legal advice to the city and all officers and departments.
• Prosecutes and defends suits for and on behalf of the city in all courts.
• Prepares all contracts, bonds, and other legal instruments for the city.
• Renders opinions on all legal matters submitted by city officials.
• Supervises a staff of attorneys.
• Attends meetings of the city council and renders opinions on the legal effects of actions taken and proposed.

**REQUIRED KNOWLEDGES, ABILITIES, SKILLS AND OTHER ATTRIBUTES**
Extensive knowledge of city codes and charter provisions and the general laws of the city and state. Extensive knowledge of the sources of legal reference. Extensive knowledge of court procedures and rules of evidence. Ability to organize, interpret and apply legal principles and knowledges to particular circumstances. Ability to supervise the preparation of difficult and important cases. Ability to evaluate work performed by subordinates. Ability to prepare and try cases. Ability to establish and maintain harmonious working relationships with other department heads and governmental officials. Ability to perform legal planning and to advise the City Council and City Manager on the formulation of legal policy.

**ACCEPTABLE TRAINING, SCHOOLING AND EXPERIENCE**
Graduation from a recognized law school and seven years of legal experience, three of which must have been in municipal law and of a progressively difficult nature; or any combination of training and experience which provides the required knowledges, abilities and skills.

# BALTIMORE, MARYLAND
## DIRECTOR, DIVISION OF PLANNING

### CHARACTERISTICS OF THE CLASS
Under administrative direction, develops and administers technical plans and programs for urban renewal; and does related work as required.

### EXAMPLES OF DUTIES
Develops technical plans and programs for urban renewal; schedules and controls all planning activities; develops and executes agency policies relating to area and project planning, site selection, land use, area design, and area programming; interprets and executes governmental policies and legislation pertaining to planning aspects of the urban renewal program; evaluates and controls all planning operations; coordinates planning activities with the comprehensive general planning performed by the Department of Planning; develops working relationships and liaison with public and private agencies and with advisory services concerned with the total urban renewal program; provides technical advice and assistance with such groups as required; through subordinate supervisors, directs the activities of technical personnel, such as architectural designers, area and site planners, cost estimators, and research personnel; may act for superior in his absence.

### MINIMUM QUALIFICATIONS
*Training and Experience:* Master's Degree in architecture or city planning and eight years of increasingly responsible professional experience in the field of city planning, architecture, urban renewal, redevelopment, or related work, five years of which must have been in an executive or high-level administrative capacity; or equivalent combination of training and experience.

*Knowledge and Skills:* Thorough knowledge of the principles of city planning as related to urban renewal programs; good knowledge of architecture and urban redevelopment; ability to plan and administer large-scale programs affecting the environment of the city population; ability to prepare reports; ability to obtain cooperation from individuals and groups.

---

# LANSING, MICHIGAN
## HUMAN RELATIONS DIRECTOR

### NATURE OF WORK
This is administrative work with responsibilities in the area of human relations.

Work involves the responsibility of the administration and management of a program of investigation, education, and counseling in minority group problems, the area of civil rights of these minority groups, and the projection of research and analysis of all minorities, racial and ethnic groups of the community.

Work of this kind and its activities is governed by the policies of a Commission and supervision is over one or more employees.

EXAMPLES OF WORK
(Any one position may not include all of the duties listed, nor do the listed examples include all tasks which may be found in positions of this class.)

Plans, organizes, and directs all the activities of the department and reviews the work of his staff.

Makes final reviews of all problems and approves the continuity of same, or recommends modifications.

Makes major problem area investigations, with or without the aid of staff, and writes reports on these findings.

Attends various meetings and gatherings, preparing and making speeches on matters relating to minority group problems.

Performs various research, evaluates data and keeps continuing records of these statistics.

Makes recommendations to the Commission relative to minority group matters.

Participates as a mediator in cases of problems involving minority groups.

Cooperates with and executes liaison work with all organizations participating in minority group needs. This includes all governmental units as well as other organizations.

Performs related work as required.

REQUIREMENTS OF WORK
Extensive knowledge of the social and psychological forces pertinent to the integration of minority groups into the economic and cultural life of the community.

Thorough knowledge of the economic energies at work in the community that affects the well-being of the minority group.

Thorough knowledge of resources available to further the objectives of the Human Relations Commission and local ordinance.

Thorough knowledge of all civil rights laws.

Ability to sustain existing standards in the evaluation and handling of problems requiring needed action.

Ability to execute good personal relations with the public and civic organizations as well as commissions and departments of the local government.

Ability to gather and analyze social and economic information and to prepare and present reports relative to the information.

Ability to speak and write effectively.

DESIRABLE EXPERIENCE AND TRAINING
Experience in social programs with a recognized organization, and graduation from a four year college or university with a major in the social sciences.

## Public Agencies—Financial Operations

### FORT WORTH, TEXAS
#### CITY SECRETARY—TREASURER

DISTINGUISHING FEATURES OF THE CLASS
This is staff administrative work of a difficult and responsible nature in connection with the filing and recording of City records and the custody of City monies, funds, and securities. The work is performed in accordance with established laws, rules and regulations but the employee works with considerable independence in determining work methods to carry out assigned duties. The work is performed under general supervision.

EXAMPLES OF WORK (Illustrative only)
• Attends meetings of the City Council with responsibility for keeping minutes of the proceedings.
• Keeps all records pertaining to the office of the City such as ordinances, contracts, and deeds.
• Serves as the custodian of all monies, funds, and securities of the City, entailing receiving, receipting, depositing, and reporting on monies collected.
• Serves as paymaster issuing pay checks, and as ex-officio clerk of the corporation court, entailing supervision of a clerical force engaged in maintaining records of the court.
• Directs the work involved in conducting municipal elections.
• May serve as secretary-treasurer of the Fireman's Retirement Fund.

REQUIRED KNOWLEDGES, ABILITIES, SKILLS AND OTHER ATTRIBUTES
Considerable knowledge of the City Charter and of the laws governing the operation of the City government; considerable knowledge of City administrative problems, processes and relationships; considerable knowledge of modern office procedures, practices and appliances; working knowledge of accounting principles; ability to maintain a wide variety of administrative records in conformity with statutory requirements; ability to plan and direct the activities of clerical assistants; ability to establish effective working relationships with City officials and the general public.

ACCEPTABLE TRAINING, SCHOOLING AND EXPERIENCE
Graduation from a four year college or university with major work in business or public administration and seven years' experience in clerical and administrative work of which two years shall have been in a supervisory capacity, preferably in accounting; or any equivalent combination of training or experience which provides the required knowledges, abilities and skills.

---

# A MAJOR SOUTHERN CITY
## DIRECTOR OF FINANCE

DEFINITION
To perform administrative work directing the financial management program for the City; and to do related work as required. Employee has wide latitude in interpreting and applying policies, rules and regulations, and performance is measured by total results.

EXAMPLES OF DUTIES
Plans, directs, and coordinates the fiscal management program of the City; participates in the planning and development of overall fiscal objectives and provides consultative services in fiscal management; plans and directs the continuous review and analysis of fiscal operations, needs, and resources; appraises, adjusts, and correlates budget needs among programs and functions; directs the collection of City taxes and business license fees and other assessments; manages investments; provides city-wide services in the development, coordination and operation of grant programs; directs payroll operation; directs a program of budget administration including the preparation of the capital and annual operating budgets, budget analysis, and recommendations and forecasting; confers with agency and other City officials and local and federal representatives on fiscal management and problems affecting the agency's fiscal policies and controls; directs the preparation of financial statements and reports; may serve as officer on several public agency boards; advises mayor and council regarding fiscal matters.

SELECTION REQUIREMENTS

*Education and Experience*
Any combination equivalent to graduation from college in an appropriate curriculum and thorough administrative or supervisory experience related to this class of work.

*Selection Factors*
    Principles and practices of governmental accounting and budgeting.

Principles of governmental program financing and bond issuance.
Principles of organization, administration and supervision.
Principles and practices of office management.
Principles and practices in the preparation and revision of accounting systems and documents.

# LANSING, MICHIGAN
## FINANCE DIRECTOR

NATURE OF WORK

This is diversified and highly responsible administrative and professional accounting work in directing the activities of a large municpal Finance Department.

This employee is responsible for organizing, directing and coordinating the activities of the various units and sections of the Finance Department involved in all phases of accounting, collecting, and purchasing. This employee coordinates this work through conferences and meetings and recommends to the Mayor and City Council all matters of important budget and financial needs.

EXAMPLES OF WORK

(Any one position may not include all of the duties listed, nor do the listed examples include all tasks which may be found in positions of this class.)

Is the administrative official directly responsible for the effective functioning of the Finance Department sections and units.

Confers with and advises city officials, department heads, and others regarding financial matters.

Supervises and directs the employees of the accounting section of the division, planning, organizing and reviewing the efforts of this staff.

Serves as a member of various boards and committees providing professional assistance to such organizations and to the general public.

Supervises the preparation of municipal programs and projects and reportings relative to finance, and is responsible for reporting Finance Department activities.

Supervises specialists and technicians reviewing planning, and research in procedures, methods, services, and internal accounting problems by means of conference or review.

Plans and organizes all materials and accounting for the purpose of investments of municipal funds, and reports such investing and proceedings to the Mayor and City Council.

Approves or delegates the responsibility for issuing approvals for all contracts, vouchers, and financial transactions, and confers with supervisors on special events outside of routine transactions.

Supervises departmental budgeting and aids Mayor in his annual presentation as well as counseling the municipal council when requested in budget hearings.

Performs related duties as required.

## REQUIREMENTS OF WORK

Extensive knowledge of the principles and practices of modern accounting and finance administration.

Extensive knowledge of modern management practices and thorough knowledge of accounting and data equipment.

Extensive knowledge of processes methods and procedures involving office management relative to their values, and priorities pertinent to application for data processing.

Ability to prepare and submit concise, accurate written and verbal reports of a complex nature governing financial investments, transactions, recommendations for modifications and budgetary activities of a departmental or municipal scope. Ability to establish and maintain effective working relations with subordinates, other officials and the public.

## DESIRABLE EXPERIENCE AND TRAINING

Extensive administrative and professional experience in the service of a large organization, with some governmental experience desirable; graduation from a recognized college or university with a degree in business administration or accounting supplemented preferably with additional studies in management and/or accounting or an equivalent combination of experience and training.

---

# BALTIMORE, MARYLAND
## DIRECTOR, DIVISION OF ADMINISTRATION

### CHARACTERISTICS OF THE CLASS

Under direction, is responsible for the preparation and administration of the operating and project budgets and the direction of the purchasing, personnel, and all general administrative services of the Baltimore Urban Renewal and Housing Agency; and does related work as required.

### EXAMPLES OF DUTIES

Administers the budget system of the agency; develops and installs budget methods and procedures; reviews and analyzes budget needs and determines the necessity of expenditures; coordinates budgets with program goals and directs the preparation and compilation of budget data prior to submission to the appropriate Federal agency and to the Board of Estimates; establishes standards for materials, supplies, and equipment; plans and administers a program of procurement for the Housing Authority and coordinates urban renewal purchases with the Bureau of Purchases; plans and directs the personnel and training program of the agency; develops and maintains a comprehensive program for the organizational, procedural, and administrative planning of the agency; develops and directs a records management system; organizes and directs a centralized messenger, mail, reproduction, and filing system; certifies the payrolls of the agency; directs all other central office functions required to service the daily operations of the agency.

MINIMUM QUALIFICATIONS

*Training and Experience:* Graduation from a university or college of recognized standing and eight years of responsible experience in business or public administration, including personnel and purchasing responsibilities, three years of which must have been in a supervisory capacity in the preparation, analysis, and control of budgets and the development of budget procedures; provided that graduate work in business or public administration may be substituted on a year for year basis for the experience requirement, not including the supervisory budget experience.

*Knowledge and Skills:* Thorough knowledge of the principles and techniques of budgetary planning and control; considerable knowledge of the principles and practices of public and business administration, including personnel and purchasing; ability to deal effectively with the public; ability to develop and install modern budget methods, procedures, forms, and records; administrative ability.

---

# FORT WORTH, TEXAS
## TAX ASSESSOR—COLLECTOR

DEFINITION

Under general direction, plans, promotes, and administers the activities of the City Tax Collector's Office; and does related work as required.

CLASS CHARACTERISTICS

This is a division head position under the administrative direction of the Finance Director. The incumbent is responsible for planning, organizing and directing the appraisal of taxable property and the collection of taxes and revenue producing licenses. The development of procedures and regulations necessary for the effective and equitable assessment of property and the collection of taxes in the city are part of the functions of this class.

## EXAMPLE OF DUTIES
Exercises overall administration of the Tax Department, with responsibility for the assessment of taxable property in the city, the preparation of tax rolls, the collection of taxes, and the collection of revenues generated by licenses and/or special assessments; working through subordinate supervisors' plans, coordinates and directs the activities of a staff of appraisers and a clerical force engaged in the preparation of tax rolls and statements to taxpayers and the work involved in the collection of delinquent taxes; supervises and coordinates record keeping and accounting activities; may be required to make new assessments, increase assessments, or correct errors in tax assessments; adds and/or deletes property from assessment rolls; answers complaints by mail and at the counter, explaining assessment procedures to the public; attends meetings and conferences as required; prepares statements, analysis, and statistical summaries of assessing work performed; trains subordinate staff members in the work of the department; investigates complaints; answers correspondence and prepares special reports.

## MINIMUM QUALIFICATIONS
*License:* Possession of a valid Texas Driver's License.

*Education:* Graduation from an accredited college or university with major work in business administration, economics, engineering or a related field.

*Experience:* Five years of progressively responsible property appraisal and tax collection work, three years of which must have been in a supervisory capacity.

*Special Requirements:* Must have attained the designation of a Certified Texas Assessor.

*Substitution of Experience for Education:* Experience in real and/or personal property appraisal, building cost estimation, and/or building inspection may be substituted for the required education on a year-for-year basis up to a maximum of four years.

*Knowledge of:* Principles, laws and standards applying to the assessment of personal property, land and improvements; organization and management principles and practices, with particular reference to the assessment and collecting of taxes; modern office methods and procedures, with special reference to the property and fiscal records of the city.

*Ability to:* Plan, organize and direct the work of subordinates; analyze factors which would tend to influence the value of property and to exercise sound judgment in the determination of property values; write clear and concise reports; establish and maintain an effective working relationship with other city officials and the general public.

## Public Agencies—Operations

## A MAJOR SOUTHERN CITY
### DIRECTOR OF PUBLIC WORKS

DEFINITION

To do professional administrative and technical engineering work relative to the planning and maintenance of a complete public works program for the city and to do related work as required. Employee has wide latitude in interpreting and applying policies, rules and regulations, and performance is measured by total results.

EXAMPLES OF DUTIES

Plans, directs and coordinates the design and construction of all public works including streets, sidewalks, and drainage structures; plans for long-range public works programs; prepares annual operating and capital outlay budget for the Department of Public Works; conducts special studies relative to public works development; responsible for the development and maintenance of a comprehensive traffic control program for the city; confers with various administrative officials and public groups on proposed public works programs; plans and directs the collection and disposal of waste; confers with division heads on proposed projects and improvements; coordinates the funding of various public works program involving federal, state, and local expenditures; prepares regular and special reports to the Mayor and City Council relative to the design, construction, and funding of public works projects and programs.

SELECTION REQUIREMENTS

*Education and Experience*
Graduation from college in an appropriate curriculum, and thorough experience related to this class of work.

*Selection Factors*
Principles of public works, engineering, design, and construction.
Principles of municipal public works administration.
Laws and regulations governing municipal public works.
Methods of traffic engineering and control.
Administrative techniques.
Supervisory methods.

*Licenses or Special Requirements*
Registration as a professional engineer.

# BALTIMORE, MARYLAND
## CHIEF, DIVISION OF SANITATION

CHARACTERISTICS OF THE CLASS
Under direction, is responsible for all activities of the Division of Sanitation in the Bureau of Utility Operations, Department of Public Works.

EXAMPLES OF DUTIES
Directs the cleaning of public streets, lanes, alleys, and markets, the collection and removal of ashes, garbage, and rubbish, and the operation of incinerator plants and sanitary landfills; directs the operations of the animal shelter; coordinates the activities of all sections of the division; recommends policies pertaining to operations, methods, and procedures; may assume duties of the bureau head in the latter's absence.

MINIMUM QUALIFICATIONS
*Training and Experience:* Graduation from a university or college of recognized standing, with a degree in engineering, and seven years of responsible experience in the cleaning of streets and in the collection and disposal of solid wastes, four years of which must have been in a responsible administrative capacity; provided that a master's degree in engineering may be substituted for two years of the nonadministrative experience requirement; or equivalent combination of training and experience.

*Knowledge and Skills:* Thorough knowledge of solid waste collection, street cleaning, and refuse disposal methods and equipment; administrative ability.

# CITY OF DALLAS, TEXAS
## MANAGER OF SECURITY
### (*Grade 16*)

DISTINGUISHING CHARACTERISTICS
Building Services Department division manager responsible for maintaining security of all facilities of the City's agencies. An employee in this classification is the City's Chief of Security operations and coordinator of all security activities including internal police and fire protection as well as protection from sabotage. Employee is responsible for hiring, training and performance of all security guard personnel. Assumes wide latitude in developing work methods and procedures in his area of responsibility. Plans and objectives are worked out in conference with department head.

TYPICAL DUTIES

1. Coordinates and administers City's security division operations; implements policy to insure protection of City facilities and property, and safeguard of employees while they are on City premises; implements and insures compliance with rules and regulations established for protection of facilities, property and personnel. Assures that rights of individuals, while at work, are upheld in accordance with municipal ordinances.

2. Provides program and policy to provide identification cards for employees and passes for other persons associated with City facilities including establishing requirements for and implementing issuance of suitable identification credentials.

3. Establishes and administers procedures, systems and methods for internal security activities in conformance with City police; coordinates the function of internal security with City's uniformed police service.

4. Directs activities associated with investigation in the sense of surveillance to confirm or prove false suspected theft or falsification of records.

5. Performs related work as assigned.

MINIMUM EXAMINING REQUIREMENTS

*Education:* Bachelor's degree or equivalent.

*Experience:* Six years experience as an F.B.I. special agent, as a member of United States Armed Forces responsible for maintenance of maximum security of military base requiring higher than normal security measures, industrial security or other experience of this difficulty and complexity.

*Acceptable Equivalency* (for Education)

Two years of college plus nine years experience as an F.B.I. special agent as a member of United States Armed Forces responsible for maintenance of maximum security of a military base requiring higher than normal security measures, industrial security or other experience of this difficulty and complexity.

*Abilities Required to Perform Work*

Must have extensive knowledge of fire and police protection systems and procedures; general knowledge of laws pertaining to property and individual rights; thorough knowledge of principles of industrial or governmental security regulation relative to prevention of sabotage and theft; knowledge of personnel procedures and human relations necessary to administer large security organization; ability to plan, organize, staff, direct and control activities of large organization.

*Working Conditions and Hazards*

Normal office conditions.

*Promotes from:* Security Manager 14

*Promotes to:* Not yet established.

# FORT WORTH, TEXAS
## POLICE CHIEF

### DEFINITION
Under administrative direction to plan, direct and coordinate all activities and operations of the Police Department in enforcement of laws, ordinances and regulations; and to do related work as required.

### CLASS CHARACTERISTICS
This is highly skilled administrative work involving immediate responsibility for the planning, development and direction of a complete program of police administration. Work is subject to administrative review but the incumbent has complete internal control over police activities and personnel and exercises wide discretion in administration of the department.

### EXAMPLES OF DUTIES
Plans, directs, inspects, and exercises general supervision over activities of the entire department; formulates and enforces departmental rules, regulations, work methods and procedures; reviews activities and reports of officers; may direct investigation of major criminal offenses, cooperates with County, State and Federal Officers in the apprehension of wanted persons; supervises the preparation of reports for City Manager, National Safety Council and Federal Bureau of Investigation; prepares budget estimates and controls expenditure of all departmental funds; determines personnel policies and broad training requirements and makes decisions on all appointments, promotions, dismissals and disciplinary actions made in the department; consults with division heads and advises on departmental problems.

### MINIMUM QUALIFICATIONS
*Education:* Graduation from high school or attainment of a satisfactory score on a G. E. D. test.

*Experience:* Two years experience as a "bona fide" police officer in the State of Texas.

*Knowledge of:* Municipal police administration and organization; technical and operating principles, practices and problems of law enforcement and crime prevention activities; laws governing custody of persons, search and seizure and rules of evidence.

*Ability to:* Plan, assign and coordinate the work of varied divisions within a City Police Department; analyze police problems and formulate policies and procedures; direct and evaluate the work of subordinate officers and personnel, establish and maintain effective working relationships with fellow employees and the general public.

# LANSING, MICHIGAN
## FIRE CHIEF

NATURE OF WORK

This is responsible administrative supervisory and technical work in directing the activities and personnel of a municipal Fire Department.

This work involves responsibility for the direction of all fire control and prevention activities of a municipality including the development, through study and consultation with other officials, of planning and training for the protection of life and property within the municipality.

This work requires a wide knowledge of departmental administration, modern fire control and fire prevention methods and techniques used in making determinations of work problems encountered.

Administrative details include purchase recommendations for supplies and equipment, preparation of budget estimates, control of expenditures and assignment and supervision of personnel and equipment.

This employee consults with the Board on over-all policy and planning, and with the Mayor and municipal council on budget matters, but has independence in the supervising of technical operations and performance relative to results achieved.

EXAMPLES OF WORK

Plans departmental operation with respect to equipment and personnel and supervises through subordinates the executing of plans or assignments.

Is advised by assistant chief, verbally and by written reporting, of problems and status of personnel, property, and operations of the department; takes action, or orders such actions, on the information received for the purpose of improving departmental operations.

Assigns personnel and equipment to such duties and uses as the service requires and evaluates the need for and recommends the purchase of new equipment and supplies.

Responds to fires of a major size, personally directing activities within the fire area, checking responsibilities and reassigning or adding more equipment and personnel.

Supervises the inspection of buildings, properties and fire hazards and the enforcement of prevention ordinances, either personally or by occasional checks, or by review of the bureau's work.

Supervises and reviews the operation of the departmental training program.

Prepares, by supervision and review, the preparation of the departmental budget and supervises expenditures.

Supervises and reviews a maintenance and repair program for departmental equipment.

Appears publicly giving talks relative on prevention and safety.

Performs related work as required.

REQUIREMENTS OF WORK

Thorough knowledge of modern firefighting methods and ability to apply this knowledge to fire control and prevention programs.

Thorough knowledge of the geographic layout of municipality, location of streets, hydrants, and important structures.

Ability to assign, direct, and supervise personnel in effective fire control techniques and to anticipate unusual fire conditions and hazards relating to fire control operations at large, and dangerous or unusual fires.

Ability to lead and direct men effectively, maintain discipline, promote harmony, and maintain effective working relationships with staff, departmental personnel, municipal officials, and the public.

Ability to prepare clear and concise reports and to project verbally to groups and gatherings.

Physical strength and endurance; the ability to meet such specific physical standards as may be established by competent authority.

DESIRABLE EXPERIENCE AND TRAINING

Considerable supervisory experience in fire control; graduation from a standard high school preferably supplemented by special training in fire control and equipment.

# LANSING, MICHIGAN
## CIVIC CENTER MANAGER

NATURE OF WORK

This is administrative, promotional, and supervisory work in managing and furthering the activity and use of a municipal auditorium and facilities.

This employee is responsible for all phases of management of this civic facility including promoting its use, making arrangements and scheduling rentals, ticket promotion, temporary personnel placement, and the setting of equipment for each use.

This employee is responsible for the safety and convenience of the public, the supervision of all personnel, and maintenance of buildings and equipment.

This employee is required to be present, or assure an immediate supervisor's presence, during all primary activities; his work is supervised by a commission but the work is performed with a latitude of independence.

EXAMPLES OF WORK

Rents auditorium and other vacant rooms for public use and events according to fixed rate schedules and determines scheduling of use.

Arranges scheduling of road shows of a variety of kinds, aids in ticket promotion, prepares pertinent contracts, and supervises allied arrangements for use of the facilities.

Checks and audits all financial transactions, rentals and leases, and audits ticket sales when providing personnel for this use.

Directs or assigns supervision of maintenance and custodial staff and plans and recommends building and equipment changes and improvements.

Maintains and executes by personal appearances the facilities of the center. Provides information on the ability of center to serve the public.

Maintains professional and public relations with occupants, prospective renters, and the public using the facilities for the purpose of creating a sustaining relationship.

Performs related work as required.

REQUIREMENTS OF WORK

Considerable knowledge of methods and requirements in presenting public entertainments and attractions including a variety of events.

Considerable knowledge of business practices in the field of bookings, production, and building management.

Considerable knowledge of building maintenance practices and safety requirements for buildings involved in large scale attendances.

Knowledge of bookkeeping and office work.

Ability to organize, instruct, and direct groups of temporary employees in varied responsibilities and duties.

Ability to establish and maintain effective working relationships with personnel, organizational representatives, and the general public.

DESIRABLE EXPERIENCE AND TRAINING

Considerable experience in public relations, business, or auditorium management with responsible work in varied bookings and arrangements preferred, as well as experience in supervision of maintenance of a large building; graduation from a standard high school supplemented by college level courses in business management or any equivalent combination of education and experience.

*Public Agencies—Urban Affairs*

# CITY OF DALLAS, TEXAS
## SOCIAL WORKER
### *(Grade 14)*

DISTINGUISHING CHARACTERISTICS

This is experienced and/or supervisory professional social caseworker classification responsible for (1) supervising a group of subordinate social workers engaged in interviewing and counseling persons requesting social welfare services; (2) interviewing and processing a large volume of applicants who have complex and multiple problems. An employee in this class is given wide latitude in developing work methods and procedures for his organization. Supervision may be exercised over subordinate social workers or clerical personnel.

TYPICAL DUTIES

1. Plans, assigns, and supervises work of subordinate social workers and aides; develops and maintains professional standards of casework services and evaluates performance of subordinate employees.

2. Holds periodic conferences with subordinate workers for continued training and instruction on procedural and technical matters and to review casework progress.

3. Maintains contact with various service agencies to ensure efficient handling of multi-problem cases.

4. May handle heavy load of complex cases; identifies problems and recommends services; arranges appointments and refers applicants to proper agencies; may arrange transportation; follows up to assure applicant receives proper attention.

5. Prepares written reports of program activities and accomplishments.

6. Performs related work as assigned.

MINIMUM EXAMINING REQUIREMENTS

*Education:* Master's degree in social work or other closely related behavioral science field with concentration in social work; or Bachelor's degree in social work or other closely related behavioral science field with concentration in social work and two years experience in social work in a position equivalent to Social Worker 10 will substitute for Master's degree.

*Experience:* Two years progressive professional social work experience.

*Acceptable Equivalency:* (Promotional examination only)

Completion of City's social work special development program and two years social work experience in a position equivalent to Social Worker 10 will substitute for Master's degree.

*Abilities Required to Perform Work:*
Must be able to form and sustain good work relationships and to encourage social adjustment in others.

Must have thorough knowledge of principles and practices of social work. May need knowledge of personnel procedure and human relations necessary to supervise a group of subordinate social workers.

*Working Conditions and Hazards*
Normal social worker office and field conditions; possibly subjected to variety of communicable diseases.

*Promotes from:* Social Worker 12

*Promotes to:* Social Worker 16

---

# CITY OF DALLAS, TEXAS
## SOCIAL WORKER
### *(Grade 16)*

DISTINGUISHING CHARACTERISTICS
This is advanced supervisory, administrative, and highly experienced professional social caseworker classification applying intensive and diversified knowledge of social casework principles and practices in broad areas of assignments and related fields. Typically, this level of difficulty arises from the large size of the program.

An employee in this class makes decisions independently relative to casework problems and represents the organization in conferences to resolve important questions and plan and coordinate work. Employee receives supervision and guidance only in the sense of establishment of overall objectives, critical issues, new concepts, and matters of policy. Employee supervises, coordinates, and reviews work of a staff of social caseworkers.

TYPICAL DUTIES
1. Supervises staff of social workers, community workers, and clerical personnel; assigns duties and coordinates activities of staff; assists staff through individual and group conferences in analysis of case problems and improving their diagnostic and helping skills; evaluates performance and indicates action; develops and implements policy in collaboration with director.
2. Performs related work as assigned.

MINIMUM EXAMINING REQUIREMENTS
*Education:* Master's degree in social work or other closely related behavioral science field with concentration in social work; or Bachelor's degree in social

work or other closely related behavioral science field with concentration in social work and two years experience in social work in a position equivalent to Social Worker 10 will substitute for Master's degree.

*Experience:* Four years progressive professional social work experience.

*Acceptable Equivalency:* (Promotional examination only)
   Completion of City's social work special development program and two years social work experience in a position equivalent to Social Worker 10 will substitute for Master's degree.

*Abilities Required to Perform Work:*
   Must have administrative ability necessary to administer a large social work program. Must have knowledge of personnel procedures and human relations necessary to supervise a large staff of social workers and clerical personnel.

*Working Conditions and Hazards:*
   Normal office and occasional social worker field conditions.

*Promotes from:* Social Worker 14

*Promotes to:* This is top level social worker position.

---

# LANSING, MICHIGAN
## HOUSING DIRECTOR

NATURE OF WORK
   This is administrative work directing the activities of a staff performing varied functions in the supervision of private dwelling and housing projects, their occupancy and maintenance.
   This work involves liaison with federal, state, and other agencies and this employee interprets and supervises regulations while assigning phases of details to staff.
   Work includes conferences and meetings with staff, agencies, and the public and involves continued supervision of several efforts continuously.

EXAMPLES OF WORK
   (Any one position may not include all of the duties listed, nor do the listed examples include all tasks which may be found in positions of this class.)
   Plans and organizes initial processes and solicits approval for programs and projects relative to housing for deprived families and individuals.
   Contacts outside governmental agencies specifically to obtain necessary endowments and prepares or causes to be prepared all required statistics and data relative to regulations toward receiving such aid.
   Supervises the placement of families and individuals in private units, or in

municipally controlled housing projects, and reviews by consultation or written reports all activities of these placements.

Discusses finances and construction with approved agencies and contractors, and supervises progress in these allied fields.

Coordinates federal agency funds with municipal officials and advises and recommends to these officials federal requests and regulations.

Prepares and executes public appearances and individual consultations with the public relative to the department and its activities.

Inspects field work and projects, talks with field personnel and prepares public relations information relative to departmental activities and progress.

REQUIREMENTS OF WORK

Thorough knowledge of socio-economic problems of municipalities and acquaintance with governmental agencies and their authority to aid in housing problems.

Knowledge of municipal finance methods and procedures and some knowledge of municipal administration.

Ability to manage and direct a staff of subordinates and to maintain detailed and varied projects.

Ability to speak and write accurately and concisely.

Ability to maintain effective working relationships with staff, city officials, and agency representatives.

DESIRABLE EXPERIENCE AND TRAINING

Considerable experience in social services and graduation from a recognized college or university with course work in social science or allied fields or any equivalent combination of experience and training.

# BALTIMORE, MARYLAND
## DIRECTOR, DIVISION OF NEIGHBORHOOD DEVELOPMENT

CHARACTERISTICS OF THE CLASS

Under administrative direction, develops and administers the neighborhood rehabilitation program of the Baltimore Urban Renewal and Housing Agency; and does related work as required.

EXAMPLES OF DUTIES

Conducts studies to determine the needs of urban renewal areas; establishes plans and policies for community organization activities in urban renewal areas; is responsible for establishing standards and procedures to be followed in determining the feasibility of rehabilitating area structures; directs operations in renewal area field offices; makes field trips to review rehabilitation progress and inspect problem areas; coordinates activities with city and private agencies; reviews proposed housing code revisions and amendments, recommending policies on these changes to superiors; appears before various city commissions and boards to explain policies on rehabilitation; promotes private participation in rehabilitation in renewal areas; appears before the public to explain the rehabilitation program.

### MINIMUM QUALIFICATIONS

*Training and Experience*
Graduation from a university or college of recognized standing, preferably with a degree in business administration, public administration, or the social sciences, and eight years of experience in business or public administration, four years of which must have been in a supervisory capacity with responsibility for a major program in rehabilitation, urban renewal, public housing, or other closely related field; provided that graduate work may be substituted on a year for year basis for two years of the nonsupervisory experience.

*Knowledge and Skills*
Thorough knowledge of the principles and techniques of public administration; thorough knowledge of the principles and techniques of rehabilitation; ability to plan and organize a large rehabilitation program; ability to conduct sociological surveys; ability to obtain the cooperation of individuals and citizen and business groups; administrative ability.

## Public Agencies—
## Management Information Systems

### FORT WORTH, TEXAS
#### DATA PROCESSING MANAGER

### DEFINITION
Under general direction to supervise both administrative and technical operations of all data processing activities within the municipality.

### CLASS CHARACTERISTICS
This is skilled supervisory work over both administrative and technical areas of the data processing unit. The incumbent bears final responsibility for such allocated tasks as planning, personnel evaluation, scheduling, analysis programming and production, and for coordinating these tasks. Further, he provides liaison with other municipal units at the departmental head level, develops

improved systems, and participates as a permanent member of the Data Processing Committee.

## EXAMPLES OF DUTIES
Plans, organizes, and develops procedures for the data processing unit; confers with department heads or their representatives in planning for the application of data processing methods to departmental records problems; directs the preparation of annual budget requirements; supervises the preparation of programs, operating instructions, and operating manuals; assigns personnel, schedules work, allocates system time, and prepares and maintains work schedules; sets up and maintains in-service training for data processing personnel; supervises flow of work to see that necessary production levels are maintained and that assignments are completed on schedule; establishes a system of records of operational results to determine equipment utilization and efficiency; determines equipment and supply needs of the department; evaluates long-range administrative data requirements of agencies.

## MINIMUM QUALIFICATIONS

*Education:*
Graduation from an accredited college or university with major course work in mathematics, business administration or a related field.

*Experience:*
Five years of progressively responsible experience in electronic data processing operations, two years of which must have been in a supervisory capacity, with special training in systems planning and basic computer systems.

*Knowledge of:*
Data processing methods; techniques, limitations, and equipment; statistics, accounting and/or corporate finance; systems planning; production scheduling, form design, and control requirements; operator and machine production rates; effective supervisory techniques; and general office management methods and equipment.

*Ability to:*
Plan, devise, and institute machine records procedures; develop data processing systems and modify them for efficient operation; analyze complex data processing problems and institute effective programming procedures; plan, organize, and supervise the work of subordinates; adapt accounting and statistical reports to computer processing operations; submit clear, concise reports in oral, written or graphic form; establish and maintain effective working relationships with fellow employees and the public.

*Hospitals—Officers*

---

# BALTIMORE, MARYLAND
## DIRECTOR OF BALTIMORE CITY HOSPITALS

CHARACTERISTICS OF THE CLASS
Subject to administrative approval, administers, directs, and coordinates all activities of Baltimore City Hospitals; and does related work as required.

EXAMPLES OF DUTIES
Reviews and evaluates existing policies, procedures, and work methods and makes necessary changes and improvements; develops standards and methods and makes necessary changes and improvements; develops standards and methods for measurement of efficiency of hospital activities; assures that care of patients is of high professional level; meets with department heads to coordinate their activities and formulate the total program of the hospital; determines lines of authority and responsibility; coordinates activities of hospital staff to prevent overlapping and duplication of functions; prepares the hospital budget and approves the ordering of necessary equipment and supplies; directs public relations activities, explaining hospital program and policies to community groups, the press, and the general public; applies tested techniques of hospital administration and recommends the adoption of new policies and procedures.

MINIMUM QUALIFICATIONS

*Training and Experience:*
Graduation from a graduate school of recognized standing with a master's degree in hospital administration, and eight years of experience in hospital administration, the last four years of which must have been as assistant director of a voluntary, municipal, or state hospital; or equivalent combination of training and experience.

or

Graduation from a medical school of recognized standing, four years of postgraduate training in medicine, including chief residency, and two years of experience in hospital administration; or equivalent combination of training and experience.

*Knowledge and Skills:*
Thorough knowledge of hospital administration; working knowledge of personnel and business administration, public relations, and plant maintenance; administrative ability.

# METHODIST HOSPITAL OF INDIANA, INC.
*(Indianapolis)*
EXECUTIVE DIRECTOR

GOALS
1. To administer the corporation and the operation of the hospital through staff of specially trained personnel and with established policies, standards and procedures to the satisfaction of the Board of Trustees.
2. To institute controls enabling each area of activity to function without immediate administrative direction, but within the limits of established policies and standards.
3. To serve as the hospital's representative to the church and community and conduct a continuous public relations program.
4. To participate in state and national organizations instrumental in developing and giving guidance to health care programs, policies and legislation.
5. To develop a program for physical plant changes and expansion and for professional growth of the staff.
6. To keep up to date on trends in the hospital field and transfer this knowledge to members of staff and to the public.

SUPERVISION RECEIVED
Under the authority of the Board of Trustees assumes complete responsibility for carrying out their policies and regulations.

SUPERVISION EXERCISED
Exercises executive authority in directing the hospital and its several functions through a staff of professionals and with the advice of specially equipped committees.

TYPICAL FUNCTIONAL RESPONSIBILITIES INCLUDE:
1. Administering the corporation and the hospital to the satisfaction of the Board of Trustees.
   a. Develops and coordinates an administrative organization plan and staff to carry out the plan.
   b. Generates enthusiasm and cooperation of the Board, personnel and medical staff through application of sound management techniques.
   c. Presides at various meetings of staff personnel and special committees to obtain guidance, provide leadership, and coordinate the activities of these groups to the best interest of the hospital.
   d. Delegates authority and responsibility for the execution of the hospital's many departments and functions.
2. Instituting a system of controls that enables each area of activity to function without direct supervision from the Executive Director.

a. Recruits and employs a competent staff.
b. Develops clear cut lines of authority and channels of communication.
c. Establishes operating policies and procedures.
d. Establishes standards of service, performance and budgetary controls.
3. Representing the hospital to the church and community and conducting a public relations program.
    a. Serves on various church and civic committees as official hospital emissary.
    b. Talks before various groups to present the hospital's "story" and create community pride in the hospital.
    c. Plans and participates in a program for obtaining gifts and grants for the hospital.
    d. Serves as a professional in setting patterns of health care and the church's role in the health and welfare ministry.
4. Participating in state and national organizations in developing health care programs and policies including Blue Cross Board and the American Hospital Association.
    a. Works with organizations responsible for developing and guiding legislation concerning health care and health care economics.
    b. Participates in state and national organizations that help to guide and set health care policies and procedures.
    c. Serves as a consultant to U. S. Surgeon General.
5. Developing a program for continuous up-dating of plant and staff to meet the needs of the public.
    a. Anticipates the needs of the community for hospital service and plans for alterations and expansion to meet those needs.
    b. Provides opportunities for education, research or other means of professional growth and advancement for personnel at all levels to meet the future needs of the hospital.
6. Keeping up to date on trends in the hospital field and passing this knowledge on to the staff and public.

## *Hospitals—Operations*

---

# METHODIST HOSPITAL OF INDIANA, INC.
### (*Indianapolis*)
### NURSING SUPERVISOR (DAY)

GOALS
1. To direct patient care activities of two or more nursing units.
2. To advise Nursing Administration of requirements and major problems for units supervised.
3. To be continually aware of the condition and needs of the patients.
4. To assist in the planning for the patient care activities of the nursing units supervised.

SUPERVISION RECEIVED
Under the general supervision of an Assistant Director; within the professional guidance of the physicians; and within the guidance of hospital and nursing policies.

SUPERVISION EXERCISED
1. Exercises general supervision over two or more head nurses and through them unit nursing personnel.
   a. Evaluates the work performance of head nurses and assistant head nurses, and reviews evaluations prepared on other employees.
   b. Approves pay increases, terminations, transfers and promotions.
   c. Arranges and approves vacation schedules.
   d. Sits as a member of promotion committees.
   e. Counsels employees on personal and work problems.
   f. Directs the orientation of new employees to areas of responsibility.
   g. Participates in the in-service education program and the student clinical education program.
2. Guides and assists the head nurses in providing for the work load of the units.
   a. Assists in planning work assignments and recommends assignment changes.
   b. Approves work schedules developed by head nurses.
   c. Directs the temporary reassignment of personnel between units supervised to meet day-to-day work loads and emergencies.
3. Exercises administrative supervision of the supervisors of obstetrics, pediatrics, and psychiatry.

TYPICAL FUNCTIONAL RESPONSIBILITIES INCLUDE:
1. Directing the patient care activities of two or more nursing units.

  a. Maintains an up-to-the-moment appraisal of unit capability and requirements.
  b. Provides guidance to head nurses in matters of scheduling, patient care problems, and special patient care.
  c. Assists the head nurse in planning and organizing the day's activities.
  d. Provides for the adequate staffing of each nursing unit on an hour-by-hour basis.
  e. Maintains an up-to-date knowledge of patient care techniques, drug changes, and nursing procedures, and instructs nursing personnel in such areas.
  f. Counsels head nurses regarding hospital and nursing policies and procedures, and interprets policies and regulations.
2. Reviewing and advising Nursing Administration of patient care problems and needs, and recommends changes in policy and procedure.
  a. Investigates reports of incidents, suspected infections, and patient complaints, and resolves problems or makes recommendations for action.
  b. Plans for and orders equipment and supplies required by the units.
  c. Provides for the securing of special equipment.
  d. Makes recommendations to Assistant Director regarding changes of procedure or policy thought desirable.
3. Maintaining contact with and remaining aware of the condition of the patients.
  a. Maintains an up-to-the-moment appraisal of patient conditions and needs.
  b. Visits critically ill patients daily and as necessary.
  c. Appraises physician of special nursing problems and secures guidance for handling.
  d. Advises head nurses in matters of patient care and assists in bedside care as required.
  e. Counsels visitors and relatives regarding patient conditions and needs.
4. Assisting the Assistant Director in the planning of patient care activities in areas such as:
  a. Plans and recommends annual operating budget.
  b. Projects nursing unit staff needs.
  c. Investigates and studies trends in units and recommends practices and techniques.
  d. Develops and prepares a variety of daily, monthly and annual reports.
5. Carrying out other responsibilities such as:
  a. Coordinating nursing activities with other hospital departments.
  b. Sitting as a member or chairman of a variety of advisory and social activities committees.
  c. Conducting group tours and interested persons through areas of responsibility.

# MERCY CATHOLIC MEDICAL CENTER
(*Darby, Pennsylvania*)
## PATIENT CARE COORDINATOR

PRIMARY FUNCTION
Evaluate and plan nursing care with relation to type, quality and quantity, in order to provide a high standard of nursing service. Supervise and coordinate activities of units for which responsible.

*Main Equipment:* All types of patient care equipment.

*Main Materials and Supplies:* Records, reports, office supplies, medications, and solutions.

*Source of Supervision:* Associate Chairman, Nursing Service.

*Direction Exercised:* Head nurses, staff nurses.

MAIN DUTIES AND RESPONSIBILITIES
In accordance with approved policies, procedures, and schedules:
1. Supervise personnel assigned to nursing units for which responsible. Provide for the nursing care of patients within the units. Evaluate patient care and plan the kind and amount of nursing care in relation to the objectives of nursing service. Coordinate the efforts of the health team in planning patient care. Study needs and interpret same to immediate supervisor. Assign responsibility and delegate authority to subordinate personnel. Promote conformity to departmental policies and procedures. Give guidance and direction to personnel.
2. Select personnel for nursing care of patients within the unit. Determine qualifications of personnel for unit staffing and recommend personnel for transfers and promotions. Assign and reassign personnel within units to meet needs.
3. Guide head nurse in implementing policies. Provide means for communicating policies to personnel. Serve as a member of various nursing service organization committees. Participate in in-service and related activities.
4. Assist immediate supervisor in planning for allocation and utilization of space and equipment.
5. Contribute to the establishment of a budget which will allow for adequate personnel, supplies, equipment, and physical facilities within the unit. Interpret and justify nursing need. Determine needs based upon past experience and future plans. Explore priority needs with personnel. Establish priorities.
6. Communicate with Medical Staff in reference to patient care or nursing service activities.
7. Relieve immediate supervisor when necessary.
8. Perform other related duties as assigned by immediate supervisor.

# METHODIST HOSPITAL OF INDIANA, INC.
*(Indianapolis)*
### DIRECTOR OF CHAPLAINCY SERVICE

GOALS
1. To symbolize the religious dimension present in the hospital.
2. To recommend policies and procedures relative to hospital, church and community relations.
3. To provide consultation and guidance to administrative and medical personnel and to patients.
4. To administer the pastoral care activities in the hospital community.
5. To serve as staff consultant to hospital personnel when such services are sought out.
6. To participate in all pastoral duties and pastoral education programs when subordinates assigned to these responsibilities require assistance.

SUPERVISION RECEIVED
Under direction of the Administrator and functional guidance of the Executive Director.

SUPERVISION EXERCISED
Exercises administrative authority over an Associate Chaplain and Researcher for a Smoking Project for Clinical Pastoral Education.

TYPICAL FUNCTIONAL RESPONSIBILITIES INCLUDE:
1. Providing a climate or atmosphere that creates an atmosphere of person-centered activity and a Christian approach within the hospital.
2. Recommending policies and procedures relative to hospital-church relations.
   a. Provides guidance on moral and ethical dimensions.
   b. Recommends programs providing for pastoral needs of patients, personnel and students.
3. Providing consultation and guidance.
   a. Serves the religious needs of hospital personnel including students through a staff and in person.
   b. Provides for the spiritual need of patients when requested through a staff and in person.
   c. Participates in educational programs in identifying patient spiritual care needs.
   d. Trains clergymen in the art of Clinical Pastoral Counseling.
4. Administering the pastoral care activities in the hospital community.
   a. Coordinates the relationship with the religious community and supporting churches.
   b. Coordinates the in-hospital service of the local pastor.

    c. Assists in creating an atmosphere of patient-centered activity and a Christian approach within the hospital.
5. Serving as staff consultant to hospital personnel when services are requested.
6. Participating in all pastoral duties and pastoral educational programs when assistance is needed by subordinates.

# BARNES HOSPITAL
## (*St. Louis, Missouri*)
### SUPERVISOR, PHARMACY MANUFACTURING

JOB SUMMARY

Under the direct supervision of the Chief Pharmacist, supervises Pharmacist Technicians and Aides in manufacturing area of Pharmacy. Assists in directing Pharmacy policies and procedures in accordance with established policies of department and Hospital. Implements decisions of Administration pertaining to the Pharmacy. Manufactures and dispenses medicines and preparations according to formulas developed by department and utilized in the institution. Prepares and sterilizes injectible medication manufactured in Hospital, and also manufactures pharmaceuticals. Performs related duties as required.

OPERATIONAL GUIDELINES
1. Responsible for the preparation and sterilization of injectible medication, including irrigation solutions, manufactured in Hospital.
2. Supervises the manufacture of pharmaceuticals, dispensing of drugs, chemicals, and pharmaceutical preparations.
3. Supervises the filling and labeling of all drug containers issued to services.
4. Maintains a perpetual inventory of injectible medications, irrigation solutions, and manufactured pharmaceuticals as well as which drugs, chemicals, and pharmaceutical preparations have been dispensed.
5. Maintains file of specifications for purchase of chemicals.
6. Establishes and maintains, in cooperation with Accounting Department, a system of records and bookkeeping in accordance with policies of Hospital for charges to patients, and control over requisitioning and dispensing of drugs and pharmaceutical supplies.
7. Plans, organizes, and directs Pharmacy policies and procedures in accordance with established policies of Hospital.
8. Must be accurate in use of chemical and pharmaceutical equipment for compounding and dispensing drugs and medicines.
9. Must be accurate in accounting for, diluting, and handling of alcohol.

QUALIFICATIONS

1. Must have completed four year course in an accredited college leading to a degree of Bachelor of Science.
2. One year previous experience in a Pharmacy desirable. On-the-job orientation can be accomplished.
3. Good physical and mental health.
4. Must be willing to work with realization that errors may have serious consequences to patients.
5. Must be able to give undivided attention to details over extended periods of time.
6. Must have a memory for details and be alert to detect errors in compounding.
7. Must be able to cooperate with other employees and have the ability to supervise subordinate workers.
8. Must be able to plan operation and work schedule of department.
9. Follows standard formulas, but makes frequent decisions in a variety of technical matters.
10. Must be familiar with professional and commercial phases of pharmacy and have the ability to utilize all necessary reference books and textbooks related to medicine and pharmacy.
11. Must know pharmacy and chemical techniques.

---

# METHODIST HOSPITAL OF INDIANA, INC.
## (*Indianapolis*)
### DIRECTOR, NUTRITION AND DIETETICS

GOALS

1. To administer the operation of the Department of Nutrition and Dietetics through a staff of specially trained dietitians and within the established policies of the hospital and departmental policy, to the satisfaction of the management of the hospital.
2. To establish controls for assuring nutritional adequacy and efficiency of operation, acceptability of dietetic service to patients, medical and administrative staff.
3. To coordinate the dietetic program with the other clinical activities in the hospital and to make available to the medical staff the specialized knowledge of the field of nutrition and dietetics.
4. To organize and implement an ongoing formal educational program for dietetic interns; educational programs for dietary personnel, nursing personnel, house staff and patients.

5. To plan and implement the development of a research program in the areas of food service administration, clinical nutrition, and Public Health.

SUPERVISION RECEIVED

Under direction of Assistant Administrator and within the operating policies of the hospital.

SUPERVISION EXERCISED

1. Exercises general supervision over intermediary supervisors and, through them, the employees of the Department of Nutrition and Dietetics.
   a. Makes final decision on all personnel actions.
   b. Plans and executes departmental performance evaluation system.
   c. Supervises the planning of work assignments and work schedules.
   d. Organizes, directs and approves therapeutic, administrative, educational and research programs.

TYPICAL FUNCTIONAL RESPONSIBILITIES INCLUDE:

1. Gives administrative direction to the formulation and service of regular and modified diets to patients, employees, physicians and public; food service for special events as authorized by Administration; instructing patients in the requirements of prescribed diets; development of research and investigative studies regarding the use of diet in the treatment of disease; educational programs for dietetic interns and in-service personnel; performing consulting or advisory work for the medical and administrative staff.
   a. Directs planning of the master menu.
   b. Plans, supervises and controls the purchase, storage and utilization of all food items and supplies relating thereto.
2. Investigates, plans and recommends feeding systems, equipment requirements and staffing requirements.
3. Guides and motivates a staff of personnel having a wide variety of backgrounds, to excel in job performance.
4. Participates in employee health program on matters relating to diet.
5. Develops dietary operating policies and procedures, establishes lines of authority responsible for development and implementation of the diet manual.
6. Delegates authority to various dietitians to carry out the program.

# MERCY CATHOLIC MEDICAL CENTER
*(Darby, Pennsylvania)*
## EXECUTIVE HOUSEKEEPER

PRIMARY FUNCTION

Direct and administer housekeeping program and maintain Hospital in clean and orderly condition.

*Main Equipment:* Mops, dust mops, utility items, buffer, vacuum cleaner, and related cleaning equipment.

*Main Materials and Supplies:* Various cleaning supplies.

*Source of Supervision*: Associate Director.

*Direction Exercised:* Supervisory personnel, service workers.

MAIN DUTIES AND RESPONSIBILITIES

In accordance with approved policies, procedures, and schedules:

1. Supervise the activities of supervisory personnel, service workers and other personnel assigned. Responsible for planning, scheduling and assignment of employees.
2. Make work performance standards known to all subordinates in order that they are aware of what is expected of them and consequently can be properly rated on their performance.
3. Demonstrate new equipment and methods, and conduct on-the-job training for new employees, and other employees as necessary.
4. Report need for repair or maintenance to equipment, fixtures, facilities or furniture to Maintenance Department.
5. Responsible for the control of odors, and may engage the services of the exterminator in controlling pests, as required.
6. Spot-check work while in progress and upon completion, checking all areas for cleanliness of floors, glass, bathroom fixtures, furniture and apparatus, observing quality and quantity of work accomplished, and advises employees of conditions that do not meet the standards of the Medical Center.
7. Investigate unduly heavy consumption of supplies to detect waste; and makes periodic inventories, computes consumption, estimates needs, and prepares written requisition for supplies.
8. Make every effort to provide coverage for cleanliness of all areas at all times as a preventive measure against infection; and concurrently promotes good will and public relations from the standpoint of the patient and visitors, since cleanliness radiates cheer and provides a pleasant atmosphere.
9. Instruct new employees, and other employees as necessary, to observe safety precautions in cleaning electrical equipment, and proper use of step ladders in order that employees may avoid personal injury. Also instructs and makes certain that subordinates comply with instructions in the place-

ment of cleaning equipment so as not to obstruct traffic and prevent injury to any persons who may be in contact with the particular area.

10. Consult with supervisors and head nurses of various departments, in an effort to resolve any problems concerning subordinates who are assigned to the particular departments.
11. Responsible for interpreting, and clarifying policies of the Hospital to subordinates.
12. Responsible for suggesting adaptations to existing methods, standards, and equipment or new applications.
13. Maintain contact with Department Heads and Supervisors of various segments of the Hospital, in an effort to coordinate the services of the Housekeeping Department; and to resolve problems affecting the work and personnel of the Housekeeping Department.
14. Operate area of responsibility within approved budgets.
15. Keep informed about the most effective ways to get results through others.
16. Keep abreast of latest technical developments affecting scope of responsibility.
17. Make recommendations to immediate superior about how methods and procedures can be improved.
18. Perform other related duties as assigned by authorized personnel or as required to meet emergency situations.

---

# BARNES HOSPITAL
(*St. Louis, Missouri*)
## MANAGER, LAUNDRY

DUTIES BY EXAMPLE

Responsible for the entire operation of the Laundry Department including the Linen Room, Sewing Room, wash area, sorting area, finishing, mending, manufacturing of new items, and distribution of textiles throughout the entire hospital area. Interviews and selects new employes, directs their orientation and training on the job. Assigns duties, schedules workloads, and installs new methods to insure maximum efficiency. Requisitions replacements for worn or damaged articles or textiles, supplies, and equipment as needed. Maintains necessary records such as those on employee attendance, production, inventory, etc. Investigates new laundry equipment and intra-departmental procedures for possible application to the Laundry Department. Recommends changes or additions to the Laundry operation. Prepares departmental reports and budgets. Performs related duties as required.

PERFORMANCE REQUIREMENTS

*Responsibility For:* Cleanliness of laundered articles. Maintaining level of clean linens and uniforms. Mechanical functioning of equipment. Training new employees, and determining workloads. Preparation of departmental reports and budgets.

*Physical Demands:* Stands, walks, and sits most of working day.

*Special Demands:* Ability to accept responsibility for directing functions of department, supervising others, and working under stress during peak loads. Alertness to maintain even flow of work, preventing bottlenecks, and eliminating hazards to personnel. Considerable initiative and judgment involved in selecting and training workers, scheduling operations, and assigning tasks to meet peak load periods, revising methods to lower laundry costs, and securing cooperation of workers.

QUALIFICATIONS

*Education:* High school graduate with courses in mathematics, chemistry, general science, and physics is required. Graduation from a Laundry School covering courses in laundry operation and maintenance, supplies, cost computing, together with specialized courses in Industrial Engineering and Laundry Management is preferred.

*Training and Experience:* Five years' previous experience in supervisory capacity. Must have knowledge of modern steam laundry procedures, textiles, chemicals, and laundry machinery and equipment. Should be able to make time and motion studies, chemical PH and titration values. Ability to train and supervise workers while maintaining good worker morale. Ability to apply principles of personnel management to the selection and placement of workers.

*Job Knowledge:* Knowledge of the processes and details of laundry operation and service.

## *Hospitals—Financial*

# METHODIST HOSPITAL OF INDIANA, INC.
### (*Indianapolis*)
## DIRECTOR OF FINANCIAL MANAGEMENT AND CONTROLLER

GOALS

1. To develop for the hospital the necessary financial policies and controls for the protection of the assets.

2. To administer all approved accounting and financial control activities for the hospital.
3. To provide the Executive Director and Board with financial guidance.
4. To keep abreast of economic and social trends as they affect the finances of the hospital.
5. To provide for the purchase and inventory control of supplies and equipment.

SUPERVISION RECEIVED
Under the direction of the Executive Director and within the policies of the Finance Committee.

SUPERVISION EXERCISED
1. Exercises general supervision over the Managers in the Division and through them the employees of the Finance Division.
   a. Makes the final recommendation for salary increases within hospital policy.
   b. Reviews all dismissals of employees made by supervisors to determine fairness of action.
   c. Approves vacation schedules, reviews promotions and insures that all personnel policies are carried out.
2. Exercises policy direction over the carrying out of the accounting functions throughout the hospital and wherever there is a financial impact.

TYPICAL FUNCTIONAL RESPONSIBILITIES INCLUDE:
1. Developing, planning and recommending the accounting approach for the financial problems of the hospital to protect the assets.
   a. Formulates and recommends, to the Executive Director and the Board, accounting and budgetary policies; practices, procedures and controls.
   b. Designs accounting systems and records for the hospital for use under present and planned conditions.
2. Directing, administering and maintaining approved uniform accounting and control activities throughout the hospital for the purpose of obtaining sound financial information, controlling operating and capital expenses, and maintaining required records.
   a. Maintains a system of business procedures and controls of the nature of general accounting, cost accounting, budgetary control, insurance coverage, signing authorities.
   b. Directs and approves all tools required for financial programs such as charts of accounts and related prime accounting forms.
   c. Coordinates the accounting function with all other areas of the hospital.
   d. Directs the planning and execution of internal audits.
   e. Supervises or personally handles all tax matters, including the preparation and filing of necessary tax returns.
3. Providing guidance for the Executive Director and the Board in decisions

having a significant financial impact, and for the Division Directors and Managers in their individual areas.

    a. Prepares and analyzes or guides the preparation of statistical and accounting information.

    b. Provides required financial summaries, reports and all necessary financial interpretation of hospital functions.

4. Maintaining an awareness and keeping a continuous appraisal of economic and social forces and other influences and interpreting their effect upon the hospital's financial programs.

5. Providing for the purchase and inventory control of supplies and equipment.

    a. Approves the procedures for the purchase of supplies and equipment.

    b. Approves procedures for the receipt, handling and distribution of supplies and equipment.

    c. Provides for the storage and issue of supplies and equipment.

    d. Provides for the inventory and control of supplies and equipment, and the maintenance of appropriate related records.

6. Carrying out other responsibilities such as:

    a. Directs and coordinates all procedure manuals in Purchasing, Receiving, Stores, Patient Accounting, Corporate Accounting, Gift Shop.

    b. Decides on varying from established policy regarding payroll problems of employees where not involving Personnel Department.

    c. Participates in the Finance Committee activities.

    d. Determines the cash flow for such necessary reasons as capital expenditures, purchasing, payroll.

    e. Coordinates with other Division Directors and Department Heads in procedures, working tools, etc. that affect finances.

    f. Handles personally the purchasing of insurance coverage of various kinds such as: liability, asset protection, malpractice.

    g. Approves or personally handles all large contract purchases.

---

# MERCY CATHOLIC MEDICAL CENTER
*(Darby, Pennsylvania)*
## DIRECTOR, FISCAL AFFAIRS

PRIMARY FUNCTION

Directs treasury, accounting and financing activities for the Medical Center and its divisions. Has specific responsibility for sponsoring and coordinating necessary and appropriate accounting and statistical assistance to all departments of the business.

*Main Equipment:* Telephone, office-type equipment.

*Main Materials and Supplies:* Records, reports, office-type supplies.

*Source of Supervision:* Executive Vice President, MCMC.

*Direction Required:* All personnel, fiscal affairs, MCMC.

MAIN DUTIES AND RESPONSIBILITIES

In accordance with approved policies, procedures, and schedules:

1. Direct the Controller in providing and directing procedures and systems necessary to maintain proper records and to afford adequate accounting controls and services.
2. Acts as custodian of the funds of the corporation.
3. Appraises the corporation's financial position and issues periodic financial and operating reports. Directs and coordinates the establishment of corporate budget programs.
4. Coordinates expenditure programs with forecasted cash flow.
5. Directs, consolidates, and analyzes all cost and plan economy analyses together with other statistical and routine reports, including any desirable analysis of the monthly departmental reports.
6. Directs the Controller in the preparation of reimbursement and government reports originating in the accounting division, and signs such returns and reports.
7. Makes financing arrangements with third party contracting agencies and banking institutions.
8. Negotiate settlements on cost contracts with third parties.
9. Implement and monitor contractual arrangements with physicians and executive personnel.
10. Recommend level of capital expenditures, and changes in charge rates.
11. Perform other related duties as assigned by immediate supervisor.

---

# METHODIST HOSPITAL OF INDIANA, INC.
## (*Indianapolis*)
### CREDIT MANAGER

GOALS

1. To carry out the credit and collection policies and keep monetary losses at a minimum.
2. To organize and administer a system for collection of accounts.
3. To supervise and train personnel performing credit and collection functions.
4. To provide the final judgment on treatment of difficult or "special" cases, keeping in mind both the financial well-being and the public image of the hospital.
5. To provide the Controller with credit policy recommendations.

SUPERVISION RECEIVED

Under the general supervision of the Assistant Controller, Office Manager. Works within well defined policy limits but with considerable latitude for judgment.

SUPERVISION EXERCISED

Exercises direct supervision over an Assistant Credit Manager and two or more supervisors, and through them the interviewers, clerks, billers and other employees in the Credit Department.

TYPICAL FUNCTIONAL RESPONSIBILITIES INCLUDE:

1. Administering the credit and collection policies—keeping monetary losses at a minimum.
   a. Providing an interviewing process for obtaining pertinent credit information from patients either at time of admittance or as soon as is practical.
   b. Personally approving the more desirable credit risks without question and interviewing the more complicated or most distraught patients, usually involving quasi-legal matters.
   c. Approves courtesies to employees, ministers, physicians, student nurses, etc., within framework of policy.
   d. Arranging payment plans.
2. Organizing and administering a collection system.
   a. Supervising collection and mailing of follow-up letters following an established procedure.
   b. Reviewing the 90-day listings and taking appropriate action.
   c. Approving and processing accounts to bad debts, including selection of accounts, signing journals and supervising the preparation of trays for posting.
   d. Processing and endorsing notes to banks.
3. Supervising and training credit and collection personnel.
4. Providing the final judgment on handling of difficult or "special" cases.
   a. Determining how far to press for collection in the more difficult cases.
   b. Establishing limits of action to be taken without injury to the hospital's public image.
5. Keeping abreast of the economic conditions of the area at all times and recommending to the Controller changes in hospital credit and collection policy based on the conditions as changes take place.

## Hospitals—Personnel
## and Employee Relations

# METHODIST HOSPITAL OF INDIANA, INC.
*(Indianapolis)*
### ASSISTANT EXECUTIVE DIRECTOR,
### PERSONNEL AND EDUCATION

GOALS
1. To provide and maintain an adequate and efficient work force.
2. To administer an effective, well-rounded personnel program within the hospital.
3. To serve as liaison with developmental and educational programs in various colleges in the area and with governmental manpower development projects.
4. To fill in for the Executive Director in the absence of the Executive Director and Administrator or as assigned.
5. To serve as liaison between employees and management and board of trustees.
6. To keep abreast of new developments in the personnel and Health Care Educational field.

SUPERVISION RECEIVED
Under general direction of the Executive Director. Works within clearly defined policies, but many are of his own making. Has a great deal of latitude for initiative and judgment.

SUPERVISION EXERCISED
Exercises administrative authority over a staff of personnel specialists concerned with hospital personnel, nursing personnel, safety and education, work measurement and methods, and employee health.

TYPICAL FUNCTIONAL RESPONSIBILITIES INCLUDE:
1. Providing and maintaining an adequate and efficient work force.
   a. Recruits and screens personnel for employment at all levels.
   b. Provides a well planned program for orientation and general up-grading of personnel through training and in-service education.
2. Administering an effective personnel program within the hospital.
   a. Assists in developing and interpreting personnel policies.
   b. Establishes a system of communication for discriminating policy and personnel information throughout the hospital.
   c. Maintains adequate records and reports as required by government agencies and the hospital administration.
   d. Administers employee benefit plans, safety and health programs.

e. Provides for proper manpower and budget controls through salary and wage administration, work measurement and man-hour budgets.
3. Serving as liaison with developmental and educational programs in various colleges in the area. Works with local, state and federal projects on manpower development.
4. Acting for the Executive Director in his and the Administrator's absence or as may be designated by the Executive Director.
5. Providing and serving as the necessary liaison between the hospital employees and the hospital administration.
6. Keeping abreast of new developments and changes in the Personnel and Health Care Educational field.

# MERCY CATHOLIC MEDICAL CENTER
(*Darby, Pennsylvania*)
## DIRECTOR OF PERSONNEL

PRIMARY FUNCTION
Develops, implements and coordinates policies and programs covering the following: employment, employee relations, wage and salary administration, indoctrination and training, placement, benefits and employee services. Originates policies and activities which will provide a balanced program throughout all locations of the Medical Center.

*Main Equipment:* N/A; Telephone.

*Main Materials and Supplies:* N/A.

*Source of Supervision:* Executive Vice President and/or President.

*Direction Required:* All employees assigned to Personnel Department.

MAIN DUTIES AND RESPONSIBILITIES
In accordance with approved policies, procedures, and schedules:
1. Directs the interpretation and application of established personnel policies throughout the Medical Center.
2. Formulates and recommends personnel policies and objectives of the Medical Center.
3. Responsible for administration of wage and salary policies and structures, and for personnel rating programs. Provides adequate personnel through employment office. Protects interests of employees in accordance with Medical Center's personnel policies.
4. Maintains over-all supervision of the Medical Center's recruitment, placement and training programs.

5. Exercises general supervision over all Medical Center benefit programs and services.
6. Conducts a continuing study of all personnel policies, programs and practices to keep the Medical Center abreast with current practice and informed of new developments.
7. Directs the preparation and maintenance of such reports as are necessary to carry out functions of the department. Prepares periodic reports to the President and/or Executive Vice President, as necessary or requested.
8. Directs and maintains various activities designed to promote and maintain a high level of employee morale.

---

# METHODIST HOSPITAL OF INDIANA, INC.
*(Indianapolis)*
## DIRECTOR OF EDUCATION AND TRAINING

GOALS
1. To plan, organize, administer and direct the daily operations and long range program of the Education and Training Department.
2. To plan, implement and maintain a program of supervisory and management development.
3. To plan, implement and maintain an orientation program for new employees.
4. To supervise and coordinate special education and employee up-grading programs.
5. To provide professional consultation on training and education to other hospital departments, and formal education programs.

SUPERVISION RECEIVED
Under the direct supervision of the Assistant Executive Director, Personnel—Education.

SUPERVISION EXERCISED
Exercises direct supervision over the employees of the Education and Training Department. Interviews and selects applicants referred by the Personnel Department. Carries out disciplinary actions, including discharge, under general hospital policies. Has authority to delete trainees during their training period.

TYPICAL FUNCTIONAL RESPONSIBILITIES INCLUDE:
1. Planning, organizing and directing the daily operations and long range programs of the Education and Training Department:
   a. Determines training needs in consultation with department heads.

   b. Provides skill training for Nursing Assistants, Ward Secretaries and Unit Secretaries and similar positions which may later be assigned.

   c. Develops course content, training methodologies, course materials and training aids.

   d. Develops schedules and work assignments for departmental employees.

   e. Trains departmental employees to carry out their assigned function.

   f. Evaluates the work of the department and its employees to determine whether objectives are being met.

   g. Maintains close liaison with department heads to be certain their employees are receiving the training necessary to do an efficient job.

   h. Develops a budget and other controls to insure the department is being operated on a sound fiscal basis.

2. Planning, implementing and maintaining a program of supervisory and management development.

   a. Develops, in cooperation with department heads, a continuing program of supervisory training. The program should prepare the new supervisor with the knowledge and skills of leadership. The continuing supervisory training program should be designed to reinforce leadership, knowledge and skills and efficient management techniques.

   b. Provides hospital managers, including administrators, department heads, and assistant department heads, with a continuing program of individualized development.

3. Planning, implementing, and maintaining a program of orientation for new employees.

   a. Provides a program of orientation to new employees which will give them the information necessary to be effective members of the work force and which will motivate them to remain in the employ of the hospital. New employees should be informed of the goals and objectives of the hospital, the role of their department in achieving these objectives, the benefits and responsibilities of hospital employment, and the rules and regulations which affect their employment and the safety rules of the hospital.

4. Supervising and coordinating special education and employee up-grading programs.

   a. Directly supervises the Personnel Assistant, Special Education, in his activities in these programs.

   b. Advises and consults with department heads on special education and employee up-grading programs.

   c. Consults with governmental and private agencies on development of special education programs and obtaining financial support for such programs.

   d. Coordinates special education training program with programs offered in public schools.

5. Providing professional consultation on training and education to other hospital departments and formal education programs.

a. Cooperates with the Audio-visual Department in the development of greater utilization of Audio-visual techniques.

b. Investigates and recommends use of programmed instruction as judged feasible.

c. Investigates and recommends use of simulation devices in education and training.

d. Works cooperatively with other hospital departments in solving problems through education and training.

e. Trains instructors in formal educational programs within the hospital as requested.

f. Provides consultation as requested to formal programs of instruction affiliated with the hospital.

## *Hospitals—Administration*

## METHODIST HOSPITAL OF INDIANA, INC.
### (*Indianapolis*)
### ADMINISTRATIVE DIRECTOR, MEDICAL EDUCATION

GOALS

1. To provide management for personnel and office relating to Medical Education.

2. Coordinates administrative activities such as schedules, reports, meetings, policies, procedures, equipment and budgeting as these relate to Medical Education, the Outpatient Department, the Emergency Room, the Family Practice Center and the Heart Station.

3. Provides administrative liaison with the House Staff Council to the office of Medical Education and with the Hospital Administration.

4. Coordinate and where necessary formulate required reports for the House Staff. Must maintain up-to-date descriptions and summaries of educational programs for each service.

SUPERVISION RECEIVED

The Administrative Director for Medical Education is directly responsible to the Vice President of Medical Education.

SUPERVISION EXERCISED

The Administrative Director is responsible for all actions of an administrative nature pertinent to Medical Education and its related hospital functions. The

Administrative Director has direct supervision over the Administrative Assistant and Office Supervisor for Medical Education.

TYPICAL FUNCTIONAL RESPONSIBILITIES INCLUDE:
1. Generates sufficient background data to answer numerous and varied required reports. He must be able to organize information which succinctly presents the facts and which would require review and possible minor revisions.
2. Must provide administrative liaison between the department of Medical Education, the Educational Committee chairmen and the House Staff Council. The Administrative Director has to relate to a wide variety of professional individuals maintaining workable relationships and at the same time exercise reasonable judgment and authority. Provides administrative liaison between the department of Medical Education, with the Hospital Administration and other departments of the hospital.
3. Develops budgets for Medical Education and Outpatient Departments. These include but are not limited to supplies, equipment and man-hour budgets.
4. Investigates cost areas through recognized cost accounting techniques.

# MERCY CATHOLIC MEDICAL CENTER
## (*Darby, Pennsylvania*)
### DIRECTOR OF PUBLIC RELATIONS

PRIMARY FUNCTION
Develop and administer a public relations program designed to effect and improve understanding by employees and the public of the Medical Center's objectives and achievements. Responsible for the administration of policies covering the broad field of public relations activities, including public and employee information.

*Main Equipment:* Telephone and office-type equipment.

*Main Materials and Supplies:* Office-type supplies.

*Source of Supervision:* Executive Vice President, MCMC.

*Direction Exercised:* Asst. Director, Public Relations, Director of Community Relations, Secretary, Photographer.

MAIN DUTIES AND RESPONSIBILITIES
In accordance with approved policies, procedures, and schedules:
1. Develop a public relations program for approval by the President. Administer such activities throughout the Medical Center. Coordinate all

public relations programs by keeping those concerned informed and by providing necessary counsel and assistance.

2. Directly supervise and be responsible for the Medical Center's Community Relations and Photographic Departments.

3. Direct the preparation and release of publicity, and maintain sound relations with the press, national magazines, radio, television and other media. Make arrangements for interviews between Medical Center executives and press, radio and television representatives.

4. Provide assistance to Medical Center personnel in speeches, letters and articles which are to be made public.

5. Recommend the employment of outside public relations counsel as needed, and supervise and appraise the performance of such counsel.

6. Review and approve from the public relations point of view all public statements and speeches, radio and television scripts and articles prepared by employees or public relations counsel on behalf of the Medical Center; advise of material in conflict with public relations policy and suggest necessary changes.

7. Review and approve from the public relations point of view all hospital advertising, other than routine employment ads. Direct the preparation of institutional advertising copy designed for promotion of the Medical Center name and goodwill.

8. Draft, in consultation with others, annual reports, special advertising, and other Medical Center material; coordinate printing and distribution of these materials.

9. Handle preparation and the issuance of Medical Center bulletin to employees concerning the Medical Center and its activities as well as other matters of general interest to them. Supervise editing, publication and distribution of employee newspaper.

10. Counsel on the selection of trade, professional and service organizations in which the Medical Center should participate and recommend best qualified Medical Center representatives for each organization. Serve as contact with organizations soliciting advertising or the Medical Center's financial support of charitable or civic undertakings.

11. Arrange for executives to talk before local groups to inform them about the Medical Center, and its role in the community; for representation on community organizations, and on various health related committees.

12. Prepare budget for the Public Relations Department, including the Community Relations and Photographic Departments.

13. Provide public relations counsel and service to the executives of the Medical Center; collect and circulate public relations material; collect and maintain data on the Center; hande miscellaneous inquiries about the Medical Center; and assist as required in other Medical Center activities.

14. Perform other related duties, as assigned by immediate supervisor.

*Hospitals—*
*Management Information Systems*

## MERCY CATHOLIC MEDICAL CENTER
*(Darby, Pennsylvania)*
### COORDINATOR OF MANAGEMENT INFORMATION SYSTEMS

PRIMARY FUNCTION
Direct the electronic data processing activities of the Mercy Catholic Medical Center. Provide management direction and leadership in computer applications development and computer operations of the Medical Center. Provide advice and counsel to management concerning the application of computing techniques to Medical Center requirements.

*Main Equipment:* Telephone, data processing equipment.

*Main Materials and Supplies:* Office-type supplies.

*Source of Supervision:* Executive Vice President.

*Direction Exercised:* None.

MAIN DUTIES AND RESPONSIBILITIES
In accordance with approved policies, procedures, and schedules:
1. Analyze management needs regarding information retrieval, control data and expanded use of computing and data processing equipment in Medical Center operations and processes.
2. Provide guidance and counsel to officers in the examination and definition of objectives for existing or proposed Medical Center systems and in the design of improved systems utilizing computing and data processing equipment.
3. Recommend the location, type, size and equipment for data processing installations including applicable machine programs within the limits of Medical Center policy. Recommend the staffing of each data processing location consistent with the work load. Assist in the selection of and supervise training of personnel within the limits of Medical Center and divisional salary and administrative policy.
4. Direct the preparation and installation of data processing procedures and systems, including the design of source documents, technical direction of processing operations and assistance in the format of management reports.
5. Establish machine schedules to obtain maximum utilization of equipment. Prepare equipment utilization reports as required.
6. Maintain professional contacts with other Medical Center research bodies and equipment manufacturers concerning computer applications and equipment.
7. Direct the continuing review of present Medical Center systems and methods and the formulation of new and revised systems, examining techniques in use and determining appropriate changes to effect improvements, reduce costs and enhance efficiency on a Medical Center basis.

# A Vertical Series of Managerial Position Descriptions in Manufacturing at the Plant Level

For those readers who are particularly interested in manufacturing, one company's managerial position descriptions at the plant level are presented below.

---

PLANT MANAGER, LARGE PLANT

OTHER TYPICAL TITLES: Works Manager, Factory Manager, Operations Manager, General Manager (Small Division)

PRIMARY PURPOSE OF JOB (Why the Company has this job):
To provide the overall management, direction and coordination of plant operations. To meet planned production schedules at the lowest possible cost, consistent with quality requirements, while attaining the maximum return on assets managed consistent with long-term Company objectives.

RESPONSIBILITIES (Major responsibilities for which incumbent is held accountable):
1. Formulate plant policies consistent with Company and divisional policies and objectives with respect to operating efficiency, manufacturing costs, product quality, scheduled performance, planning for short and long-term growth, new product developments, industrial relations, profit improvement and expense control, and plant security.
2. Maintain production schedules to meet forecasted sales requirements in a manner consistent with the efficient use of plant capacity.
3. Direct and develop key subordinate managers to provide a professional, profit-oriented management group.
4. Review actual versus planned operations to assure efficient accomplishment of objectives in order to: (a) keep top management informed of any deviations from plan and (b) to recommend corrective actions.
5. Represent the Company to the local community.
6. Meet financial targets including costs, budgets and return on assets.

REPORTS TO: Vice President—Operations

DIRECTS WORK OF (Representative positions directly supervised):
Superintendent—Assembly Operations, Superintendent—Machining Operations, Superintendent—Manufacturing Services, Manufacturing Engineering Manager, Materials Manager, Personnel Manager. Dotted line responsibility for: Quality Control Manager, Plant Controller, Plant Accountant, and Resident Engineer.

KNOWLEDGE AND SKILLS REQUIRED (What the incumbent must know to function in his job: education, specialized technical knowledge and skills, managerial skills, skills of negotiation and persuasion):

*Education:* Bachelor's degree required. MBA or advanced degree work desirable.

*Experience:* Eight to twelve years general management experience. A minimum of five years experience in manufacturing management.

*Skills:* Thorough knowledge of manufacturing operations with demonstrable managerial skills in organizing, analyzing, planning and communicating. Emphasis on ability to motivate both technical/professional or highly experienced subordinate managers.

USE OF KNOWLEDGE AND SKILLS (Decision making—extent to which individual can commit Company OR problem solving—creative thinking, decision influencing, etc., which focus on difficulty of mental application):

*Decision making:* Can commit internal plant operations within general guidelines and production schedules. May commit capital expenditures up to $15,000.

*Problem solving:* Must possess ability to select proper alternative solutions recommended by subordinate managers, considering both financial and operational implications.

SCOPE AND IMPACT OF THE POSITION (Consider number and level of people supervised, annual budgets, sales volume, markets-business development, control of financial resources, goods purchased, etc.):

*Human resources:* Directly supervises seven Department Managers; indirectly supervises 3,000 employees.

*Physical and Financial Resources:* Assets managed $ _____ Sales volume of products produced $ _____ to $ _____ Annual budget of $ _____

*Future Growth and Profitability:* Responsible for planning future plant growth and directing annual program to offset inflation in labor and material costs.

## SUPERINTENDENT, MEDIUM PLANT: COMBINED ASSEMBLY, MACHINING AND/OR FABRICATION

OTHER TYPICAL TITLES: Plant Superintendent, Manufacturing Superintendent, Assistant Plant Manager, Production Manager

PRIMARY PURPOSE OF JOB (Why the Company has this job):
To direct and control all production operations within the plant through subordinate managers to meet established production schedules at the lowest possible cost within engineered quality specifications. To direct support activities (e.g., maintenance, tool room), to provide adequate staff to meet schedules and to provide proper care of manufacturing equipment.

RESPONSIBILITIES (Major responsibilities for which incumbent is held accountable):
1. Plan and organize an adequate labor force to meet operational objectives and, through subordinate managers, direct manufacturing operations to meet production schedules based on sales forecasts and the desired level of quality within cost objectives.
2. Recommend and implement annual operating budgets and establish necessary controls to meet financial objectives; and personnel, capital equipment and tooling cost goals.
3. Maintain a safe and orderly operation of plant manufacturing facilities for a three-shift operation.
4. Coordinate overall manufacturing operations with plant and divisional support groups.
5. Recommend changes in plant facilities, capital equipment replacements, new processes and tooling to meet further requirements.
6. Provide management development opportunities for subordinate managers.
7. Interpret and implement Company and plant policies and procedures.

REPORTS TO: Plant Manager

DIRECTS WORK OF (Representative positions directly supervised):
Department Managers (General Foremen)

KNOWLEDGE AND SKILLS REQUIRED (What the incumbent must know to function in his job: education, specialized technical knowledge and skills, managerial skills, skills of negotiation and persuasion):

*Education:* Bachelor's degree or equivalent course work at college level (e.g., through night school).

*Experience:* Three to seven years in manufacturing management. Must have experience or detailed knowledge of: manufacturing engineering, manufacturing planning and scheduling, quality control techniques, managerial accounting and equipment/tooling maintenance.

*Skills:* Ability to motivate subordinate managers and proven leadership and organizational ability. Should possess high degree of employee relations skills.

USE OF KNOWLEDGE AND SKILLS (Decision making—extent to which individual can commit Company OR problem solving—creative thinking, decision influencing, etc., which focus on difficulty of mental application):

*Decision making:* Commits shop operations within production schedules and guidelines established by Plant Manager. Decisions have a major impact on short-term costs and efficiency and a long-term impact on plant operations (e.g. personnel relations, maintenance of equipment, quality of facilities, and quality of product).

*Problem solving:* Must be able to deal with problems at all levels of line supervision to insure the manufacture of products to precise specifications with changing technological requirements and within tight schedules. Must be able to effectively coordinate subordinate line managers and plant support functions.

SCOPE AND IMPACT OF THE POSITION (Consider number and level of people supervised, annual budgets, sales volume, markets-business development, control of financial resources, goods purchased, etc.):

*Human resources:* Directly supervise and appraise the performance of six subordinate Department Managers; indirectly supervises work of 750 to 850 production employees.

*Physical and Financial Resources:* Assets managed $ _____ to $ _____ equipment. Annual operating budget of $ _____ to $ _____.

---

DEPARTMENT MANAGER, LARGE PLANT:
ASSEMBLY OPERATIONS

OTHER TYPICAL TITLES: Department Foreman, General Foreman

PRIMARY PURPOSE OF JOB (Why the Company has this job):
To maintain, direct and train an efficient work force for a department to assemble portable electric power tools. Directs the fitting, aligning and adjusting of parts and sub-assemblies to meet finished product requirements including the repair of units which fail to meet specifications. Through production supervisors, in a three-shift operation, is responsible for meeting established

production schedules, maintaining quality to meet specifications, meeting efficiency goals within established budgets, and maintaining good personnel relations.

RESPONSIBILITIES (Major responsibilities for which incumbent is held accountable):

1. Organize and, through subordinate supervisors, hire, train and discipline an efficient work force to accomplish assigned departmental objectives.
2. Direct, through subordinate supervisors on a three-shift operation, all work of department to meet established production schedules within quality specifications.
3. Assign and spot-check work of department to insure consistency with skill levels and maximum productive efficiency.
4. Maintain costs within assigned budgets.
5. Maintain safe and orderly working environment.
6. Recommend need for machinery and tooling maintenance, changes in work force, replacement or addition of new equipment and tooling.
7. Assist plant service groups (e.g., Manufacturing Engineering, Purchasing, Production Planning) as required to insure modern and efficient operations.

REPORTS TO: Manufacturing Superintendent

DIRECTS WORK OF (Representative positions directly supervised):
Shift Supervisors (second-line supervision for second and third shifts).
Production Supervisors (first-line supervision).

KNOWLEDGE AND SKILLS REQUIRED (What the incumbent must know to function in his job: education, specialized technical knowledge and skills, managerial skills, skills of negotiation and persuasion):

*Education:* High or Trade school graduate (minimum requirement).

*Experience:* Practical knowledge (3 to 5 years) of assembly operations. Should be familiar with engineering standards, scheduling techniques, practices followed in machining, sub-assembly, maintenance and stores departments, Company budgeting and reporting techniques.

*Skills:* Must possess managerial skills to direct line organization and apply Company policies and practices. Should have thorough technical knowledge of assembly operations including necessary operations to meet quality specifications.

USE OF KNOWLEDGE AND SKILLS (Decision making—extent to which individual can commit Company OR problem solving—creative thinking, decision influencing, etc., which focus on difficulty of mental application):

*Decision making:* In conjunction with Superintendent, commits department to production schedules. Can influence decisions to use new methods or equipment.

*Problem solving:* Must insure smooth work flow by assisting line supervisors in overcoming problems which affect production, cost reduction projects, changes in equipment, tooling and standards changes.

SCOPE AND IMPACT OF THE POSITION (Consider number and level of people supervised, annual budgets, sales volume, markets-business development, control of financial resources, goods purchased, etc.):

*Human resources:* Directly supervise (develop and evaluate performance of) 15 to 20 subordinate supervisors. Indirectly supervise 200 to 350 assembly department personnel.

*Physical and Financial resources:* Assets managed (including assembly lines and related equipment fixtures and tooling) total value $ _____ to $ _____. Annual operating budget—$ _____ to $ _____

---

## DEPARTMENT MANAGER, LARGE PLANT: MACHINING OR FABRICATION OPERATIONS

OTHER TYPICAL TITLES: General Foreman, Department Foreman, Manufacturing Supervisor

PRIMARY PURPOSE OF JOB (Why the Company has this job):
To maintain scheduled production requirements, quality specifications, insure high level of employee relations, meet budget standards, assure maximum use of manpower, equipment and materials, and assist subordinate supervisors in carrying out their responsibilities. Recommend need for machinery and tooling maintenance, changes in work force, replacement or addition of new equipment and tooling.

RESPONSIBILITIES (Major responsibilities for which incumbent is held accountable):
1. Organize and, through subordinate supervisors, hire, train and discipline an efficient work force to accomplish assigned departmental objectives.
2. Direct, through subordinate supervisors, on a three-shift operation, all work of department to meet established production schedules within quality specifications at maximum productive efficiency.
3. Maintain costs within assigned budgets.
4. Maintain safe and orderly working environment.

5. Recommend need for machinery and tooling maintenance, changes in work force, replacement or additions of new equipment and tooling.
6. Monitor standards and efforts to improve standards, monitor scrap control and spending on rework, and take corrective actions as required.
7. Maintain good morale in department and insure employee performance reviews are made on time as well as implement plant employee relations programs.
8. Assist first-line supervisors in meeting cost-reduction goals.
9. Assist plant service groups as required to insure modern and efficient operations.

REPORTS TO: Manufacturing Superintendent

DIRECTS WORK OF (Representative positions directly supervised):
Shift Supervisors (for first, second and third shifts) and Production Supervisors (first-line supervisors).

KNOWLEDGE AND SKILLS REQUIRED (What the incumbent must know to function in his job: education, specialized technical knowledge and skills, managerial skills, skills of negotiation and persuasion):

*Education:* High or Trade school graduate (minimum requirement).

*Experience:* Five to ten years of progressive responsibility in machining and related manufacturing assignments (minimum of 2 years in supervisory position). Should be familiar with engineering standards, scheduling techniques, Company budgeting and reporting techniques.

*Skills:* Must possess managerial skills to direct line organization and apply Company policies and practices. Should have thorough technical knowledge and skills in general machining operations including grinding, milling, drilling, sheet metal and finishing.

USE OF KNOWLEDGE AND SKILLS (Decision making—extent to which individual can commit Company OR problem solving—creative thinking, decision influencing, etc., which focus on difficulty of mental application):

*Decision making:* Can commit department on three shifts within general guidelines and production schedules.

*Problem solving:* Must insure smooth work flow by removing problems in departmental operations. Must recognize and recommend solutions to technical or managerial problems within department (with emphasis on machining and tolerance problems). Must work with service groups on cost reduction projects, changes in equipment, tooling processes or standards and the training of direct and indirect personnel.

SCOPE AND IMPACT OF THE POSITION (Consider number and level of people supervised, annual budgets, sales volume, markets-business development, control of financial resources, goods purchased, etc.):

*Human resources:* Directly supervises 12 to 15 subordinate supervisors. Indirectly supervises 100 to 200 departmental personnel including leadmen and set-up men.

*Physical and Financial resources:* Assets managed (machinery and related equipment fixtures and tooling) $ _____ to $ _____. Annual operating budget, $ _____ to $ _____

---

## DEPARTMENT MANAGER, LARGE PLANT: MAINTENANCE FUNCTIONS

OTHER TYPICAL TITLES: Maintenance General Foreman, Maintenance Superintendent, Maintenance Supervisor, Plant Engineering and Maintenance Supervisor, Plant Engineering Supervisor

PRIMARY PURPOSE OF JOB (Why the Company has this job):
To plan, organize, direct and control the plant facilities maintenance operation to include maintaining all mechanical and electrical equipment, buildings, utilities (including water and disposal system where applicable) and plant services (including custodial and groundskeeping).

RESPONSIBILITIES (Major responsibilities for which incumbent is held accountable):
1. Direct and coordinate, through subordinate supervisors, the activities and operations of his department(s), on a two- or three-shift operation, at the most economic cost and at maximum efficiency, seeking to improve productivity through improved methods to meet pre-planned maintenance objectives.
2. Estimate manpower requirements for required skills, select, hire and train qualified personnel to perform the work in the department(s).
3. Plan, design, install, test, operate and maintain utility systems including electrical and steam power, heating and air conditioning, ventilation, compressed air, gas, water and waste disposal systems.
4. Cooperate with all line and staff departments so that schedules and programs may be executed as planned including preventative maintenance schedules, lubrication schedules, and overhaul schedules.
5. Develop and recommend improved work methods and standards.
6. Perform periodic facilities maintenance inspections to ensure work performed is within specified quality standards.
7. Ensure proper care and use of equipment in his department(s).

REPORTS TO: Manufacturing Services Superintendent

DIRECTS WORK OF (Representative positions directly supervised):
Electrical, Mechanical, Utilities and Plant Services Supervisors.

KNOWLEDGE AND SKILLS REQUIRED (What the incumbent must know to function in his job: education, specialized technical knowledge and skills, managerial skills, skills of negotiation and persuasion):

*Education:* High School graduate (minimum requirement) and advanced technical school training in electrical distribution, plumbing, heat and ventilation, motors and hydraulic systems (desirable).

*Experience:* Three to seven years practical experience in progressively responsible maintenance department positions. Should have minimum of two years supervisory experience. Should have experience with plant and equipment layout, repair and assembly of precision equipment and controls, and the preparation of project proposals for management approval.

*Skills:* Must possess high degree of managerial skills to direct various maintenance mechanics and custodial personnel. A strong mechanical aptitude is a prerequisite.

USE OF KNOWLEDGE AND SKILLS (Decision making—extent to which individual can commit Company OR problem solving—creative thinking, decision influencing, etc., which focus on difficulty of mental application):

*Decision making:* Can commit department in removing production bottlenecks or in making utility repairs of an emergency nature affecting entire plant operations.

*Problem solving:* Must insure rapid repair of production machinery or utility equipment that has an overall effect on production such as electricity, compressed air or refrigeration. Must be able to plan and give priorities to activities which affect plant operations on a day-to-day basis. Must cope with environmental noise, air pollution, water pollution, heating, ventilating and air conditioning, waste removal and high failure rates of production machinery through engineering projects aimed at eliminating problem areas. Should recognize employee needs to insure healthy and safe working conditions in entire plant.

SCOPE AND IMPACT OF THE POSITION (Consider number and level of people supervised, annual budgets, sales volume, markets-business development, control of financial resources, goods purchased, etc.):

*Human resources:* Directly supervise 4 subordinate supervisors and indirectly supervise 91 personnel on a three-shift operation.

*Physical and Financial resources:* Directly responsible for the maintenance and operating condition of $ _____ in plant and equipment. Annual operating budget of $ _____

## PRODUCTION SUPERVISOR, ALL PLANTS:
## ASSEMBLY OPERATIONS

OTHER TYPICAL TITLES: Assistant Foreman, Line Supervisor, Assembly Supervisor, Foreman

(Note: this is a first-line supervisor position.)

PRIMARY PURPOSE OF JOB (Why the Company has this job):
To maintain, direct and train direct labor assembly units, consisting of approximately 30 to 40 personnel for maximum efficiency in both quality and quantity. Review performance, maintain and enforce personnel and safety policies. Meet efficiency goals and budget expense targets.

RESPONSIBILITIES (Major responsibilities for which incumbent is held accountable):
1. Organize, train and discipline an effective direct labor work force to meet departmental objectives and provide objective evaluations of employee performance.
2. Maintain and direct assembly units in an efficient manner to meet production schedules within budgeted costs.
3. Assemble units to specifications and bill of material for assembly and packing of units.
4. Maintain an orderly and safe work area.
5. Train personnel to work as a group in meeting efficiency objectives.
6. Assist in the maintenance of tools and equipment for an efficient line operation.
7. Enforce Company personnel and safety policies.
8. Work with staff departments to maintain production schedules and to assist in meeting cost reduction and quality improvement objectives.

REPORTS TO: Shift Supervisor (second-line supervision, not Department Manager) in large plant. Department Manager (with no intermediate level of supervision) in medium and small plants.

DIRECTS WORK OF (Representative positions directly supervised):
Line specialists, repairmen, packers, product assemblers, set-up personnel.

KNOWLEDGE AND SKILLS REQUIRED (What the incumbent must know to function in his job: education, specialized technical knowledge and skills, managerial skills, skills of negotiation and persuasion):
*Education:* High School or equivalent (minimum requirement).

*Experience:* Three to four years in assembly operation. Must be familiar with Bill of Material listing, engineering standards (operation and prints), production scheduling practices and other shop paper. Should have some supervisory experience (e.g., as a leadman) and be familiar with Company policies and procedures.

*Skills:* Must possess managerial skills to direct labor force to meet management objectives. Must be able to effectively motivate production workers.

USE OF KNOWLEDGE AND SKILLS (Decision making—extent to which individual can commit Company OR problem solving—creative thinking, decision influencing, etc., which focus on difficulty of mental application):

*Decision making:* Supervisory decisions within guidelines for personnel and safety policies, production schedules, engineering, and departmental requirements. Interprets but does not make policy decisions for employees supervised.

*Problem solving:* Recognize and recommend solutions to technical problems within operations. May work with service groups to improve assembly of new units, tools, cost reduction, processes, and the training of direct labor work force. Must insure smooth work flow by proper balancing of assembly lines and timely (quick) maintenance of tooling and equipment.

SCOPE AND IMPACT OF THE POSITION (Consider number and level of people supervised, annual budgets, sales volume, markets-business development, control of financial resources, goods purchased, etc.):

*Human resources:* Directs, develops and evaluates performance of 30 to 40 employees.

*Financial and Physical resources:* Responsible for efficient operation of equipment and tooling valued at $ _____. Budget responsibility: participates in establishment of budget with Department Manager and is responsible for controlling costs to meet budget goals during the year.

---

## PRODUCTION SUPERVISOR, LARGE PLANT:
## MACHINING OR FABRICATION OPERATIONS

OTHER TYPICAL TITLES: Shop Foreman, Production Foreman, Machining Department Foreman, Steel Machining Foreman, Shift Supervisor, Shift Foreman, Assistant Foreman

(Note: this is a first-line supervisor of technically trained employees.)

PRIMARY PURPOSE OF JOB (Why the Company has this job):
To directly supervise production employees in meeting established production schedules within quality, budget and efficiency standards and to perform necessary first-line supervisory functions for the personnel assigned. To insure that employees under his direction meet quality costs and efficiency standards.

RESPONSIBILITIES (Major responsibilities for which incumbent is held accountable):
1. Organize, hire, train and discipline an efficient work force to meet departmental objectives.
2. Assigns work to individual employees to insure consistency with their skills and the productive efficiency of assigned machining groups.
3. Interpret and implement Company and plant policies and procedures as well as maintain the safety and health of assigned personnel.
4. Meet budget and efficiency goals.
5. Meet departmental goals for the control of scrap and rework costs.
6. Recommend to his supervisor machinery and tooling requirements including maintenance needs.
7. Assist staff support groups (e.g., engineering, purchasing, production planning or maintenance) to expedite any changes in departmental operations.
8. Develop and train, through continuous evaluation and appraisal, a technically-oriented work force.
9. May assist in establishing and setting-up machinery for new production jobs, obtaining the necessary tooling and preparing necessary set-up charts.

REPORTS TO: Shift Supervisor (second level of supervision, not Department Manager)

DIRECTS WORK OF (Representative positions directly supervised):
Machine operators and related production personnel.

KNOWLEDGE AND SKILLS REQUIRED (What the incumbent must know to function in his job: education, specialized technical knowledge and skills, managerial skills, skills of negotiation and persuasion):

*Education:* High School graduate or equivalent (minimum requirement). Trade or technical school courses desirable.

*Experience:* Three to seven years in machine shop operation. Some experience as a leadman desirable.

*Skills:* Should be familiar with engineering standards, production scheduling practices, blueprint reading, various checking gauges for quality control and general machine shop processes. Must possess managerial skills needed to direct production employees.

USE OF KNOWLEDGE AND SKILLS (Decision making—extent to which individual can commit Company OR problem solving—creative thinking, decision influencing, etc., which focus on difficulty of mental application):

*Decision making:* Supervisory decisions within guidelines for personnel and safety policies, engineering and departmental requirements. Interprets but does not make policy decisions for employees supervised.

*Problem solving:* Must have technical knowledge to diagnose machining problems. Must recognize and recommend solutions to complex technical or supervision problems within department. Must apply technical knowledge to control scrap, rework and meet budget guidelines.

SCOPE AND IMPACT OF THE POSITION (Consider number and level of people supervised, annual budgets, sales volume, markets-business development, control of financial resources, goods purchased, etc.):

*Human resources:* Directly supervises 15 to 25 production employees.

*Physical and Financial resources:* Responsible for efficient operation of equipment and tooling valued at $ _____. Participates in establishment of budget of from $ _____ to $ _____

---

## QUALITY CONTROL MANAGER, ALL PLANTS

OTHER TYPICAL TITLES: Quality Assurance Manager

PRIMARY PURPOSE OF JOB (Why the Company has this job):
To assure product quality in manufacturing operations. To provide leadership in implementing corrective action for quality problems and for controlling quality costs.

RESPONSIBILITIES (Major responsibilities for which incumbent is held accountable):
1. Determine man, machine and process capabilities and utilize this information to assure development and implementation of economically sound methods of control for existing and proposed procedures.
2. Provide analysis of quality related problems, communicate to affected functions, and implement corrective action.
3. Evaluate, interpret, review and make temporary modifications of the quality plans and standards to assure understanding and effectiveness in economical control of defined standards and quality levels.
4. Identify needs for quality information equipment. Implement necessary maintenance and calibration procedures for such equipment and maintain required records.

5. Perform test and inspection (visual, mechanical and electrical) in accordance with Quality Plans in the areas of incoming material, manufactured parts and components, assembly, finished product, etc. Maintain required records.
6. Control disposition of non-conforming material and finished product in accordance with established procedures. Chair Material Review Board meetings.
7. Manage and maintain a balanced organization possessing flexibility, technical skills, experience in quality control technology to effectively support short and long range requirements.
8. Perform appraisals, salary reviews and work within prescribed budgets.

REPORTS TO: Director, Product Reliability & Quality Assurance

DIRECTS WORK OF (Representative positions directly supervised):
Process Control Engineers, Quality Control Engineers, Test and Inspection Foremen

KNOWLEDGE AND SKILLS REQUIRED (What the incumbent must know to function in his job: education, specialized technical knowledge and skills, managerial skills, skills of negotiation and persuasion):

*Education:* B.S. Degree (Engineering) or equivalent experience.

*Experience:* Practical knowledge (3 to 5 years) of manufacturing operations. Specialized experience (2 to 3 years) in total quality control technology with knowledge of inspection methods, test equipment, statistical analysis, etc.

*Skills:* Problem analysis, integration of functional activities, strong individual personality and objectiveness.

USE OF KNOWLEDGE AND SKILLS (Decision making—extent to which individual can commit Company OR problem solving—creative thinking, decision influencing, etc., which focus on difficulty of mental application):

*Decision making:* Commits daily on outgoing quality and safety levels of Company products. Constantly involved in rapid decision making on various quality problems. Must maintain balance between product quality and production schedules and costs.

*Problem solving:* Requires high degree of problem analysis and implementation of necessary corrective action. Must integrate activities and influence decisions of other functions for such implementation to assure standards of product quality.

SCOPE AND IMPACT OF THE POSITION (Consider number and level of people supervised, annual budgets, sales volume, markets-business development, control of financial resources, goods purchased, etc.):

*Human resources:* Directs, develops and evaluates performance of 5 to 8 subordinate technical supervisors. Indirectly supervises 30 (small plant) to 70 (large plant) inspection personnel.

*Budgets:* $ _____ to _____ annually.

*Future Growth and Profitability:* Influenced by product quality in the field—partly reflected by the magnitude of warranty costs, product recall costs, liability claims, etc.

# A Sample of Executive Positions in an Insurance Company

For those readers who are particularly interested in insurance company's managerial positions, the following descriptions are provided from one insurance company.

---

## SENIOR VICE PRESIDENT AND TREASURER

*Reports to:* President and Chief Executive Officer

POSITION PURPOSE
To provide meaningful and sound financial and business planning for the maximization of investment earnings through the distribution of assets into types which will contribute to the achievement of short and long-range profit and growth objectives, and the preservation of capital.

DIMENSIONS
    Employees:
    Payroll:
    Assets:

NATURE AND SCOPE
The Senior Vice President and Treasurer reports to the President and Chief Executive Officer as do the Vice President and General Counsel; Senior Vice President, Corporate Services; Senior Vice President, Equity Products; Senior Vice President, Corporate Planning and Investment Policy; Senior Vice President, Individual Insurance Operations and Sales; Senior Vice President, Group Insurance and Pension; Senior Vice President, Actuarial Services; an Internal Auditor; a Director of Public Relations and a Vice President who is an assistant to the Chief Executive Officer.

The incumbent as Senior Vice President and Treasurer participates broadly in all current and proposed financial operations of the Company through providing recommendations to the President and Chief Executive Officer and other members of management, not only from a financial perspective but from a business viewpoint. The incumbent's fiduciary responsibility encompasses the

377

overall planning of the investment program and the selection of investment risks to be considered by the Finance Committee (bonds, stocks, mortgages, equities and correspondence mortgages) including size, risk levels, equities, etc. He meets weekly with the Finance Committee to consider investment recommendations, and to keep the Committee abreast of all pertinent market conditions.

In his function as the Treasurer, he participates in money management and regularly reviews the investment of funds to assess the allocations of monies for the direct mortgages, bonds, and stocks and correspondent loan department. Close liaison is maintained with the various departments with respect to expected cash flow. He also is personally involved in the movement and investment of excess funds ranging from two and one-half M to 20 M which is invested at lowest risk by the incumbent. Additionally, the position supervises the systems for accounting reports as they are necessary in the preparation of the asset side of the annual statement as well as the federal income tax returns. The position also continually reviews the existing investment portfolio to ensure maximum returns on investable assets and reviews the insurance coverages for the corporation.

The position directs, implements, and controls the financial program under the general direction of the Finance Committee through the determination of levels of risk, credit levels of possible investments, etc. The incumbent secures Finance Committee approval of investment programs and determines and arranges for the receipt of financial and accounting reports necessary for appraisal and control of the financial aspects of business. He also must continually maintain communication lines within the various departments, banks and other financial sources to avoid misunderstandings concerning money and money flow.

He additionally is generally responsible for typical personnel functions such as training (Home Office and Field) and technical development of staff, salary increases, etc. Another aspect of this position is the public relations within the Company as well as the public outside; for example, he may offer investment suggestions to customers as a matter of good public relations.

The following activities are under the incumbent's direction:

*Direct Mortgages*—under the direction of the Vice President, this group is responsible for the acquisition of F.H.A. and V.A. single family housing loans and commercial loans for properties, buildings, etc. This is accomplished through a Home Office staff of 5, and a field staff in 20 offices which are to maintain contact with local and national brokers and any other possible business sources.

*Correspondent Mortgages*—headed by a Vice President, he and his staff are charged with the acquisition of mortgage loans on individual dwellings from mortgage loan correspondents. These are usually V.A. and F.H.A. loans.

*Bonds and Stocks*—directed by a Second Vice President, this position and staff are charged with the responsibility of selecting new investments and of the gathering of sufficient data to present to the Finance Committee for approval of new bond and stock investments. When the securities are approved, this group is responsible for the continued maintenance of the account. They are also charged with the responsibility of the purchase and sale of stocks, fixed income securities, and bonds at maximum investment return.

PRINCIPAL ACCOUNTABILITIES
1. Participate in the overall corporate planning objectives by formulating sound short and long-range financial planning and business strategies which will meet goals of growth and profitability.
2. Create and maintain an effective organization capable of achieving maximization of financial resources available to the Company.
3. Ensure the protection of Company assets at optimal cash positions through effective procedures and sound financial control.
4. Provide optimal returns from investable assets through appropriate setting of risk factors.
5. Develop and provide sound and timely counsel and recommendations to the Finance Committee to enable them to anticipate problems and have opportunity in time to take effective action.
6. Fulfill the Company's investment policy to ensure the meeting of all legal and governmental obligations.
7. Develop and provide necessary data sources to enable the annual report, financial statements, and the federal income tax to be prepared within appropriate time schedules.
8. Select, develop and train an organization of sufficient staff quality and suitably motivated to achieve short and long-range objectives which will assure continuity of management and specialized skills.

---

## SENIOR VICE PRESIDENT, GROUP INSURANCE, PENSIONS AND CLAIM

*Reports to:* President and Chief Executive Officer

POSITION PURPOSE
This position is responsible for contributing to the overall growth and profitability of the Company through effective planning and management, primarily in the group and pension area, to meet the overall Company goals and profit objectives.

DIMENSIONS

| | |
|---|---|
| Employees: | Pension: |
| Payroll: | Life and Health Insurance: |
| Operating Budget: | Life Insurance in Force: |
| Premium Insurance Per Year: | |

NATURE AND SCOPE

This position reports to the President and Chief Executive Officer as do the Senior Vice President, Corporate Planning and Development; Senior Vice President, Equity Products; Senior Vice President and Secretary, Corporate Services; Vice President and General Counsel; Senior Vice President, Individual Operations and Sales; Senior Vice President and Treasurer; Senior Vice President, Chief Actuary; an Internal Auditor; Director of Public Relations; and a Vice President who is an assistant to the President and Chief Executive Officer.

The incumbent is responsible for ensuring the effective and profitable operations of the group insurance and pension area through establishment and maintenance of proper underwriting standards; sharing with actuarial the setting of competitive yet profitable rates (including contribution to surplus); prompt and accurate issuance of policies; timely and accurate claims services and the profitable operation of 39 group sales offices throughout the United States.

Included under this position purview are development and implementation of plans for increases in profits (new products and operating cost reduction, increase in sales, etc.), implementation of policy and claim payment guidelines, development of managerial personnel, recruiting and training of field forces, marketing plans, and development and coordination of inter-department unity.

In addition, the incumbent personally reviews policies or renewals of over $1 MM and is directly involved in financing, rate setting and underwriting problems for the business which involves $35–40 MM of premium income. He also participates with members of the executive staff in strategic, overall Company planning and goal setting.

Another dimension of the incumbent's position which is increasing in importance is the area of government involvement in insurance. This is primarily, at this time, medical and health insurance, and requires preparation of recommendations and proposals which represent the Company to certain organizations and, through industry associations, to legislative bodies in the federal government and state governments to ensure that the Company's insurance position is properly represented.

In addition to the regular inter-departmental communication, coordination, and the handling of typical personnel problems, the incumbent actively participates on the following committees: the Finance Committee, Chairmanship of the Claims Committee, Chairmanship of Group Sales Committee, Marketing Committee, Group Field Salary Committee and Home Office Salary Committee, and other civic and community groups.

The incumbent has the following staff reporting to him:

*Vice President, Group Sales*—With his staff of 250 employees, he is held responsible for the meeting of production and sales goals for group pension and life and health insurance. Included under his area are the proper staffing and training of group office and sales personnel in varying parts of the country as well as the coordination of salaries, bonuses, hiring, firing and other typical personnel functions, office space, utilization and development of promotional material, expense approval, technical advice and counsel, employee recruiting, the recommending of plans for expansion of territories, and recommendations for product development.

*Second Vice President, Claims*—Under his direction with a staff of 250 employees, he is responsible for accurate calculations and prompt payment of individual and group, life, health and disability claims from the varying offices, and the development and enforcement of consistent claims policies, practices and procedures which are utilized by claims policy operations. In addition, he is responsible for collecting all of the data of payments, the accuracy of statistical data for all claims payments, the accurate record maintenance to be utilized by actuarial and underwriting departments. This area is also responsible for the staff audit function twice yearly for the claims paying offices, and is responsible for the management of personnel and facilities necessary for efficient claims handling. The incumbent is also charged with providing claims training to his staff to ensure accurate and efficient operation.

*Second Vice President, Life and Health*—This position and his staff of 320 are held responsible for the operation of 6 group divisions which comprise Group Life and Health Administration. They are responsible for nearly all home office group life and health activities, for example, accounting, underwriting, proposal analyses, proposal preparation, contract revisions, contract issue and preparation of material for installations, some field training, sales assistance and account executive work. They also work with actuarial and sales in product development and product pricing.

*Second Vice President, Pensions*—This position and his staff of 165 are held responsible for the operation of 4 pension divisions which comprise Group Pension Administration. They are responsible for nearly all home office group pension activities, for example, accounting, underwriting, proposal analyses, proposal preparation, contract revisions, contract issue and preparation of material for installations, some field training, sales assistance and account executive work. They also work with actuarial and sales in product development and product pricing.

*Second Vice President, Pensions*—This person is an investment specialist with a broad understanding of group pension. He provides advice and counsel to companies to enable them to invest their pension funds or establish pension plans. He prepares and presents materials to the Board of Directors or officers of a corporation and prospective pension groups to sell the Company's products. He also develops educational material to aid in the training of group sales personnel in investment policy and results.

*Group Actuary*—With his staff of 33, he is responsible for providing technical support in the group department through application of group dividend formula to contracts, preparation of a portion of the annual statement (as it pertains to group lines of insurance), preparation of pension contract rates, development of proposal cost factors of prospective sales and operations within the group department, and other special projects and actuarial functions as assigned.

PRINCIPAL ACCOUNTABILITIES
1. Jointly with the Senior Vice President, Actuarial, establish actuarial soundness by adequate rates, reserves and retentions, to ensure continual growth and profitability of the group and pension operation.
2. Ensure continued effectiveness, profits and development of division through timely and proper planning of objectives, operations, policies, and procedures.
3. Participate in corporate planning to provide for the development of short- and long-range overall goals and objectives.
4. Provide direction and leadership to ensure that the financial results of group products are consistent with Company goals and will provide customer satisfaction.
5. Establish and maintain methods of record keeping which will ensure that timely and accurate data are readily available for utilization of management at lowest costs.
6. Select, develop, train and direct a competent and motivated staff to ensure continuity of management and technical skills.
7. Provide management with timely and accurate reports to enable them to take prompt action when necessary.
8. Establish and maintain rapport through all levels of management to ensure cooperation and information about other areas of the Company.
9. Participate on committees and representative state and governmental groups to ensure that the Company is properly represented to its various publics.
10. Provide leadership and direction in establishing and maintaining a field organization which will operate efficiently at lowest costs to increase sales and provide customer satisfaction.

---

DIRECTOR OF PUBLIC RELATIONS

*Reports to:* President

POSITION PURPOSE
To develop, implement and administer a program to win continuing approval

and respect of the Company's various publics—policyowners, employees, suppliers, the general public and local, state and national governments.

DIMENSIONS
    Employees: 4
    Payroll:
    Budget:

NATURE AND SCOPE
Reports directly to the President. The Public Relations Director's prime responsibility is as a staff assistant to the Chief Executive Officer who is unavoidably the Company's number one public relations policy maker. It is the Public Relations Director's responsibility to develop, largely on his own initiative, a total program which is implemented on a project-by-project basis. Areas of specific responsibility include all advertising (national and local), communications with policyowners, publicity, corporate identification, community relations, employee communications, intra-company public relations services, speeches, literature and Company contributions.

In a Company of an institutional nature, most often advertising is placed under the direction of public relations. The Public Relations Director's responsibility is to develop the underlying advertising philosophy of the Company and develop a program which considers both national and local aspects. On the national program he works with a large nationally-known advertising agency in all aspects of creativity, media selection and administration of a program. Management's role is to accept, reject or modify the recommended program. During the past three years the budget for this program has changed from approximately $ _____ to approximately $ _____ annually. In local advertising his responsibility is to develop and administer a program for all field situations (both individual and group) providing creative and mechanical services. *All* advertisements must be approved through Public Relations.

Gaining publicity for the Company includes local, state, regional and national use of all mass media and is aimed at making the Company better known and/or building the prestige of our Company and its representation in their own localities. The Public Relations Director handles inquiries for the media, including press conferences, if necessary, regarding Company activities. He prepares "position" statements stating the Company's position on questions of timely public interest to be used as press releases and/or to inform officers and employees who may be questioned by persons outside the Company. Further, he attempts to develop occasions which can be used to make management individuals more "visible", thus adding to the prestige of the Company.

A new responsibility recently approved by the Company's Chief Executive Officer has to do with legislative liaison with state representatives in Congress. In coming months the Public Relations Director will be establishing contact with legislative assistants who serve our state senators and state representatives in order to develop a channel of communication with respect to federal legislation involving areas of our business.

As secretary and a member of the three-man Contributions Committee, established by the Company's Board of Directors, the Public Relations Director has the responsibility of researching and presenting contribution requests. Generally he is the individual appealed to by the various organizations who request Company funds and he has a certain amount of discretion in making small contributions. Budget for Company contributions is approximately $ _____ annually and will climb within the next few years since it is based on a formula related to assets and premium income.

The Public Relations Director is a member of the Committee on Corporate Identity. He headed the project to develop new corporate identification system and now has a prime responsibility for policy making in connection with ongoing Corporate Identity Programs. He keeps current with the symbol and other graphic representations of the Company and, working with the Committee, helps to maintain a control over the use of such symbols.

A small, but growing area of responsibility for the Public Relations Director is to represent the Company in various industry oriented organizations such as the Institute of Life Insurance which is the communications and public relations arm of the insurance industry.

Another area of responsibility which the Public Relations Director deals with is communications with policyowners. He helps to develop and prepare the Annual Report and quarterly reports in cooperation with the Actuarial Department. He also develops, reviews and recommends use of premium notice stuffers and other informational material going to policyowners. Furthermore, he handles many general complaint letters which are addressed to the President and maintains a continuing review of letters and forms of all types used in corresponding with policyowners. Another area of interest is research with policyowners to determine their opinions of the Company to be used to suggest guidelines for future public relations efforts.

Organizing a Community Relations program covering participation by Company and employees in community and civic activities is another aspect of the Public Relations Director's duties. This area includes the use of Company building facilities by outside groups, participation by employees in community drives, Home Office tours, development of relationships, governmental agencies, various community groups and other business organizations, includes the preparation of printed materials and audio-visual materials.

Another area of activity deals with employee communications. This includes developing, supervising and improving the program including publications, bulletin boards, letters sent to employees, etc.

An effort is made to provide an "editorial service" for Company officials. This includes such things as assistance in the preparation of speeches and preparation of supporting materials such as slides, filmstrips, pamphlets, etc. for same.

It involves the preparation and use of any material in connection with communicating with the public in a non-technical manner. Some other examples of this include recruiting booklets, booklets describing our Investment Operation, and booklets describing the Corporation in general.

PRINCIPAL ACCOUNTABILITIES

1. Assisting with, advising on, administering, reviewing and approving all advertising developed in the Company's name whether it be local, regional or national so that advertising dollars are used to the best advantage.
2. Publicity on a local, state, regional and national basis through the use of press, magazines, television and radio aimed at making the Company better known and building the prestige of our sales force in their own localities.
3. Preparing news releases regarding Company activities or setting forth the Company's position on questions of timely public interest in order to enhance the general prestige of the Company; handling all media relations.
4. Participating in the control and use of the Company's symbol and other graphic representations in all Company literature, forms, signs, etc., in order to achieve the maximum benefits from such identifications.
5. Reviewing, developing and improving communications with policyowners in an effort to encourage better Company-policyowner relations.
6. Organizing and participating in a community relations program intended to encourage the involvement of both the Company and employees in community and civic activities.
7. Supervising a program of employee communications in order to inform the employees as well as promote esprit de corps.
8. Providing an "editorial service" to assist management in presenting information to the public.
9. Working with various departments developing literature about the Company or any specific operation of the Company (i.e. recruiting booklets, booklets describing the investment operation, etc.) in order to obtain material that can be used in a public relations way.
10. Handling most administrative details as one of three members of the contributions committee in order to aid in proper placement of the contributions and promote better community relations.
11. Develop channels of communication with state and Federal legislative representatives in order to present our position on legislation involving areas of our business.

AUDITOR

*Reports to:* President

POSITION PURPOSE
Performs the auditing function for the Company to aid management in developing effective internal controls and ascertaining compliance with them to properly safeguard the assets of the Company.

DIMENSIONS:
   Employees: 5
   Payroll:

NATURE AND SCOPE
This position reports to the President. Reporting to the incumbent are five persons in the Auditing Department. Two of them are at the functional title level of Auditing Associate and two are at the level of Auditing Assistant.

The incumbent has the responsibility to develop and implement an internal audit program in the Company. He assists management in developing internal controls which prevent fraud and maintain the reliability and accuracy of the accounting and other financial records. The emphasis is on the prevention of fraud rather than its detection.

The decision to initiate an audit of a particular area is made by the incumbent. The area of the Company chosen is usually one that has a relatively high potential for a financial loss, such as the Claims Divisions, Policy Loan, Cash Surrender, Purchasing, areas where checks are disbursed, and Payroll. Audits can be made in any area of the Company including Ordinary, Group, Investment, or Corporate Services.

When an audit is to be made in an area, the incumbent discusses his intentions with the officer in charge. After completion of the audit, a written report is prepared for the head of the operating area with a copy to the officer in charge. Recommendations are made, when necessary, regarding how to improve the financial controls in this area. Efforts are also made to persuade the Department to implement the recommendations.

The audit consists of a review of the accounts and the procedures in the department being audited and taking representative samples of transactions. It is impossible to check every entry, so the attempt is to review the controls and develop a system which removes temptation and prevents any wrongdoing. While the emphasis is on financial matters, the incumbent is responsible to report to management any matter which is not in the best interest of the Company. In addition, the audit ascertains the extent of compliance with established policies and procedures, and the extent to which Company ledger assets are ac-

counted for and safeguarded. Also, the audit determines the reliability of accounting records, insurance account transactions and related data.

In the event that defalcation is discovered, the incumbent is responsible to conduct an investigation to obtain a complete set of facts regarding the matter. He may work closely with an attorney from the Law Department in bringing the case to a conclusion. Another responsibility is to complete special projects related to the auditing functions which are assigned by the President or other members of management.

The incumbent coordinates his activities with the outside auditors from the state insurance commission and a private accounting firm. The private firm works primarily with financial statements and is required by law. By developing a strong internal auditing program, it is expected that the work of the outside auditors and the costs to the Company can be reduced.

The internal audit function is a developing one in the Company since it was just initiated recently. For this reason, a major responsibility of the incumbent has been to obtain ideas and set up audit procedures as well as formulate policy. He has visited several other insurance companies with internal audit programs and has studied available literature on the subject. He is attempting to develop an understanding by the management of the various functions that auditing is an aid to allow them to more effectively discharge their responsibilities.

The actual audit may be made by the incumbent, but ordinarily is delegated to one of his subordinates. He assigns projects, trains his staff, gives advice, reviews progress, makes salary recommendations, and performs the various management functions for the department. These actions by the incumbent are not ordinarily reviewed or approved by others.

A key aspect of the position is the reporting relationship to the President, which insures an independent approach to the review and appraisal of accounting and financial records and internal controls. In practice, contact with the President is infrequent. However, when a problem cannot be resolved at a lower level, it is always possible to refer it to the President. Written reports are prepared quarterly for the President and annually for the Executive Committee to keep them informed of operations in the Auditing Department. Generally, the incumbent has almost complete freedom in determining who to audit, how to conduct the audit, what recommendations to make, and how to manage and utilize his staff.

It would be preferred that the person in the position have a strong accounting background along with some management experience. A wide background in various areas of the Company would also be helpful. Participation in professional activities such as the Internal Institute of Auditors would aid in keeping abreast of developments in the insurance industry and the entire field of auditing.

PRINCIPAL ACCOUNTABILITIES
The incumbent is responsible for the following end results:

1. Develop and implement an internal audit program in the Company that meets the needs of management and is of a quality consistent with other major life insurance companies.
2. Conducts audits to establish whether internal controls are adequate and the extent to which the assets of the Company are accounted for and safeguarded.
3. Ascertain the extent of compliance with established policies and procedures and determine the reliability of accounting records and insurance accounts to properly protect the interest of the Policyowner and the Company.
4. Manage the Department in a manner to most effectively utilize the capabilities of the staff.

---

## REGIONAL DIRECTOR OF AGENCIES

*Reports to:* Senior Vice President

### POSITION PURPOSE
To direct, control, and supervise the Managers in the Southeastern Region so that Company products will be effectively merchandised.

### DIMENSIONS
    Agents & Brokers:
    Premium Income:
    Volume from Southeastern Region:

### NATURE AND SCOPE
This position reports to a Senior Vice President as do five other Regional Directors of Agencies, a Director of Brokerage Agencies, a Vice President, four Second Vice Presidents, a Sales Superintendent, a Director—Health Insurance Development, and a Director of Special Markets.

Reporting to this position are the 11 Agency Managers in the Southeastern Region. This region includes Florida, Georgia, Alabama, Mississippi, Tennessee, North Carolina, South Carolina, and Virginia.

The number of full time agents in an established agency will vary from about 3 to 40. In addition there may be part time agents and brokers selling the Company's products (including life insurance, health insurance, MUP, annuities, and variable products). These are primarily individual insurance products although the agents may also sell the Company's group life and health and pension products. Besides the Agency Manager, there may also be Senior Agency Supervisors, Agency Supervisors, Unit Managers, Unit Supervisors, and Agency Trainers who devote all or a portion of their time to management activities.

A major function of the position is to recruit and select managers for newly established agencies or for existing agencies where vacancies arise due to retirement, disability or other reasons. This may involve a promotion from within the Company or hiring someone from outside the Company. The incumbent screens candidates in an attempt to select one or more meeting the Company's standards for successful managers. In the screening process (brief multiple choice tests, preliminary investigation of past performance, personal and business history, credit report, medical report, etc.) the incumbent determines whether a candidate meets the "standards". He then interviews—in depth—the candidates who satisfy his screen evaluation. One—or more—of the candidates may then be brought to the Home Office for Career Analysis Procedure (CAP). The CAP team, which usually includes the incumbent, makes a recommendation based upon the total information gathered about the candidate. This information is reviewed by the Ordinary Sales Committee and the incumbent who reach a decision to make a position offer or not to the candidate.

The incumbent is responsible for the training and development of the field management personnel in his region. This involves training using the techniques of "showing, coaching on-the-job, observing, and appraising" in all functions of agency management including recruiting and selection of agents, sales training, agent supervision, and techniques of motivation. He promotes continual professional development for managers and agents. He participates in managers' workshops and field management meetings.

He supervises the operations of the agencies. He counsels, encourages, and motivates the managers and evaluates their progress. He makes recommendations to the Senior Vice President regarding starting salaries for new managers and salary increases for established managers. (Final approval of salaries is by the Ordinary Sales Committee or the Executive Committee.) He develops jointly with new managers (occasionally may also include other managers) the Management Achievment Program (MAP) which specifies the objectives for manpower, premium income, and training, and recommendations for personal and professional development. He also conducts annual planning conferences with each manager with special emphasis on goals for manpower growth, premium income, the manager's personal compensation—and how these goals will be attained. The incumbent serves as a liaison between the agencies and the Home Office, attempting to coordinate with the Home Office departments and resolve any problems (such as service) which arise. He has the authority to promote the personnel within the agency to the Unit Manager, Unit Supervisor, and Agency Trainer titles. A particular challenge of this position is to motivate new managers.

This position is responsible for sales results from these agencies. The incumbent recommends to the Senior Vice President the annual objectives for new premium, volume and manpower for each agency. He keeps abreast of sales results and takes corrective action to improve sales when necessary. In addition to life insurance, he promotes individual health insurance, group life and health and pension products, variable products and Multiple Underwriting Plans (MUP).

It is necessary to travel frequently in this position. The purpose of these trips includes recruiting and selection of management personnel, training, supervising and motivating managers, making agency visits when required (preferably at least once per quarter) and the end of the year planning conference. He makes suggestions for improvement to the manager and needs to get him to recognize the problem and take corrective action. After the visit, the incumbent prepares a brief report for the Senior Vice President summarizing the visit and indicating the areas of strength and weakness in the agency and the action taken.

This position participates in staff meetings of the Regional Directors of Agencies which are held about eight times per year. Through these meetings and in discussions with his superior, he participates in the development of the overall sales policy and objectives for the Agency . . . Sales and Marketing . . . operation. He represents the Company in a public relations function with speeches at underwriters' meetings, CLU seminars, etc.

The incumbent is free to manage his region and plan his work activities without frequent consultation with his superior. He is accountable for manpower development and sales results in this region consistent with the overall Company objectives. He determines the methods used to achieve the desired results within the framework of established Company procedures. It is necessary for the person in this position to have a thorough knowledge of the Company's products, plus experience and ability in sales and sales management. Professional development activities, such as CLU, are desirable for this position.

PRINCIPAL ACCOUNTABILITIES
1. Plan, develop and maintain a regional sales and marketing program that will produce a quality and quantity of sales (with appropriate product mix) consistent with the Company's objectives and budget allocations.
2. Train and develop managers and other agency personnel so that they improve their performance, become knowledgeable and skillful regarding management, Company products, sales and marketing techniques, and as a result, their professional competence is adequate and they perform at a high level.
3. Recruit and select management personnel who have the skills . . . or can be trained to acquire them . . . to develop successful agencies.
4. Counsel, motivate and encourage the managers so that their capabilities can be fully utilized.
5. Plan (long-range and short-range, 3 years—18 months), recommend quotas, analyze results, and take corrective action to make certain that sales results are in accordance with the overall sales and manpower objectives of the Company.

6. Assist managers and the Home Office staff, through leadership by example, in helping to motivate the agents.
7. Use human relations skills skillfully to successfully solve many of the "people" related problems inherent in this position.

---

## SECOND VICE PRESIDENT

*Reports to:* Senior Vice President

### POSITION PURPOSE
Manage the Group Pension administration function to ensure that customers are provided satisfactory service at a competitive cost, and that the Company's financial results from this line are satisfactory in terms of established objectives.

### DIMENSIONS
    Employees:
    Payroll:
    Operating Budget:
    Group Pension Premium:
    Group Pension Assets:

### NATURE AND SCOPE
This position reports to the Senior Vice President in charge of group and claim operations. One Vice President, three other Second Vice Presidents and the Group Actuary also report to this superior.

The incumbent directs all Home Office Group Pension activities except sales activities and the technical services provided by Group T (such as valuations and dividend calculations). Activities directed include all accounting, underwriting, preparation of proposals, preparation of contracts and revisions, and preparation of new case installation materials including employee booklets for Group Pension cases. The incumbent is responsible for the performance of the Group Pension line both in terms of customer satisfaction (which depends on quality of service and its price) and the Company's financial results.

Many of the incumbent's duties impact on both customer satisfaction and financial results since the two are often closely related. An example is product development which must be directed at customer needs as well as financial results. The incumbent is jointly responsible (with the Group Actuary) for initiating development of new products, establishing objectives to be met by the products, reviewing and stimulating progress on projects, and reviewing final results. His experience as an underwriter and as a contract writer is important, as well as his technical knowledge of product design. This duty involves considerable contact with other areas of the Company, particularly Group Sales, Legal and Actuarial. An important aspect of product development is "selling" the other areas on the advisability of the new product. In connection with his product development responsibilities, the incumbent is a member of the Group Actuarial Projects Coordination Committee which meets about twice a month to establish priorities on actuarial projects in group insurance.

This position is responsible for the financial results in the Group Pension line. Objectives in terms of rate of asset growth and level of surplus contribution have recently been established for this line by top Company management. The growth rate depends partly on sales activity so responsibility for meeting this goal is shared with the head of Group Sales. Since recent results have been close to the established objectives no drastic changes in operation were required, but the incumbent is responsible for suggesting and initiating any changes in his area which will be needed to meet the objectives in the future.

This position is responsible for providing the quality of customer service required to maintain the Company's competitive position in the pension field. On his own initiative the incumbent establishes timing standards for the various operations performed in his area. He receives monthly reports evaluating performance in terms of these standards and consults with his subordinates to attempt to resolve any problems revealed.

High quality customer service requires a well-trained staff of adequate size and a satisfying work atmosphere. In cooperation with his subordinates, the incumbent projects staff requirements five years into the future based on the volume and type of business he foresees. These projections permit orderly hiring and training of staff as well as serving as a basic input to the budgeting process in Group Pension. The incumbent attempts to maintain staff satisfaction and develop the stronger young career employees by exposing them to a variety of jobs within the Group Pension area. This program is aimed at developing future managers for the Group Pension area and other areas of the Company in addition to improving current service.

The incumbent serves as case coordinator for certain large pension cases. Cases with over $ _____ in assets or $ _____ in annual premium are assigned to case coordinators. Case coordinators serve as contact points between the Company and its large pension customers. They stay aware of all nonroutine activity on cases assigned to them. This can include following up on customer problems or requests to ensure prompt action, reviewing the design and administration of plans, suggesting any necessary or desirable changes in plans, and maintaining close customer contact to prevent loss of cases.

The incumbent is a member of the Job Evaluation Committee which meets four to eight times yearly to establish salary ranges for all non-officer jobs.

Two Assistant Secretaries report directly to this position. They serve in line capacities. One directs the administration of existing Group Pension cases. The other directs the Group Pension divisions which handle new business, provide sales support and handle the pension version of renewal underwriting. The incumbent is in close day-to-day contact with his subordinates so no formal system of staff meetings is necessary.

The incumbent participates in a monthly staff meeting involving his superior and the officers reporting to his superior. At this time he submits a short written report covering staff and operational problems and competitive developments in his area. He reports events of major financial significance to his superior as well as major personnel problems, but there are no well-defined limitations on his freedom to act.

PRINCIPAL ACCOUNTABILITIES:
The incumbent is responsible for the following end results:
1. Direction of the Group Pension administration function to ensure that financial results from this line are satisfactory and the quality of customer service is maintained at a competitive level.
2. Direction of and participation in product development in Group Pension to ensure that the Company will maintain its competitive position in the pension field.
3. Projection of staff requirements in the Group Pension area to permit orderly hiring and training of staff as well as accurate budgeting.
4. Service as case coordinator for certain large pension cases to avoid the loss of these cases to competitors.
5. Service on the Job Evaluation Committee to ensure competitive and internally consistent salary ranges for non-officer jobs.
6. Service on the Group Actuarial Projects Coordination Committee to assist in initiating and setting priorities on group actuarial projects as a means of maximizing use of available talent.

---

SECOND VICE PRESIDENT

*Reports to:* Senior Vice President and Secretary

POSITION PURPOSE
Direct the general accounting and control functions for the Company so that financial transactions are properly accounted for and the necessary financial information is available to management.

DIMENSIONS
   Employees:
   Payroll:
   Total Company Disbursements:

NATURE AND SCOPE

This position reports to the Senior Vice President and Secretary as does a Vice President (Planning and EDP) and a Second Vice President (Personnel and General Services). Reporting to this position is an Assistant Secretary, an Assistant Planning Secretary, and a Supervisor.

The incumbent is in charge of accounting functions for the Company. A partial list of his responsibilities includes: general ledger accounting, control of incoming and outgoing funds, bank reconcilements, suspense accounting, agency expenditure ledger account, EDP accounting planning, payroll, consultant for accounting of subsidiary corporations, preparation of Annual Statement, general expenses and budgeting, accounting and financial reports to Company management, and contact with outside auditors.

These functions may be done personally by the incumbent or delegated to subordinates. He has the overall management responsibility for the department including hiring, training, reviewing progress, and making or reviewing salary recommendations. His staff is composed of two Officers, two persons at the Supervisor level, five persons in "career" positions, and fourteen others in clerical positions.

An Assistant Secretary, reporting to the incumbent, is responsible for budgeting and expense allocations. This includes accounting for all of the expense items listed in Exhibit V of the Annual Statement, which amounted to about $ _____ in 19 ___. The budget system was introduced _____ which includes individual budgets at the division or department level. As this system was being established, the incumbent was intimately involved in reviewing, approving, and offering advice on the procedures for this new system. He maintains responsibility for the overall successful operation of the budget system and continues to review results from it.

A computerized accounting system is being developed under the direction of an Assistant Planning Secretary, who reports to this position. The incumbent will become deeply involved in this project during the systems design phase. It is anticipated that this system will provide improved, more meaningful, and more quickly available management information and that there will be a resulting labor savings.

The Supervisor, reporting to the incumbent, is in charge of the persons in clerical positions who handle the day-to-day general accounting functions. This includes general check writers who prepare 600–700 checks per day; including investment pay outs, general expenses, cash surrenders, etc. There is a separate payroll unit which handles all Home Office payroll records and prepares the payroll for the Company. A cash room operation processes bank deposits for the Home Office and is responsible for the balancing of drafts from the banks and for following up on outstanding checks. Other functions include the daily posting of the general ledger, the responsibility for control of the suspense account, the reporting of the daily cash position to the Investment Department, and the auditing of travel expenses.

A number of monthly reports are generated in this department including figures on income and disbursements, policy exhibit figures, cash generated, total assets, and various reports for trade associations. The incumbent originally designed most of these reports and may review them before submission to management. In addition there are reports on inter-company cost comparisons prepared by the Assistant Secretary. All of these reports are coordinated with the Management Information Committee of the Company.

An Actuary and the incumbent share the responsibility for the preparation of the Annual Statement. There is a massive amount of information which is compiled into the Statement and much of the worksheet preparation and other calculation work is delegated to others in the Company. The incumbent helps to coordinate all of this activity and personally prepares many of the exhibits in the Statement and shares the responsibility for the accuracy and the meeting of legal requirements.

This position serves as a consultant on accounting matters for persons from all areas of the Company. He has a responsibility to ensure that financial controls in the Company are adequate even though he is not in a line position in charge of the department or people performing the controls. He approves any person in the Company who has the authority to approve disbursement of funds. He offers advice on tax matters. Particularly in regard to the Federal Income Tax Law, the application of accounting procedures can have a significant effect on the tax liability of the Company.

He maintains relations with the CPA firm which audits the financial statements of the Company. This includes the original recommendation to the President regarding which firm should be appointed. He also works closely, along with other persons in his department, with the State Insurance Commission auditors during their audit every third year. While the Accounting Department is independent from the Company's Internal Auditing function, the incumbent will also work with the Auditor on any accounting or control problems of mutual concern.

The incumbent has the freedom to perform these functions without ordinarily being reviewed or approved by his superior. It is necessary for the person in this position to have a thorough knowledge of life insurance accounting and it is also desirable to have a relatively wide knowledge of operations in various areas of the Company. The extensive governmental regulations and the need to set up reserves makes the accounting function in a life insurance company much different and perhaps more complex than in other types of businesses.

PRINCIPAL ACCOUNTABILITIES:

The incumbent is accountable for the following end results:

1. Perform the overall management functions for the department so that the capabilities of his staff will be most effectively utilized.
2. Perform, personally or through his staff, the general accounting and control functions, including payroll and budgeting, so that the financial transactions of the Company are properly processed and accounted for.
3. Serve as an accounting consultant to various areas of the Company so that satisfactory advice on accounting and control matters is available.
4. Furnish reports regarding various financial matters so that management is properly informed of the financial situation of the Company.
5. Prepare the Annual Statement, accurately and promptly, to meet legal requirements for doing business, to provide management information, and to provide information for tax returns.
6. Be responsible for controls of incoming and outgoing funds to ensure that these funds will be properly safeguarded.
7. Maintain contacts with and assist the CPA firm, the State Insurance Commission auditors, and the internal Auditor so that the Company can be sure of having adequate and accurate accounting records and controls.

---

## UNDERWRITING SECRETARY

*Reports to:* Vice President

POSITION PURPOSE

Manage the underwriting and new issue functions for individual life and health insurance to ensure timely completion of such functions in a manner producing good field relations and satisfactory financial results for the Company.

DIMENSIONS

Employees:
Payroll:
Operating Budget:
Volume of Individual Life Insurance Issued:
Volume "Equivalent" of Individual Health Insurance Issued:

NATURE AND SCOPE

This position reports to the Vice President in charge of individual insurance administration as do a Second Vice President, the Medical Director and an Assistant Secretary.

The incumbent directs the activities of the Underwriting and New Issue Departments. These departments select and evaluate individual risks submitted by the field, perform the clerical functions involved in the issue of individual life and health policies, handle all phases of reinsurance administration and provide underwriting assistance to the Group Department when individual lives in a group case submit individual evidence of insurability. The incumbent is responsible for the timely completion of these functions in a manner producing both good field relations and satisfactory financial results for the Company.

This position is responsible for the establishment, review and revision of underwriting rules and procedures for individual life and health insurance that affect the Company's competitive position in the industry. Certain changes, such as raising retention limits, can be made only with the approval of the Board of Directors. Other changes, such as changing non-medical limits, would be made only with the knowledge and approval of incumbent's immediate superior. Still other changes might be made jointly with another Department Head subject to review by immediate superior. (Example—raising of medical fees or changing of medical evidence requirements.) In many of these cases the incumbent is responsible for making recommendations and for implementing changes. Other changes, involving rules for evaluating military, aviation and occupational risks or for obtaining non-medical evidence of insurability, can be made on the authority of the incumbent. Any consideration of underwriting rules must take into account both field relations and impact on the Company's financial results. As a general example liberalization of underwriting rules promotes good field relations because of fewer rejections or rated policies and quicker action on applications. On the financial side liberalization produces higher claims but this may be partially offset by expense savings. It is the incumbent's responsibility to determine the net financial effect, weigh it against the effect on field relations and make a decision on future policy. The necessary financial studies often involve contact with the Actuarial Department.

Closely related to the previous paragraph is the incumbent's responsibility for approving special exceptions to underwriting rules. Examples include frequent requests to issue insurance above normal age limits and requests to modify normal procedures in the rating of policies. Such decisions require him to know not only what the rules are, but also why the rules were established and when it is safe to make exceptions. This duty also requires human relations skill since it may involve direct contact with influential managers, agents and brokers.

The incumbent may become directly involved in the underwriting decision on certain applications, particularly those for large amounts or those which are assigned high extra premium ratings. There are no rigid rules specifying when he is to be consulted. He has the authority to decide whether to issue a policy and to modify extra premium ratings. His work experience in underwriting is useful in performing this duty and those described in the two preceding paragraphs.

In cooperation with the Agency Department this position is responsible for educating managers and agents in the underwriting and new issue process. A basic understanding of this process by the field ensures fewer mistakes, quicker issue of policies and better field relations. The primary vehicles for this education are orientation meetings for new managers, agents' schools, agency field trips (one or two weeks per year), and written material for the ratebook and other field manuals. The incumbent directs these activities and may participate personally in educational sessions.

This position is responsible for all aspects of reinsurance ceded by the Company on individual risks. The incumbent negotiates contracts, studies alternate proposals, recommends which company and which plan of reinsurance should be used and recommends changes in retention limits when desirable.

The incumbent is responsible for maintaining a well-trained staff of adequate size to ensure timely and reliable completion of the duties assigned to his area. In cooperation with his subordinates he is responsible for establishing standards of performance and for measuring results against these standards. Also, he prepares a projection of staff and space requirements for the future based on his estimate of the level and nature of future business. This projection permits more accurate budgeting as well as a more orderly hiring and training program.

Three line supervisors report to the incumbent. One supervises all phases of the new issue function. Each of the other two supervises the underwriting function for a geographical area of the country. The incumbent is kept informed of work output and problems in his area by daily contact with the supervisors and by a number of periodic reports.

As noted previously, a few changes in underwriting rules must be approved by the Board of Directors. For the most part, however, the incumbent has a free hand in directing his area.

PRINCIPAL ACCOUNTABILITIES:

The incumbent is responsible for the following end results:
1. Receipt and prompt processing of individual applications for life and health insurance and accurate issuance of policies at a cost consistent with good service and anticipated mortality results.
2. Establishment, review and revision of underwriting rules for individual life and health insurance to ensure satisfactory financial results to the Company and promote good field relations.
3. Approval of exceptions to underwriting rules to ensure that the Company's interests are protected in these unusual cases.
4. Involvement in underwriting decisions on certain large or heavily rated cases, again to protect the Company's financial interests and promote good field relations.
5. Education of field manpower in the underwriting and new issue process to minimize mistakes made in the field and ensure prompt action on applications.

6. Administration of individual reinsurance cessions to ensure that the Company is adequately protected at a reasonable cost.
7. Projection of space and manpower needs to ensure timely and reliable completion of the underwriting and new issue functions by maintaining a well-trained staff of adequate size.

---

ASSISTANT SECRETARY

*Reports to:* Second Vice President

POSITION PURPOSE
Manage the Company's personnel functions, including the recruiting and hiring of the right quantity and quality of people, in order that effective personnel services are provided to the Company.

DIMENSIONS
    Employees:
    Payroll:
    Recreation Expense:

NATURE AND SCOPE
This position reports to a Second Vice President as do 8 persons in supervisor level positions. Reporting to this position are a Supervisor, 2 Personnel Associates, and a Senior Analyst (about half time).

The Personnel Department, under the incumbent's responsibility, is divided into 3 units including the recruitment and hiring of persons for career positions, the recruitment and hiring of persons for clerical positions, and the administrative section which handles a variety of functions including timekeeping and personnel records.

For the recruiting of career employees, the incumbent is assisted by a Personnel Associate and a Senior Analyst, who spend a substantial portion of their time on college recruiting activities. This recruiting function involves about 700 interviews per year in order to hire 50 to 60 people for career positions. The incumbent travels about 10% of the time and is involved in a portion of the original interviewing. He makes the final decision regarding an offer of employment for practically all persons hired at this level.

In the career recruiting process, the first step is a 6–12 month projection of needs by canvassing all line officers. From this projection, the incumbent decides where to look, how competitive to be in quoting starting salaries, how many job offers to extend considering normal acceptance rates and how to make staff assignments as far as scheduling travel timetables.

Conducting the job interview on a campus requires the interviewer to have a well rounded knowledge of the Company and to be able to make an on the spot analysis of the potential of the person being interviewed. One of the critical problems in exercising his responsibilities is knowing how many prospects to invite to the Home Office, as acceptance rates are not subject to precise definition. Once Home Office interviews (arranged by the incumbent) have been held and job offers made, he decides where to place the applicant.

It is also a function of this position to follow up after employment to see how the new employee is getting along. He is responsible for the Career Orientation Program which is a program for new employees consisting of twenty meetings presented by people from various departments. Its purpose is to briefly familiarize the new career person with various areas of the Company.

In addition to career employment, the incumbent is responsible for the hiring of the clerical staff which involves about 2,500 interviews and 400 persons hired each year. There are 3 employment interviewers and the department Supervisor who handle most of these matters on a day to day basis but the incumbent becomes involved if a decision is required on an unusual situation or on matters involving policy. This would include matters such as starting salaries, and the determination of methods of recruitment such as advertising, visits with high schools, and hiring of persons from employment agencies.

Another area of responsibility for the incumbent is the administrative section of the department which includes 3 persons in clerical positions under the supervision of the Personnel Associate. The major functions in this area include the originating and maintaining of personnel records, timekeeping for the Company, administering employee benefit data, and preparing various personnel reports. Again, the incumbent would become involved where a policy decision has to be made, where an exception to a rule must be made, or when there are proposals for changes in the personnel procedures of the Company.

The incumbent is a member of the Company's Job Evaluation Committee for persons below the officer level. Although he delegates much of the detail work, he is responsible for seeing that all of the material is available for the Committee's review, arranges meetings, and, in general, oversees the operation and application of the program.

Other responsibilities of this position which are ordinarily delegated to others in the department include the administration of the employee recreation program, the administration of the Matching Gift Program and the participation in special employment programs such as New Horizons and Community Improvement.

The incumbent is responsible for the Company's training and development program such as the LOMA courses, the Tuition Refund Program, and the Company's speech classes. It is his responsibility to review the effectiveness of the overall development program and make recommendations for changes when necessary.

This position performs a variety of other duties including administering the exempt level of the Wage and Hour Law, conducting orientation for new officers, administering the officers' parking program, checking out officers who terminate, controlling the safety deposit boxes used by officers, and personally reviewing all changes requested by employees in their benefit plan coverage. In addition, he conducts personnel research programs designed to provide a basis for auditing personnel policies and recommending changes needed to keep an up-to-date and modern personnel program.

The person in this position should have a background in personnel type work, and with the emphasis on college recruiting, needs the ability to communicate with, as well as influence, young people. In order to stay abreast of the job market, the incumbent should maintain membership in the _____ Association, participate in salary surveys by LOMA and other groups, and regularly visit with placement people and employment agencies.

PRINCIPAL ACCOUNTABILITIES

The incumbent is accountable for the following end results:

1. Recruit and hire persons for career positions which will provide for the Company's manpower needs in the future.
2. Hire the right quantity and quality of persons for clerical positions so that an effective staff is available to process the work of the Company.
3. Seek the most advantageous placement of an employee through a counseling plan to evaluate their placement, attitudes and needs.
4. Assist in the development of all personnel in the Company through the institution and administration of training and development programs.
5. Serve as a member of the Job Evaluation Committee and administer its operation to provide accurate evaluations of positions within the Company.
6. Manage centralized administrative functions, such as timekeeping and personnel record keeping, in order that these services may be performed most effectively for the Company.
7. Maintain an employee relations program of the nature and quality that will contribute to good morale.
8. To maintain, through research and recommendations, an effective and competitive overall corporate personnel program.

# A Sample of Executive Positions in an Educational Institution

For those readers who are particularly interested in an educational institution's managerial positions, the following descriptions are provided from the University of Florida.

---

## VICE PRESIDENT FOR ADMINISTRATION

### STATEMENT OF FUNCTION

Serve as chief advisor to the President on all matters pertaining to the administrative, financial and business affairs of the University. Is responsible for having a comprehensive awareness of the fiscal and financial status of an intricate complex of centers, institutes, colleges and stations unique in the University System. Serves as advisor and counsel to the Chancellor and staff of the State University System and to the Chairman of the Finance Committee of the Board of Regents on matters pertaining to business and finance of the University System. Responsible for maintenance of physical plant, administrative computer services and auxiliary services consisting of laundry, printing, bookstore and food service.

### POLICY-MAKING AND/OR INTERPRETATION

Consults, advises and maintains liaison with President, members of the University's Executive Committee and others on all matters of an administrative, financial or business nature. Attends Board of Regents meetings, conferences with Chancellor and staff of the State University System, staff of Budget Director and other representatives of state offices. Participates in policy-making decisions, and subsequent interpretation of policies, at both the State and University level and directs and coordinates through subordinate divisions the auditing, finance and accounting, purchasing, personnel, physical plant, administrative computer, and business enterprises in compliance with such policies, laws of the State of Florida, and rules and regulations of the State University System and the University of Florida.

### PROGRAM DIRECTION AND DEVELOPMENT

Participates in University planning and operating committees such as Campus Planning and Development, University Budget, University Development Intercollegiate Athletics, Boards of Directors of Sponsored Research and Staff Personnel Policies to provide business management and financial administrative leadership in the development or modification of University programs. As Treasurer of University Foundation, Inc., with the concurrence of the Finance and Endowment Committee of the Foundation, executes investment program for assets of the Foundation to produce optimum returns.

SUPERVISION

Supervision received from the President, Board of Regents and State University System in broad terms relative to overall philosophies and objectives of the University of Florida.

Direct Supervision of Divisions of Finance and Accounting, Personnel, Administrative Computer, Internal Auditing program, Physical Plant Division, and Business Manager (Purchasing Division and all Auxiliary Enterprises). Total number of division heads and employees, approximately 1,200.

LEVEL OF PUBLIC CONTACT

Maintains contact with President; members of Executive Committee; Administrative Council; faculty; staff; Budget Commission; State Personnel Board; Board of Education; Purchasing Commission; Attorney General; Board of Regents; State University System staff; federal agencies such as FHA, HUD, NIH; and with vice presidents for administration and similar positions at other institutions of higher learning throughout the United States.

MONETARY RESPONSIBILITY

Responsible for the entire fiscal operation of the University of Florida, involving all purchases and the receipt, payment, and accounting for all funds.

CONFIDENTIAL DATA

Financial records and budgetary documents are public information. However, during certain investigations and other matters concerning the operation of the University, disclosure of information could be prejudicial to the final conclusion of the matter under investigation.

OTHER CHARACTERISTICS OF POSITION

Position requires the ability to work under heavy pressure constantly and diplomacy and patience in dealing with research faculty, faculty, staff, students, and the general public.

PROVOST FOR AGRICULTURE

*Supervisor's Job Title:* President, University of Florida

GENERAL RESPONSIBILITIES

The general responsibilities of the Provost for Agriculture of the University of Florida includes the administration of the agricultural programs of the University which are organized administratively under the Institute of Food and Agricultural Sciences. The Institute is one of the largest individual and most widely dispersed administrative and budgetary units within the University System. Encompassing four major divisions—the College of Agriculture, the Agricultural Experiment Stations, the Agricultural Extension Service, and the School of Forestry—IFAS is Florida's statewide system of agricultural research and education. These programs extend into every county and community of the State.

The primary mission of IFAS is that of helping Florida to realize its maximum potential for agricultural development—programs which undergird the principal segment of the State's economy. This vital development mission is carried out through the three closely related functions of resident teaching, research and extension.

Currently, IFAS has a professional staff numbering over 740, located at 21 experiment stations and field laboratories throughout the State, in county extension offices in 66 of Florida's 67 counties, and in 19 departments on the main campus of the University. The Institute, with an annual operating budget of over $23 million, operates with a separate appropriation and budget within the University.

The Provost, therefore, administers a large, widely dispersed, diverse and highly complex operation in terms of mission, scope of programs, size of staff and physical facilities, and geographic location. In addition, the Provost has overall responsibility for guiding the University's contract programs of technical assistance in agriculture to developing nations in the tropical zones of this hemisphere and Southeast Asia.

As the principal administrator of IFAS, the Provost exercises responsibility in advising and assisting the President of the University in developing policy for the general operation of the University consistent with Board of Regents policies and State and Federal regulations.

In addition to seeking general budgetary support from State sources, as chief administrator of the Institute, the Provost works to secure grants from national foundations, industrial firms and Federal sources as well as private support from industry groups, firms, and individuals within the State of Florida.

Because the mission of IFAS is vital to the further development of agriculture, Florida's largest industry, the Provost maintains constant contact with many business groups and industry organizations throughout the State and Nation. Furthermore, he is called upon frequently to serve on various kinds of regional and national boards, committees and commissions—work which is of vital importance to the further development of the Nation's agriculture and the educational and research institutions which serve it.

SPECIFIC DUTIES

Within the framework of his general responsibilities the Provost:

(a) Formulates policies for the overall operations of IFAS consistent with Florida Board of Regents and University of Florida policies as well as the regulations of those Federal agencies with which the Institute cooperates in the administration of its research, teaching and extension programs.

(b) Prepares the budget requests for the Institute, seeks approval thereof at the University and Board of Regents levels and administers the funds provided by the Florida Legislature and budgets approved by the Florida Board of Regents.

(c) Provides general supervision for the administration of the Center for Tropical Agriculture established under a grant sponsored by the Ford Foundation and those programs of technical assistance established under contract within the Agency for International Development in the countries of Jamaica, Costa Rica, Vietnam, Nicaragua and Guyana and with the Atomic Energy Commission in the country of Panama.

(d) Serves as a member of the University Executive Committee, which is concerned with advising and assisting the President of the University in the general operation of the University and serves as a member of the University Senate, Council of Academic Deans, University Administrative Council, and on such other University committees as he may be appointed to serve by the President of the University.

(e) Works in close concert with such industry groups as the Florida Agricultural Council, the Florida Council of 100, the Florida Farm Bureau Federation, the Florida Citrus Mutual, etc. in the development of Florida agriculture. In addition, he is in constant contact with various other agricultural commodity groups throughout the State and such State agencies as the Florida Department of Agriculture and such Federal agencies as the Federal Extension Service, the Cooperative State Research Service, etc.

(f) Serves on the Executive Committee of the SHARE (Special Help for Agricultural Research and Education) Council, which is a program aimed at advancing agricultural higher education through private investment and is an integral part of the University of Florida Foundation, Inc.

(g) Serves in regional and national organizations, such as the Southern Regional Education Board, the Agricultural Division and Executive Committee of the National Association of State Universities and Land-Grant Colleges and Universities, Board of Directors of the National 4-H Foundation and many others. He is frequently called on to serve on such national study and advisory groups as the joint University–U.S. Government Committee appointed by the Secretary of Agriculture to study and make recommendations concerning the future role and scope of the Cooperative Extension Service.

RELATIONSHIPS OR CONTACTS WITH OTHERS
Daily contacts with various administrators in the University System of Florida, and the Federal Government, leaders in the agricultural industry of the State and the Nation, etc. ranging from the President of the University, to the Chancellor of the University System, to the Commissioner of Agriculture, to the presidents of many industry organizations throughout the State and Nation.

---

PROVOST

STATEMENT OF FUNCTION
Administers the affairs of the J. Hillis Miller Health Center within the provisions of State law and in accordance with the policies of the University of Florida and the Board of Regents.

POLICY-MAKING AND/OR INTERPRETATION
Responsible directly to the President for formulation and interpretation of policies relating to health services for students, and for health education, research and services through the facilities of the J. Hillis Miller Health Center.

PROGRAM DIRECTION AND DEVELOPMENT
Responsible directly to the President for developing and directing programs related to health education, research and service under auspices of the J. Hillis Miller Health Center and the Department of Student Health.

SUPERVISION
This position reports directly to the President of the University. Supervision is limited to broad policy guidance only.

General policy supervision and guidance provided to the Deans of the five colleges of the Health Center, to the Director, Teaching Hospital and Clinics, and to the Director, Department of Student Health.

LEVEL OF PUBLIC CONTACT
Daily or frequent contact with President or Vice Presidents of the University, and with members of the State Legislature, members of the State and national

advisory committees, members of the Board of Regents and staff, and chairmen or members of various national professional societies.

### MONETARY RESPONSIBILITY

Incumbent has ultimate responsibility for administration of over thirty-and-one-half-million-dollar annual budget. Consequence of error could result in serious breach of service to public and/or to health educational programs in the State of Florida under auspices of the University.

### CONFIDENTIAL DATA

Incumbent is responsible for all confidential data received at the University relating to Patient Care activities within the Teaching Hospital and/or the Student Infirmary. He also shares with top University administrative figures such business related information as may be confidential in nature subject only to disclosure by the President or his designee.

---

## VICE PRESIDENT FOR STUDENT AFFAIRS

### STATEMENT OF FUNCTION

The Vice President for Student Affairs serves as a staff officer, advisory to the President, and is responsible for all matters pertaining to the educational experiences of students outside of the classroom and for the general welfare of all students. He serves as a liaison between the Office of the President and other University administrative offices as they deal with students and the self-government processes of student groups.

### POLICY-MAKING AND/OR INTERPRETATION

Initiates, coordinates, and implements policies for University relative to personal, cultural, and general welfare of students. Advises, and in some instances acts for, the President in matters relating to students.

Serves as a member of the President's Executive Committee and the President's Advisory Council where University-wide policy is formulated.

### PROGRAM DIRECTION AND DEVELOPMENT

Formulates, develops, coordinates, implements and directs University policies and programs relative to programs concerned with all aspects of student nonclassroom activities. Directs those departments within the University concerned with the general welfare of students. Counsels students and student groups on personal, social, cultural and welfare problems.

SUPERVISION
Reports directly to the President of the University of Florida

*Directly Supervises:*

| | |
|---|---|
| Office for Student Development | Assistant to Vice Pres. for Student Affairs—2 |
| Division of Housing | Dean—1 |
| J. Wayne Reitz Union | Assoc. Dean—1 |
| Student Financial Aid | Asst. Dean—4 |
| Graduate Placement Office | Director—5 |
| Coordinator for Disadvantaged | Coordinator—2 |
| Coordinator for Student Conduct | Staff Assistant I—1 |
| Student Publications | |

LEVEL OF PUBLIC CONTACT
Confers, counsels and advises students, faculty, staff and parents regarding the activities and programs of the student body; counsels and advises student leaders and faculty committees responsible for administration of various areas.

Confers and counsels with various state agencies, councils, and commissions.

Confers and counsels with groups outside the University community.

Prepares and delivers speeches and talks to various civic, educational, professional and interested community groups on matters of general student welfare.

MONETARY RESPONSIBILITY
Responsible for budget of Student Affairs (salaries, expense, OCO).

CONFIDENTIAL DATA
Responsibility for all student files which contain confidential personal and academic information.

Much of conferences with individual students or student groups involves matters which are highly confidential.

Conferences with other University administrative staff and faculty, law enforcement officers, federal agencies, civic authorities, etc., are concerned with matters that are confidential.

Many of the above might have serious repercussions if premature disclosure of the matters under discussion were to be made public.

OTHER CHARACTERISTICS OF POSITION
The most unique feature of this position is the necessity of preparedness for the unexpected. Any unusual or out-of-the-ordinary happening affecting the students would be reflected in the work of this office.

Patience, stamina, sensitivity to other people and their problems, a religious orientation and dedication, a successful career in some academic discipline, administrative ability, ease in meeting people and capacity for public presentations are requirements for this position.

BUSINESS MANAGER

STATEMENT OF FUNCTION
Responsible to Vice President for Administrative Affairs for planning, budgeting and directing the operation of the Purchasing Division and Auxiliary Services, including Campus Shop and Bookstore, Food Service, Laundry Division, Printing Division, Vending Services, Campus Mail, Traffic and Parking program, including shuttle bus operation. The office also has general staff duties as assigned by the Vice President for Administrative Affairs.

POLICY-MAKING AND/OR INTERPRETATION
Assists Vice President for Administrative Affairs in coordinating and administering finance, accounting, internal control, data processing, purchasing, personnel, and physical plant division programs.

Consults and meets with University committees on management and operation of Reitz Union, advising on matters of business budgeting and finance.

In absence of Vice President for Administrative Affairs, attends Executive Committee, Administrative Council and other meetings.

In absence of Vice President for Administrative Affairs, assumes responsibilities for all business and financial matters of the University.

Assists Vice President for Administrative Affairs in answering correspondence, telephone inquiries, complaints from citizens, faculty, staff, students, industry.

Prepares items for submission to the Board of Regents.

PROGRAM DIRECTION AND DEVELOPMENT
Directly responsible for developing and directing programs involving Purchasing and Auxiliary Services as identified in 2 above.

SUPERVISION
The Vice President for Administrative Affairs generally approves projects and policies before they are released; however, there is little or no supervision of methodology or day-to-day activity.

*Supervision exercised:*
    Director, Purchasing Division—14.0 employees
    Director, Auxiliary Services—171.5 employees *
      * Does not include food contractor employees.

LEVEL OF PUBLIC CONTACT
Chancellor, members and staff of the Board of Regents, including Architect; Budget Director and his staff; Attorney General; representatives of state and federal governments, both elected and appointed; city and county officials; ad-

ministrative staff and faculty of this and other institutions of higher learning; businessmen and the general public; members of the student body—frequently.

### MONETARY RESPONSIBILITY
Responsible through Director of Auxiliary Services for generation and expenditure of approximately $ _____ as follows: (1) Campus Shop and Bookstores, $ _____; Printing Division, $ _____; Traffic and Parking, $ _____; Food Services, $ _____; Vending, $ _____; Laundry Division, $ _____; Campus Mail, $ _____; Purchasing, $_____.

### CONFIDENTIAL DATA
Although budgetary and financial data are public information, some actions taken during the absence of the Vice President for Administrative Affairs are confidential, and disclosure would be prejudicial to the successful operation of the University.

### OTHER CHARACTERISTICS OF POSITION
Position demands an honest, responsible person with great moral strength, but of equal importance the incumbent must possess a calmness of mind, a genial disposition, and the propensity for observing the University and its operations as seen by students, faculty, staff, alumni, taxpayers and visitors due to the wide range of services and activities for which this position is responsible.

---

## DIRECTOR, PHYSICAL PLANT DIVISION AND CAMPUS ENGINEER

### DUTIES AND RESPONSIBILITIES
The Director of Physical Plant Division and Campus Engineer is the chief executive and administrative officer of the Division and is responsible for formulating, developing, and administering policies, rules, and regulations governing Division activities of more than 700 employees.

Through his assistant directors and department heads, directs and coordinates the detailed activities relating to Police Department, Maintenance Department, Grounds Department, Janitorial Department, Transportation Department, Heating Plants, Sewage Treatment Plant, Drafting and Mapping, Central Stores, Safety Officer, Civil Defense Coordinator, Telephone Coordinator, Locksmith and Key Shop, and Accounting Office.

Administers through the Assistant Director for Maintenance the Maintenance Department which is responsible for preventive, routine, and major maintenance of buildings, utilities, and other physical facilities; construction of minor buildings and additions, alterations, and renovations to departmental facilities and equipment.

Administers through the Assistant Director for Engineering the engineering planning and estimation of major repairs and the construction of minor buildings, additions, alterations, and renovations to departmental facilities and equipment. Also administers through the Assistant Director for Engineering the Heating and Sewage Treatment Plants and the Grounds Department.

Administers through the Assistant Director for Services the Janitorial, Police, and Transportation Departments; Central Stores, Agency Civil Defense Coordinator, and Division internal service functions: purchasing, personnel, and accounting.

Administers through the Assistant to the Physical Plant, the Telephone Exchange and Locksmith Shop.

Plans and directs the expansion of roads, parking lots, utilities, and landscaping to meet new building construction needs. Includes these factors when budgeting insofar as they are done by Physical Plant Division forces rather than the State Road Department and outside contractors.

Initiates and directs the preparation of personnel, capital, and operating budgets for the Working Capital Fund and Educational and General accounts of the Division, and recommends those budgets in final form to the Vice President for Administrative Affáirs. Manages expenditures from budgeted funds to accomplish maximum effectiveness of Physical Plant Division in support of the function of the University.

Advises on the site planning of new buildings and facilities, additions to older ones, traffic patterns involved, availability of utilities, desirable landscaping, and the availability of Division services.

Advises on new building construction from the standpoint of features which experience has proven most economical to maintain and service.

Chief liaison for the University with Florida Power Corporation, Southern Bell Tel & Tel, and Gainesville Gas Company; liaison for the Division with members of the Board of Regents and Legislative committee members. Liaison between the Division and the Planning Department, Zone Architect, Architect to the Board of Regents, and other architects and consulting engineers working on University projects.

Serves on the following University committees: Space Utilization, Campus Planning and Land Use, Fraternity and Sorority House Plans and Construction, and Civil Defense.

Represents this unit of the University with governmental agencies and other representatives; official spokesman for the Division to press and other news media.

Member of Board of Trustees of the Gainesville Municipal Waste Conversion Authority, Inc. Represents the University in this function. Serves on the Executive Committee of the Authority as Secretary.

Member of the Interinstitutional Physical Plant Committee of the State University System. Together the Committee members develop budgeting standards, exchange information, and develop uniform approaches for the State University System.

## DIRECTOR OF PERSONNEL RELATIONS

### STATEMENT OF FUNCTION
Responsible for all aspects in employee relations activities involving the staff employees of the University and responsible for providing services to the faculty community in terms of administering and counseling in the areas of fringe benefits and the processing of faculty personnel actions.

### POLICY-MAKING AND/OR INTERPRETATION
Responsible for recommending, implementing and interpreting all policies in regard to employee relations for the staff employees within the Board of Regents regulations and State and Federal laws applying to employee relations. Works with University Policy Committee, consisting primarily of Deans, which makes recommendations to the Vice President for Business Affairs, or in case of fringe benefits answers to the Executive Committee of the University through the Vice President. The scope of policy-making and interpretation is University-wide.

### PROGRAM DIRECTION AND DEVELOPMENT
In conjunction with the staff of the Personnel Division develops University employee relations programs that carry out University policies. Programs cover all facets of employee relations and include all staff employees in the University, and programs which are appropriate for the faculty include all faculty positions.

### SUPERVISION
Supervise two assistant directors and a secretary.

*Supervision received:*
Vice President for Business Affairs. Supervision is of a general nature covering the review and approval of major changes in programs and policies.

LEVEL OF PUBLIC CONTACT
Regular contact with all levels of administration of the University. External contacts with local, State and Board of Regents staff officials.

MONETARY RESPONSIBILITY
Responsible for departmental budget of approximately $ _____ plus responsibility for administration of Workmen's Compensation and administration of Wage and Hour matters and classifications which could amount to considerable amounts of funds if responsibility mishandled.

CONFIDENTIAL DATA
The nature of personnel administration, by necessity, includes knowledge of personal confidential information regarding individuals, changes in plans of the University and changes in the organization which if disclosed could bring embarrassment to the University and increase the difficulty of the operation of the University.

OTHER CHARACTERISTICS OF POSITION
This position requires the ability and integrity to satisfy many different elements of the University and at the same time awareness of an over-all need for action in employee relations activities which will strengthen the University's image and operation which may not always be understood or accepted by all persons affected. The position requires ability to sell intangible ideas which result in tangible results and benefits which manifests itself in specific programs being enacted which will enhance the employer-employee relationship.

---

DIRECTOR, UNIVERSITY COMPUTING SYSTEMS

STATEMENT OF FUNCTION
Operation of the Administrative Computing Center through general or direct supervision of Systems and Programming manager, Technical manager, and Operations manager. Coordinate with various administrative users to insure adequate support for their projects. Responsible for control and development of administrative computer systems.

POLICY-MAKING AND/OR INTERPRETATION
Policy is formulated in regard to computer applications. Requires responsibility in the interpretation of new, or changes to existing, policies, rules and regulations in regard to computer systems. Encourage changes to existing policies

that would enable more efficient computer applications that may effect University department level or state level.

## PROGRAM DIRECTION AND DEVELOPMENT

Involved in committees that affect computer system development on University and state level. As a member of the largest University in the system, it is imperative to contribute to long range planning of computer systems. Since the Administrative Computing Center has developed computer systems that affect nearly all phases of management, it is important to be aware of the interrelationship of the many applications.

## SUPERVISION

Little or no supervision required. Contacts are for special projects or need for management information.

*Title of supervisor:* Vice President for Business Affairs.

*Supervision exercised:*

    Manager of Systems and Programming   1
        1. Programmers
        2. Systems Analyst
        3. Systems Programmers
    Manager of Computer Operations        1
        1. Operations
        2. Setup Control
        3. Keypunch
    Secretary                             1

## LEVEL OF PUBLIC CONTACT

| CONTACT | FREQUENCY | SCOPE |
| --- | --- | --- |
| Vice President | Infrequently | Special requests or approval of projects |
| Directors | Frequently | Development of computer systems |
| Other Campus Contacts | Infrequently | Development of computer systems |
| Legislator Auditor | Infrequently | Special reports |
| IBM | Frequently | Computer matters |
| Management Information System (Board of Regents) | Frequently | Computer matters |
| Electronic Data Processing Division (State) | Infrequently | Computer matters |

## MONETARY RESPONSIBILITY

This Division's budget is approximately $ _____ per year. This Division has the responsibility to prepare accurate and timely reports as requested which will enable various users to fulfill their missions in an efficient manner. Errors could result in completely erroneous information for management and affect decision-making process.

## CONFIDENTIAL DATA
Certain types of information are considered confidential.
1. Payroll records
2. Income records
3. Detail expenditures
4. Student grades
5. Student permanent records.

The Division considers all information the property of the users and any disclosure must be through the users of the Computing Center.

## OTHER CHARACTERISTICS OF POSITION
Constant development of newer and advanced computer system for more efficient management. Bring to the attention of management in other areas the need to use data processing and try to stimulate the staff to think ahead. There are 42 employees in the Division who require attention from time to time. A very dynamic phase of management with constant awareness of near and future developments.

# Managerial Group Position Descriptions

In some organizations, the board of directors, the executive committee, the management committee, the budget committee, the finance committee, the building committee, or some other top executive group is the "managing personality." It controls the entire business and has authority to make binding decisions on the spot. For this reason, at least a few organizations write position descriptions for the board or the committee, regarding it collectively as doing a continuous and highly important "job." Descriptions of boards of directors and of very important committees with considerable authority have been included in this report from this survey and from the 1958 report.

---

## A MACHINERY MANUFACTURER
### BOARD OF DIRECTORS

FUNCTIONS OF THE BOARD OF DIRECTORS

The Board of Directors, as trustees of the owners of the business, have the responsibility of keeping a proper balance among the interests of the stockholders, employees, customers, and the public; and, because of their experience and past accumulated administrative know-how, have the additional responsibility of seeing that management gets things done in accordance with the broad over-all objective of operating the Company on a profitable basis.

Among its principal functions, the following are included:
1. To secure competent executives to operate the Company and to insure the continuation of able management.
2. To consider and approve broad policies, such as the manufacture of new products, acquisition of new manufacturing facilities, changes in distribution methods, price changes, and relations with consumers, distributors, labor, and government.
3. To check executives and the results they have secured; that is, by analyzing financial results, such as sales volume, profits, and competitive position.
4. To supervise, control, and act on important matters, such as capital structure changes, large loans, and dividend payments.
5. To review and approve capital and operating budgets.
6. To approve selection of general counsel and formal action required by law.
7. To establish the salaries of senior executives, approve bonus and pension plans, and control all other policies relating to payments to executives.

8. To make discerning inquiries of members of general management at Board meetings.
9. To present an outside, detached point of view.
10. To inspect properties and review actual operations.
11. To request inside and outside audits and secure professional services, such as management consultants and public accountants.
12. To see that the Company is legally operated.

A checklist as to the relationships of limits of authority between the Board of Directors and general management has been prepared and is part of the Company Organization Manual as a further clarification regarding their respective areas of responsibility and authority.

The above implies a strong Board capable of supervising and directing the activities of general management, confining, in the main, however, its activities to the formulation of broad policies without any line authority except as exercised through the President. It also implies that the Chairman of the Board under this definition is the chief executive of the Company and the sole privileged individual who can exercise any line authority over management through the President.

# A LARGE AUTOMOBILE MANUFACTURER
## BOARD OF DIRECTORS

Manage and control the business and property of the Company; and exercise all such powers of the Company and do all such lawful acts and things which are not by statute, the Certificate of Incorporation, or the By-Laws required to be done by the stockholders, including the functions summarized below:

1. Elect the officers of the Company.
2. Appoint members of the Executive Committee and other committees of the Board, excepting the Administration Committee.
3. Fix from time to time the salaries of officers and executives, except as power may be conferred by the By-Laws upon the Audit and Compensation Committee to fix salaries for members of the Board or the Administration Committee.
4. Make all such regulations as are deemed expedient concerning the issue, transfer, and registration of stock certificates of the Company.
5. Determine who shall be authorized to make and sign bills, notes, acceptances, indorsements, checks, releases, receipts, contracts, conveyances, and all other written instruments executed on behalf of the Company.
6. Publish and submit to the stockholders an annual statement of the financial condition of the Company, including consolidated income and surplus accounts and a consolidated balance sheet for the preceding fiscal year.

7. In its discretion, submit for approval or ratification by the stockholders at any of their meetings any contract or act of the Board or of any officer, agent, or employee of the Company.
8. Determine the amount and manner of payment of any dividends paid by the Company.
9. Fix, periodically, the amount of the Company's working capital, and set aside out of net profits or surplus such amounts as are deemed necessary to safeguard and maintain adequate working capital, or as reserves for contingencies, repairs, maintenance, revaluation of profits, equalization of dividends, or for other purposes.
10. Purchase, or otherwise acquire for the Company, property, rights, or privileges at such price or consideration as is deemed proper, and pay therefor in money, stock, bonds, debentures, or other securities of the Company.
11. Create, make, and issue mortgages, bonds, deeds of trust, trust agreements, or negotiable or transferable instruments or securities, secured by mortgage or otherwise.
12. Appoint any person or corporation to accept and hold in trust any property or interest of the Company.
13. Delegate any of the powers of the Board in the course of the current business of the Company to any standing or special committee or to any officer or agent, and appoint any person the agent of the Company, with such powers (including the power to subdelegate) and upon such terms as it deems proper.
14. Remove any officer or transfer the powers and duties of any officer to any other person.
15. Confer upon any officer the power to appoint, remove, and suspend subordinate officers and agents.
16. Adopt, subject to stockholder approval when required by law, and administer any retirement, group insurance, or similar plan.
17. Make and change regulations, not inconsistent with the By-Laws, for the management of the Company's business and affairs.
18. Make and alter the By-Laws.

# A LARGE PHARMACEUTICAL FIRM
## BOARD OF DIRECTORS

### OBJECTIVITY AND PHILOSOPHY

The primary responsibility of the Board of Directors, as defined by New Jersey law, is to manage the business of the Company. To carry out this responsibility, the Board membership provides a balance between directors who are also officers of the Company and so-called external or "outside" directors, who represent general fields of interest to the Company, especially the scientific field. The present number of "outside" directors is eight, compared with four directors who are also operating officers, reflecting the philosophy that "outside" directors comprise the majority on the Board.

Four Board committees have been established to facilitate the operation of the Board. The Executive Committee, the committee of the Board with the broadest field of interest, consists of three "outside" directors and three directors who are also officers, including the President of the Company as Chairman. The Finance Committee membership is independent of operating management and consists solely of "outside" directors, although Company financial officers are invited to attend meetings regularly. The Scientific Committee consists of two "outside" directors and two directors who are also officers, one of whom, the President of the Company, serves as an ex officio member. The Stock Opinion Committee consists of three "outside" directors, plus two directors who are also officers, all of whom are ineligible to participate in the Stock Option Plan.

GENERAL RESPONSIBILITY
The Board of Directors is responsible for determining policies, goals, and philosophies of the Company and for seeing that they are carried out by the officers; for electing and appointing the Chairman of the Board and the officers of the Company and the fixing of their responsibilities; for authorizing the President and other Company officers to act for or on behalf of the Company in performing delegated responsibilities as prescribed in the Corporate Resolutions of the Board; for establishing committees of the Board and defining their responsibilities; and in general for directing the management and control of the business, finances, property, and concerns of the Company.

*Responsible to:* The Stockholders.

FUNCTIONS
1. *Objectives.* Determines the general objectives, goals, and philosophies of the Company; and guides the development and operation of the business toward their accomplishment.
2. *Policies and Programs.* Formulates or approves broad policies for execution by the President and other officers, and approves programs proposed by Company officers.
3. *Organization.* Elects the Chairman of the Board and other officers specified in the By-Laws; appoints, upon recommendation of the Executive Committee, other officers of the Company; establishes committees of the Board; and fixes the responsibilities and authority of Board committees, the President, and other Company officers to act for or on behalf of the Company in the operation of the business.
4. *Stockholders.* Considers and approves for submission to the stockholders all proposals which are recommended for stockholder action; and gives final approval of the periodic reports to stockholders.

5. *Capital Investments.* Authorizes directly or through appropriate delegations the making of new capital investments and the sale and exchange of assets.
6. *Profit Distribution.* Determines the distribution of profits; and authorizes dividend actions.
7. *Appraisal.* Reviews and appraises the results of Company activities and performance of management to insure the protection of the rights and interests of stockholders.
8. *Auditing.* Appoints outside auditors upon the recommendation of the Finance Committee; and provides direct access at all times for reports and recommendations from the outside auditors and the Controller of the Company on any matters they may wish to bring to the attention of the Board.
9. *Executive Compensation.* Approves compensation to be paid all officers and directors, as well as to all other employees in cases involving monthly compensation of $2,000 or more.
10. *Advice to Management.* Provides advice and consultation to the Company's officers on general matters affecting the management of the business.

MEETINGS
The fourth Tuesday of the month. Meetings are attended by the Directors, the Secretary of the Board, and a representative of the Company's outside legal counsel. The Board will also from time to time request other officers and employees to attend the meetings, and in particular the Controller and the Treasurer will be available for all Board meetings.

# A MANUFACTURER OF MACHINERY
## FINANCE COMMITTEE

1. PURPOSE
   The purpose of this policy is to establish a Finance Committee and to define broadly its objectives, its membership, and its method of operation.

2. THE FINANCE COMMITTEE AND ITS OBJECTIVES
   The Finance Committee will review and study the financial structure of the Company, its financial needs, its financing methods, its credit terms, its borrowing practices, and its financial budgets, for the purpose of recommending to the President adequate programs for attainment of a sound and balanced Company financial structure which will support an optimum rate of Company growth and profit. These results will be sought through
   1. Review of financial policies and their administration.
   2. Review of credit and collection policies and their administration.

3. Review of financial budgeting practices and administration to ascertain their effect on the Company financial structure.
4. Ascertainment and recommendation of sound short-term and long-term Company financial objectives, such as
   a. Required rate of capital expenditure.
   b. Required amount of working capital.
   c. Required total operating funds.
   d. Preferred methods of financing.
   e. Return on capital employed.
   f. Required gross profit margins.
   g. Required rate of expenditures for research and development.
   h. Attainable financial ratios.

In its work the Committee will make full use of available Company staff services to develop the factual data upon which its conclusions and recommendations are based. Financial performance standards thus developed, when properly approved and expressed arithmetically in ranges of satisfactory performance figures, will be recommended for inclusion in the management guides of affected, responsible executives. Therefore, such recommended financial performance ranges must be attainable under and consistent with overall Company planning.

3. MEMBERSHIP
Membership of the Finance Committee will be as determined or amended by the President.

4. FREQUENCY AND LOCATION OF MEETINGS
Frequency and location of meetings will be established from time to time by the Chairman.

5. AGENDA
Any Committee Member may furnish to the Committee Secretary suggestions of matters which could be put on the agenda of a Finance Committee meeting.

## AN AIRCRAFT MANUFACTURER
### PLANNING COMMITTEE

FUNCTION
To integrate the planning of engineering, manufacturing, sales, and finance into over-all Company plans and objectives to govern the selection of products, the application of effort, and the use of facilities.

SCOPE

The Committee will devote its efforts to over-all Company endeavor. It is a sub-committee of the Policy Committee and an advisory body to that Committee and the President.

RESPONSIBILITIES

The Committee will advise the Policy Committee and the President with respect to:

1. Research and development programs to be undertaken by the Company.
2. The type of work and projects which should be solicited and accepted by the Company.
3. General instructions to serve as guides to the operating groups in the acceptance of business. Recommendations on specific projects not governed by outstanding general instructions, when such matters are referred to the Committee.
4. The allocation of work among the various geographic or product divisions of the Company.
5. General policies governing items to be subcontracted.
6. General facility requirements and recommendations as to specific items deemed advisable by the Committee or referred to the Committee for consideration.
7. Any other matters which the Committee deems pertinent to the above matters or which are referred to the Committee for consideration.

AUTHORITY

The Committee will have the authority to request information and studies deemed necessary for carrying out the assigned responsibilities.

STAFF SUPPORT

Each member of the Committee will be expected to furnish staff support for analysis of matters considered within the scope of his own functions. Staff support relating to facilities, work load, and capabilities will be furnished by the Office of the Senior Vice President.

MEMBERSHIP

Vice President–Administration.
Vice President–Engineering.
Vice President–Finance.
Vice President–Manufacturing.
The Vice President–Engineering is Chairman of the Committee, and the Vice President–Finance is Vice Chairman.

# SEATTLE–FIRST NATIONAL BANK
## BUILDING COMMITTEE

MEMBERS

President (Chairman)
Administrative Assistant to EVP
Corporate Secretary

Manager, Bank Properties
Manager, Branch Development
Manager, Market Research and Development

MISSION

To establish policies and priorities concerning the bank's building program and decide on major real property transactions.

RESPONSIBILITIES

Reviews annually project priorities established under the "Capital Budgeting" process, considers priorities for non-branch projects, and recommends a total expenditure for property and buildings for the year ahead to Interim Committee.

Approves proposals for building projects (new buildings and remodelings) involving a total project cost between $50,000 and $500,000 and endorses those over $500,000 to the Interim Committee for approval as to general concept. Reviews those under $50,000 as reported by Manager, Bank Properties.

Approves purchases, leases, and sales of real property involving commitments totaling between $50,000 and $300,000 and recommends those over $300,000 to the Interim Committee. Reviews those under $50,000, as approved by Manager, Bank Properties.

Reviews progress on all building projects quarterly, considers changes in priorities to meet altered circumstances, and directs changes in plans or approves additional expense when costs exceed original estimates by 10% or more.

Reviews periodically policies covering maintenance, rental and lease of bank space to tenants and establishes guidelines for rates and terms in regard to major buildings.

BASIC RULES

Committee meets monthly.

Corporate Secretary serves as secretary.

An agenda, listing all matters to come before the Committee and accompanied by copies of major proposals, is to be in the hands of Committee members two days before meeting date.

# Bibliography

**Books**

Belcher, David W., *Compensation Administration* (Englewood Cliffs, N.J.: Prentice-Hall, 1974).

Burack, Elmer H., *Strategies for Manpower Planning and Programming* (Morristown, N.J.: General Learning Press, 1972).

———— and Walker, James W., eds. *Manpower Planning and Programming* (Boston, Mass.: Allyn and Bacon, 1972).

Cemach, Harry P., *Work Study in the Office,* 3rd ed. (Croydon, Surrey, England: MacLaren and Sons, Ltd., 1965).

Corson, John J., and Paul, R. Shale, *Men Near the Top: Filling Key Posts in the Federal Service* (Baltimore: The Johns Hopkins Press, 1966).

Dailey, Charles A., *Assessment of Lives* (San Francisco, Calif.: Jossey-Bass Inc., 1971).

David, Paul T., and Pollock, Ross, *Executives for Government* (Washington, D.C.: The Brookings Institution, 1957).

Famularo, Joseph J., *Organization Planning Manual* (New York: AMACOM, 1971).

Fine, S. A., and Wiley, W. W., *An Introduction to Functional Job Analysis* (Kalamazoo, Mich.: W. E. Upjohn Institute, 1971).

Finkle, Robert B., and Jones, William S., *Assessing Corporate Talent* (New York: Wiley-Interscience, 1971).

Glaser, Barney, ed., *Organizational Careers* (Chicago, Ill.: Aldine Publishing Co., 1968).

Jennings, Eugene E., *The Mobile Manager* (Ann Arbor, Mich.: Bureau of Industrial Relations, University of Michigan, 1967).

Odiorne, George S., *Personnel Administration by Objectives* (Homewood, Ill.: R. D. Irwin, 1971).

Phillips, Victor F., Jr., *The Organizational Role of the Assistant-To* (New York: AMACOM, 1971).

Ross, E. E., *Encyclopedia of Job Descriptions in Manufacturing* (Milwaukee, Wis.: Sextant Systems, Inc., 1969).

Sayles, Leonard R., and Chandler, Margaret K., *Managing Large Systems* (New York: Harper and Row, 1971).

Stanley, David T., *The Higher Civil Service* (Washington, D.C.: The Brookings Institution, 1964).

Strauss, George, and Sayles, Leonard R., *Personnel: The Human Problems of Management,* 3rd ed. (Englewood Cliffs, N.J.: Prentice-Hall, 1972).

Stroh, Thomas F., *Managing the New Generation in Business* (New York: McGraw-Hill Book Co., 1971).

U.S. Department of Labor, Manpower Administration, *Handbook for Analyzing Jobs* (Washington, D.C.: U.S. Government Printing Office, 1972).

Wortman, Max S., Jr., and Luthans, Fred, eds., *Emerging Concepts in Management,* 2nd ed. (New York: Macmillan, 1975).

**Articles**

Akalin, Mustafa T., and Hassan, M. Zia, "How Successful Is Job Evaluation— A Survey," *Industrial Engineering,* 3, No. 3 (March 1971), pp. 32–36.

Ansoff, H. Igor, and Brandenburg, R. G., "The General Manager of the Future," *California Management Review,* 11, No. 3 (Spring 1969), pp. 61–72.

Annett, J., and K. Duncan, "Breaking Down the Task," *Personnel Management,* 2, No. 5 (May 1970), pp. 28–32, 34.

Atwood, Jay F., "Position Synthesis: A Behavioral Approach to Position Classification," *Public Personnel Review,* 32, No. 2 (April 1971), pp. 77–81.

Bassett, Glenn A., "Manpower Forecasting and Planning: Problems and Solutions," *Personnel,* 47, No. 5 (September 1970), pp. 8–16.

———, "The Qualifications of a Manager," *California Management Review,* 12, No. 2 (Winter 1969), pp. 35–44.

Battalia, O. William, "The Mad Hatter World of Executive Titles," *Business Management,* 37, No. 12 (March 1970), pp. 22, 42.

Baum, Bernard H., and Sorensen, Peter F., Jr., "A 'Total' Approach to Job Classification," *Personnel Journal,* 48, No. 1 (January 1969), pp. 31–32.

Bennett, Corwin A., "Toward Empirical, Practicable, Comprehensive Task Taxonomy," *Human Factors,* 13, No. 3 (June 1971), pp. 229–235.

Brown, Pamela, "Jobs in the Test Tube," *Personnel Management,* 3, No. 1 (January 1971), pp. 34–36.

Brumback, Gary B., "Consolidating Job Descriptions, Performance Analysis, and Manpower Reports," *Personnel Journal,* 50, No. 8 (August 1971), pp. 604–610.

——— and Vincent, John W., "Jobs and Appraisal of Performance," *Personnel Administration,* 33, No. 5 (September 1970), pp. 26–30.

Burack, Elmer M., "Meeting the Threat of Managerial Obsolescence," *California Management Review,* 15, No. 2 (Winter 1972), pp. 83–90.

Cassidy, Edward W., and Kelly, James H., "Rewarding Professional Growth," *Compensation Review,* 3, No. 1 (First Quarter 1971), pp. 34–38.

Charles, A. W., "Installing Single-Factor Job Evaluation," *Compensation Review,* 3, No. 1 (First Quarter 1971), pp. 9–21.

Chowdhry, Kamla, "Selection of Executives and Administrators: Implications of Recent Research," *Personnel Journal,* 48, No. 2 (February 1969), pp. 102–107.

Coleman, Bruce P., "Research Manpower Resources Planning," *Research Management,* 16, No. 4 (July 1973), pp. 28–32.

Collett, Merrill J., "Re-Thinking Position Classification and Management," *Public Personnel Review,* 32, No. 3 (July 1971), pp. 171–176.

Cox, Arne, "Personnel Planning, Objectives and Methods Presentation of an Integrated System," *Management International Review,* 8, Nos. 4–5 (1968), pp. 104–114.

Cramer, J. J., Jr., and Strawser, Robert H., "Perception of Selected Job-Related Factors by Black CPAs," *CPA Journal,* 42, No. 2 (February 1972), pp. 127–130.

Dauw, Dean C., and Fredian, Alan J., "Executive Career Guidance," *Personnel Administration,* 34, No. 2 (March–April 1971), pp. 26–30.

Dayal, Ishwar, "Role Analysis Technique in Job Descriptions," *California Management Review,* 11, No. 4 (Summer 1969), pp. 47–50.

Dean, Burton V., Reisman, Arnold, and Svestka, Joseph A., "Job Evaluation Upholds Discrimination Suit," *Industrial Engineering,* 3, No. 3 (March 1971), pp. 28–31.

Desi, G. R., "Task Assignment: Does the Right Man Get the Job?" *Supervisory Management,* 12, No. 6 (June 1967), pp. 33–35.

Dressel, Wayne A., "Coping with Executive Mobility," *Business Horizons,* 13, No. 4 (August 1970), pp. 53–58.

Dumas, Neil S., and Muthard, John E., "Job Analysis Method for Health-Related Professions," *Journal of Applied Psychology,* 55, No. 5 (October 1971), pp. 458–465.

Evans, J. S., "Contrasting Task Analysis Procedures in Consultancy-Based and Survey-Based Research," *Human Relations,* 24, No. 2 (April 1971), pp. 139–148.

"First Step in Getting a Good Man: Sound Job Description," *Iron Age,* 209, No. 25 (June 22, 1972), p. 25.

Gayle, John B., and Beam, Maurice E., "Use of Overstrength Spaces in Personnel Management," *Management Services,* 7, No. 3 (May–June 1970), pp. 29–36.

Henley, J. S., "Salary Administration: A Look to the Future," *Personnel Management,* 4, No. 4 (April 1972), pp. 28–30.

Hodge, Billy J., and Johnson, Herbert J., "An Employee's Role: The Impact of Three Different Views," *Supervisory Management,* 15, No. 8 (August 1970), pp. 18–20.

"Is Your Ablest Assistant Locked in Your Desk?" *Business Management,* 33, No. 8 (November 1967), pp. 57–60, 62–68.

Jack, Thomas B., "A Salary Administration Plan for the Small Employer," *Personnel Journal,* 52, No. 6 (June 1973), pp. 467–469.

"Job Description: Key to Hiring Right Man," *Industry Week,* 173 (April 10, 1972), pp. 60–61.

Kemple, Robert J., and Meade, Thomas M., "Find the Man to Fill Your Spot," *Industry Week,* 171 (December 13, 1971), pp. 28–31.

Laughlin, Thomas C., and Kedzie, Daniel P., "Organization Planning," *Best's Review* (Life Ed.), 73, No. 3 (July 1972), pp. 70–73.

Ludwig, Steven, "Tying Job Appraisal into the Business," *International Management,* 25, No. 7 (July 1970), pp. 31–32.

Lutz, Carl F., "Efficient Maintenance of the Classification Plan," *Public Personnel Management,* 2, No. 4 (July 1973), pp. 232–241.

——— and Ingraham, Albert P., "Design and Management of Positions," *Personnel Journal,* 51, No. 4 (April 1972), pp. 234–240.

Mann, Karl O., "Characteristics of Job Evaluation Programs," *Personnel Administration,* 28, No. 5 (September 1965), pp. 45–47.

McCormick, Ernst J., Jeanneret, Paul R., and Mecham, Robert C., "A Study of Job Characteristics and Job Dimensions as Based on the Position Analysis Questionnaire (PAQ)," *Journal of Applied Psychology,* 56, No. 4 (August 1972), pp. 347–368.

Melcher, Robert D., "Roles and Relationships: Clarifying the Manager's Job," *Personnel,* 44, No. 3 (May 1967), pp. 33–41.

Moment, David, and Fisher, Dalmar, "Managerial Career Development and the Generational Confrontation," *California Management Review,* 15, No. 3 (Spring 1973), pp. 46–55.

Muther, Richard, and DeMoor, Ray J., "Planning an Organization Structure," *S.A.M. Advanced Management Journal,* 38, No. 1 (January 1973), pp. 28–33.

Patten, Thomas H., Jr., "Evaluating Managerial Positions by Evalograms," *Personnel Administration,* 29, No. 6 (November–December 1966), pp. 17–26.

"Position Description: A Key to Finding Good Executives," *Best's Review* (Life Ed.), 73, No. 3 (July 1972), pp. 78–79.

Prahalis, C. P., "Put It in Writing," *Sales Management,* 103, No. 24 (December 1, 1969), pp. 50, 52.

Price, Karl, "Characteristics of Corporate Executives: A Research Note," *Academy of Management Journal,* 15, No. 3 (September 1972), pp. 378–381.

Prien, Erich P., and Ronan, William W., "Job Analysis: A Review of Research Findings," *Personnel Psychology,* 24 (1971), pp. 371–396.

Rakich, Jonathon S., "Job Descriptions: Key Element in the Personnel Subsystem," *Personnel Journal,* 51, No. 1 (January 1972), pp. 26, 42–45.

Sauer, Robert L., "Selecting the Best Job Evaluation Plan," *Industrial Engineering,* 3, No. 3 (March 1971), pp. 16–21.

Schiffhauer, Joseph A., "Developing Human Resources Through an Employee Upgrading Program," *Personnel Journal,* 51, No. 3 (March 1972), pp. 199–203.

Seamans, Lyman H., Jr., "What's Lacking in Most Skills Inventories?" *Personnel Journal,* 52, No. 2 (February 1973), pp. 101–105.

Stevens, Robert I., "Time Distribution Chart: A Technique for Job Analysis," *Journal of Systems Management,* 23, No. 10 (October 1972), pp. 40–41.

Stuart, Walter, "Automated Job Description and Evaluation of Computer-Related Occupations," *Journal of Data Management,* 7, No. 9 (September 1969), pp. 33–35.

Suskin, Harold, "Personal Competence Rating," *Personnel Administration,* 35, No. 3 (May–June 1972), pp. 62–69.

Vance, Paul M., "How to Write an Accurate Job Description," *Supervisory Management,* 15, No. 9 (September 1970), pp. 9–11.

Walker, James W., "Models in Manpower Planning," *Business Horizons,* 14, No. 2 (April 1971), pp. 87–95.

Walsh, William J., "Writing Job Descriptions: How and Why?" *Supervisory Management,* 17, No. 2 (February 1972), pp. 2–8.

Ward, Derek, "Job Evaluation in Local Government," *Personnel Management,* 5, No. 7 (July 1973), pp. 34–35, 39.

Weber, Wesley L., "Manpower Planning in Hierarchical Organizations: A Computer Simulation Approach," *Management Science,* 18, No. 3 (November 1971), pp. 119–144.

# Index by Kinds of Position